Rogers Mary Eliza

Domestic Life in Palestine

Rogers Mary Eliza

Domestic Life in Palestine

ISBN/EAN: 9783337291051

Printed in Europe, USA, Canada, Australia, Japan

Cover: Foto ©Andreas Hilbeck / pixelio.de

More available books at **www.hansebooks.com**

DOMESTIC LIFE

IN

PALESTINE

BY

MARY ELIZA ROGERS.

———◇———

CINCINNATI:
PUBLISHED BY POE & HITCHCOCK.

R. P. THOMPSON, PRINTER.
1865.

AUTHOR'S PREFACE.

WHILE residing in Palestine, I was placed in circumstances which gave me unusual facilities for observing the inner phases of Oriental Domestic Life. I mingled freely with the people, of all creeds and classes, and daily became better acquainted with their habits and modes of thought. The women especially interested me, and I gleaned many facts concerning them, which have never hitherto been published, and probably have never been collected.

The pleasure which my Notes and Journal afforded to members of my home-circle, on my return to England, led me to think that, possibly, my countrymen would like to gain a further insight into the mysteries of Eastern life. Hence it was that I resolved to publish this volume. In compiling it I have avoided, as much as possible, those subjects with which the public are already familiar. Descriptions of well-known places are only given when they are necessary to form an introduction or background to those scenes of real life which I have attempted to portray.

To avoid complication, I speak of the people of

Palestine generally as Arabs; for, though they are a mixed race, they all call themselves "Arabs" or "Sons of the Arabs," and Arabic is their mother-tongue. I classify them only according to their creeds; but I may here mention, that the Christians of the land are said to be of pure Syrian origin, while the Moslems are chiefly descended from the Arabians, who settled in the towns and villages of Syria and Palestine in the seventh and eighth centuries.

In preparing this volume for the press, I have had the valuable assistance of my brother, Mr. E. T. Rogers, Her British Majesty's Consul at Damascus, and have enjoyed the opportunity of personally consulting him. He has suggested a few alterations in the orthography of Oriental titles and names of persons and places, and has added a few notes of explanation, which are distinguished by his initials.

M. E. R.

21 Soho Square, London.

CONTENTS.

CHAPTER I.

From London to the Levant—Yâfa, the ancient Joppa, in sight—The Quarantine Boat—Landing in Palestine—The Quarantine Station—Breakfast in Yâfa—Arab Ladies' Toilette—Salutations and Kisses—Sit Leah and her First-born Son—Fruit Gardens of Yâfa—"*Ai-wa!*"—Guest-chamber at Ramleh—Lepers—The Hill Country of Judea—"Village of Grapes"—"Fountain of Birds"—Jewish Builders and Greek Gardeners—First Sight of Jerusalem—Arrival at the Talibiyeh—Tent Life, and the Consul's Children..........................PAGES 17–40

CHAPTER II.

Jerusalem—Church of the Knights of St. John—Glow-worms—Bishop Gobat's Encampment—Holman Hunt's Goat—Sunday on Mount Zion—Bazars and Shopkeepers—Girls of Bethany and Siloam—A Wandering Madman—Moresque Buildings—View from the Seraglio—European Homes in Jerusalem—Native Servants—A Whirlwind at Night—The Convent of the Cross—Mosaic Pavement................................41–55

CHAPTER III.

Learning Arabic—Carriage Roads—Ride to Bethlehem; that is, Beit Lahm—The Convent and its Shrines—Population of Beit Lahm—The Carver of Beit Lahm—His wife and Child—The Vail of Ruth—"The Mother of Joseph"—Description of House and Furniture—Note on Mark ii—The Fields of Boaz—Milk Grotto Miracles—Girls of Beit Lahm—Bedouins on the Move—The Gardens of Solomon—The Cottage in the Valley—Urtás—The Reservoir—Aqueducts and Chariot Roads—Reeds—Remedy for Musketo Bites......................................56–74

CHAPTER IV.

Rainbows and Bee Catchers—Philip's Fountain—A Runaway Horse—Katrine and her Delusions—Start for Háifa—The little Lame Girl of

Kubâb—Siesta at Ramleh—The Abyssinian Slave—The Bedouin's Song to his Camel—Sunday at Yáfa—"There cometh a Shower"—Exhibition of a Performing Goat—Circumcision—Making Bread—Scenes in an Arab Sailing Boat—The Custom-house at Tantûra—Ruins of Dora and Athlite—A Wedding Party—Cradles—"Locusts and Wild Honey"—The Monks of Mount Carmel—Hâifa..............................PAGES 75-99

CHAPTER V.

Greetings at the Gate at Night—Our House and Servants—The Poor Widow's Petition—People of Hâifa—Siege of Hâifa—Retreat of the Tirehites—Help from an English Ship—A False Alarm—Wedding at the Greek Church—Wedding Procession—Songs and Dances—Going forth to meet the Bridegroom at Night—Professional Bride Dressers—Turkish Baths—Kohl and Henna—Angelina and the Clergy of Hâifa—Denunciation of Black Lace Mittens—The Bazar on a Night of Rejoicing—Jane Eyre and Arab Story-tellers—An important Question—Yassin Agha and his two Wives—Mohammed Bek and his Wife Miriam—Sheikh Abdallah and his seven Wives—"The Holder of the Keys"—A Hint to Polygamists—A Divination Dictionary, or Dream Book—My Dream interpreted—Hannah and Penninah—A Market Garden—African Maniac among the Tombs.....................................100-126

CHAPTER VI.

To Nazareth; that is, Nâsirah—The River Kishon—"Daughters of Sound"—A Village Oven—The Birthplace of Saleh's Mare—Hidden Treasures and Treasure Trove—Necromancy and Clairvoyants—Saleh's little Sister—Congregation at the Latin Church—Costumes of the People of Nâsirah—Reputation of Nâsirah—Willow-pattern Cheese-plates—A Hint to Decorators—Mount Tabor—Erinna, the Hermit, and "his Man Friday"—Reeds and Inkhorns—Dinner by the Streamlet—Sephoris—The Crusaders—Stephani's Guest-chamber—Dances, Songs, and Supper—The Greek and Latin Clergy—Castle of Shefa 'Amer—The Governor's Harem—Lament of the Senior Wife—Native Schools—Jewish Synagogue—The Olive Harvest—Cotton Fields in the Plain of 'Akka—Productiveness of the Plain......................................127-160

CHAPTER VII.

"New brooms sweep clean"—Death at Midnight—The Moslem Bier—Armenian Remedies for Cholera—Note on the "Early and Latter Rain"—Panic in Hâifa—"The Yellow Wind"—Suleiman the Tailor—Quarantine at the Convent—A Dream and its Consequences—"Imps of the Yellow Wind"—Rain—Our new House—Contents of the

Store-room—Reverence for Bread—Death of Ibrahim—Funeral Procession—The Mother's Grief and Death—Funeral Service—The Widower Khalil and his Young Bride—Elias Sekhali—Government of Syria—Death of Elias—The Widow and her Children—Songs and Lamentations for the Dead—Funeral Dances—Death of Khalil—Funeral Orations ....PAGES 161-185

CHAPTER VIII.

Sparrows on the Housetops—Grass-grown Roofs—"Poterium Spinosum"—The Crown of Thorns—Harvest on the Roofs—My Bedouin Visitors—Katrine Sekhali and her Cousin—The White Mare and the Sapphire Bead—Our Egyptian Groom Mohammed—The Wandering Herdsmen—Bedouin Depredations—The Horse-Guards of Galilee—Supper with Salibh Agha—Salibh Agha's little Son—Wrestling—A Home at Shefa 'Amer—Women at the Bakehouse—The Lizard—Bedouin Eyesight—A Gazelle Hunt—A Bedouin Dinner—Crabs on the Seashore—Moslem and Christian Prayers at Sunset—Persecution of Jews—Characteristics of Arab Children—My Moslem Teacher—Explanation of the Use of the Rosary—A Moslem Freethinker—Christening of Jules Aumann—Fête at the French Consulate—The African Foot Messenger—Saleh Bek's Good-by...186-214

CHAPTER IX.

Katrine and her Scapulary—Preparations for a Journey—A Bedouin Encampment—Bedouin Women—Bedouin Bread-making—Moslem Villages—Seeking a Night's Lodging—Women of Kefr Kára—The Blind Man's Questions—Conjecture Concerning the "Nativity" and the "Manger"—Morning Visitors—An Encampment of Gipsies—Jugglery and Gymnastics—Government of Nablûs—Arrabeh—The Divan—The Harem—Helweh the Youngest Wife—Dinner:. Starch and Conserve of Roses—Curious Inquiries—A Marriage Portion—Songs of Rejoicing—Discussion about the Queen of England—A War Song—A Mother and her Infant Son—Preparation for a Night's Rest in the Harem—The Lord's Prayer and the Moslem Women—Moslem Prayers and Salutations—Scenes at Midnight in the Harem—Morning Visitors......215-255

CHAPTER X.

From Arrabeh to Senûr—Castle of Senûr—Ibrahim Jerrar's Portrait—The Harem in the Castle—Approach of Turkish Cavalry—Hostilities prevented—To Nablûs—A Price for the Head of Ibrahim—Marriage among the Samaritans—Selâmeh, the aged Priest—The Samaritan Synagogue—Home of Habib and Zora—Anithe the Betrothed—Samaritan Laws and Customs—The Priesthood—The Passover—Samaritan

Women—Character of the Samaritans—Yakûb esh Shellabi—Letter from Priest Amran—The Widow and her Son—The Schoolmaster in search of a Wife—The Betrothal—Protestants of Nablûs—The Bazars—Sheikh Mûssa—Visit to the Governor of Nablûs—Test for Building Stone—Sheikh Mûssa's Ideas about Wisdom and Folly—Jacob's Well—Search for a Bible at the Bottom of the Well—Joseph's Tomb—False Alarm—Little Zahra and the Violets—Oriental Enjoyments—Brothers and Sisters—Ibrahim Pasha and the Woman of Sefurieh—Wit Rewarded—Dinner with Daûd Tannûs—The Women's Apartments..PAGES 256–296

CHAPTER XI.

To Jerusalem—Priest Amran and the Greek Catholic—My Escort—A Dangerous Road—Valley of Figs—Darkness—The Lost Track—Alone on the Hill-top—The Nimbus—Arrival at Jerusalem at Midnight—Jerusalem in the Spring—Rain—Flowing of the Kedron—En Rogel—Course of the Kedron—Easter in Jerusalem—Birth of the Imperial Prince of France proclaimed—Fête at the French Consulate—Outbreak at Nablûs—Attack on the Christians—Rescue of the Rev. S. Lyde—Celebration of Peace—Sham Fight—Sieges of Jerusalem—The Holy Fire—Greek and Armenian Pilgrims—"Bishop of the Holy Fire"—Fight of the Fanatics—Turkish Soldiers—Confessions of a Greek Priest—Truth—Fire Worshipers.................................297–329

CHAPTER XII.

Peasant Girls—Harvest of Roses—Caverns—Rules for the Observance of Ramadan—Sir M. Montefiore's Schools for Jewesses—Sale by "the Uncounted Group"—Urtâs—Peter Meshullam—An Arab Encampment—Dar el Benât, the House of Girls—Solomon's Harem—My Home on Mount Olivet—The Sheikh of El Tûr—His Wives and Children—A Moslem Funeral—Tombs of the Prophets—Skirmishes on Olivet—Farewell Fête at Urtás..330–359

CHAPTER XIII.

Abu Ghôsh—Art and Poetry of the Modern Arabs—Education of Native Girls—The Sea-shore and the Sanctuary—Moslem Call to Prayer—Edwin Arnold—Melon Harvest—Ruins of Cæsarea—The River of Crocodiles—A Fable—Wreck of an Arab Boat—Hebrew Boy adopted by Bedouins—Stone Quarries—Prayers at a Moslem Village—Village Supper—A Piano at Háifa—My Moslem Friends from Arrabeh—Saleh Bek and his Children—Home of the Gardener's Daughter—Chess—New Ideas in Saleh Bek's Harem—Helweh's Questions—Jews—An Earthquake—Widow and her Children—Day of Ill-luck—Feast of "Sainte Barbe"—Force of Custom—Helweh and her First-born Child—Saleh Bek's Perplexities about the Education of his Daughters—Thoughts about Moslem Women—Missionaries—The Day of Congratulation—Society for the Diffusion of Useful Knowledge—Yassin Agha's Petition and Proposal...PAGES 360–398

CHAPTER XIV.

Fête of the Corpus Domini—The Bahjeh—Furrah Giammal and her Love-Letter—Lebibeh in her New Home—Carmella and her African Attendant—Women of Damascus contrasted with the Women of Háifa—Bastrína—Winter at Jerusalem—Surreya Pasha—Houses of Jerusalem numbered—Russian Influence in Palestine—Dr. Levisohn and the Samaritan Pentateuch—Visit of Prince Alfred—Refugees from Arrabeh—Appeal for Protection—Dakhal—Prisoners from Arrabeh—The Governor's Demand for my Protégés—His Forbearance—The Boys taken Prisoners and conveyed to 'Akka—Farewell to Háifa—Miss Bremer—Russian Steamer—Fête of the Grand Duke Constantine—The Bishop's Benediction—Feast for the Pilgrims—The S. S. Demetrius—Jew of Aleppo—Collision—Rabbi Shaayea's Timidity—"Hallo, Jack!"—The Captain and Solomon—Shaayea Missing—Fruitless Search for Shaayea—Official Inquiry...399–436

INTRODUCTION.

During a recent brief sojourn in London, I had the pleasure of meeting, several times, the genial and talented writer of this volume; and received from her the exclusive privilege of republishing her work on this side of the Atlantic.

The old land of Canaan is still dear to the Church, and, although so many volumes of travel and research in that region have been written, we take up the new with undiminished interest. The land is to all Christians more like *home* than any other spot on earth. The most precious memories, the purest love, the most blessed hopes of life, are the products of that Gospel which first budded and bloomed in Canaan. The names of its cities, and valleys, and streams, and mountains, are reminders of the most wonderful and thrilling incidents which the history of the world records. Think of Bethlehem, Nazareth, Jordan, and Jerusalem; put your finger on Tabor and Olivet, as you scan the sacred map, and how are you overwhelmed with sacred recollections! Each name starts through your mind a marvelous panorama.

Canaan is also the type of the eternal land toward which with insatiate longing we daily journey.

Blessed Canaan! While the memory and love of Jesus linger in the hearts of men, and while hope points to the "rest prepared for the people of God," thy cities and mountains shall be dearer to the Christian than his native land or the home of his childhood.

The struggle raging to-day between rationalism and Evangelism imparts additional interest to the old geographical center of historic Christianity. He who represents the New Testament records as mere myths is confronted by the stubborn denial of the land itself, as it stands to-day, a monument and testimony to the literal accuracy of the Holy Book. Sacred names cling to the ruins that crown every hill-top. Caves, tombs, temples, mosques, fountains, pools, and roads, are burdened with sacred associations. The land singularly retains its geographical conformation, its primitive and Scriptural modes of architecture, dress, labor, and social habits. It might easily have been utterly desolated and depopulated, and its remains scattered to the four winds. It might have been richly cultivated, and under the full flowing tide of civilization its traces of earlier times might have been completely covered up and rendered unrecognizable. But God has kept the land. Over the hills of Gibeon and the vale of Aijalon has the sun of progress stood still, and, while the rest of the world has been moving onward, Palestine yet lingers among the earlier centuries, and amidst its sacred and venerable scenes we feel the presence of an ancient dominion. The mummy wrappings of Mohammedan domination have providentially preserved it till this age of skepticism, that it may testify to the reality of a Divine revelation. It is a memorial land, seamed and scarred with the rough handling of centuries, but bearing still the legible imprint of the Divine finger. Its terraced hills yield a vintage of sacred memories. Its valleys flow with streams of testimony. Every rock cries out in bitter remonstrance against the unbelief of men. Every stone voices the praise of God. Palestine is more than a land of memories. It is a memorial land, as well.

Every volume that illustrates this harmony between the land and the book is an invaluable contribution to sacred literature. The field is still open. We sometimes think, for example, that the topography of Jerusalem is an exhausted subject. But we forget that the Jerusalem of to-day stands upon a mass of ruins and debris thirty or forty feet in depth. What a kindling of the fires of antiquarian controversy, and what valuable developments are yet in store for us when the Crescent wanes from Zion, and the city becomes another Pompeii for excavation and research!

In no department of eastern exploration does the Bible student acquire more instructive lessons than in that pertaining to the domestic habits of the people. The Scripture narrative enters largely into the details of social life. The old customs have not changed materially, and one can to-day reproduce the incidents of social life so graphically described in the Bible. Abraham still sits in the door of his tent; Ruth gleans after the reapers on the plains of Bethlehem, and on these plains shepherds keep watch over their flocks by night. Isaac meditates at eventide. Rachel descends from her camel and covers her beautiful face with the ample vail before she meets her lord. The marriage feast is still kept in Cana. The mourners with wailing follow the bier to the grave. Salutations are exchanged among the people as in the days of Abraham and Christ.

The seclusion of the women, through the jealousy of their lords, renders it quite difficult for the casual traveler to gain access to the inner courts of Oriental houses. Conversation with the ladies of the harem is a thing impossible. Missionaries do not enjoy much greater facilities than transient visitors. They are the bearers of a new and hostile religion, and harem doors are securely shut against them.

It is in the fullness of the information, which Miss Rogers gives us concerning these unexplored Moslem homes, that we find the chief value of her work. She possesses rare qualities of character, and during the three years of her residence in Palestine enjoyed the amplest facilities for the observations she desired to make. Her brother was British Consul at Hâifa, and was popular among the natives from Nazareth to Jerusalem. She was scrupulously careful never to offend the religious prejudices of the people, and as she was their guest, not only received from them the most cordial hospitality, but was permitted to converse freely with women of all classes and ranks. Miss Rogers is an artist, and many a time won her way to hearts of sheikh and warrior by her accurate sketches; the wit of her pencil now and then provoking bursts of merriment from the immovable old Orientals who entertained her. This artistic gift renders her descriptions graphic and circumstantial, thus fairly photographing on her pages the domestic scenes she presents. Of quick perceptions, unwearying perseverance, an inexhaustible stock of good-humor, a heart full of humanity, with a frank and fearless manner, she was admirably adapted to perform the work she undertook.

With special pleasure do I call the attention of the

American public to this unpretentious and entertaining volume, believing that it will not only furnish pleasure to every reader, but that it must contribute to the clearer understanding of the Scriptures, and serve as another bulwark in defending historic Christianity against the vain speculations and unholy plottings of rationalism and infidelity.

J. H. V.

TRINITY PARSONAGE,
Chicago, Ill., Jan., 1865.

DOMESTIC LIFE IN PALESTINE.

CHAPTER I.//
FROM LONDON TO YÂFA.

THE good-byes and farewell greetings on board the Rhine, at London Bridge, on the night of the 14th of June, 1855, need not be recorded here. At midnight the tide was favorable, the bell rang, the steam was up, lingering friends hurried away, and I found myself alone with my brother. He had been enjoying a few months in England, after having spent more than six years in consular service in Syria, and I had gladly consented to accompany him, on his return to his official duties. We landed at Boulogne the next day, and arrived at Marseilles, in time to embark by the Egyptus, on the morning of the 21st of June. We passed through the Straits of Bonifacio on the 22d, at midday; and on Sunday, the 24th, spent a few hours ashore at Malta.

On Thursday morning we landed at Alexandria, and after seeing Said Pasha's palace, Cleopatra's needle, and Pompey's pillar, went on board the Tage, on the evening of Friday, the 29th. It was crowded with passengers, Greeks, Syrians, Turks, and Jews, who were leaving Alexandria on account of the outbreak of cholera there. The sunset-gun flashed from the fort as the steamer glided out of the harbor.

We remained on deck till a late hour, listening to the animated songs of the Greek sailors, who were celebrating the festival of their patron saint, Paul. The deck passengers were trying to make themselves comfortable for the night, and soon men, women, and children, Moslems, Christians, and Jews, wrapped up closely in carpets, cloaks, and wadded quilts, looked like gigantic chrysalises crowded together in the moonlight.

We were in the cozy little deck saloon soon after dawn on the following day; and, when the sailors came to wash the decks, I was sorry to see the motley crowd of sleepers disturbed, and pushed hither and thither, as they tried to save themselves and their baggage from saturation.

We watched the sun rise out of the sea, which was suddenly changed from gray to gold, while the lead-colored sky was crimsoned—but the land I was longing to see was not in sight.

The next morning, July 1st, I was roused by the joyful news that we were approaching the shore, and was soon on deck, looking with strange delight and emotion over the blue sea to the coast of Palestine, stretching far away north and south in low, undulating lines. The picturesque walled town of Yâfa—the ancient Joppa—was immediately before me, with its white stone-houses built down to the water's edge, and rising one above another on a rounded hill sloping to the sea.

My brother said, "Look far into the east, a little toward the south, where the sun has just risen. Those distant hills which are now almost lost in bright mist are the hills of Judea, 'the hills round about Jerusalem,' and from their summits you will have the first view of the Holy City. They are separated from these low coast hills by the broad, fertile plains of Sharon and Philistia." He reminded me how the pines and cedars of Lebanon were brought "*in floats by sea to Joppa*," and thence carried up to Jerusalem, for the building of the Temple.

This ancient port, with its bustling quay, its large convents, tall minarets, palm-trees, and extensive gardens, is the only cheerful and animated spot on the somewhat monotonous coast, which runs in an almost unbroken line from the bold headland of Mount Carmel, about fifty miles north, to the ruins of Gaza, forty miles south.

We were soon at anchor just outside a semicircular belt of rocks, some of which rose dark and high out of the water, while others had sunk beneath its surface, and were only indicated by the dashing of the surf over them. This rocky belt stands like a barrier in front of the town, and forms a natural harbor of about fifty feet in width, but it is only entered by small boats, and affords no protection in bad weather. Tradition connects the names of Perseus and Andromeda with these rugged rocks. Two Austrian war steamers were at anchor near to us. They were waiting the pleasure of the Archduke Maximilian and his suite, who were then in Jerusalem. A few merchant vessels, Greek and French, were also to be seen, and little Arab boats were plying to and fro.

A quarantine boat, containing an officer and *garde de santé*, was towed along side, and baskets of oranges, apricots, and lemons, were taken on board. A beautiful branch of an orange-tree, covered with glossy leaves, and laden with ripe fruit, was handed to me. It was a difficult matter to get into the little quarantine boat destined to convey us to the shore, for the breeze was fresh, and a heavy swell disturbed the sea. The Arab sailors in the towing boat would not touch the boat they were employed to tow, even to render necessary assistance, lest they should be compromised, and imprisoned in the quarantine station. After many vain attempts, we, with two Franciscan monks, and our baggage, were lowered clumsily into the clumsy boat, and narrowly escaped a fall into the sea; and when free from the Tage, we were dragged along boisterously. The little towing boat was quite hidden from us now and then, as it bounded over a wave, leaving us on the other side of it. As we approached the belt of rocks, I felt that it was impossible to escape being dashed to pieces, and while steering through the narrow pass I was silent with fear;

but the seeming danger was soon over. Within the belt, the water was smooth as a lake, and once more I looked with delight on the scenes around me. There are two openings in the line of rocks; one toward the north, and one due west. We had entered at the latter; I felt the boat grating on the rocks beneath us.

It was now half-past eight, and the quays were already crowded with people, mostly in the brilliant native costumes, but there were a few Franks in the usual Levantine dress, which is white from head to foot. Flags were waving from the consulates and from the convents, as well as from the ships, for it was Sunday, and the place had quite a holiday appearance.

We passed in front of the town, toward the quarantine station, which is an isolated building, a little distance beyond the walls on the southern side.

Friendly voices from the shore welcomed my brother, in Arabic, Italian, French, and English. When we arrived opposite to our destination, the boat was dragged toward the sands, and the *garde de santé*, who wore only a coarse shirt and a girdle, jumped knee-deep into the water, caught me in his strong arms, and ran splashing through the sandy sea. When we came to land he still ran on, and would not release me till he placed me in charge of another *garde*, at the foot of the rude steps, leading up the sandy cliff, to the quarantine station. Then he hastened back to the boat for my fellow-travelers, carrying them one after the other to *terra firma*.

I had wondered how I should feel on first landing in Palestine, but this proceeding quite took the romance out of the event. I almost forgot I was in the Holy Land, while fully realizing the fact of being a prisoner. As soon as my brother and the monks joined me, we were led up the steps, to a door, which admitted us to a square inclosure, formed of low, flat-roofed buildings of stone, in a dilapidated state. In the center of the square, a wooden shed covers a deep well, and tall, large-leaved, thriving mulberry-trees throw a thick and welcome shade round it. The station was unusually full, owing to the outbreak of cholera in Egypt.

Our fellow-travelers, the Franciscans, were quartered on some ecclesiastical pilgrims, and lodged eight in one room.

The only chamber which was unoccupied opened into a little court-yard in the left-hand corner of the square, and that was allotted to us. It was by no means a pleasant lodging, but we determined to make the best of it. It was about twelve feet square. The floor was of stone. The walls were whitewashed; and the door, which was formed of rough planks, had no fastening inside. A casemented window, with half the glass out, looked toward the north, and showed us the blue sea, the rocky shore, and the southern wall of Yâfa with its curious profile of flat-roofed houses, rising step by step one above the other, with here and there a minaret or a palm-tree. Groups of children were playing under the trees near to us. The prospect without somewhat compensated for the desolate picture within.

There was nothing in the room but our luggage, our *garde de santé*, with his long stick, thousands of flies, an ant's nest, and ourselves.

I sat in the narrow window-seat, while my brother threw himself on the portmanteaus and boxes. For some minutes we could only laugh at each other, and at the ridiculous position in which we were placed. However, if we had not been in excellent health and good spirits, it would have been a serious matter.

Fortunately my brother was no stranger there, so help was at hand. Mr. Kayat, the English Consul—a native of Syria—sent his dragoman, who soon provided us with matting, mattresses, and wadded quilts, of which we made a sort of impromptu divan.

Soon afterward our kind friend, Mr. Graham, of Jerusalem, came to see us. He stood outside the window in the presence of the *garde*, who watched us continually. If our visitor had touched our hands, he would have been obliged to share our quarantine lodging. Mr. Graham lent us some of his tent furniture, cooking utensils, etc., and made our abode more comfortable.

When we sent to the market for provisions, we had to put the money in a cup of water to prevent infection, but we certainly looked more wholesome than any of the dirty little half-naked messengers who executed our commissions, and by whose aid we obtained fowls, goat's milk, coffee, rice, fruit, and vegetables, at a very reasonable rate.

There were two rooms in addition to ours opening into the court-yard. One was occupied by a party of Moslem travelers, and the other by the Franciscan pilgrims. The court-yard was in shade and cooler than the rooms, so with one accord we all took breakfast there.

The Moslems, after pouring water over their hands and feet, spread their carpets, prayed, and then sat round a dish of rice, butter, and tomatoes, putting their hands together into the dish. They ate rapidly and in silence, then washed their hands, and smoked chibouques and narghilés. The monks, who spoke French, Italian, and Spanish, invited us to share some of their conserves and sirups.

When the heat of the day had passed, we were allowed to take a walk, accompanied by a *garde*, to prevent our contact with human beings.

We gladly descended the steps of our prison, and reached the broad sands. The sun was going down, tinging the sea and the sky, and the white walls of Yâfa, with a red glow. We walked along the shore toward the south, with drifted sand-hills, more or less covered with vegetation on our left, and the waves of the sea approaching us on our right. We saw the skeleton of a camel half-sunk in the sand, and found many shells, and dorsal bones of cuttle-fish. About a mile from the quarantine station the beach was entirely composed of shells, most of them broken. The rocks, which form natural jetties, or rise up out of the beach, seem to be a sort of conglomerate of sand and shells, in every stage of hardness. These rocks were in appearance all alike, yet some masses were as firm and hard as marble; while other parts crumbled easily, and the imbedded shells separated from the sand with very little difficulty. When the sun had quite disappeared, the *garde* turned homeward, and we obediently followed. The town was already illuminated, and lights were reflected on the quiet water from the ships at anchor. The stars shone brightly, for night succeeds day very rapidly in this latitude, and there is scarcely any evening twilight.

The boy who acted as our cook and waiter had prepared our evening meal. It was spread on the ground under the mulberry-trees. A lantern stood on a large block of stone close by, and threw a flickering light upon the various dishes. The salt, which was very coarse and pungent, was served in a smooth hollow shell, to which the boy called our attention, that we might applaud the contrivance. We seated ourselves on a mat of reeds. Red ants, three-quarters of an inch long, were swarming around, and cats came running out of the darkness, eager to share our meal.

Many pilgrims and Bedouins were sleeping on the ground, in the open air, and mattresses were spread on the flat roofs or terraces of the buildings around.

No female servants are employed in the establishment, and there were no women among our fellow-prisoners. While my brother strolled in the starlight, smoking, I prepared our room as comfortably as possible under the circumstances. Even from our discomforts we extracted amusement, and at the same time learned some useful lessons in the distinction of the real and fancied necessaries of civilized life.

The next day the quarantine doctor, a Frenchman, sent word that he would visit us, to ascertain the state of our healths.

Presently he appeared in the little court-yard, with three official attendants. They stood opposite our doorway, carefully avoiding contact with ourselves and the other inmates of the quarantine. He greeted us with a profusion of compliments on our healthful appearance, and congratulated us on having obtained the best room in the station, and especially on having it entirely to ourselves! He left us with stately bows, and, kissing his hand, said, "I shall have the pleasure to give you *pratique* to-morrow."

On July 3d, at half-past seven, we were set at liberty. We gladly mounted the steps at the back of the quarantine station, traversed the extensive burial-ground, and passed the Government storehouse, a large building outside the town, where a crowd of camels were waiting to be relieved of their burdens, and women, vailed and shrouded in white drapery, were standing in groups, with baskets of mulberries and grapes balanced on their heads. On our left hand were the moated and battlemented walls of Yâfa, and on the other, gardens of orange and lemon trees, palms and pomegranates, which threw a checkered shade upon the sandy ground. We soon came to the broad road, just outside the town-gate, where camels and peasants, mules and muleteers, were congregated, and a bustling market of fruit and vegetables was being held. Booths and tents, sheltering turbaned and tarbouched smokers, were pitched under tall trees; and the itinerant vendors of coffee, sherbet, and glowing charcoal—ready to light the hundreds of pipes and narghilés around—seemed to be in great request.

In passing under the archway into the town, we had to walk carefully, to avoid getting entangled in the camel-ropes. I was glad to find shelter from the burning sun in the bazars, which are long arcades, shaded overhead with cloth or matting, with little open shops on each side. In many of them were shoemakers, cutting out yellow morocco slippers, or heavy red leather boots—tailors, marking out graceful patterns for gold embroidery—pipe-makers, modeling red clay bowls for chibouques—all seated on their heels, on little platforms, about two feet from the ground.

In another part of the bazar, the silks of Aleppo and Damascus, the cottons of Manchester, and vails of Constantinople and Switzerland, were exposed for sale, the shopkeepers, gravely smoking, reclined at their ease among the gay wares. The barbers' shops and the coffee-houses were much larger and more frequented than any of the others. I met no women in the bazars, men and boys do all the marketing in the towns of the Holy Land.

We descended a narrow, ruinous street of stairs, to the English Consulate, which was at that time close to the seaside. We were kindly welcomed, and led across a court to a square and vaulted stone chamber, with a deep raised recess in a rudely-built casemented balcony, looking on to the sea. A cozily-cushioned divan and a Turkey carpet made this a most pleasant retreat; and there, freed from the restraints of quarantine, I soon felt quite at home with Mrs. Kayat, a native of Syria, who, with Eastern hospitality, said, "This house is yours; order all things as you will."

Her young sister, Furrah, spoke English pretty well—thanks to the American mission-school of Beirût. She wore a white muslin dress, open to the waist, and exposing a thin net shirt, which did not conceal her neck and bosom, and through the semi-transparent skirt her full Turkish trowsers of blue silk could be seen. Their mother was dressed in a black velvet jacket, seamed with silver, and a soft, white silk skirt.

A number of gentlemen were in the body of the room, a step below us. They, as well as the ladies, were smoking narghilés. Strong coffee, without milk, and in tiny cups without handles, held in silver filigree stands exactly of the size and shape of common egg-cups, were handed round. After taking a cup, it is customary to incline the head slightly, raising the hand to the forehead, and thus to salute the host or hostess, who, in return, does the same to the guests.

An Arab breakfast was prepared, and a large party assembled to partake of it, including three beautiful little girls, the Consul's children, in a pretty costume, half European and half Oriental. A large dish of rice, boiled in butter, with pieces of fried meat imbedded in it, formed the staple dish. Vegetable marrows, filled with mince-meat and spices in place of the seeds which had been scooped out; some excellent fish, minced meat and rice rolled up in vine leaves, and dressed like small sausages; a happy *mélange* of meat, tomatoes, pine seeds, butter, and eggs; followed by roast fowl and a good salad; and a dessert, composed of all the fruits that the garden of Yâfa could furnish, gave me a very favorable impression of the Summer resources of a town on the coast of Palestine.

At about midday, after this meal, nearly every one of the family sought rest, lounging on the divans or musketo-curtained beds, to smoke or to sleep.

When the sultry hour of noon had passed, Mrs. Kayat invited me to go with her to see her cousin, Sit Leah, and her newly-born infant son. The ladies were soon ready for the walk, for the universal outdoor dress is very simple. A soft muslin vail, about a yard square, of showy pattern and many colors, is thrown over the head and face. A scarf or shawl girdle is fastened round the waist, and then a fine calico sheet, about two yards or more square, is put on like a cloak, but drawn up high over the head, and folded neatly on the forehead, brought under the chin, crossed over the breast, and, overlapping down the front, hides the dress entirely. It is tucked into the girdle in front, so as to lift it about three inches from the ground— at the back it is allowed to fall quite smoothly in a straight line to the heels. The hands are kept inside and hold the sheet, so that only the colored mask of muslin over the face is visible. No individual could be recognized in this disguise, except by some peculiarity in the manner of walking or singularity of figure. Yellow or red shoes, turned up at the toes, complete the costume.

My readers may easily imitate this costume with a sheet

and a colored silk handkerchief for a vail, and thus form a good idea of the general outdoor appearance of the women in the chief towns of Palestine. It must be remembered, however, that not a vestige of crinoline is to be seen, and full, soft trowsers, with sometimes a skirt over them, a jacket, and a shirt, is all that is worn under the *izzar* or *sheet*.* The three shrouded ladies led me out, and a kawass, not unnecessarily, went before to clear the way; for in the narrow streets of stairs, with their tortuous turnings and broken steps, it is well to have notice of the coming of a frisky horse, a heavily-laden mule, or a ponderous camel.

At the arched entrances of some of the large houses I noticed fragments of granite columns, marble bases, carved capitals and cornices, which had probably been transported from the ruins of Ascalon. They are used as stepping-stones for mounting and dismounting.

We entered a low doorway, and found ourselves in a court-yard, where a group of negresses were busy washing. They took me by surprise by seizing my hands, kissing them, and pressing them to their ebony foreheads. I soon learned to be on my guard, and to draw my hand away firmly but courteously, in time to elude the embrace; for I observed that this is the way the act of submission is expected to be received. The refusal to accept the kiss shows that you do not wish the individual who proffers it to humble himself before you.

However, under certain circumstances, the case is different; for instance, if a person asks forgiveness of you, or protection, or any favor, your refusal to allow him to kiss your hand or your feet is a sign that his request is not granted.

Priests always exact this homage, and it is very readily paid to them; but laymen, who invariably allow it, generally gain the *sobriquet* of "*Khouri*"—priest.

---

* Is this the kind of sheet referred to in Judges xiv, 12-18, where Samson says, "If you find out my riddle I will give you thirty sheets, and thirty changes of garments?"

We ascended a stone staircase to a terrace leading to two rooms. We entered the first, a pretty little square whitewashed room, draped with pink and white muslin. In one corner was a bed, made on the floor, and a narrow mattress, about a yard wide, ran round the other sides of the room. Cushions covered with damask were leaning against the walls, and thus a comfortable lounge was formed. A Turkey carpet concealed the stone floor. Several ladies were seated *à la Turque*, on the divan, smoking narghilés, the long flexible tubes of which radiated from the group of large red Bohemian glass bottles, which stood bubbling and sparkling in the center of the room. On the low bed a young mother was reclining. Her dark wavy hair, unbraided, escaped over the embroidered pillow. Her red tarbouche was decorated with folds of blue crape and everlasting flowers, her pale hands rested on the crimson silk wadded quilt, and her striped Aleppo yellow and white silk dress contrasted well with the dark brilliancy of her fever-bright face and eyes. I took her hand in mine, and she said, "Welcome, my sister; my lips must be silent, but my heart is speaking to your heart." She lifted up a tiny blue velvet lehaff—quilt—embroidered with silver thread, and revealed a baby boy of a few days old. I took him in my arms. The ladies with one accord said, "May you soon have the joy of holding in your arms new offspring of your father's house! May your brother soon be married, and be blessed with many sons!"

The infant I held in my arms was so bound in swaddling-clothes that it was perfectly firm and solid, and looked like a mummy. It had a band under its chin and across its forehead, and a little quilted silk cap on its head, with tiny coins of gold sewed to it. The outer covering of this little figure was of crimson and white striped silk; no sign of arms or legs, hands or feet, could be seen.

Leah's sister-in-law, whose head was much decorated with jewelry and artificial flowers, took the child from me and placed it in a swing cradle, draped with pink and white muslin, and everlasting flowers. She covered the little creature with such heavy quilts, that it seemed in danger of suffocation, then she closed the curtains round it, till there was no aperture left at which a musketo could enter.

After sherbet and coffee had been handed round by a black servant, I was led to the next room, where I found my brother with Habîb Nasîr, the husband of Leah, the proud father of a first-born son. I congratulated him, and his reply was a wish that I might soon have to congratulate my brother on a similar occasion. This is the customary answer.

In each of the rooms there were modern Greek pictures of sacred subjects, rude imitations of ancient Byzantine art, proclaiming that Habîb was a member of the Greek Church.

I returned to the consulate to prepare for our journey toward Jerusalem, Mr. Graham and Mr. H., a wanderer from the Crimea—then the seat of war—who had just arrived by Austrian steamer, having arranged to travel with us. When our luggage was in the care of the muleteers, and our horses were ready, we took a slight collation of goat's-milk cheese, fruit, sweetened starch, and native wines, in Mrs. Kayat's room, seated on the cushioned floor, round a low table inlaid with mother of pearl.

After taking leave of our kind host and his family, we mounted at their door, their blessings and good wishes ringing in our ears, "Go in peace, and return to us in safety; return speedily; peace be with you." The children and servants echoed the words till we were out of sight. An old man, in a coat of many colors, shaped like a sack, and with a curious mosaic-looking vandyked pattern on the back of it, led my horse up the steep streets of stairs, through the crowded bazars, and out of the town gate, which we had entered in the morning. It is in the middle of the east wall, and is the only land gate. I must here remind my younger readers that wheeled carriages are not used in Palestine. I never saw even such a thing as a wheelbarrow there; in fact, the roads are so bad that such conveyances would be useless; so people always travel on camels, or mules, or donkeys, or on horses, as we did. It was now about six o'clock, and just outside the gate the inhabitants of Yâfa were enjoying their pipes in the shade of the city, for the sun was going down toward the sea. Others were riding and galloping along the broad sandy road, which led us to a pleasant bridle path between hedges of a gigantic kind of cactus—the opuntia—the large, fleshy, thick-jointed stems of which were fringed with yellow flowers, promising a rich harvest of prickly pears. These formidable hedgerows rising from two to eight, and sometimes even ten or twelve feet in hight, were wreathed with graceful creepers, the briony, the clematis, and the wild vine twining their tendrils together. Our Crimean friend suggested that such a cactus hedge would prove an impenetrable barrier to advancing cavalry. This pleasant sandy path led us for three or four miles between beautiful fruit gardens, where the palm-tree, laden with golden fruit, towered high above all other trees. Oranges, lemons, pistachios, apricots, almonds, and mulberries were ripening. The pomegranate-tree showed its thick clusters of scarlet flowers, and acacias, locust-trees, tamarisks, silvery olives, and broad-leaved fig-trees flourished. It was about half-past six when we reached the open country beyond the extensive and well-cultivated gardens of Yâfa. The sun was going down behind us, over the sea. The far-away hills toward which we were journeying, east by south, were crowned with glowing red, while purple night shadows were rising rapidly. We passed through fields of mallows and gardens of cucumbers, with tents or little stone lodges for the gardeners scattered here and there.

The sun went down. Vultures and kites were sweeping through the air. As the darkness increased, our little party, consisting of six muleteers, our servants, and ourselves, assembled together to keep in close company for the rest of the way.

We could distinguish parties of field-laborers and oxen

at rest by the road-side, and sometimes we came to a rude thrashing-floor, where, by the light of a bonfire of weeds and thorns, we saw Rembrandt-like groups of rough-looking, half-clad peasants, some of them sleeping, and others lighting their long pipes with the fragrant embers. Our muleteers were singing monotonous and plaintive songs, only interrupted now and then when the jogging mules disarranged their burdens by jolting against each other, and the drivers would cry out, "*Ai-wa! Ai-wa!*" an interjection of very flexible signification, which answers nearly to our "Now then!" when used deprecatingly, or to "All right," or "Go on," under more favorable circumstances.*

We rode on in the darkness over an undulating plain, occasionally passing a well, a tomb, a little sleeping village, or a grove of ancient olive-trees, and reached Ramleh at half-past nine.

We had been invited to pass the night at the house of one of the principal Christian Arabs of the town, and soon met his servants and lantern-bearers, who had been watching for us. They led the way up a flight of stone steps to a small square court, round which lofty stone chambers were built.

Our host then conducted us to the guest-chamber, "a large upper room, furnished" with divans and cushioned window-seats.

His wife—a handsome and stately-looking woman, in rich Oriental costume—came to salute and welcome us. She took me to a long vaulted stone chamber, where two mattresses were spread on the floor; one was for me, and the other for two negresses who were appointed to attend me. Supper was spread for our party in an arched recess of the court, by two Abyssinian men-servants, who waited on us with intelligence and alacrity.

Presently, two awkward but good-natured-looking, black, woolly-headed, tall, white-robed, shoeless girls, led me to

* "Aiwa" is probably an abbreviation of "Al Wallah," a very significant oath.—E. T. R.

my room. They poured hot and cold water alternately over my feet and hands, and did all they could to make me comfortable. After a few hours rest, I rose by the light of the moon, which streamed in at the wide, unglazed, arched window.

The hinges, locks, and door-handles throughout the house were of beautiful design, somewhat resembling Italian work of the sixteenth century.

By the time the muleteers were roused, and our horses were in readiness for the journey, the sun had risen, and we hastened away. The market-places were already busy with buyers and sellers. The gardens of Ramleh are extensive and fertile; the date-palm, especially, flourishes there. The soil is sandy.*

Just outside the town, under a clump of tamarisk-trees, sat a group of dirty-looking Arabs, in picturesque rags. As we passed, they rose from their stony seats, and advanced toward us, holding out little tin cups for alms. I then perceived that the poor creatures were lepers! Their faces were so disfigured that they scarcely looked human; the eyelids and lips of some were quite destroyed, while the faces of others were swollen into frightful masses. It was the saddest sight I ever saw.

The families afflicted with this terrible and hereditary disease intermarry, and sometimes the immediate offspring are free from any appearance of it, but it is sure to revive in the succeeding generation; some of them appear quite healthy till they are nineteen or twenty, but they feel themselves to be a doomed race, and live quite apart from the rest of the world, subsisting almost entirely on charity—for often their fingers rot off and render their hands useless.†

In return for the few piasters we gave them, they cried, in hoarse whispers, "May it return to you tenfold!" "Peace

---

* "Ramleh" is the Arabic word for sandy; Arab names of places are very frequently descriptive.

† They live in special quarters in four towns in Syria; namely, Jerusalem, Damascus, Ramleh, and Nablûs, whither those born casually elsewhere are sent as soon as the disease has thoroughly shown itself. They are better off than

be with you!" We passed through fertile fields and orchards, overtaking peasants leading oxen or laden camels, or shepherd boys guiding flocks of goats to pasture land. Though the sun was low, and sent our shadows in long lines behind us, yet the rays were fierce with light and heat. The fields of sesame—called *simsim* in Arabic— looked very pretty. It is a tall, bright-green plant, with upright stems, garnished with blossoms, somewhat like the fox-glove, white, shaded with pink. The seeds yield a very fine oil, almost equal to olive. Blue chicory, yellow flax, the hardy goat's beard and convolvulus, of many tints, large and small, bordered the road. We soon reached an uncultivated part of the undulating plain, where the ground was burned up and cracked into deep, wide fissures, and where large blocks of stone, like cromlechs, cast their shadows. I watched numbers of green lizards and strange reptiles, running rapidly in and out of the cracks, and under and over the rocks, pausing sometimes, opening their eyes of fire to the sun, and nodding their large heads quaintly. Wild ducks were flapping their wings above our heads. Camels every now and then passed in strings of three or four together, their drivers bending and touching their foreheads gracefully as we passed. Some of the peasants wore scarcely any clothing. Flocks of goats and cattle were browsing on the scanty burned-up pasture, and the shepherd boys were piping on rude instruments made of cane or reed. At half-past eight o'clock we were in the shelter of the hills, and paused for a few moments at the entrance of a woody and rocky valley, called Wady-'Aly. Some Arabs brought us a supply of good water, in leather bottles. Mr. Finn, Her Britannic Majesty's Consul at Jerusalem, had sent his kawass there to meet and welcome us, and to lead the way, for in the hill country a skillful pilot is required. Wild

beggars in general, for they have foundations, "Wakf," and it is deemed a great act of charity by all classes of Orientals to do any kindness to these afflicted people. Those of Damascus, being chiefly Christians, were all killed, or, from their helpless condition, perished in the flames during the massacre and conflagration in the Summer of 1860.—E. T. R.

fig-trees, dwarf oaks, and thorns, grew among the rocks, and thousands of larks, disturbed by our approach, rose high into the air, but they did not sing the sweet song of the larks of our cornfields.

We passed over steep hills, wild and rocky, with treacherous stones slipping from under the feet of the often-stumbling horses. Sometimes the passes were so narrow that we had to ride singly, watching the leader carefully in his ins and outs among bushes and rocks. On the summits of many of the rounded hills there are ruins and large hewn stones, which have given rise to much discussion among Biblical topographists. We saw traces of terraces, and of former careful cultivation every-where, but the Winter torrents have been allowed to sweep away the protecting stones, and the rich, red loam is washed down, so that in many places large masses of bare limestone are exposed; but wherever the earth rests, however scantily, there is vegetation. Wild fruit-trees, shrubs, and aromatic herbs, thorns and thistles, prove the natural fertility of the soil. Even out of the small handfuls of earth washed into the holes and crevices of the rocks, tiny flowers spring, especially the wild pink and crane's-bill. We took zigzag paths up the faces of hills which looked almost perpendicular. Sometimes we gained a hight commanding views of the Great Sea and the plain of Sharon on one side, and the hills which concealed the city of Jerusalem on the other; then again we were in a narrow valley, or closed in by a seemingly impassable amphitheater of hills. Here and there our road was along ledges, so narrow—with a rocky ravine below, and a hill rising abruptly like a wall above—that we took the precaution of sending our leader to the end of the pass, to see that the way was clear, and to keep it so till we could traverse it. Eagles and vultures swept through the air. The sky was intensely blue, and the sun very powerful. Sparrows and finches were twittering among the trees.

At about ten o'clock we dismounted by a little *tell*, or

mound, in the center of a triangular space, where three valleys meet. Here there is a well of sweet and excellent water, and round it olives, figs, locust-trees, and evergreen oaks grow. A party of Bedouins were watering their camels at the stone trough connected with the well. Under the pleasant tree-shadows we rested, and on a bank of wild thyme and sweet marjoram we spread our simple provisions—"a basket of Summer fruit," a few thin cakes of flour, and some new wine. At the entrance to an extensive cavern, in the base of a hill opposite to us, a group of peasants were sleeping. The cave, like many smaller ones which we had seen, had been fashioned originally by nature, but man had at some period or other smoothed the inner wall, and made a dwelling there.

When we remounted, we passed through a partially-cultivated district. Groves of olive-trees bordered the dry bed of a Winter torrent, and patches of vines, and vegetables, and stubble-fields appeared on the terraces, till we came to higher and steeper hills in the neighborhood of Ajalon, covered with sage and wild lavender. The heat was sensibly increasing till about noon, when a pleasant breeze arose. This is generally the case in the hill country in the Summer time, the breeze rises at about twelve, lasts for an hour or two, and cools the air. We came into a cultivated region again, announcing a village near, and soon saw the white walls of the square castle-like houses of Abu Ghôsh, on a hill-side, and the fine ruins of an ancient Christian church to which a Franciscan convent was formerly attached. We dismounted at its large arched entrance; the groined roof and clear-story, supported by tall massive columns, are in good preservation. This building is now used as a stable and khan, but has often served the purpose of a fortress. It is very long since it echoed the litanies of the Franciscans, for they were expelled about the middle of the thirteenth century, when the sultan of Egypt conquered Jerusalem.

A cousin of the robber chief, the celebrated Abu Ghôsh,

is now sheikh of the village, and it is his policy to be very polite to Frank travelers.

We rested for a little while on the step of the church door. A group of women were drawing water from a well. We watched them as they walked one after the other toward the village, with the replenished jars poised perfectly on their heads. Herds of cattle and flocks of goats on the surrounding hills, richly-cultivated orchards and vineyards, and a few palm-trees, proclaimed this little village rich and flourishing. It is now called Kuryet el'-Enab, "village of grapes," the ancient Kirjath-Jearim probably.

A few hills more or less difficult were traversed. One, which seemed only fit for goats and conies to ramble over, we descended on foot, sliding over slabs of stone as smooth as polished marble, and leaping from rock to rock, over thorns and briers, till I was tired, and glad to mount again. Then we came to a pleasant terraced road, made on the slope of a hill, looking down into a fertile valley, where an Arab village has risen on the site of an ancient Roman colony, the record of which is preserved in the modern name Kolônieh. Traces of an amphitheater and fortifications were pointed out to me. We crossed to the opposite side of the valley, and pursued our way along a rocky ledge, till we came to a spring of living water, gushing from a rock above into a trough, which overflowed constantly. The water finds its way through ducts into the valley below. Maiden-hair, delicate creepers, and ferns, grew around, and thousands of birds congregated there—it is called the *Fountain of birds*. We, as well as our horses, enjoyed the deliciously cool water. We rode on again, and soon crossed an ancient Roman bridge, built over a water-course. There are the remains of a Jewish city by this stream, and local tradition says that David took from its bed the pebble which gave the death-blow to Goliath. Large stones, carefully hewn and beveled, are scattered in heaps, and half concealed by hawthorn bushes, wild rose-trees, fruit-laden blackberry brambles, and tall thistles. Others appear among rough unhewn stones, in the low walls which mark the boundaries of the vineyards and orchards near at hand. No doubt these large stones were once portions of stately palaces and strongholds, erected by skillful Hebrew builders long ago. Amos said, "Ye have built houses of hewn stone, but 'ye shall not dwell in them; ye have planted pleasant vineyards, but ye shall not drink wine in them."

The Arabs have a proverb in common use, which says, "The Jews built; the Greeks planted; and the Turks destroy." It is true that in nearly every town or village or deserted ruin in Judea, some traces of the massive architecture of the Jews—whose forefathers had served their toilsome apprenticeship in Egypt, among pyramids and temples—are discovered, sometimes serving as the foundation of Roman citadels and theaters, which in their turn have fallen to give place to the Moorish arch or minaret, and the mud-built hovel of the peasant; while all the ancient olive-trees, which stand in regular and equidistant rows, forming avenues in all directions, are said to have been planted by the Greeks, and present a striking contrast to the wild wood-like picturesqueness of younger olive plantations now fruitful and flourishing, as well as to the still more ancient trees now falling to decay.

Presently Mr. Graham said, "Now, Miss Rogers, prepare yourself for a treat. When we reach the summit of this hill, our eyes shall behold the city of the Great King." I quickened my pace, forgot my fatigue, and was soon on the hill-top, pausing to look around me, requiring no guide to point out the long, low line of battlemented wall, with a few domes and minarets rising above it, crowning the table-land of a hill which stood in the midst of hills, and I knew that I was looking on Jerusalem, "builded as a city," and "the mountains round about her." The afternoon sun was shining from behind us, brightening the white walls of the city, the gray-green tints of Olivet, which rises just beyond, and the long chain of the far-away mountains of Moab, seen here and there through openings in the Judæan hills. The

Mount of Olives, "which is before Jerusalem on the east," says Zechariah, is separated by slight depressions into three distinct parts. On the central and highest point a white-walled Moslem village stands, with olive and mulberry trees clustering round it. Near the summit of the northern hill, a little isolated square stone tower is conspicuous, and when Mr. G. pointed it out, he invited me to pay him a visit there, for it was his Summer retreat, and was commonly called "Graham Castle," by Europeans in Jerusalem.

We descended into a long, narrow, stony valley; but the view from the hill-top we were leaving was already photographed on my brain, and I have never lost the impression. Though I have seen Jerusalem under more beautiful aspects, and from more favorable points of view, the first sight had its peculiar charm.

We left the Yâfa road, and made our way toward the Talibîweh, where Mr. Finn, the English Consul, encamps in Summer time. It is about a mile west of the city. We rapidly approached a low, rough stone wall, inclosing a large tract of partially-cultivated land, on a gradually-sloping hill, looking toward Jerusalem. On the highest part of the ground a small square stone building stood, with seven or eight tents pitched near to it, among rocks, young trees, and shrubs. This I found was the consular encampment, and gladly I dismounted there, at four o'clock, P. M., welcomed by the Consul and his family.

The stone house consists simply of one lofty double-vaulted chamber, which serves for dining and general sitting-room, with veranda-sheltered seats outside it, looking toward the east. An arched recess—or *lewan*, as it is called in Arabic and Turkish—looks toward the west, and consequently is in shade in the morning. Kitchens and offices occupy the third and fourth sides. It was built by Jewish laborers, of a red and yellowish stone, from a quarry on the estate, and is not plastered either inside or out.

Mrs. Finn led me across a rough path, among little patches of newly-cultivated red earth, where melons, cucumbers, and vegetable marrows, were flourishing. Young castor-oil trees, palms, and oleanders, were springing up between large masses of rock. In their shelter the sweet basil, pinks, roses, as well as many English seedlings, were being coaxed into existence, making a cheerful though wild-looking garden round the pretty Egyptian tent prepared for me, the ropes of which were attached to some vigorous olive-trees, of two or three years' growth. I found my luggage already there, for the muleteers had arrived an hour or two before us. The blue tent lining appliquéd with black and scarlet borders, in patterns of good design, on the white canvas, the crimson cloth carpet, and simple tent furniture, looked bright and cheerful; while the views of the Bethlehem plain, Mount Zion, and Jerusalem, from the tent door, delighted me.

We passed the evening pleasantly with Mr. and Mrs. Finn, talking over our journey, and planning future ones. Their children were eager to show me their treasures, and to take me to all the memorable spots in the neighborhood they knew so well, for they were born in, and had scarcely ever been out of sight of Jerusalem. "I will take you to Olivet, and to the top of Mount Scopus, and then you can see the River Jordan and the Dead Sea," said Skander, the eldest boy; and little Constance added, "Mamma, may I take Miss Rogers to see Judas's tree, and the Garden of Gethsemane, and may we go to Bethlehem and to Solomon's Pools?"

These children, who had grown up amid such scenes, and who had learned to speak Arabic simultaneously with English, interested me exceedingly, evincing in all they said and did the effect of the influences around them. I showed to Constance an engraving of an English seaside view, and she immediately said, pointing to a castle, "There's the tower of David;" and again, pointing to the bathing machines, exclaimed, "These are the tombs of the kings, and there is the Dead Sea," the only sea which she had ever seen. After tea, the little ones were led by their pleasant-looking Armenian nurse, Um Issa, to the nursery tent, and Skander, wishing me good-night, added, "Do not be afraid if you hear the jackals crying and barking, they will not come to our tents; but we hear them every night, and they wake the dogs, and the horses, and the donkey, and then sometimes they all make a noise together." At an early hour Helwé, a woman of Bethlehem, brought in the lanterns which were to light us to our several tents. Mrs. F. led me to mine, and showed me how to secure it; while her niece warned me to look well at my clothes, and to shake them before putting them on in the morning, to get rid of ants or spiders, or perhaps a scorpion, which might creep into them at night. I watched the lanterns as they dispersed over the grounds to the different tents, and soon fell asleep amid the scenes and sounds that were so strange to me. It was difficult to realize the fact that I had left London only three weeks before.

CHAPTER II.

JERUSALEM.

IN the early morning, childish voices called me to come to breakfast in the lewan, on the shady side of the house. The sun was shining brightly over the city and the hills, but the western walls and slopes were still in shade.

After breakfast, we went to the sitting-room, which was almost as simply furnished as a hermitage, with rustic tables, camp stools, matting, and a few rough shelves for books and toys.

I sat on the doorstep, and looked over a rocky, thorny slope to a ridge which I was told marked the course of the valley of Hinnom, beyond which rose the western wall of Jerusalem; the turreted and massive-looking tower of David, and the Yâfa gate, breaking its monotony.

The Anglican church and consulate, with its pointed façade and strikingly modern appearance, the large white-domed Armenian convent, a minaret, a few palm-trees, pines, and cypresses, was all I could see of the Holy City, for it slopes eastward.

On my right hand was the plain of Rephaim. It spreads southward toward a rounded hill, which is crowned by the convent of Mar Elias. Long lines of camels, troops of horsemen, flocks of goats, vegetable-laden asses, and groups of peasant women, with baskets or bundles on their heads, were coming and going all day, along the broad road which crosses this plain, and vultures and eagles swept through the air.

In the afternoon I rode out with my brother. We went down into the stony valley of the Convent of the Cross, passing the white-walled newly-restored Greek convent, and made our way, among rocks and thorns, to the valley of Hinnom, well planted with olives, figs, and pomegranates. We ascended the hill leading to the Yûfa gate, meeting many people on foot and on horseback, who were just starting for a stroll before sunset. We passed under the deep, pointed archway, through the vaulted chamber in the great gate, along by the wall and deep moat of the citadel or tower of David, and then turned down a narrow passage, leading to the consulate, which adjoined the English church. Here we dismounted, and I felt a strange joy when, for the first time, my feet stood within thy gates, O Jerusalem!

Mr. Bartlett has made the streets of the Holy City so familiar in his "Walks about Jerusalem," and "Jerusalem Revisited," and Mr. Murray's invaluable Hand-Book gives its topography and statistics so perfectly, that I will refer my readers to those sources, and only give a slight account of the city as I saw it.

My brother led me back to the open space in the front of the citadel, where a daily market is held in the early morning. We passed a large open café, where soldiers and groups of Moslems were smoking. The Latin convent, a large, well-built stone edifice, is opposite the citadel; its long, flat roof serves for a terrace, where a number of monks and boys, in black robes, were walking in monotonous procession. The Anglican bishop's town-house overlooks the market-place, out of which we turned into a bustling street, paved with gradually-descending shallow steps, so smooth and worn, and so scattered with melon-parings and other vegetable refuse, that it was difficult to find a sure footing. On each side there were Arab shops, the owners of which were folding up their gay wares, or stowing away baskets of dried fruit or trays of pipes preparatory to closing for the night, for it was past the eleventh hour. We turned up Christian-street, the first turning on the left, where, besides the truly Oriental barbers' shops, the coffee-houses, pipe-makers, and bakers, there are several European establishments, kept by Maltese, and Italians, and Germans, pretty well supplied from London and Paris with ornamental as well as useful and necessary articles of dress; though, as may be anticipated, a large per centage is charged. We met crowds of Moslems, Spanish and German Jews, Bedouins, Greeks, and monks of many orders. I heard my brother greeted and welcomed by name, in various languages, by passers by, for he was well known in the city, where he had passed several years as *cancelière* in the British Consulate. We made our way to the Church of the Holy Sepulcher, and paused in the square court-yard in front of it, to look at its beautiful façade. Two arched doorways, side by side, with deep intricate moldings enriched with ball flowers, are divided by a magnificent cluster of five marble columns. The center and outside columns are green and the others white. The capitals are foliated, and richly carved. There are friezes across the doorways from the spring of the arches. The one to the right, over the door which is bricked up, is of ornamental scroll-work, with boys playfully introduced in arabesque style. The frieze over the left door, which is the only entrance to the church, is a well-carved alto-relievo picture of Christ's Entrance into the City, and the Last Supper, not exactly agreeing in character with the other frieze. We then went to the ruins of the Church of the Knights of St. John, near at hand. We passed under a wide low Norman arch, rich with zigzag and dog-tooth moldings, marble columns, and carved capitals. We climbed over a dust-heap, where vegetables and dead bodies of dogs and cats were rotting, where flies and fleas were regaling themselves, and half-naked, wretched-looking children were playing and munching melon parings. We crossed a court-yard, full of abominations, assailed by barking and snarling dogs, but tempted on by the strange beauty of this neglected relic of ancient chivalry. We found three high walls of the outer edifice standing, and within them there were divisions which indicated three distinct compartments; one is used as a tannery, and in the others we saw skeletons of asses and horses; for, when animals die in the neighborhood, their carcasses are dragged into this desecrated place to be devoured by dogs or vultures. We climbed over burning lime and rubbish to a rather treacherous stone stairway, which led us to a gallery above, corresponding with the cloisters below. Here there are two large windows with stone tracery, mullions, and moldings of early English character, in pretty good preservation.

Notwithstanding the offensive surroundings, I paid several visits to these interesting ruins. The style, for the most part, is like the Norman architecture of Sicily, while other parts of the ruins remind me of our early English style. The building altogether seems originally to have been built to serve the purpose of a fortress as well as an ecclesiastical retreat. It is said to have been founded in the eleventh century, as a place of rest for pilgrims to the Holy Sepulcher. It rapidly and continually grew in importance till the middle of the thirteenth century, when Christian influence was suddenly overthrown, and all its monuments destroyed, or allowed gradually to decay, as in this instance. Above the Norman door which we had entered I remarked a rich bas-relief of groups of figures, emblematic designs, and monograms, quaintly carved; but this has lately been so roughly used that it is now almost defaced, and future travelers will be puzzled to find it. When I revisited the spot in 1859—four years afterward—I found the door blocked up, and the space in front of it closed in and converted into a store or shop, for the sale of glass beads and bracelets made at Hebron. We shook the dust from our feet, and strolled a little way along the Via Dolorosa, till we were warned by the deepening shadows, and the evening cries from the minarets around, that the sun had gone down. We hastened through the streets and bazars. The little shops were nearly all deserted by their owners, and shut up for the night.

Our horses were waiting at the gate, which was kept open for us. A few stragglers were hastily entering in, but immediately after we had passed out, the heavy doors were closed, to be opened no more till sunrise.

The stars were coming out as we rode homeward, across the valley of Hinnom, and through an inclosed plantation belonging to the Greek community, in the center of which, by a well, under the trees, sat a group of Arabs in a circle on cushioned mats, singing lustily, and swaying their bodies to and fro slowly, in time with the monotonous tune which they sang. A large lantern, hanging from a tree-branch above, lighted up the figures and their many-colored garments, producing striking effects of light and shade.

We were soon on the Talibîych grounds. An immense number of vividly-bright glow-worms bordered the rocky path which led toward the house. I found that by placing a few of them together, on a stone or cool place, I could see to read by the green light which shone from their lantern-like bodies.

The next morning we rode down the Valley of the Cross, and over hills covered with rocks, poterium spinosum, and brambles, toward the little village of Lifta, near to which, in a beautiful olive grove on a terraced hill-side, Bishop Gobat and the Rev. H. Crawford had encamped with their large families. Their tents were picturesquely distributed under the shade of large trees.

There was no house on the grounds to serve as a retreat or shelter in the heat of the day, as on the Talibîych, but the trees under which Mrs. Gobat's pretty drawing-room or day tent was pitched, served almost as effectually as a protection from the sun. Sofas, cushions, easy chairs, writing tables and work tables, children with their dolls or lesson books, made the place look quite homely, and took away the idea of the transitory nature of tent life. Mrs. Gobat gave me a hearty welcome there, and introduced me to her friends who came from the surrounding tents, and to the children, who left their studies or their play to welcome us.

A large party was soon assembled in the tent and on the sofa under the opposite tree. After a luncheon of fruit and bread, olives, and cheese, Mrs. Gobat smoked a narghilé, evidently enjoying it, and I date the taste which I acquired for tumbac from the experimental pipe which I smoked with her. Coffee, mulberry sherbet, and bon-bons were handed around by Abyssinian servants in Arab style. Mrs. Gobat's fine, hearty-looking children, and the fair little Crawfords, seemed thoroughly to enjoy tent life. They showed me their swing in the mulberry-tree, and their attempts at architecture with the heaps of stones around. They led me eagerly from tent to tent, the kitchens, pantries, and school, and to the neat little bed tents, and then pointed out some of the finest points of view. Neby Samuel, the tomb of the "Prophet Samuel," was conspicuous on the summit of a conical hill, rising abruptly in the distance on one hand, and in another direction the widespreading valley, with a little village and its surrounding fields, vineyards, and thrashing-floor could be seen. A beautiful white goat followed us wherever we went. It was the goat which Mr. W. Holman Hunt used as his model while finishing his well-known picture—the Scapegoat. Two had died in his service, but this one became quite tame, and would answer to his call; he gave it to these children when his picture was completed. The loud, shrill cry of the cicalas was heard from every olive-tree, and I was assured that at night their noise is loud enough to keep people unaccustomed to it awake.

I spent several pleasant days in this retreat on various occasions; such as a social dinner-party at the Bishop's, when he presided at a long table under the trees, or a cheerful tea-party at the Crawfords', in their tents, partly by the light of the moon, and partly by the light of lanterns hanging in the trees, or round the tent-poles. In these *réunions*, and at similar entertainments at Mr. Finn's, I made the acquaintance of most of the European members of the Protestant community of Jerusalem. Sometimes we strolled about the grounds in little companies, visiting the vineyards and the bright-green sumach plantations below, or the thrashing-floor above, and the few scattered stone and mud hovels, roofed with tree-branches, which were the homes of the peasant guardians of the ground. In one of these little nooks we saw a stone handmill and two women working it, grinding corn.

The Europeans of Jerusalem, especially those who have children, or who have been accustomed to temperate climes, generally encamp thus from June to September, and select a site about a mile or more from the city, so that the gentlemen can go into town every day, while the ladies and children rarely do so except on Sunday. This is one of the pleasantest phases in the life of the European resident in Jerusalem, and it may be justly attributed to Mr. Finn, for he was the first who ventured thus to trust himself and his family in the open country. His little stone house on the Talibîyeh—of which he was the architect, while Jews were its builders—was the first and for a long time the only private dwelling-house outside the city; whereas now, 1862, buildings of importance and commodious dwelling-houses are rapidly rising on the hills round about Jerusalem.

On Sunday, July 8th, we had a pleasant early ride into town, and the chimes of the church bells welcomed us. Flags were hoisted at all the Consulates. Ladies and children from distant encampments were alighting at the doors of the Anglican church from sleek and gayly-trapped donkeys. The congregation consisted of about a hundred Europeans, including children, and about half as many Arabs and Jewish converts. The transepts were occupied by the children of the diocesan schools, all in simple European dress, but it was easy to distinguish the bright, intelligent countenances of the Jewish children—the gentle and amiable-looking little Abyssinians—the long-headed Copts—the precocious and handsome Arabs—and the pretty little Armenians, in spite of their uncharacteristic costumes.

The glare and heat were excessive, so I gladly accepted shelter at Mr. Nicolayson's till the cool of the day, and we rode to the Talibîyeh a little before sunset. Crowds of Arabs in holiday costume were strolling on the Medan, a large extent of table-land north-west of the city, where the troops are exercised. It is the favorite promenade of the citizens.

The men's dresses were picturesque and various in the extreme, and of every tint and color, from the somber robes of the procession of monks, to the gorgeously-embroidered jackets of the Turkish officers and *employés*, the high-pointed hats and long gabardines of the Jews, the bright sashes and turbans of the Moslem gentleman, and the light-braided suits and red tarbûshes of the Christian Arabs. The women, who kept in groups quite apart from the men, sitting under the olive-trees or strolling into the valley below, were all shrouded in sheets, and whether Jewish, Christian, or Moslem, the only variety in their dress depended on the color of the vail or mask, and the form or color of the shoes. Some of the ladies wore European shoes, others had socks and pointed slippers of yellow leather. The black slaves wore only red or yellow slippers, and thus could be distinguished from their mistresses. A few of the ladies carried gay parasols embroidered with spangles.

By starlight we wandered to the high ground behind the Talibîyeh. We could see watch-fires on many of the hills around and on the Bethlehem plain, and heard in the still night air echoes of the clear shrill voices of far-off shepherds, who were "watching their flocks by night," and giving signals perhaps to their fellow-watchers.

On Tuesday, 10th, I again rode into town, walked down Christian-street and through the chief bazars, now descending a dirty crooked street of stairs, now passing under narrow archways, dark and dusty, and through wide, lofty arcades or bazars, where the butchers' market, the bread, fruit, grain, and leather markets were respectively held.

The shopkeepers were crying to the passers-by, "Ho, every one that hath money, let him come and buy!" "Ho, such a one, come and buy!" But some of them seemed to be more disinterested, and one of the fruiterers, offering me preserves and fruit, said, "O lady, take of our fruit without money and without price; it is yours, take all that you will," and he would gladly have laden our kawass with the good things of his store, and then have claimed double their value. In a street leading to one of the bazars, a number of peasant women and girls from Bethany and Siloam were selling vegetables and fruit. They did not wear the white shroud of the townspeople. Their dresses were chiefly of indigo-dyed linen, and made like long shirts, girdled with red shawls or sashes. Their heads were covered with colored handkerchiefs or shawls, or white towels, so arranged as partially to conceal their faces, which were very dark and tattooed with blue stars and dots on the forehead and round the lips. Their dark eyes looked larger and darker on account of the kohl on the eyelids, and the black pigment on the eyebrows. They wore colored glass bracelets—made at Hebron—silver anklets, and some of them had necklaces of coins and silver rings. A very striking-looking young Siloam girl said to me, taking hold of my dress, "Taste of the fruit of our gardens and our vineyards, O sister!" My brother, by accident in passing a shrouded yellow-booted figure in the crowded street, slightly disarranged the folds of her izzar, and he said, "Your pardon, Ya Sitti"—*O my lady!* She answered, "Say not, '*Ya Sitti*' to me; say it rather to the queen of heaven." We met a large number of people afflicted with ophthalmy, and partial or entire loss of sight; but deformed persons are comparatively rare in Palestine.

In one of the most bustling bazars we saw a tall, gaunt man gesticulating in the midst of a crowd. He was almost naked, for he wore only a ragged strip of sackcloth round his loins. He carried in one hand a long, stout staff, and in the other a large stone. His vehement exclamations, excited manner, and fiery eyes reminded me of the descriptions of the prophets, as well as of the possessed of demons in days of old. His hair was long and wild, and his beard hung to his waist.

He cried out in Arabic, "The city shall be made desolate, fire shall consume it, because of its wickedness," etc.; and, notwithstanding his violent maledictions, and the weapons he carried, the people around did not interfere with him or molest him. He was evidently mad—or *majnûn*, as the Arabs say—and my brother told me that he had for years been a tolerated wanderer in the bazars, and wherever he went an idle crowd followed him. He lived on charity. The Orientals invariably treat with kindness and consideration those who are thus afflicted, believing them to be under the especial protection of God. It is imagined that they have a greater knowledge of spiritual things in proportion to their want of it concerning things of this life; in fact, in the East, a "madman" and a "prophet" are almost synonymous terms.

We entered the quiet, picturesque, but narrow street, in which the Prussian Consul resides. Pointed arches, with groined and fretted roofs, cross it here and there, and fine buttresses support some of the houses, which are built of large, well-hewn, beveled stones, put together with lead instead of mortar. The deep-arched entrances, canopied with dropping fretwork, are good examples of the Moresque style. Low stone divans, or benches, just within the portals were occupied by stately-looking armed servants, or black slaves. There are many alabaster tablets and friezes let into the walls, over doors, or under oriel windows, or in arched recesses, on which Arabic inscriptions and monograms are elaborately carved in slight relief, and in some cases illuminated in red, blue, and gold. The graceful Oriental characters, with their flowing lines, are well adapted for this sort of ornamentation, and are very extensively used in the exterior as well as interior decorations of Moresque buildings. Ancient carved capitals, near to the doorways, served as stepping stones; and in many places horses were haltered to large perforated blocks, which projected from the walls.

We made our way along the Via Dolorosa, pausing, sometimes, while a long line of donkeys, laden with stones or brushwood, jogged by, enveloped in a cloud of dust; or when a string of unwieldy camels, bearing melons to the market, almost blocked up the way.

We met the colonel of the Turkish cavalry, and several officers. They kindly invited me to mount the rude steps leading to a broad and elevated terrace of the Seraglio, or Pasha's Palace. From this central and lofty spot, I first gained a general idea of the city, and the surrounding hills. The building on which I stood was partly formed by the north wall of the Haram, or Great Mosque inclosure; and thus, looking toward the south, I overlooked its entire area, which is almost equal in extent to one-quarter of the whole city. In its center the well-known Kubbetes-Sakhara, or "Dome of the Rock," stands.

The beautiful cupola, resting on a circular base, crowns a wide-spreading octagonal building, each side of which is ornamented with six lofty arches, and the lower part is faced with bright enameled tiles of many tints. This building is on a large square platform, raised considerably above the other parts of the inclosure, and is approached from six points by broad flights of steps, which lead to light and graceful entrances, divided by three or four elaborately-carved columns and pointed arches. There are many little praying niches and stone canopies, supported on columns, and alabaster pulpits on the platform, as well as in the grass-grown inclosure below, where the white stone walls and domes are relieved by the dark beauty of the cypress and the silvery shade of olives, and some few shrubs in flower. A beautiful grove of trees leads to the Mosque-el-Aksa, which is in the southern part of the area, where its long and gabled roof, large dome, and Saracenic façade are conspicuous. Groups of white-turbaned Moslems sitting in the tree-shade, solitary devotees at the little shrines or niches, and the slow pacing of Turkish sentries or black slave guardians of the Holy Place, gave some animation to the otherwise picture-like stillness of the scene.

The contrast is very great between this bright spot on Mount Moriah and the other part of the city, which is traversed by a valley and covered with irregular masses of white-domed and terraced buildings, relieved here and there by a tree, a church, or a minaret. The extreme southern quarter is the most desolate, and is inhabited by the Jews. The south-west portion is chiefly thronged by Armenians, where their convent stands, white and conspicuous, and marks their quarter distinctly. The north-west quarter—*the highest*—is more frequented by Franks; and the Church of the Holy Sepulcher, the Latin convent, the Protestant church, and various consulates, proclaim it. The north-east is the Moslem quarter. The patches of open land within the city are, in some places, used as drying-grounds for indigo-dyed linen; while others have become public dust-heaps or dunghills. I could trace the battlemented walls of the city, now following the downward sweep into the valley, and then rising in an irregular line to crown the hights of Zion.

After we had lingered there for some time, fascinated by the scenes around, the military governor led us to a divan, where we took coffee and sherbet. He excused himself for not taking refreshments with us, for it was Ramadan, the month in which Moslems fast from sunrise to sunset daily.

We then called on several European families—English, German, Greek, and Russian. The vaulted stone chambers in which we were generally received were cool and pleasant even at midday, and so furnished as to combine Oriental and Western luxuries. In the deep, arched recesses and broad window-seats, soft cushions were arranged and loose muslin drapery floated from the open windows, fanning the air. Glowing Turkey carpets and Egyptian matting covered the stone floors. The newspapers, bookcases, pictures, pianos, and little works of art or knickknacks, proclaimed that Europeans had made homes there; while on the terraces, and under the columned corridors, English flowers appeared among the native oleanders and jasmines, shaded by vine-covered trellises. But in these Europeanized houses, European servants are very rare. Almost every-where Abyssinian men-servants are sought in preference to natives, for they are intelligent, attentive, and faithful; and the hardy, but somewhat self-willed, Bethlehem women are in great request as house-servants, for they are clean and comparatively careful. I perceived that the training and management of a staff of Oriental attendants is one of the chief difficulties that European ladies have to contend with.

July 15th was a very sultry day. We all retired early to our tents, fatigued with the heat. About midnight I was aroused by the violent movement of my light tent bedstead, and a loud murmuring noise. My first thought was that an earthquake was disturbing the hills; then I fancied that some wild beast was near; and, lastly, I came to the conclusion—which proved to be the right one—that my tent was in danger of being carried away by a whirlwind. It had blown open in two places, and its yielding walls beat against the light frame-work of my bedstead.

The noise of the flapping canvas, the tightening and straining of the tent ropes, the rustling and snapping of the young trees, and the continuous rocking, kept me awake for a long while. I quite expected to be left shelterless, for I was on the highest part of the grounds.

On the morning of July 16th there was a general fixing and repairing of tents, and a search for hammers and tentpegs, for all the canvas dwellings had been more or less disturbed by the wild wind of the preceding night. At sunrise, the air was soft and warm, but clouds were being driven from the north in large masses, burnished by the morning sun. A south-west wind had driven those clouds from Egypt a day or two before, and now, unbroken, they were chased back again to their source, the mighty Nile. We wandered through the grounds, replanting the uprooted trees, and supporting the fallen ones, for none had escaped injury.

Before breakfast, I rode with my brother to the Convent of the Cross, in the lonely valley to which it gives a name. The convent has been lately very thoroughly restored by the Greeks, to whom it now belongs; and an excellent college has been established there for about forty or fifty students. It was formerly the property of the Georgians, and was founded by them in the fifth century, on the very spot where grew the tree which furnished the wood of the cross. This is, at least, the tradition which our monkish attendant gravely told as he led us into the church, a fine building, about seventy feet long, with a groined roof supported by four massive piers. The walls are covered with curious frescoes; and the altar-screen contains a pictorial history of the sacred tree, from the time it was planted by Abraham and Lot, till it was hewn down and formed into a cross. As sculpture is strictly forbidden in the Georgian and Greek churches, all the decorations depend on color; but in some of the pictures there was a compromise, the figures being cut out in thin wood, and mounted on appropriate backgrounds. The nimbus, in almost every instance, is formed of pure gold, and stones and jewels are introduced in the adornment of the dresses.

In the center of the church is a large square pavement of mosaic, the finest I met with in Palestine. Quaint birds, curious figures, and Christian symbols are represented, and in the lozenge-shaped spaces left by the intersecting lines of the frame-work of these devices, most beautiful designs are introduced. The tesseræ of which this pavement is composed are about three-quarters of an inch square, and are black, white, red, blue, and yellow. We hastened back to breakfast. The blue sky was flecked with fleecy clouds fastly moving, and the mountains round us were checkered with their shadows. One moment a hill was crowned with sunlight, the next it was all in shade. The flocks of goats browsing on the hill-sides, and peasant women making their way to the city, laden with vegetables, bowls of milk, and baskets of fowls, animated the landscape. L. and the children returned with me to the convent, where I spent the whole day, drawing delightedly some of the curious mosaic pictures. (I will refer those who take an interest in early Christian art to No. 878 of the Builder, published December 3, 1859, in which some examples of these are given from my sketch-book.) Considering that these buildings were deserted and left in ruins for two or three centuries, it is surprising that so much of the ancient work remains in good preservation. We were led to a cavern under the altar, and the identical spot where the sacred tree grew was pointed out to us in a damp and dark recess. We saw some workmen destroying an ancient Georgian MS. They were using the parchment to make bags for their dry powdered colors, and willingly gave me a few sheets. The garden terrace of the convent is roofed with trellis-work covered with vines, and the rich fruit hung above us in heavy clusters. We strolled home on foot, gathering bright-blue borage, wild pinks, and geraniums.

A red, cloudy sunset was followed by a calm moonlight night, only disturbed by prowling jackals, noisy hyenas, and wild dogs without, and buzzing musketoes within. In the morning I found the tent curtains saturated with dew, and the garments which had been hanging there during the night were too damp to be put on with safety.

CHAPTER III.

AROUND ABOUT JERUSALEM.

In the mean time all my leisure hours were spent in studying Arabic. The little ones at the Talibîyeh were never tired of adding to my vocabulary, which I practically applied whenever an opportunity arose, such as during the visits of Arab guests or work-people, and in my daily intercourse with the native attendants, whose voices rapidly grew familiar to me. Some of the elder women-servants were very demonstrative and affectionate, and often when I uttered a request, or gave directions in some newly-acquired words, they would reward me, (?) or testify their delight by clasping me in their arms and kissing me. I had been accustomed to hear Arabic spoken for a year or more, so the sounds were not strange to me.

On the 17th of July, after a quiet day of study, I started with my brother for Beit Lahm—that is, Bethlehem—the sun was going down, and purple shadows were swiftly rising in the eastern sky. We made our way over a rocky, pathless slope, and a few fields of sesame, till we reached the broad level road which traverses the fertile plain of Rephaim, where the Philistines were routed by David. This road is about a mile in length, and is the only place remaining in the neighborhood of Jerusalem fit for a carriage drive, though in many spots traces may be seen of ancient roads, telling of the time when "King Solomon had four thousand stalls for horsemen and chariots, and twelve thousand horsemen, which he bestowed in the chariot cities and at Jerusalem."

We passed over the plain quickly, the kawass galloping before us, and soon came to a spot where no carriage could have served us. Our horses stumbled over smooth slabs of rock and loose stones as we rose on to the rounded and terraced hill on which stands the Convent of Mar Elias, or Elijah, a massive building of gray masonry, in the midst of olive groves and flourishing plantations. A moon of three days old and her attendant star shone in the clear blue sky, just above the silvered tree-tops. We paused on the hill to rest our panting horses, and to look around us. Southward we could see the picturesque town of Bethlehem, white and gleaming. Between the hills to the east we caught glimpses of the Dead Sea, and the Moab mountains beyond. Turning to the north we saw, brightened by the moonlight, the southern wall of Jerusalem, and the buildings on the brow of Mount Zion; and on the west an olive grove bounded the view. The kawass brought me some water, in a curious little two-handled cup of red pottery, from the stone reservoir provided for travelers by the good monks of Mar Elias.

We then descended abruptly into a valley by a declivity which would have terrified me a week or two before; but I had become accustomed to rough riding on the rude hills round about Jerusalem. We reascended, and swept round hill-sides covered with well-kept terraces of fig and olive-trees. The rude parapets supporting the rich earth were garnished with hanging creepers and luxuriant foliage, which threw dark but delicate shadows on the white limestone. Here and there we saw rows of quaint-looking ravens, perched on the rock ledges tier above tier; some of them silent and motionless, others nodding their heads together as if in consultation. A pleasant bridle-path, half-way up the western boundary of a broad valley, led us toward the white walls and flat-roofed houses of Bethlehem. We passed under a pointed archway, and between low, scattered buildings, till we entered a high-walled, gloomy street. Looking down on our left, we caught glimpses through the open doors of family groups, in lamp-lit rooms, built a few steps below the level of the road. Cheerful-looking women and children and stern-browed men strained their eyes, looking out of the light into the darkness, to try to see us as we passed—the clattering of our horses' feet over the stones having broken the stillness of the place. We came again to an open terrace, and could see the hill-side above and below dotted with houses, on the flat roofs of which many families were already sleeping. From the unglazed windows flickering lights were shining. Clusters of trees grow here and there throughout the town. The Church of the Nativity, surrounded by convent buildings, rises like some baronial castle, gloomily and grandly, on the steepest side of the hill.

We passed under a deep arched way, which led us into the Convent Court, where we alighted, and were kindly welcomed by the Latin recluses, who were expecting us. The Spanish Consul of Jerusalem and his wife were there; with them and the Superior, and a few well-educated Spanish and Italian monks, we passed the evening pleasantly in the divaned reception-room. After an excellent supper we were shown to our several apartments. The Superior led me to a large, vaulted, gloomy chamber, in which I felt quite lost, when the heavy door closed upon me and I was alone. There were eight closely-curtained iron bedsteads in the room, and I peeped rather timidly into every one. A small lamp of red clay, like a deep saucer, with a lip on one side shaped to support the lighted wick, stood in a little niche; but its feeble red glow was almost lost in a stream of moonlight which fell from the grated, unglazed window above the door, glancing on the walls and the white curtains, and throwing a patch of checkered light on the stone floor. I was a martyr to musketoes that night, and as soon as daylight appeared through the grated window I rose, and wandered about the corridors, meeting the monks on their way to morning prayer, and witnessing the distribution of bread to the poor convent pensioners who crowded to the gates. The women carried away their provisions in the corners of their linen vails, but the men and boys put their loaves of bread in the bosom of their open shirts, their girdles supporting the burden.

On meeting my brother we went, guided by one of the Latin monks, to the Church of the Nativity, built by the Empress Helena, in A. D. 327. It is said to be the oldest monument of Christian architecture in the world. The shafts of the forty columns which support the fine architrave and decaying roof are each of a single piece of marble, more than two feet in diameter, about sixteen feet in hight, and surmounted by elaborately-carved capitals. These may have formed a part of some more ancient building. It has been suggested that they were brought from the ruins of the Temple at Jerusalem. The upper part of these columns are frescoed with Greek and Byzantine figures of saints and martyrs, while lower down are some curious sketches and monograms, by crusaders perhaps, or pilgrims of the Middle Ages. Above the columns and on the walls there are remains of ancient mosaic pictures of glass, and stone, and metal. I could make out groups of figures, views of cities, strange devices, and ornamental borders. They had been recently discovered under plaster-work, and were being ruthlessly scraped away, when an English traveler put a stop to .the destruction by pointing out to the Superior the value and interest of these relics.

Here the Greeks, Latins, and .Armenians have their several shrines and services, and they sometimes have very fierce conflicts about them. We went down into the Grotto of the Nativity, so well known through dioramic and other pictures, with its silver lamps, its fumes of incense, silken tapestries, and gilded saints. On the floor in front of the altar a star marks the spot said by tradition to show the very place where Christ was born; but I was not moved with mysterious awe; it was not here that I realized the scene in the manger; and surrounded as I was by priests, in their gorgeous robes, and pictures, and treasures, from France, Italy, Spain, and Greece, I could scarcely even believe that I was in Bethlehem.

We visited the convent schools. In one room fourteen handsome, intelligent-looking Bethlehem boys were learning Italian. They showed us their exercises and translations, and sang a Latin hymn to the Virgin, giving a peculiarly Oriental twang to the last sounds of every line. Another school-room which we entered was crowded with younger boys, learning to read and write Arabic; but they were dirty, disorderly, and noisy, and we did not linger there.

After taking breakfast with the Latin Superior—who related to us stories of recent miracles wrought in the sacred grotto, with earnestness and simplicity, as if he thoroughly believed what he said, and wished us to benefit by it—we hastened away, and walked through the steep streets and passages, and among the scattered buildings of the town. It is almost entirely peopled by Christian Arabs, of the Latin, Greek, and Armenian Churches, and they number altogether about three thousand two hundred.* They cultivate their fields and terraced gardens with care, and send large supplies of vegetables and fruit to Jerusalem every day; but one of the principal occupations of the Bethlehemites is the carving of various articles in mother-of-pearl and olive-wood.

We inquired for a young man, an orphan, whom my brother knew to be one of the most skillful carvers in the town. The neighbors who guided us to his door said:

---

* There was formerly a considerable Mohammedan quarter in Bethlehem; but after the insurrection of the people in 1834 it was entirely destroyed. The houseless Moslems fled and distributed themselves over the neighboring country, some settled in Moslem villages, and others enlisted. A few took to tent life, and have ever since wandered about like the Bedouins, except that they retain their custom of observing religious forms and ceremonies, fasts and feasts, more strictly than nomadic tribes usually do. During the month of Ramadan, they select a spot for their encampment within sight of Jerusalem, that they may see the flash of the gun fired from the citadel at sunset, to announce the moment when Moslems may break their fast.

Some of these scattered Moslems, however, are by degrees returning, to settle in Bethlehem.

"Be glad, and enter in with joy, for this is to-day a house of rejoicing." We found the carver at his work, seated on the floor. He rose up with evident delight to receive my brother, who had formerly protected him, and helped to establish him in business. He said, "Welcome, O my master! thank God that he has led you back to this land, to see the fruit of your goodness, the work of your hand. You have built up my house, you have made me to rejoice, you have given me a son!" My brother replied, laughingly, "You speak in riddles darkly, make your words plain, O my friend." The carver took up a handful of tools, saying: "O my protector, you gave me these tools—these tools brought me gold—the gold brought me a wife, and my wife brought me a son, on the night of the new moon!"

He had once been in my brother's service, and during that time showed decided taste for carving, which my brother encouraged by giving him a little instruction in the art, and some English tools.

Round the room, and hanging on the white-washed walls, were a number of small inlaid mother-of-pearl table-tops, about half a yard square, intended for the stands or stools on which coffee and preserves are placed in Oriental establishments. Carved rosaries, crucifixes, cups, and crosses, of olive-wood, decorated the place. The carver showed us, with especial pride, some large flat shells, on which he had sculptured pictures of sacred subjects and holy places; and some beads carved in bitumen, from the shores of the Dead Sea. During the past Easter he had reaped a goodly harvest, for the pilgrims eagerly buy these objects, and, when they are blessed by the priests, preserve them as relics. The English travelers, too, had bought a great number of paper knives, bracelets, and brooches, made at my brother's suggestion—the original sketches for which the carver had preserved with loving care, and with new expressions of gratitude he showed them to me, saying, "Peace be on his hands." While speaking, he was especially bright and intelligent-looking. His long dark-blue and red-striped coat, his crimson girdle, and red and yellow shawl head-dress, twisted into turban-form, became him well. He invited me to see his wife and child. I delightedly rose and followed him across a little square court-yard, partly sheltered by matting, supported by planks and tree branches, and partly by a vine, which traveled over a rude trellis-work. In one corner of this court were a large number of oyster-shells from the Red Sea, some of them a quarter of a yard in diameter; lumps of bitumen, from the wilderness of 'Ain Jidy; and pieces of rock, from Jerusalem, of red and yellow tints. The carver pointed these out to me as his stock of raw material. A pile of fine melons, and a row of water jars, stood on one side, while a bleating sound drew my attention to the other, where a fatted lamb stood munching mulberry-leaves. Into this central court the four rooms of the house opened; but, as it is built on a hill-side, the shop floor is a step or two below the level of the court, while the room opposite to it is raised considerably. We mounted a few steps, and my host left me at the open door of this upper chamber, within which, seated on a mat, was a pretty-looking woman, with a round, childish, cheerful face. Perfectly unembarrassed by my unexpected appearance she rose, and, after placing her hand on her breast, and then carrying it to her forehead, she said, "Be welcome, and be pleased to rest here." This was the carver's wife. An elder woman, whom I afterward found to be her mother, placed some pillows for me on a small carpet, and then took a little swaddled figure from a curtained rocking-cradle of red painted wood. She placed it on the skirts of my dress, saying, "Behold the gift of God!" I took the little creature in my arms. His body was stiff and unyielding, so tightly was it swathed with white and purple linen. His hands and feet were quite confined, and his head was bound with a small soft red shawl, which passed under his chin and across his forehead in small folds; to this a moldering relic of St. Joseph, in a crystal case, was attached. His mother wore a long blue linen shirt, rather scanty, and opening in front to the waist, a straight short pelisse or jacket, of crimson and white striped silk, and a shawl girdle. A long thick white linen vail hung over her head and shoulders, and partly concealed her stiff tarbûsh or cap, which was ornamented with a row of small gold coins, and a few bunches of everlasting flowers. The elder woman wore a heavy shirt or smock of blue linen, the wide hanging open sleeves of which exposed a tattooed and braceleted arm. Her long white linen vail fell from her head over her shoulders, in graceful folds to her feet, which were naked. In such a vail as this Ruth, the young Moabitish widow, who three thousand years ago gleaned in the fertile fields of the broad valley below, may have carried away the six measures of barley, which her kinsman, Boaz, the then mighty man of wealth of Bethlehem-Judah, had graciously given to her, saying, "Bring the vail that thou hast upon thee, and hold it; and when she held it, he measured six measures of barley, and laid it on her, and she went into the city." Ruth iii, 15.

I asked the young mother her name; she answered, "Miriam is my name;" but her mother said, "Not so, she is no longer Miriam, but 'Um Yousef' [mother of Joseph,] for a son is born unto her, whose name is Joseph."

It is the universal custom in the East, for a mother to take the name of her first-born son, with the prefix of "*Um*"—mother—such as *Um Elias*, mother of Elias; or *Um Elia*, mother of Eli, whence perhaps came such names as *Em*ma, *Emi*ly, and *Am*elia. On the same principle the father's name is changed as soon as he has a son, whose name he adopts, with the prefix of "*Abu*"—father. It is a source of great distress and disappointment to parents if they are, for want of a son, obliged to retain their respective names.

The little mummy-like figure in my arms began to show signs of life, by uttering a feeble sound, in the universal language of babyhood. The mother took it from me, and before holding it to her bosom she reverently kissed a small silken bag, embroidered with gold, and then pressed it to her forehead. In answer to my look of inquiry, she explained, partly by words, and partly by signs, that the little bag, which hung from her neck, contained a piece of crumbling white stone, from a grotto near to Bethlehem, sanctified by the milk of the Blessed Virgin, which once overflowed there, and mothers eagerly procure it, to place in their bosoms as a charm.

The room in which we sat was very simply furnished. It was nearly square. The floor was of stone, and the walls were whitewashed. On a broad, high shelf running round three sides of it, many articles of native crockery and earthenware, drinking cups, jars, lamps, and metal dishes, were ranged. A mat of reeds, a carpet about as large as a hearth-rug, and several pillows or cushions were on the floor. A large red box, with brass hinges and ornaments, served as the wardrobe of the family. The red cradle, a large metal basin and ewer, and a few small coffee-cups, on a low stool or stand, of inlaid mother-of-pearl and dark wood, garnished the room. In a deep, arched recess, opposite to the door, a number of mattresses and wadded quilts were neatly piled up. In genuine Arab houses no bedsteads are used, and consequently no rooms are set apart expressly for bedrooms. Mattresses are spread any where, in the various rooms and courts, or on the terraces, according to the season, or to the convenience of the moment; and the beds and bedding are rolled up and put away during the day, in recesses made for them. Thus, with a pretty good stock of mattresses and lehaffs, a large number of guests may be entertained any night, at a moment's notice. The room was well ventilated by two large square openings, near the ceiling, opposite to each other, one being just over the door, and the other over the recess for the mattresses.* I took a cup of coffee and some sugar-plums,

---

* This sort of bed could easily have been carried away by the sick man of Capernaum, to whom Christ said—as recorded in the second chapter of Mark—" Arise,

and then said, "Good-bye," or rather, "God be with you," to Miriam. The elder woman led me back across the court, pointing to a kitchen on one side, and to the well-filled store-room on the other. She drew her long white vail across the lower part of her face, as we entered the workshop. She kissed my brother's hands, and then served us with coffee and preserves. Our servants now arrived with the horses, and we left the workshop of the Bethlehem carver. His parting words, "The peace of God be with you, O my protector;" and the answer which my brother gave, "God's blessing be upon you and upon your house," reminded me of the salutations exchanged by Boaz and the reapers, long ago, in one of the fields at the foot of the hill we were descending, where we could see oxen treading out the corn on the numerous thrashing-floors.

We approached the particular spot which local tradition connects with the names of Ruth and Boaz; but it was enough for me that they had met somewhere in that broad and fertile valley, and that the town of Bethlehem, though changed, was the very town in which Ruth rejoiced over her first-born son; where the sorrows of Naomi were turned into joy, and "the women, her neighbors, rejoiced with her." We stood in the midst of little groups of men, women, and children. Some were attending to the mules

and take up thy bed and go thy way into thine house;" and if the houses of Capernaum were built like most of the houses of the present day in the towns of Palestine, the uncovering of the roof referred to in the fourth verse of the same chapter, admits of an easy explanation. The inner court of the house is usually more spacious than any of the surrounding rooms, and often there are platforms or benches of stone on each side, spread with carpets and cushions, used as divans during the day and as sleeping places at night. To such a court Christ may have retreated when the crowd increased. We may imagine him there, with the wondering people round him, and the crafty and scornful scribes seated near on the divan—all sheltered from the hot sun by some kind of matting or canvas, supported on a trellis-work of tree-branches and planks, more or less secure. When the sick man was carried by his friends to the house where Christ was preaching, "they could not come nigh to him for the press," so they very naturally went on to the terrace or house-top, and "uncovered the roof" of the court, that is, they removed the matting which sheltered it, and then they "broke up" the trellis-work and let down the bed whereon the sick of the palsy lay. If an ordinary house-top had been broken up, the wooden beams, and the masses of earth and stone of which it is composed, would in falling have endangered the lives of those below.

and oxen on the thrashing-floor; others were gleaning and weeding in the neighboring fields; and the noisiest and most active were busy loading some kneeling camels with sacks of grain. Assisted by the contemplation of this busy scene, and the remembrance of the incidents of the morning, I could fully realize the beautiful story of Ruth. We crossed a field of Indian corn, to pause for a moment under the shade of the clump of trees, said to mark the spot where the shepherds were keeping watch over their flocks by night, when the "good tidings" were proclaimed. The place is now called the "Shepherds' Garden," and is in the keeping of the monks of Bethlehem. We rose on to the hill-side again, and peeped into the Milk Grotto, in which tradition says that Mary rested on the eve of her flight into Egypt. It is a cave in a very white limestone rock, and has been undergoing excavation for centuries, on account of the before-mentioned supposed virtue of the stone. Fragments of it are treasured in all parts of Syria, and in many countries of Europe. I have often seen it used successfully. It seems to me, that the mere fact of not being provided with this relic will, in nervous subjects, occasion a deficiency of milk, and in such cases herbs and other medicines, wise women and doctors, are resorted to in vain; but whenever a portion of this crumbling stone can be procured, through the hands of a priest, tranquillity is restored, and favorable results follow. In this way many so-called miracles may be accounted for.

We rode on southward toward Urtâs, passing over terraced hills, where the vines, and olives, and fig-trees grew luxuriantly, and little white stone watch-towers peered out here and there, in commanding positions, from the midst of the thick foliage. Near to the winding bridle-path we saw now and then a cottage or hut made of rough, unhewn stones, and roofed with tree-branches, standing in a garden of cucumbers, or tomatoes, or a choice vineyard. One of these rude dwellings was being clumsily repaired by a group of boys, who had been gathering stones and sticks

for the purpose, and were shouting merrily over their work.
From another of these little huts there came forth, as if by
magic—for it did not look capable of containing them—
five young Bethlehem girls. Three of them were very
pretty, brilliant brunettes — the others rather fair. All
looked strong and hearty, with rich color and large clear
eyes. They advanced, half-shyly, half-daringly, to peep at
us as we passed. Their simply-made, loose purple linen
dresses, girdled below the waist negligently; their long
wide sleeves, revealing bronzed and braceleted arms; their
coarse white linen vails thrown back from their foreheads
and hanging over their shoulders; and their naked feet,
were in perfect harmony with the pastoral scenes around.

I was very thirsty, so I called to one of them, saying,
"Water me with water, O my sister!" Immediately a red
and black two-handled porous earthenware vase of antique
form was handed to me, and when I had drank of the cool,
tasteless water it contained the girls around said, "May
God make it refreshing to you, O lady!" And, prompted
by my brother, I gave the customary answer, "God preserve you!" We inquired whence came the delicious water,
and they answered, "From the well over against the town."
So perhaps we had tasted of the very water which David
sighed for when he said, "O, that one would give me of
the water of the well at Bethlehem, that is at the gate!"
We gave the girls a backshîsh, and they gave us their
blessings as we rode away.

The men and boys whom we met, or saw working in
the orchards above or the plains below, wore nothing but
short coarse white shirts, girdled with broad red leather
belts, ornamented with stitching and embroidery. Their
heads were protected and adorned with bright-red and
yellow-striped shawls, tastefully bound round their tasseled
tarbûshes, the crowns of which were bleached by the sun.
A few of them wore red, pointed, clumsy-looking, but picturesque boots. Nature, however, provides admirably for
the shoeless and furnishes a hardy and ever-growing horny

case, which is insensible to the sharpness of stones and thorns, and to the roughness of the stubble-field.

In the valley below we saw broad fields of green millet and broom-corn—a strong grass about five or six feet in hight, of which brooms are made—but all the wheat and barley had been cut, and mules and oxen were busy on the thrashing-floors.

On the eastern side of this valley the hills were uncultivated, and on the neglected terraces wild fig-trees, evergreen oaks, and thorns grew. In the breaks between these hills we had occasional glimpses of the Dead Sea, calm, and blue, and bright in the sunshine, and the long range of Moab beyond; its channeled and furrowed hills bounded the view, and met the sky in an almost level line.

The sun was very powerful, for it was the fifth hour, between ten and eleven o'clock. We protected our heads from sunstroke by winding round our hats long strips of muslin, after the fashion of turbans, which are the most suitable head-dresses for hot countries.

We left all traces of cultivated land presently, and came to hills which were clothed with thorns and thistles, wild thyme and sage, except where the scanty soil had been washed away from the grayish-blue slab-like rocks.

As we descended into the valley of Urtâs by a pathless steep, we paused to watch a long line of camels, and a considerable body of Bedouins, who were entering it from a narrow wady just opposite. They were preceded by three sturdy-looking men mounted on horses, and carrying spears about twelve feet long, garnished with tufts of ostrich feathers.

They were evidently on their way to seek some favorable site for a Summer encampment, for they were accompanied by a large number of women and children, who rode in clumsy cradles or panniers on the foremost camels, while the rest were laden with black hair tents and bundles of tent-poles, cooking utensils, water jars, mats, and sacks of provisions. Goats, sheep, and a few donkeys brought up the rear, pausing only to drink at the little shallow pools of water which rested in natural and stony basins in the middle of the valley, bordered with fresh green grass and flowers. The tinkling of the camel bells, and the wild, plaintive, monotonous song of the women, rang in our ears long after the primitive procession had passed out of our sight. No doubt those wanderers pitched their tents and made themselves at home by sunset, near to some stream or fountain of sweet water. Their dusky dwellings up they quickly rear, and build a village in an hour's space.

When we reached the bottom of the valley, and had passed a bold, projecting, and caverned rock which causes an abrupt turn in its course, I was startled with delight and surprise at the picture before us—the loveliest I had seen in the East.

No wonder that Biblical topographists agree in calling Urtâs the site of the gardens of Solomon, and no wonder if Solomon selected this valley for his especial retreat, and made this part of it his pleasure-ground. It may have been more magnificent in his time, when the now fallen and shattered columns supported stately buildings, and the terraces were paved with the now scattered tesseræ; but it could not have been more beautiful and refreshing even in those golden days; for here the pomegranates still yield their pleasant fruit; the vine flourishes; the fig-trees put forth their green figs around the fountain of gardens— the well of living water. Vegetable marrows, cucumbers, melons, and tomatoes carpet the bed of the valley with their broad leaves and glossy fruits, and fields of lentils, beans, potatoes, millet, and patches of golden maize, blossoming tobacco and sesame in excellent order, proclaim the agricultural skill of the successor of Solomon. Higher up in the valley is a splendid orchard, where peach, apple, pear, and plum-trees flourish side by side with the more common fruits of the country, watered by sparkling streams which intersect the gardens and orchards like silver threads.

We followed a narrow bridle-path, raised a little above the bed of the valley. This led us to a solitary stone house, built up against the abruptly-rising hill on the right. Here we dismounted, and were kindly welcomed by its occupants—Mr. Meshullam and his family—the present cultivators and shareholders of this favorite spot. They are of Jewish birth, but have become Christians, and are under British protection. We rested under an immense fig-tree, on a divan of rocks and stones, built round its massive trunk, and covered with carpets and cushions. Opposite to us was a wide arched portal or lewan, the approach to the house. A wooden locker, and two stone benches or raised seats, covered with mats, occupied its three sides. It is used as a Summer sitting-room. Above the rude door leading to the inner rooms were a number of badger-skins hanging to dry, and some foxes' tails, and tusks of wild boars—trophies of the courage and skill of the young Meshullams. Bunches of Indian corn, and some large dried gourds of a golden tint and cup-like form, were suspended from the arched roof, with a few captured birds in cages, and a large lantern.

The room within was just as simple. We dined there with Mr. Meshullam and his family, and Mr. Henry Wentworth Monk, who for two years had lived there, almost a hermit's life, his only constant companion a Greek Testament, and his chief intercourse with the world the *Times* newspaper. He spent nearly all his time in the open air, entering the house only to sleep and to eat. His lifelike portrait, by Holman Hunt, appeared in the Royal Academy Exhibition in 1860.

Our hostess, Mrs. Meshullam, an Italian Jewess, told me she could only give us an Italian peasant's dinner, as she had not expected us that day; but the savory soup of lentils and other vegetables, the dishes of fried beans, the potato fritters, omelettes, and fruit, needed no apology.

After dinner, Mr. Meshullam's sons kindly led us up the rocky hill-side to the ruins of Urtâs. Scattered blocks of stone, fallen columns, foundations of houses, and broken walls alone remain. A few wild Arabs of the Thamari tribe haunt these ruins and the caverns in the limestone hills which rise behind them, attracted by the spring which gushes impetuously from a rock overgrown with mosses and ferns, and overshadowed with fine trees. The water falls in a large body, splashing and bubbling, into a square reservoir, where a group of little Bedouins stood enjoying shower-baths. A few men were bathing their feet and washing their hands, in preparation for prayer.

From this basin the water escapes into a lower and large reservoir, where a number of Urtâs women and girls were washing their white and purple linen shirts, and their tattered vails, in primitive style, folding them, and placing them on smooth slabs, just under the surface of the water at the margin of the pool, and then beating them with flat stones, which they held in their hands. Little naked, bronzed children were luxuriating there, and wriggling about like tadpoles. The girls called to me to come down into the reservoir, to bathe my feet. The rough stone walls inclosing these pools were tapestried with ferns, cresses, delicate creepers, and liverwort.

We followed the course of the stream, and, with it, descended into the valley between the low stone walls which inclose the plantations of olive, fig-trees, lemons, and pomegranates. We had to make our way cautiously, now on one side, and then on the other, of the rocky bed of the swiftly-flowing stream.

The pleasant sound of the rushing waters—the songs of the goldfinches—the sight of the blossoming and fruitful trees in the garden below, inclosed by steep hills, covered with aromatic herbs—the breezy air, laden with the heliotrope-like scent of the fig-trees, and tasting of the wild flowers and herbs around—delighted us. King Solomon could scarcely have enjoyed such scenes more completely, when he, long ago, went into the garden and invited his beloved to come and eat the pleasant fruits. "Awake, O north wind! and come, thou south! blow upon my garden, that the spices thereof may flow out."

The stream led us to the bottom of the valley, and then took its way rather more gently in a narrow bed, bordered with grass and brook-lime speedwell, close to the hillside, which was festooned with masses of maiden-hair and mosses of the most vivid green. We walked on a raised stone path, or viaduct, across the gardens, and passed through a field of tall broom-corn, every stem of which was crowned with a plumy tuft, and wreathed with convolvulus, pink and white. We saw a number of gardeners at work, in the employ of Mr. Meshullam. He has a shop in Jerusalem, exclusively for the sale of the fruit and vegetables from this spot. He has introduced many fruit-trees and vegetables which had never before been cultivated in the East; and they thrive well, especially the seeds and slips from America. Were it not for the vigorous protection afforded to him by Mr. Finn, however, he could not resist the encroachments of the Arab tribes in the district, and the fruitful valley would soon be a desert.

After taking leave of the Meshullams, we rode up the valley to see the three great pools, one above the other, which collect the springs of the neighborhood. The largest and lowest is 582 feet long, and 50 feet deep; the next is 423 feet long, and 39 feet deep; the upper one is 380 feet long, and 25 feet deep. Clear blue water half filled these tanks—a precious reserve for the dry season. The bottom of the upper pool is higher than the top of the next, and so with the second and third. They are partly formed of excavations in the rock, and partly of immense hewn stones. These are called Solomon's Pools; and he perhaps thought of them, and of his gardens at Urtâs, when he said, "I made me gardens and orchards, and I planted trees in them of all kinds of fruits; I made me pools of water, to water therewith the wood that bringeth forth trees." No doubt the fountain and streams which supply these pools found their way down the valley of Urtâs to the Dead Sea, and wasted their sweet waters in the bitter lake, till a Solomon's hand restrained them, and led them into these great reservoirs, and built the famous duct round hill-sides, over plains, and across valleys, to convey the water to the Temple on Mount Moriah. Even now the fountain opposite to the Mosque-el-Aksa is thus supplied. Sometimes, it is true, the supply is scanty there, owing to the careless keeping of the aqueduct; for men water their horses at the various openings, and otherwise waste the water, before it can reach the city. Every new Pasha does his best to enforce strong measures to prevent this abuse, but generally gives up the attempt after a short time.

We rode homeward, following, as nearly as we could, the course of the aqueduct. At every opening we saw the running water framed in a mass of delicate maiden-hair and moss; at several of these places women were, contrary to the law, washing their clothes, and filling their water-jars. It strikes me, that there may have been a chariot-road by the side of this aqueduct, in ancient times, and it may have served as a sort of coping or parapet to it. No chariot-road is to be found there now, and in some places the path is difficult even for a mule; yet, when we consider what damage the torrents of one Winter will effect, we may wonder that the torrents of centuries have not proved even more destructive than they have.

Roads in this land must have required peculiar attention and care. In the Talmud it is said that, before the going up of the tribes, three times a year, to Jerusalem, the roads leading to it were prepared. "Prepare the way of the people; cast up the highway, gather out the stones, take up the stumbling-block out of the way of my people." I can imagine the kind of preparation required in obedience to this command; how the rocks, and stones, and *débris* of the hills, washed down by the Winter rains, were cleared away; how the fallen tree-trunks were gathered up and supported; and the broken edges of the road and the holes formed by the bursting of springs were blocked up; and I see, in fancy, the chariot-roads winding round terraced hills, and through vineyards, pleasant gardens, and pasture-land in the plains, as they did in the days when such kings as Solomon the magnificent ruled, or when Uzziah the lover of husbandry reigned. (See 2 Chron. xxvi, 10, 11.)

The sun had gone down in red, and gold, and purple splendor when we quitted the tortuous course of the aqueduct. We lost the cheerful sound of the running stream, whose waters were flowing freely toward Jerusalem; and we took a more direct route, turning toward the Convent of Mar Elias. We mounted the hill, and then galloped quickly over the plain of Rephaim, meeting long strings of unladen camels gently jolting along, and numbers of Bethlehem peasants and women, returning homeward, with their empty baskets poised on their heads. They had been selling fruit and vegetables in Jerusalem.

It was dusk when we reached Talibîyeh. We found that some poor Jews had been employed there throughout the day, to make a sort of veranda or shelter of reeds in front of the little stone house, and it proved a very pleasant retreat. The reeds used were from the banks of the Jordan. They are about an inch and a half or two inches in diameter, and twelve or thirteen feet in hight, with a plumy tuft at the top, like a miniature palm-tree. It is very likely that this kind of reed is referred to in the history of the Crucifixion, where it is said, "And straightway one of them ran and took a sponge and filled it with vinegar, and put it on a reed, and gave him to drink." Matt. xxvii, 48.

Thoroughly tired, but well pleased, I went to my tent; and, according to the advice of the Armenian nurse, bathed my feet and arms with milk and vinegar, to allay the irritation caused by the musketoes, which had tormented me in the convent at Bethlehem. It proved an effectual remedy, and I recommend travelers to try it.

CHAPTER IV

FROM JERUSALEM TO HÂIFA.

It was our intention to remain only a short time in Jerusalem, but my brother had been detained on consular business, and was appointed to attend Kamîl Pasha on an expedition to Hebron, to quell a serious insurrection there.

I was left in the care of my good friends at the Talibîyeh, where I enjoyed excellent opportunities for improving myself in Arabic, and gleaning information about the people of Palestine. Every day brought some new delight. I visited all the places of interest in the neighborhood, sketching and making notes, and had the privilege of accompanying Sir Moses and Lady Montefiore when they explored the Moslem mosques and shrines on Mount Moriah.

Mr. W. Holman Hunt was then busy in his studio on Mount Zion, and there I watched the progress of his wonderful picture of the "Meeting in the Temple," and with delight looked through his portfolios and sketch-books. On the 21st of August I went to Hebron, and after spending a few days with my brother at the Pasha's camp, I returned to the Talibîyeh; but of these pleasures I will not pause to speak in detail here.

On the 9th of September, at sunrise, a shower of rain fell, the first I had seen in Palestine. It lasted only half an hour, and seemed quite local. Low down among the hills rainbows, one within another, spanned the valleys, and produced a most beautiful effect. Soon after the rain was over, a cloud of birds appeared coming from the north, their strange snapping cries sounding louder and louder as they approached. They were bee-catchers, bright-colored birds of the swallow kind. A strong north wind soon carried the rain clouds and the birds far away, and cooled the air, which had been very sultry.

On September 11th, Miss Creasy—who had long been resident in Jerusalem—took me to see Philip's Fountain, which is about two hours south-west by west of Jerusalem. We started early, with one kawass, and rode over the rocky hills to the Convent of the Cross before the dew had disappeared. We met large companies of "fellahîn"—peasant women—flocking to the city with fruit and vegetables. Most of them wore blue linen shirts, white cotton vails, which fell over their shoulders, and crimson girdles fastened very low. The foremost were carrying a great variety of cucumbers and vegetable marrows, and the fruit of the dark egg-plant, which is pear-shaped, of a deep violet-red color, and very glossy. A group of girls, who balanced on their heads baskets of grapes from the Greek gardens, made a beautiful picture; trailing branches and tendrils of the vine were hanging over their shoulders. We went down a narrow valley, newly planted with mulberries and vines by the enterprising monks of the Greek convent. On the summit of a steep hill, on our right, we saw the picturesque little village of Mâlihah, and large kilns for preparing charcoal were burning on the rock ledges or terraces below it.

We entered the Wady-el-Werd, or Valley of Roses—well named; its broad bed, for above a mile, is like a thicket of rose-bushes, cultivated for making rose-water and conserves. Beyond this garden, which attracted thousands of birds to feast on its crimson berries or hips, we found fig-orchards, blackberry-bushes, and walnut-trees. On our left hand we saw the remains of an ancient building, large hewn stones, excavations in the native rock, a few fallen columns, and a small stone fountain called Ain Yalo, or the Spring of Ajalon. We were following the course of the ancient road "which goeth down from Jerusalem to Gaza." Long ago,

Queen Candace's eunuch traversed it, riding in his chariot; but the Romans kept "the way" in repair then; no chariot could pass it now. It is little better than a track for mules, and runs along a sort of terrace half-way up the hill on the left-hand side of the valley. Rugged rock ledges were above and below us, and a few flocks were feeding on the scanty herbage and thorns, but down in the bed of the vale there were thrashing-floors and stubble fields. About a mile beyond Ain Yalo we came to Ain Haniyeh, a fine spring of pure water, commonly called Philip's Fountain. Two pilasters, with richly-carved Corinthian capitals, flank a semicircular apse, formed of very large, carefully-hewn stones. From a deep, arched recess or niche, in the middle of this apse, a large body of water gushes and falls with great force into a small basin, which overflows into a stone reservoir below, and then forms a narrow stream which finds its way into the valley. I climbed over immense blocks of stone, assisted by a shepherd boy, and gathered some of the maiden-hair and mosses which festooned the arched mouth of the fountain. Indications of a much larger apse can be traced just beyond; and exactly opposite the fountain, at about forty paces from it, there is a fragment of the shaft of a column nearly six feet in diameter, but only about five feet high. A few shafts of smaller columns are to be seen in a neighboring field. The villagers around carry away the hewn stones which are found here to build their little watch-towers, or to repair their houses. Local tradition says that this is the very fountain to which the eunuch referred when he said to his teacher, Philip, "See, here is water! What doth hinder me to be baptized?" Some boys and girls, wilder looking than the shaggy goats which they led to drink at the fountain, crowded around me as I sat on the great column, sketching the scene before me. My horse, in the mean time, less obedient than the chariot of the eunuch, had broken away from the block of stone to which he was tethered, and was running at full speed into the valley. Loud cries and shouts from the boys brought, from all directions, volunteers to pursue the runaway, and, after some little time, the frightened animal was caught, in a circle of the noisiest, wildest-looking little fellows I ever saw, and to whom the few piasters which I distributed was a fortune.

We returned by a rather different route, and passed another fountain, more simple than the others, but very picturesque, and formed chiefly of blocks of unhewn stone. Women were washing their linen shirts and vails in the reservoir, and a number of rough, desperate-looking men were lounging idly round it. They looked over my paper while I sketched the fountain and a few figures. One of them said, "If we were to fetch all the men of the valley, and all the men of the hills, they could not do that." They seemed, by their remarks, to fancy that drawing was a sense or faculty peculiar to the Franks. They were clamorous for backshîsh, and followed us for some distance, muttering, grumbling, and disputing among themselves. After they had given up the pursuit, I found that I had lost my pocket-book, containing papers of value. I galloped back to Philip's Fountain, though the rays of the sun were very powerful. I explained my loss to the shepherd boys, now my firm allies, then I rode back to the other fountain, where I found the group of men who had followed us, standing as if in consultation. I felt certain that they had my book. I told them I came from the English consulate, and asked them to help me in my search. They so positively declared that my book was not lost there, that I felt more convinced than ever that they had found it. Presently I tried the effect of a small piece of gold, which I offered to the finder. In a moment one of the men drew my book from his girdle, and rather hesitatingly placed it in my hands. I feared he might repent, so I immediately gave it to the kawass to take charge of, and we very thankfully rode away. These men were all fully armed, and dressed in coarse scanty clothing. They looked as if a trifle would excite them to mischief and to deeds of daring. When we were far enough from them, we sat down and took our lunch, which we had provided before setting out. We rested under a walnut-tree during the hour of noon, and did not reach the Talibîyeh till three o'clock, where we were anxiously awaited, for the Gaza road is not considered a very safe one. In the arched recess at the back of the house, figs from Urtâs, strung together, were hanging in the sun to dry. One of the servants, sitting in the shade, was busy stripping off the flag-like envelopes of large ripe ears of Indian corn, or maize. She told me that she was going to make a mattress of the dried husks for one of the men-servants; and added that poor people, who can not afford to buy cotton wool, make their beds of the outer skins of onions, thoroughly dried and sweetened by exposure to the sun, and sewed up in coarse linen cases.

On the following day, my brother returned from Hebron, and was at last free to leave Jerusalem and start for his vice-consulate at Hâifa. A few days were spent in making preparations for the journey. I engaged Katrîne, a widow of Bethlehem, as my attendant. She was highly recommended to me as a faithful and affectionate woman, but with the serious drawback that she was subject to fits of mental derangement. In the year 1834, when her native town was the scene of rebellion, her husband and little sons were murdered in her presence in their beds, and alarm and despair disordered her mind.* (Who can calculate how much harm of this nature will be the result of the late massacres in the Lebanon and Damascus, and how many weakened intellects will be transmitted to succeeding generations? Men survive the sight of open warfare on the battle-field; but who can wonder that women become mad with rage and terror, who see their sons and fathers murdered in their homes?)

In a day or two Katrîne was quite at home with me. She had known my brother for years, and fancied that he

* See note, page 60.

and I were her own children. She often told me curious stories of our childhood, fictions of her imagination. This delusion, however, made her happy, and caused her to be a most devoted servant to us.

On the 14th of September I was roused before sunrise by the tinkling sounds of mule bells, which reminded me that our journey was planned for that day. All was bustle and animation at the camp. Groups of Arab servants were seated among the rocks. Bags and baggage were strewed around. Tents and tent poles were being removed and packed, and mules and muleteers stood waiting for orders. Mr. Finn was about to make a tour with his niece and a friend, and had arranged to travel with us as far as Yâfa.

After a great many delays, all the attendants were in readiness by eleven o'clock; but it happened that my brother, who had gone into Jerusalem early on business, was detained, and consequently kept a prisoner there, for it was Friday, the Moslem Sabbath, and the city gates are always closed on that day during the hours of morning prayer, and we knew, therefore, that he could not on any consideration be released till noon. (This custom is rigidly observed, owing to a prophecy which declares that the Holy City will be invaded and conquered at Sabbath prayer-time.) So the Consul with his party started, leaving us to overtake him at Yâfa; and I spent one more evening with Mrs. Finn and the little ones at the Talibîyeh. We had nothing to detain us the next day, and at half-past three I rose by lantern and starlight, gathered a branch from the olive-tree above the tent which had been my resting-place for ten weeks, breakfasted with Mrs. Finn, and rode away, well mounted, just as the first gleams of light appeared in the eastern sky.

A Moslem kawass led the way, and my *soi-disant* mother, Katrîne, a Latin Christian, closely vailed and wrapped in a red Arab cloak, sat, à *la cavalier*, on the broad pack-saddle of a nimble little donkey, and two laden mules, in the care of a muleteer, followed. Although our attendants were of conflicting creeds, they fraternized very well on the way.

We did not pause till we came to the Fountain of Birds, where a peasant boy brought us fine grapes, and helped us to give our animals water. The orchards around were now in their full beauty, bright with pomegranate fruit and blossom. The rich green fig-trees, wet with dew, smelt like heliotropes, and were garlanded and interlaced with richly-laden vines. Little birds were rustling the silvery leaves of the olive-trees, and they now and then swarmed forth in cheerful chirruping flight.

At eight o'clock we reached Abu Ghôsh, and while we waited for Katrîne and the muleteer—who lagged behind—I sketched the old church, and then hastened onward. At ten we rested and lunched under a tree by a well-side near to Latrone, and the kawass contrived to make us some coffee. I was astonished to find that I had traveled through the hill-country of Judea, without fear and without fatigue, by the same road which a short time before had appeared to me so full of danger and difficulty. The hills seemed to me to have been made low, and the "rough places plain." When we entered the level country, the sun was shaded every now and then by quickly-moving clouds, and a breeze sprang up from the west, pleasantly fanning our faces.

We cantered over the plain till we reached a village called Kubâb, a poor, straggling place, with a few gardens fenced with yellow-blossoming cactus hedges. We paused by a well, in a sort of farm-yard, and a lame girl handed us some water in a red jar. She made curious signs and gestures, and we soon saw that she was deaf and dumb. We gave her a backshîsh, and she limped away well pleased. A boy followed us, noisily demanding money as we rode on, but we did not give him any thing; so he ran back to the poor lame girl, threw her down, and snatched her treasure from her. She rose with difficulty, and with silent and impotent rage threw handfuls of dust after him, and when he was out of sight, she began tearing her scanty clothing. We turned back and tried to console her, but our words were useless; however, some sweet chocolate cakes were more effectual. We left her stealthily eating them, and went on our way, thinking how sad her life must be.

Before noon we entered Ramleh, leaving our servants far behind. We rode under the tall palm-trees, now laden with glossy red and golden fruit, hanging in clusters on orange-colored stalks. Strings of camels and laden donkeys crowded the dirty, dusty streets, and with difficulty we made our way to the house of an Arab friend. My brother was received with kisses and embraces by the sons of the house, and I was led by an Abyssinian slave—*a eunuch*—to his widowed mistress, a superior-looking woman, dressed in black silk garments, embroidered with gold thread. She said, "Welcome, my daughter;" and, after giving me some lemonade, took me to a pleasant chamber opening on to a terrace covered with pots of blossoming pinks and roses. She called the slave, and he immediately spread a mattress for me on the floor. Then she took off my hat and habit, and told me to "Rest in peace;" and, sitting by my side on a soft-cushioned carpet, she gently fanned me to keep away the flies and musketoes. When I awoke, after an hour or two of refreshing sleep, I found that my hostess had gone, and the slave was kneeling by my side, fanning me with a little flag made of a green split palm-frond, nicely plaited. His dark, polished face and large eyes, contrasting with his white turban, white cotton dress, and crimson silk girdle, rather startled me before I quite remembered where I was. I heard afterward that he was a favorite and confidential slave, who had belonged for many years to this family.

He poured rose-water over my hands, and led me to a court, where a genuine Arab meal was prepared for us. It consisted of boiled wheat, dressed in butter and mixed with minced meat; some fine broiled fish, in a bed of very sweet stewed apricots and rice;* and baked fowls, garnished with tomatoes, filled with rice and shreds of meat. A dessert of grapes, dates, and sweetened starch, stuck with bleached almonds, followed. After coffee and pipes we called our servants together, and at about five o'clock we mounted and rode toward Yûfa. The sun was shining directly in our faces, and we watched it gradually going down behind the low coast hills which hid from our sight the Mediterranean Sea. The crescent moon rose bright and clear, throwing our shadows in long dark lines on the sandy road before us.

We saw a little company of Bedouin Arabs sitting on the wayside feasting. As soon as we had passed they rose up and started into a run, leaping and shouting vociferously, and as we and the kawass slackened our pace to join the servants who were behind they passed us, running and dancing along, snatching off each other's white skull-caps, flinging them in the air, flourishing their sticks, throwing handkerchiefs at one another, screaming and singing. Their heads were shaved except just at the crown, where the hair was allowed to grow very long, and was plaited. The plait is generally twisted up, and quite concealed under skull-caps, tarbûshes, or kefias— that is, shawl head-dresses. The Arab costumes are familiar to most of my readers from the pictures of them in our school-books, and I need not further particularize them here.

We soon found that these wild-looking men were quite harmless. They had only lingered on the wayside to enjoy a heartier meal than usual, and had allowed their camels to go on leisurely with two or three camel-drivers, and they were running to overtake them, which they very soon did. They then pursued their way so slowly that we quickly passed them. Some of them were mounted on the unwieldy-looking animals, and their songs were already

---

* This *melange*, which is very common, always reminded me of the "broiled fish" and the "honeycomb" spoken of in Luke xxiv, 42.

subdued to harmonize with their monotonous swinging pace, and chimed softly and plaintively with the tinkling of camel bells—thus:

> "Dear unto me as the sight of my eyes
> Art thou, O my camel!
> Precious to me as the breath of my life
> Art thou, O my camel!
> Sweet to my ears is the sound
> Of thy tinkling bells, O my camel!
> And sweet to thy listening ears
> Is the sound of my evening song.

Sometimes these wanderers pass several days without taking substantial food; but, to make up for their abstinence, they eat voraciously and "make merry" when they have the opportunity. It was dark in the bridle-path between the Yâfa Gardens, but the large and many glowing watch-fires within the inclosures showed that the abundance of ripe fruit was well guarded.

We entered the gate of the town, where crowds of people were lounging. The broadest bazar was bright with lamps and lanterns; but we soon merged one by one into dark, narrow, crooked streets of stairs, and I was directed to follow the kawass closely and carefully. His large, full, white Turkish trowsers seemed to move before me by some mysterious power, without support or suspension; for the black horse which he rode was quite invisible in the darkness, and his red fez and embroidered jacket could not be seen, only now and then two shining eyes turned round to see if I were safe. I followed my ghostlike leader cautiously till we reached the British Consulate down by the seaside, where we were welcomed by our friends, Dr. and Mrs. Kayat; and Mr. Finn, who had only arrived an hour earlier, soon came to meet us. He had slept at Ramleh on the previous night, and was surprised we had made the journey from Jerusalem so easily in one day. Fire-works from a ship at anchor attracted us to the oriel window which overlooks the sea, and we sat for a long time watching the waves as they rolled toward us, crested with white foam, and with lines of phosphoric light flashing from beneath them, only extinguished by the breaking of each successive wave on the rocks.

The next day, Sunday, we went to the Rev. Mr. Krusé's house, and, in company with Mr. Finn and his party, and Dr. Kayat and his family, we heard Dr. Bowen—the late lamented Bishop of Sierra Leone—preach a most simple, earnest, and appropriate sermon. A few Arab children belonging to the missionary school, and Mrs. Krusé and her family, with the Rev. Henry Reichart, of Cairo, completed the little congregation. Some Arab ladies of the neighboring house watched us the whole time through the open window, and seemed greatly amused. The hymns were sung with much energy in Arabic, and the liturgy—read in English—was responded to by the little Arab scholars with vehemence and clearness. I spent the remainder of the day with Mr. Finn and his party, at the new and well-built house of an Arab friend. We sat on a sheltered terrace, sweet with pinks and jasmine, overlooking the terraced house-tops and the sparkling sea. Down on our left was the southern wall of the town, and the deep dry moat. Beyond it was a sloping, stony plain, where horsemen were galloping about and displaying their skill in the use of spear and musket. Further still was the large open cemetery, with a cupola, supported on arches, in the center; children were playing, and turbaned smokers were resting, under its shade. A garden of figs, palms, and tamarisks, on a gentle declivity, bordered the sandy margin of the sea between us and the quarantine station, and the white sheets or wimples of groups of women could be distinguished among the trees. Drifted sand-hills bounded the view. The sea, calm and brightly blue, broke gently along the belt of rocks, fringing them with foam. We watched the setting of the sun, the hills in the south grew rosy, violet, and gray. The western sky was covered with dark slate-colored clouds, edged with gold. The sunset-gun was fired, and we were led by our host to a covered court on the house-top to dine, by lantern light. For dessert, among other fruits, we had a dish of large ruby-colored pomegranate seeds moistened with wine, and sprinkled with powdered sugar; bleached almonds formed the border of this tempting-looking dish.

The next day I was sitting in the oriel window at the British Consulate, with the Rev. Dr. Bowen, while Dr. Kayat was engaged with an English captain and a number of Arabs in the lower part of the room. Black clouds came traveling quickly from the west, over the lead-colored sea. Dr. Bowen observed, in the words of Christ, "When ye see a cloud rise out of the west, straightway ye say, There cometh a shower, and so it is." He had scarcely uttered the words when the clouds spread and fell in a tremendous torrent. The sea swelled, and rolled heavily to the shore. The ships looked as if they would break away from their anchors, and loud peals of thunder made the casemented recess in which we sat tremble violently. The captain hastened away, fearful for the fate of his struggling ship off such a rocky coast. When the rain ceased, and the sun shone again, I rode out with Dr. Bowen to visit Mr. Jones, an American missionary, who lived in the midst of a beautiful garden, east of the town. He had done a great deal of good in teaching the Arab gardeners and agriculturists habits of order and method, but he finds them very slow learners.

At sunrise the next day rain fell in torrents, and did not clear off till noon, after which I sat in my favorite window corner with Nasif Giamal, Mrs. Kayat's brother. We saw just below us, on the rudely-constructed "parade," a crowd of men and children, assembled round a fantastically-dressed man exhibiting a goat, which had been tutored to perform some curious tricks. It stood with its four feet close together on the top of a very long pole, and allowed the man to lift it up and carry it round and round within the circle; then the goat was perched on four sticks, and again carried about. A little band of music—fifes, drums, and tambourines—called together the people from all parts of the town to witness this performance. The goat danced and balanced himself obediently and perfectly, in very unnatural-looking postures, as if thoroughly understanding the words and commands of his master. The men who watched the antics of the goat looked as grave and serious as if they were attending a philosophical or scientific lecture.

The assembled crowd had to make way presently for a long procession, preceded by horsemen carrying long spears, and firing guns. Two little boys, gayly dressed and decked with flowers, rode one behind the other on a white horse. Two large books, carried on embroidered cushions, were borne by two attendants. Women closely vailed walked by the side of the boys, singing wildly, and making a peculiar ringing noise in the throat, not unlike the neighing of horses made slightly musical by modulation. Nasif, who can speak English, told me the object of the procession, saying, "The boys are Moslems; they have suffered an infliction not observed by the Christians; the Jews have it, and also the Moslems." This explained to me that the children had been circumcised, and were now being conducted round the town in triumph.

My brother made arrangements with the owner of a little Arab boat to be prepared to take us to Hâifa, as soon as the south wind rose. Two monks of Mount Carmel begged to accompany us. We made our plans so as to be ready at a minute's notice, and spent the evening with Sit Leah. She had quite recovered, and proudly showed me her little Selim. I found that every one addressed her and spoke of her as "Um Selim," or mother of Selim, and the father was called "Abu Selim."

On Wednesday, September 19th, I was roused before sunrise, and informed that the Reis—or Arab captain—had sent for us, as the wind was favorable. With the two monks and Nasif G. we quickly went down to the quay. In the mean time the wind had shifted, and the

Reis could not undertake to steer against it; but he added, "It will veer round to the south again by midnight, and then we shall reach Haifa in eight or ten hours." It was still very early. We strolled leisurely through the town. The people were just beginning to stir. The shutters of the shops in the bazars were being lifted up—they are like flap-doors attached by rude hinges to the beams above the shop-fronts, and when opened and propped up, they form excellent shades, which are easily dropped down and secured at night.

On my return to the Consulate, I found two of the women-servants making bread, sitting on the ground at a low circular wooden board. One of them moistened some flour with water, another added salt, and a small piece of leavened dough—to "leaven the whole lump"—and then kneaded it vigorously in turn with her companion. It was left to rise, and then the two eldest daughters of Dr. Kayat divided it into portions, rolled them into little round loaves, which were carried away to the oven on large round trays made of reeds, bound together with strong grass.

We prepared ourselves for the journey, and then went to rest early, without undressing. At midnight the Reis sent for us, and immediately we went out into the darkness, with Nasif and three or four lantern-bearers. I noticed a number of men, wrapped in lehaffs, sleeping on low stone platforms, or by the side of kneeling camels, in the streets near the quay. The Mutsellim, or governor, was parading the place. Nasif told me that he did so at irregular intervals, sometimes in disguise, so as to see the state of the town at night, and to ascertain, by personal observation, whether the guards did their duty. We met the two Carmelite monks on the dark wharf, and the great water-gate was opened for us. I was somehow dropped gently into a little rowing-boat far down in the darkness below, where I was taken charge of by two brawny boatmen. After much shouting and jolting we were all huddled together, and skimmed over the water to the sailing-boat, which awaited us outside the rocky barrier. I found it was divided into three parts—the central portion being like an uncovered hold, four feet deep and eight feet square. The decks fore and aft were incumbered with the ship's tackle, and crowded with sailors, who were singing lustily. The hold, lighted by two lanterns, was matted and set apart for passengers and luggage. Our portmanteaus and carpet-bags served us for a couch, and the monks sat on their saddle-bags, wrapped in their comfortable-looking hooded robes. Poor Katrîne, who had never been on the sea before, was very much alarmed. She rolled herself up in her cloak, stretched herself full length by my side, and was happily soon fast asleep. Our kawass smoked his pipe in company with the Reis above, and an Italian, who had smuggled himself and his baggage on board, in the hurry and darkness, kept aloof with the sailors. The sky was bright with stars; the south wind was strong, and filled the sails, and by fits and starts I dozed till dawn of day. Then I roused myself, and watched the little group around me, the hooded monks sleeping soundly, my brother at my feet, leaning against a hamper, and Katrîne so enveloped that I could not distinguish her head from her heels.

The favorable wind had ceased, and the sailors were busy taking in sail. By the time the sun appeared above the low coast hills the wind had shifted to the west, and we were in danger of being driven on the rocks. It then suddenly veered to the north, and blew so violently that the Reis was obliged to cast anchor, and we were tossed on a heavy sea, near to a desolate coast, where there was no possibility of landing. By nine o'clock the sun was very powerful. An awning made of the now useless sails was thrown over the hold. We found our quarters far from comfortable, but we were determined to make the best of them. By noon the heat was intense and suffocating down in the hold, so I climbed on to the deck, and sat on a coil of rope, clinging to the mast. The strong wind and the sea spray revived me. The coast, which was every now and then concealed by the high waves, was a range of drifted sand-hills, traversed by flocks of goats feeding on the scanty patches of pasture. Not a human habitation, not even a human being was visible, and not a boat or ship was seen all day. In the afternoon the wind ceased, but the ship rocked lazily from the effect of the sea-swell, which had not yet subsided.

My brother read St. Paul's voyage to me as it is recorded in the 27th of Acts. It seemed more interesting than ever. We were not far from Cesarea, the port from which Paul embarked; and he was tossed about by contrary winds, in this sea for many days. It must have been about the same time of the year, too, during the equinoctial gales, when, as he said, "sailing was dangerous." It is distinctly explained that it was after the great Fast of the Atonement, which is held on the tenth day of the month of Tisri, and corresponds with the latter part of our month of September.

At sunset "the south wind blew softly." The sails were soon set, and in better spirits we sat down to our evening meal, and shared our chickens and preserved soup with the monks, who added their eggs, cheese, and cognac. We passed a dreamy, restless night, "sailing slowly," and in the morning were nearly opposite Tantûra. The wind had changed to north-east, so my brother insisted on landing to pursue our journey on shore. We tacked about, put out to sea, and then allowed the strong wind to drive us toward the picturesque coast. Little islands of rock and mounds of ancient masonry stood out before it, beaten by the waves. With some maneuvering the boat was brought safely to the beach, where there were plenty of Tantûra men to meet us, and carry us through the surf to the smooth yellow sands. I was delighted to find myself on firm land again; and I shall always remember St. Paul's advice to the centurion, and vote against sailing in the Levant in the Autumn.

The custom-house officer came to meet us; and, followed

by troops of men and boys, we approached the little town, which comprises about thirty or forty rudely-built houses, made of irregularly-piled blocks of hewn stone, bits of broken columns, and masses of mud or clay. The custom-house officer, Abu Habîb, guided us to his house, which consisted of one low, large, square room, lined with clay, and roofed with tree branches blackened with smoke. One half of the ceiling was concealed by matting, and the other half was picturesque with pendent branches. Small holes served as windows, and the roughly-made door was a portable one. A mattress spread on the floor was used as a divan. Jars of earthenware and metal saucepans stood against the wall. A cooking-place was built in one corner, made of large, finely-beveled, ancient stones and burned clay. Baskets of coarse salt from the sea-shore were near to it. Habîb, the son of our host, prepared coffee for us. In our presence he roasted the berries, and then pounded them in a stone mortar. A large box, like a muniment chest, with ornamental lock and hinges of wrought iron, stood near the door, and I perched myself on it to be as far away as I could from the mud floor, on which I could distinctly see a numerous assembly of large fleas dancing and hopping about. The monks, with truly monastic virtue, did not seem to mind them. Gaunt-looking women, hiding their faces with tattered white cotton vails, peeped at us, and dirty but pretty children came crowding round.

Katrine made a tour of the town, and then took me to the house which she considered the neatest and cleanest, where I rested with her and refreshed myself. The women who welcomed me were dressed in tight jackets and full trowsers, made of washed-out Manchester prints, patched all over without regard to color or pattern. Their heads were covered with mundils—squares of colored muslin; their necks adorned with coins, and their wrists with twisted silver bracelets. They were exceedingly amused with my little traveling dressing-case. They told me they had never seen a hair-brush before. They unplait their long henna-stained hair about once a week only, and *occasionally* clean it with fuller's earth, which is found near, and use small-tooth combs of bone or wood.

After some delay animals were procured; fortunately we had our saddles with us. We left our heavy luggage in the care of the Reis, and at two, P. M., we mounted and took leave of Tantûra. We made a rather ludicrous procession. The kawass, on a shaggy mule, took charge of our carpet-bags, and led the way. The two monks were mounted on donkeys, so small that their sandaled feet and heavy robes nearly touched the ground. My brother rode on an old white horse, whose head was garnished with red trappings ornamented with shells. I was put on a little pony who had lost his mane and tail, and who could not understand a side-saddle, but persisted in turning round and round to investigate the mystery; and Katrîne, on a stubborn donkey, had great difficulty in keeping up with us.

We rode northward along the shore, which was strewed with blocks of marble and hewn stones. Women and children were busy collecting in large baskets the coarse incrusted salt, which settles in the natural hollows and artificial basins of the rocks on the beach below. Large herds of cattle and goats, the chief wealth of Tantûra, grazed on the plain on our right hand just above us, which was overgrown with thorns, thistles, dwarf mimosa, and low brushwood.

A little beyond Tantûra stands the ancient Dora, or Dor, on a rugged promontory, with ruined walls all round it, at the edge of the cliff. From its center rises what appeared to me at first to be a lofty tower or castle; but on approaching it I found it was only the narrow southern wall of some long since fallen building. It stands about thirty feet high. This place is now quite abandoned, as the walls are tottering and the cliffs are giving way. The stones are gradually being removed to build up Tantûra. Opposite to these ruins, the plain was concealed from us by a low ridge of rocky hills, running close to the sandy shore, which is here and there enlivened by a group of palm-trees.

We kept close to the sea till we came, in about one hour and a half, to Athlīte, or Castellum Pelegrinum, a curious motley pile of ruins standing out on a rocky headland. The foundation stones are so massive, that they have resisted the storms of centuries, and tell of a time anterior to the Romans, who no doubt erected the fortress, built the walls, and fashioned the columns which are now falling to decay. The crusaders, too, have left some of their handiwork here—the pointed arches and the ruins of a Christian church still speak of them. Within the walls of the church, and under the shadow of the fortress, modern houses are rudely built, and inhabited by a poor Moslem population. A group of women were resting by a well of sculptured stone, just outside the walls. Opposite to this interesting place we found a narrow defile cut through the rocks, leading eastward direct from the shore to the plain. Deep ruts, for chariot wheels, were cut in the road, which was just wide enough for two horsemen to ride freely abreast. The white limestone walls rise abruptly on each side, garnished with patches of fragrant herbs and amber-colored lichen. Lintels at each end of this passage show that formerly it was protected by gates, and ruins of strong fortifications surmount it.

We passed out of this curious defile into the fertile but not very extensively-cultivated plain, or "Vale of Dor," between the mountain range of Carmel and the rocky coast-hills under whose pleasant shade we pursued our way. We could see that the two chains of hills met at an acute angle far away in the north. Now and then, natural fissures in the rocks, or little valleys made fertile by Winter torrents, revealed to us the sun and the sea.

We stopped to water our animals at a little spring, called Ain Dustrei, which forms a tiny lake, and then finds its way between the hills to the shore. A group of goatherds, with reed pipes, were assembled round a clay trough, where their flocks of goats were crowding to drink. The vegetation by this stream and fountain was wild and luxuriant. Oleanders, lupins, tall grass, and the arbutus abounded. The monks soon pointed out, with delight, the white convent of Mar Elias on the headland of Carmel.

Pleasant sounds of voices, songs, and bells, and laughter reached us, and we saw an animated little party approaching, mounted on camels, whose nodding heads and necks were decorated with beads, shells, crimson tassels, and strings of little tinkling bells. I paused by the wayside to watch them, as they slowly passed. There were thirteen camels strung together, each carrying two or three women and children, all in gala dresses, made chiefly of soft crimson silk, with white Vandyked stripes on it. On their heads, they wore scarfs or vails, of various colors and materials—silk, muslin, and wool—folded across their foreheads, just meeting the eyebrows, then thrown over the back of the head, and brought forward again to cover their faces, all but the shining eyes. The fringed or bordered ends were allowed to fall gracefully over the shoulders. Some of the women had slipped these vails, or wimples, down below their lips, so as to join in the chorus of the songs improvised by the two professional singing-women who accompanied them. My brother could perceive that it was a bridal party, by these songs, which very much resembled in style the "Song of Songs which is Solomon's." A number of men were in attendance on foot, forming a picturesque body-guard to the exalted women. They were people of one of the villages of the plain or vale of Dor, and had been to Hâifa, to purchase dresses, trinkets, and furniture for two approaching weddings, in a family of some local importance. They were scarcely out of hearing when we met another noisy group, consisting of men and boys, with a few camels, mules, and donkeys, clumsily laden with the purchases for the weddings—cooking utensils, baskets of rice, reed mats, bales of goods, and two red wooden boxes, ornamented with gilt hinges and strap-work.

The largest camel carried, high on his back, two little wooden cradles, painted blue, red, and yellow; one for each of the brides. This piece of furniture is regarded in the East as the most important and necessary item of a *trousseau;* and she is an unhappy wife who does not soon see rocking in the gaudy cradle an infant son, whose name she may take, and through whom she may become honored among women.*

As we proceeded northward, the plain was so much more narrow, that we could distinguish the deep caverns and excavations in the limestone hills opposite, which have, in turn, served as places of refuge or retreat for prophets, saints, and anchorites, banditti or robbers, and beasts of prey.

The village of Tîrch was pointed out to me, surrounded by cultivated fields and orchards. Groups of palm-trees grew here and there, and the hill-sides were clothed with dwarf oak, wild fig, and locust trees. The fruit of the locust, when ripe, is like a large crooked bean-pod, brown and glossy, filled with large seeds. It is so nutritious, that the children of the poor live entirely on it, during the season, requiring no other food, for it contains all the necessary elements for the support of life—starch, sugar, oil, etc., in proper proportion. I found it, when new, rather too sweet to suit my taste. Children seemed to enjoy it, and they thrive on it, eating the shell as well as the seeds. When this fruit is stored, it becomes somewhat dry, and less sweet, but on being soaked in honey, it is like new fruit. The Arabs all like sweet food, and of many a man of Judea and Galilee, as well as of John the Baptist, it might be said, "*His meat* [for a season] *was locusts and wild honey.*"†

Just before sunset, we reached the foot of the headland which forms the southern boundary of the bay of Akka. On its summits the convent stands. It was too late, and

---
* See page 63.

† The Arabic name for the locust-tree is "Kharub," and the beans are commonly called "St. John's bread."

we were all too tired, to go round to the usual ascent on the other side; so we urged our animals up the steep and pathless rocks, here and there overgrown with brushwood, thorns, and thistles, fit only to be traversed by goats and conies.

The monks, who had been our guests on the way, now acted as our guides and hosts, for they were on convent ground. They warned us to grasp the manes of our tired steeds firmly, as they mounted the steep ledges; and I now found the disadvantage of being on a pony without a mane. After about ten minutes difficult riding, we reached a cultivated garden, on a plateau, in front of the large, well-built convent. Frère Charles, an old friend of my brother, came out to meet and welcome us, and kissed him and the two monks again and again.

We were about six hundred feet above the plain, with a magnificent scene before us. The sun was just going down, and the Great Sea was flooded with crimson light. The bay of Akka and the plain surrounded by the hills of Galilee were on our right. The ruins of an ancient port and fortress could be seen on the level strip of land below us; and at about a mile to the right of it stood the little town of Hâifa—very interesting to me, for it was there I was to make a home with my brother, at Her Britannic Majesty's Vice-Consulate.

We spent a pleasant evening with the good monks. It was Friday; they did not let us fast, but sat by us, in pleasant chat, while we enjoyed fish, flesh, and fowl from their excellent *cuisine*. After dinner we went to the divan or drawing-room, and I looked through the convent album, which is quite a polyglot, containing the autographs of many great and celebrated characters—testimonies to the kindness and hospitality always met with here.

Three or four examples of misplaced zeal and intolerance have called forth the satire, wit, and displeasure of less prejudiced pilgrims. Frère Charles pointed out to me a few pages crossed, recrossed, and interlined by indignant commentators. He remarked that they always seemed to be particularly interesting to English people, provoking laughter and anger by turns. The pages had evidently been translated to him.

We gratefully rested that night in clean, comfortable, neatly-furnished rooms, and on French musketo-curtained beds. In the morning I heard the swell of the organ and the chanting of the monks at an early hour. A servant brought *café au lait* to my room at seven, and told me my brother had already gone down to Hâifa. Frère Charles and our fellow-travelers conducted me to the chapel, which has a finely-proportioned dome and marble floor, and a few sculptured figures in alabaster.

The ground-floor of the convent is occupied by the offices, kitchens, pharmacy, and surgery. A large portion of it is set apart for a place of shelter for poor pilgrims. The first-floor, consisting of a fine suite of lofty rooms, is nicely furnished, and prepared for travelers, who are expected to pay first-class hotel prices; but no direct charge is made. The second-floor is reached by a narrow staircase, at the foot of which an inscription, in Italian and French, proclaims that females are not admitted. The monks told me that there was an excellent library of English, Latin, French, and Italian books up there, as well as a large refectory and a great number of cells; and the terraced roof made a fine promenade for the recluses.

Presently a kawass came, bringing a horse for me, and an invitation to spend the day with Mr. Finn, whose tents were pitched just outside Hâifa; so with Katrîne, in her purple dress and white vail, by my side, and the kawass leading the way, I emerged from the convent buildings, and gradually descended, on the north-east side, by a winding path almost like a rocky staircase. The upper part of the hill was covered with wild flowers, fragrant herbs, shrubs, artichokes, acanthus, and dwarf oaks, and on the lower terraces a fine grove of olives and some fig-trees flourished.

The little town of Hâifa was in sight—flags above all the Consulates were waving a welcome to Mr. Finn and my brother. I was quite surprised to recognize so many; they were French, Austrian, Prussian, Greek, Dutch, and American, and made the place look quite cheerful. We rode through a beautiful olive grove in the plain at the foot of the hill, crossed several stubble-fields, some rocky waste land and young plantations, and found the tents of Mr. Finn under a large terebinth-tree, near to the sea-shore, not very far from the west wall of the town. Visitors were coming and going all day, and coffee and pipes were in constant requisition.

The view from the open tent, looking toward the north, was very lovely. I will try to make you see it as I saw it on that sunny afternoon. Fancy a foreground of white rocks and dark thorny bushes; then a stony bridle-path, skirting a garden which gently slopes toward the shore, so that the broad sands are quite concealed by its fruit trees, and the blue sparkling sea looks as if it came close up to the hedge of prickly pears below. On the left-hand side of the picture the sea meets the sky; but from the right a range of undulating hills, tinted with crimson, purple, and orange, extend more than half-way across it, terminating in a bold white cliff or headland, called Ras el Abiod—the "Promontorium Album" of Pliny—standing out in strong contrast to the dark-blue sky and darker sea. The opposite shore of the bay, nine miles distant, is marked by a level line of white sand, which seems to separate the sea from the green plains at the foot of the hills; and on a low promontory to the right of Ras el Abiod the proud-looking little city of 'Akka is conspicuous, and forms the central point of the picture. Above the clearly-defined summits of the hills silvery clouds are resting. Mount Hermon rises in the distance, pale and shadowy, till the sun is low, and then it is tinged with gold and violet. Four ships are at anchor on the right, and a vessel in full sail is entering the bay from the north. A man-of-war is cruising about far out at sea. A tall palm-tree on one side, and an oak and a seared, white-branched fig-tree on the other, inclose this *coup d'œil*.

The bridle-path across the foreground was enlivened by passers-by, such as troops of barefooted boys, driving donkeys laden with hewn stones, which had been taken from the ruins of the fortress, and were about to be used in Hâifa, where many new houses were in progress, and still more were planned. Camels laden with grain and melons jolted by, and a few townspeople passed backward and forward as if to peep at our tents. At sunset there came large numbers of goats and cattle, led toward the town to be secured there for the night, for it is not safe to leave them in the open country, even in the care of the well-armed herdsmen.

Hâifa is a walled town, in the form of a parallelogram, pleasantly situated close to the sea, on a gently-rising slope. A steep hill, a spur of Mount Carmel, rises immediately behind it, and is crowned by a small castle, to which I climbed with Mr. Finn, and thence looked down into the town. The houses are distributed irregularly. Those occupied by consuls and merchants are large, substantial buildings of hewn stone, with central courts and broad terraces. The poorer class of houses are of earth and rough stone, and have no upper chambers. All the roofs are flat. On each side of the little town there are fine fruit gardens, where the pomegranates and figs especially flourish. A grove of palm-trees borders the sandy shore on the east of the town.*

I returned to the convent to sleep, and after spending the next day, Sunday, with Mr. Finn at the tents, I prepared to enter Hâifa for the first time, by moonlight.

* The town of Hâifa was built where it now stands, by the famous Dhâher, governor of Acre, in the middle of the last century. The ruins of the old town of 'Hφá, Sycaminum, are still to be seen on the sea-shore just below the head of Mount Carmel, which site Dhâher found to be too much exposed to the incursions of the nomadic tribes in the plain of Athlite. Some of the elder residents remember their fathers having pointed out the position of their former residences in the old town.—E. T. R.

CHAPTER V.

DOMESTIC LIFE IN HÂIFA.

ALTHOUGH the tents were very near to the town, Mr. Finn laughingly insisted that I should not make my first entry into Hâifa on foot; so I mounted, and, with my brother and a few of his Arab friends walking by my side, traversed the bridle-path by the gardens, and approached the embattled stone gateway. Its heavy wooden doors, covered with hides and plates of iron, were thrown open for us, on their creaking hinges, by the sleepy wardens, whose mattresses were spread on stone platforms in the square vaulted chamber of the gate. They welcomed us with the words, "Enter in, in peace." We said, "May God preserve you! good-night." And they answered, "A thousand good nights to you!" but their greetings were almost drowned by the angry barking of a troop of dogs, roused by the clanging of the great doors behind us.

Within the town, wherever there was space, flocks and herds were lying down, crowded together in the moonlight; and in the narrow, tortuous, dirty, channeled streets we met now and then a moaning, miserable-looking, sleepless cow or stray donkey.

We passed a little belfried Latin chapel, shaded by a pepper-tree—just like a willow—and a simple mosque and minaret, with a palm-tree near it, and then came to a pleasant opening close to the sea-shore, where a number of camels, camel-drivers, and peasants were sleeping round the red embers of a wood fire.

I dismounted at the entrance of a house overlooking this scene, and passed under a low, arched gateway, into a roughly-paved, open court, brightened by the lamps and lanterns in the rooms all round it, the doors of which were open, for their inmates, our neighbors, were watching and waiting to see and welcome us.

I mounted a steep, uncovered, stone stairway to a broad landing, dignified by the name of terrace, leading to two square, lofty, airy rooms, with whitewashed walls and stone floors, where my brother had formerly lived for a year or more; this was to be our temporary home, and Katrîne, with the help of an upholsterer—an Arab Jew—had been very busy making it ready for us.

At the end of the terrace was a little room, in which were all the requisites for preparing pipes, coffee, and sherbets. Narghilés, chibouques, tobacco-bags, coffee-cups, and glasses garnished its walls—and Yûsef, our little coffee boy, pipe-bearer, and page, who, to his infinite satisfaction, presided over it, came out, arrayed in all his best, to kiss my hands, and evidently did his utmost to make a favorable impression on his new mistress. He had on clean, loose, white cotton drawers, a scarlet cloth jacket, a shawl girdle, and a white, quilted cotton skull-cap. Katrîne was quite content with her new quarters below, and she told me that she had unexpectedly found some cousins in Hâifa. I congratulated her, guessing, however, that this was only one of her curious delusions.

My brother's dragoman and secretary, Mohammed, his Egyptian groom, and several candidates for service at the Vice-Consulate, crowded round to welcome me, and solicit my favor and protection, in words which were exactly like quotations from the Old Testament.

An elderly Moslem woman, with an anxious, time-worn face, came, and after saluting me, said, "If now I have found grace in your sight, speak for me to my lord, your brother, that he may take my son into his service; speak now, I pray you, a word for my son, for he is my only son, and I am a widow."

Mattresses, cushions, and pillows, newly covered with chintz, placed nearly all round the rooms on planks, supported by roughly-made, low wooden trestles, a few pieces of European furniture, and a pretty well-stocked bookcase, made the place look cozy and comfortable. The boat from Tantûra arrived safely during the night with our luggage.

The next morning, September 24th, two men from Nazareth came to welcome us, and gave me a fatted lamb. Soon afterward a little party arrived from Shefa 'Amer, with a camel-load of fine water-melons; and a peasant from a neighboring village brought us some goat's milk cheese.

I must explain that these offerings are generally paid for at a rate considerably above the market price.

Saleh Sekhali, our neighbor, a Christian Arab, an intelligent, thoughtful-looking man, took breakfast with us. He told me that my brother was the only Englishman who had ever resided in Hâifa, and that I was the first English girl who had ever passed a night within the walls of the town. He said that very strange notions and opinions were held by the Arabs about English women and English society, and a great deal of curiosity was expressed by his friends on the subject. They hoped now to have an opportunity of judging for themselves by personal intercourse with us.

Saleh did not understand any European language, but he was clever and very quick of comprehension, and fond of study. He kindly volunteered to teach me Arabic, and to hear me read every day.

On inquiry I found that the population of Haîfa was, in 1854, computed thus:

Moslem	1,200
Greek Catholics	400 ⎫ Adherents of the Pope,
Latins	50 ⎬ and consequently under French patronage.
Maronites	30 ⎭
Orthodox Greeks	300
Jews	32
Making a total of	2,012

In the year 1860 the population was reckoned at about 2,300 souls. We went out and took leave of Mr. Finn, who was on the point of starting for 'Akka. His tents were all cleared away. Then we called at each of the Consulates, for among the Europeans in the Levant, the new-comer is expected to be the first caller. The French Consul—who in early youth had served in the ranks of the first Napoleon—received us heartily, and introduced me to his wife, a Syrian lady, who spoke French fluently. The Austrian Consul is a native of one of the Dalmatian Isles, and the other Consulates were held by Ionians and natives of Scio, who showed us great courtesy and kindness. The American Consular Agent is an Arab, who can speak a little broken English. The ladies of these families were all either Syrian or Greek, but they most of them spoke Italian, and welcomed me into their circle with graceful cordiality. Two other families, of French extraction, engaged in commerce, completed the European colony of Hâifa. Their houses were built in Oriental fashion, round courts, some of which were paved with black and white marble. The rooms were furnished with Turkish divans, French mirrors, consoles, and pictures. I must not omit the little Café, called the Victoria Hotel, kept by a Maltese.

Wednesday, September 26th, a party of women in white izzars, or sheets, from the court below, came early and brought me several flat loaves of bread, stamped with a cross, formed of groups of sacred monograms, $\overline{IC}$, $\overline{XC}$, NI, KI, etc., in celebration of the Greek Feast of the Holy Cross.

Presently the Greek Bishop of 'Akka visited us. He wore a long, blue cloth dress, very flowing and open, exposing an under robe of crimson silk, a crimson girdle, and black pointed shoes. He did not remove his low, brimless, black hat, which curves slightly and spreads toward the crown.

When he and his suite had retired, a letter was handed to my brother, which caused him to rise hastily and go out. I watched from the front window, and soon saw evident signs of a commotion in the town. Little groups of armed men were standing about in the open place, and passing hurriedly to and fro. In a short time I saw all the consuls in a body, preceded by their kawasses, carrying their swords and tall silver-headed sticks, going toward the Governor's castle, which was in sight. My brother ran up for a moment to tell me that Tîreh and the villages in its neighborhood had united to attack Hâifa, and three or four hundred of the peasantry were just outside the walls, attempting to effect an entrance. We were actually in a state of siege. The two gates were closed and guarded, and wherever its walls were very weak, detachments of impromptu volunteers were placed. I sat alone watching, and wondering what would happen. Men were parading the streets, making a great noise, and armed with old guns, staves, and swords of all shapes. The boys followed their example by marching about with sticks, shouting lustily, seemingly half for fun and half for fear. I could hear the firing of guns now and then from the back of the town, and the loud screams of the terrified women and children.

Girls from the neighboring houses and the court below flocked into my room, with their mothers, crying and trembling. They wondered why Madam Inglesi, as they called me, did not show any signs of fear. I tried to calm them, saying, "Be at rest, Allah is good." But they almost nonplused me by replying, "Allah is good! Praised be Allah! But the sons of Tîreh are bad!" And they refused to be comforted.

A group of heavily-armed, mounted horsemen were prancing about, as if to excite all the people to action. The consuls returned from the castle, where a council had been held. They had drawn up a protest against the Government, and signed it. I was told that four of the most venturesome of the attacking party had been shot under the south wall, and some of our townspeople had been slightly wounded. The Tîrehites had retreated; but as it was expected that they would renew the attack at night, preparations were made to resist it; for the walls of Hâifa are not very strong, and could easily be scaled or broken down.

A messenger was dispatched to 'Akka by boat to demand assistance. In the mean time my brother, at the Governor's request, procured guns and ammunition from an English ship in the port. Our room was converted into an armory, and our stairway and terrace was soon crowded with applicants for arms, which were cautiously distributed. A Government secretary stood by, making a list of the names of the volunteers thus supplied. By sunset the excitement had greatly increased, and no one seemed to think of going to rest. The consuls kept a careful look-out on the walls, and men paraded the town by moonlight, shouting, "Our swords are strong, and our trust is in God!" And the boys, with their sticks uplifted, echoed the words at the top of their voices.

Several Arab women, my neighbors, came and sat with me when my brother went out. One of them brought a favorite Arab dish of bleached and crushed walnuts and vermicelli, baked in butter and sugar. It was eaten while hot. The women all wore full trowsers and tight jackets; some were made of colored prints, and others of striped Damascus silk. Katrîne's simple Bethlehem dress was quite strange to them—they had never seen the costume before. They smoked, and chatted, and laughed, and cried by turns; and retired, hastily vailing themselves, when my brother came in at midnight to tell me that fifty artillerymen and thirty Bashi Bazûks had arrived from 'Akka in consequence of the consular protest. They were placed in proper positions as sentinels and patrols, and three or four hundred of the peasantry of a friendly village came to offer their assistance. Many of them were mounted on horses, and carried long spears; the rest had heavy guns. Altogether the little place looked quite warlike. Thus protected we slept in peace.

The next morning a large party of horsemen arrived from Shefa 'Amer and dismounted at our house; for they had come, they said, especially to protect the English Vice-Consulate.

The Tîrehites had now quite retreated, but our little town was still full of excitement. The assembled volunteers and armed peasantry were galloping about, singing and shouting, and now and then firing their guns. They seemed quite disappointed at not finding any especial use for them. The place was so well guarded that there was no longer any fear of an attack.

Just before sunset I strolled out with my brother through the quadrangle or castle-court, which was occupied by the artillery. We went out at the east gate, and through the Moslem cemetery to the fruit-gardens and the palm-grove. We were returning homeward on the sands when the loud and angry shouting of some herdsmen attracted our notice. A large number of cattle, some of which were said to be stolen property, were being led toward the town, and they were the subjects of the dispute. A crowd soon assembled, the noise increased, and an angry contest ensued, till words were followed by blows. I was led out of the way, and stationed on an embankment, thrown up years ago by Ibrahîm Pasha's soldiers. The disturbance was, naturally, misconstrued by the gallant volunteers and defenders of Hâifa. A troop of mounted peasantry issued from the gates, their long spears uplifted, the dust flying under the feet of their galloping horses, while their long striped cloaks and shawl head-dresses—kefias—streamed like flags or banners. The cattle and goats fled in all directions, and in their fright they did not seem to see where they were going, but blundered into thickets, against rocks and tombs, and into the sea. I was very nearly thrown down by some of them. More than a hundred men came out before they discovered that it was only a false alarm, and then, regretfully, they retraced their steps. Saleh, who was with us, told me to consider it as a little "fantasia," got up for my especial entertainment.

After our evening meal my brother was called away. I puzzled over my Arabic lesson for some time, and then went out on the terrace, where two of the men-servants were already sleeping. It seemed to me like a dream to be standing there alone in the moonlight, the night-silence only broken by the rippling of the waves on the shore, the bleating of my tethered lamb, and distant sounds of shouting and singing.

The next day the Pasha of 'Akka arrived. He visited each of the consuls, and then held a council at the castle. It was proposed that a force should march against Tîreh, in order to arrest and punish the plotters of the late attack on Hûifa; but it was soon made apparent that the Tîrehites had friends at Court and protectors in the Council. Some Moslems of influence in Hâifa had personal interest in the prosperity of Tîreh, for they had considerable property there, and some of the Tîrehites were largely in their debt. Through their interference and bribes, the affair was allowed to pass by almost unnoticed, notwithstanding the strongly-expressed indignation of the consuls and others.

A few days afterward, I was invited to a wedding in the Sekhali family, Christian Arabs of the orthodox Greek community. At about eight o'clock, A. M., I was led into their church, a domed building, lighted from above, and gaudy with highly-colored, distorted copies of ancient Byzantine pictures; for the Greeks, though not allowed to have images to assist them in their devotions, may have pictures, provided they are not too life-like! The body of the church, unincumbered by stalls or chairs, was already nearly filled with wedding guests, holding lighted—homemade—wax tapers; one was placed in my hands. In the center of the crowd, at a lectern, stood a priest, and, immediately before him, the bride, closely shrouded in a white izzar. A many-colored muslin vail entirely concealed her features. The bridegroom by her side, who was only seventeen, wore a suit of sky-blue cloth, edged with gold thread, and a handsome crimson and white shawl girdle. He had only once seen the face of the bride, and that was six months before, on the day of the betrothal.

The service was in Arabic, and rapidly uttered in clear

but monotonous tones. The most important part of it seemed to be the Gospel narrative of the marriage at Cana, in Galilee. While the priest was reading it, bread and wine were handed to the young man. He gave some to the girl, who, in taking it, was very careful not to expose her face. Immediately afterward, she held out one of her henna-stained hands, and a jeweled ring was placed on her finger. Two crowns, made of gilt foil, were brought by the bridegroom's-man and bride's-woman, and placed on the heads of the now married pair, who joined hands, and with their two attendants walked round and round in the midst of the people, who made way for them and sprinkled them with rose-water and other scents as they passed, singing, and shouting good wishes. By the time the circuit had been made seven times, the vails of the bride and bride's-woman were quite saturated, and the two men submitted, without the slightest resistance, to have bottles of scent emptied on their tarbûshes. As the excitement increased, the sprinkling became general, and I came in for my share. Thus ended the ceremony.

While this was going on, a continual shrill screaming accompaniment was kept up by the female friends of the bride, who were crowded together in the latticed gallery overhead. There were very few women in the body of the church, and those were near relations of the bride or bridegroom. Presently the men formed a procession, and with the bridegroom in their midst, walked out of church. A pipe-bearer, carrying a handsome chibouque, was in attendance, and he handed it to the bridegroom whenever the leaders paused to dance, or to sing some wild extravagant love-song. Rose-water was poured on his head from the roofs or windows of the houses under which he passed. Etiquette required that he should look quite calm and composed in the midst of the noise and excitement. I was told by Saleh that he preserved his dignified demeanor throughout the day, while his friends and fellow-townsmen were feasting and making merry round him, and singing bridal songs.

In the mean time, the bride, with her female attendants and companions, all vailed, and shrouded in white, walked very slowly toward her home—the home of her childhood; for she was not to go forth to meet the bridegroom till after sunset. I accompanied her. We all carried our tapers, although it was the third hour, that is, about nine o'clock, A. M. We paused now and then while one of the professional singing women improvised a solo, suitable for the occasion. All the women took up the words, and joined in chorus, as we walked on again. One verse was in allusion to the presence of a daughter of England at the wedding. It was regarded as a favorable omen. The chorus was a prayer for the peace and happiness of the English girl. We mounted a broad, covered stone staircase, and, passing through a corridor, entered a large, many-windowed room. The bride was led to a sort of throne, made of cushions and embroidered pillows, and I was placed by her side. Her white izzar and vail were taken off. She looked dreadfully faint and fatigued. She was not more than fourteen years old, with an oval face, rather large lips, and black, delicately-arched eyebrows. Her eyes were shut; for custom makes it a point of honor for a bride to keep them closed from the time she leaves the church till the moment she meets the bridegroom at night. She sat in state, in a kneeling posture, resting on her heels, while the palms of her hands were placed flat on her knees, as some Indian deities are represented. Her head-dress was almost concealed by strings of pearls, festoons of small gold coins, diamond—or paste—rosettes, and flower sprays. Her long hair, twisted with braid, hung down her back in nine plaits, heavy with little gold ornaments and coins. She wore a purple velvet jacket, very open in front, showing her crape shirt and her chest, which was actually adorned with little bits of leaf-gold! Her necklace, or collar of gold coins, was very beautiful. Her skirt of white and yellow silk almost concealed her full, yellow silk drawers. Her hands and arms were checkered with deep orange-brown henna stains; but what struck me more than all, was the glossy, shining luster of her skin.

While I had been intently watching and observing the bride, the company of women had quite transformed themselves. They had thrown off their white izzars and vails, and now appeared in all the colors of the rainbow—in all sorts of combinations. The faces of many looked as glossy as the bride's. Nearly all of them had very large dark eyes, with the edges of the eyelids blackened with kohl. Their mouths were rather wide, and revealed large, very perfect white teeth, which glistened as the teeth of wild animals do. Their complexions were generally dark, but brilliant and clear. They came forward, one by one, to kiss the bride's hand; but she remained quite passive, and did not answer any salutations. Dancing and singing commenced. A woman kept time with a tambourine, and two or three dancers stood up in the center of the room, and attitudinized gracefully but voluptuously. They began very slowly—advancing, as if reluctantly and timidly, toward some imaginary object—then retreating, only to advance again, gradually quickening both step and action. The lookers on sat round on the matted floor, in a double row, clapping their hands in harmony with the tambourine, and singing wild, passionate songs, to melodies in a minor key, in two-four time. As soon as one dancer was tired, another stood up and replaced her; and four of them worked themselves up into such a state of excitement that they looked as if they were dying, when at last they gave way. Some of the younger girls wore white calico dresses, with small gold spangles sewed all over them in clusters; others had on white thin muslin skirts, over blue or red silk trowsers, and red or black velvet jackets; and, when they danced, they held in their hands embroidered shawls, which they waved about gracefully. Sweetmeats, fruits, creams, and various dishes were served at midday.

After sunset the mother and female relations of the bridegroom came to fetch the bride; and then she com-

menced crying and wailing bitterly. This is expected of
her; and, whether she feel regret or no, she must show
signs of sorrow on leaving her home, and must also appear
unwilling to go forth to meet the bridegroom. This real
or affected reluctance is sometimes carried to such an extent
that the weeping bride has to be pushed and dragged
along very ungracefully. I have witnessed ludicrous scenes
of this kind. The vailed bride, whose eyes are still supposed
to be closed—but she does peep about a little—is
generally lifted on to a horse; and, though her new home
may be only in the next street, she makes a tour through
the town or village, riding very slowly, attended by a large
company of women and girls, carrying flaming torches, and
screaming and singing wildly.

I have often lent my horse to a poor girl that she may
thus ride in triumph, lifted up among the crowd of torch-bearers,
to meet her bridegroom; and very often, just before
midnight, I have been attracted to the window to see such
processions pass by.

Before the going forth of the bride a party of men and
women convey her *trousseau* by torch-light to her new home.
A red wooden cradle and a red box are always the most
conspicuous objects. Sometimes a small looking-glass in
a gilt frame is proudly displayed. Pillows covered with
bright-colored silks, a trayful of scented soap, a mattress or
two, and a lehaff may be seen, varying in quality according
to the rank of the bride.

On subsequent and persevering inquiry among Arab
ladies, I found out how it was that the bride's face
looked so lustrous. I learned that girls are prepared for
marriage with a very great deal of ceremony. There are
women who make the beautifying of brides their especial
profession!

A widow woman, named Angelina, is the chief *artiste* in
this department of art in Hâifa. She uses her scissors and
tweezers freely and skillfully to remove superfluous hair,
and trains the eyebrow to an arched line, perfecting it

with black pigments. She prepares an adhesive plaster of very strong, sweet gum, and applies it by degrees all over the body, letting it remain on for a minute or more; then she tears it off quickly, and it brings away with it all the soft down or hair, leaving the skin quite bare, with an unnaturally-bright and polished appearance, much admired by Orientals. The face requires very careful manipulation.* When women have once submitted to this process, they look frightful if from time to time they do not repeat it; for the hair never grows so soft and fine again. Perhaps this is one of the reasons why aged Arab women, who have quite given up all these arts of adornment, look so haggard and witch-like. In some instances this ordeal slightly irritates the skin, and perfumed sesame or olive-oil is applied, or cooling lotions of elder-flower water are used.

The bride invites her friends to accompany her to the public bath previous to the wedding day, and sends to each one a packet of henna, two or three pieces of soap, and two wax candles. Angelina is generally the bearer of the message and of these articles, which are always to be paid for. I have now and then accepted such invitations.

Bridal parties assemble and sometimes pass three successive days in the luxury of the Turkish bath. Pipes, sherbet, coffee, and other refreshments are served, and songs are sung in honor of the bride, who is, of course, attended by Angelina, and forms the center of attraction. Her hair is unbraided, she is slowly disrobed, and then, with her loins slightly girdled with crimson silk, she is mounted on high clogs, and led through halls and passages gradually increasing in temperature, with fountains overflowing their marble floors. She is placed on a marble platform, near to

---

* Did David allude to this custom—which is evidently a very ancient one—when he prayed for the physical prosperity of his kingdom and said, "May our daughters be as corner-stones, polished after the similitude of a palace?" It is only as brides or wives that they could be recognized as corner-stones, helping to build up the nation, and it is then that their faces are made to shine.

a jet of hot water. Fullers' earth is rubbed on her head, she is lathered with soap, and brushed with a handful of tow. Hot water is poured over her, freely, she is swathed in long towels, and by slow degrees conducted back to a more moderate temperature, and lastly to a fountain of cool water. Her companions in the mean time undergo the same process. Then, shrouded in muslin, crape, or linen, they sit together, smoking, till they are rested and refreshed.

The edges of the eyelids are blackened thus—a little instrument, like a silver bodkin, is dipped in water, and then into a bottle or box containing an impalpable powder called *kohl*, made of antimony and carefully-prepared soot; the blackened point is drawn gently along between the almost closed lids of the eyes. Poor people use soot alone, and apply it with pins made of lignum vitæ.*

The arms and hands, legs and feet, are bandaged with narrow tape or braid, like sandals, crossing and recrossing each other; then a paste made of moistened henna powder—the pulverized leaves of the henna tree—*Lawsonia*—is spread and bound over them, and allowed to remain on for several hours. When it is removed, the skin is found deeply dyed wherever the tape—which is now unwound—did not protect it. Thus a sort of checkered pattern is produced, and when it is artistically and delicately done—as Angelina can do it—the feet look, at a distance, as if they were sandaled, and the hands as if they were covered with mittens of a bright orange or bronze color.

Finally, early on the wedding-day, the bride is dressed in her bridal robes. Her hair is braided in what we call the Grecian plait. Small pieces of leaf-gold are stuck on her forehead and on her breast. Care is taken not to con-

---

* This process is probably referred to by Ezekiel xxiii, 40. "Ye have sent for men to come from far; for whom thou didst wash thyself, *paintedst thy eyes*, and deckedst thyself with ornaments." And it is written that Jezebel "painted her eyes," or "put her eyes in painting." And Jeremiah says, in the fourth chapter and thirtieth verse, "Though thou deckest thee with ornaments of gold; though thou *rentest thy face* [or, as it should be written, *thine eyes*,] with painting, in vain shalt thou make thyself fair," etc. So we may regard the use of kohl as a very ancient custom.

ceal any of the stars or spots tattooed on her face or chest in infancy. A line of blue dots encircling the lips is sometimes seen, and a spot on the chin is very common. A little rouge is added to highten the color of the cheeks when considered necessary.

Angelina gets into sad disgrace with the clergy of Hâifa for encouraging all this vanity, out of which she, by the by, makes a good living. She goes from one church to another for absolution, sometimes reckoning herself a Greek, sometimes a Latin, and sometimes a Melchite, according to the leniency of the respective priests.

The Arab women are very much wedded to the ancient customs of the country, and they will not abandon them, notwithstanding the persevering efforts of the priesthood.

The Greek Catholic Church vainly pronounces anathemas, and threatens with excommunication those women who tattoo themselves, and use kohl, and henna, and rouge. They will persist in doing so while they believe that it adds to their beauty, and to their powers of attraction, and in vain the noisy processions at weddings and at burials are forbidden, so long as the people believe them to be propitious. Their respect for custom is stronger even than their fear of the Church. If the priests persisted in carrying out their threats of excommunication for such offenses, their congregations would soon be scattered; so they are lenient, and thus Greek and Roman forms of Christianity are blended insensibly with ceremonies and practices so ancient that their origin even is unknown.

This is not the only difficulty which the priests find to contend with, in the pastoral care of Arab women.

In 1859 a number of black silk mittens were sold in Hâifa by a peddler from Beirût. They were a novelty to the Arab women, who were quite proud of this addition to their toilette, and displayed their mittened hands delightedly in church. The priest of the Greek Catholic community actually denounced them from the altar, forbidding the adoption of gloves, mittens, or any new and expensive luxury in their dress, and cautioned them also against exposing any part of their ornamental head-dresses in church!

I had a very interesting conversation a few days afterward with the utterer of this denunciation, and he explained to me his reason for this seemingly-strange interference about the mittens. He said that he considered it very important to check, if possible, the inroad of Frank taste among the Arab women; for, if they were to adopt the Frank dress, which requires many changes of apparel, and alters its fashions frequently, a *trousseau* would be so expensive that young men would not be able to marry, and early unions, which are so desirable in the East, would be prevented. The costly articles of a genuine Arab wardrobe last a lifetime, and are heirlooms, whereas the gala dresses of a Frank wardrobe must be renewed every year. This priest spoke feelingly; for he was an Arab, a husband, and the father of a large family of girls. It is quite clear that in matters of fashion and custom, the priests have very little influence. In towns where the Arabs have much intercourse with Europeans, they gradually adopt some of their manners, and imitate their costumes, by degrees abandoning their own.

On the 1st of October the victories in the Crimea were announced and celebrated in 'Akka. Five times during the day twenty-one guns were fired, and at night the town was illuminated, and bonfires were made on the hills which encircle the bay. In Hâifa a great portion of the lately-acquired supply of ammunition was used in *feux de joie*, the minaret and the Consulates were lighted up, and we borrowed lamps from the Jewish synagogue to deck the English flagstaff!

At night the place was very animated. We went out with Saleh Sekhali, and Mohammed Bek, a distinguished-looking, handsome Moslem, and two or three of his friends. Yûsef led the way, with "a lantern for our feet." It threw light now and then on such muddy pools, guttered streets, and heaps of vegetable refuse, that it was quite indispensable. We made our way to the narrow, ill-constructed, but well-supplied bazar, which is generally deserted at sunset, but that night the shops were all open. Pipes, red and yellow shoes and boots, embroidered slippers, Manchester prints, Damascus silks, purple linen, shawls, jars, lamps, and cooking utensils, fruit, sweetmeats, and samples of grain, were exposed by the light of a hundred lanterns. Groups of Arabs in their *fête*-day dresses were on all the counters, and in the open *cafés* and barbers' shops story-tellers and singers attracted earnest listeners. Showers of sugar-plums were thrown from one side of the place to the other, and boys were busy scrambling for them.

Mohammed Bek and Saleh, and a few Arab friends, spent the evening with us. One of them inquired what kind of stories or romances English people liked. We had recently read "Jane Eyre," so my brother began translating it to them, *au courant*, somewhat condensing it, and adapting it to Arab comprehension. The listeners were so interested that they came several successive nights for an hour or two to hear it to the end. I mention this because two years afterward, when traveling in the interior, we heard this story, somewhat altered and modified, but well told, by an Arab who did not know its source. We soon traced it to some of our guests of that night. Perhaps some future collector of Arabian tales may be puzzled by hearing the Oriental version of this *very unoriental* romance, and may fancy he has found the origin of the plot of "Jane Eyre," and rob the little imaginative recluse of Yorkshire of the credit of her wonderful power and originality. Æsop's Fables, freely translated in the same way, with the help of illustrations, gave great pleasure to our Arab friends. Our maps puzzled them, and excited their interest and curiosity, and they had faith in them when they found that by the assistance of a map of Palestine I, a stranger, could tell the names and directions of most of the towns and villages for miles around.

AN IMPORTANT QUESTION.

The Moslem guests were at first rather shy, and hardly ventured to address me; for they are not in the habit of seeing any women except their wives, slaves, and servants, and they never see any Christian women. I had been advised to avoid meeting my brother's Moslem guests for the sole reason that they seclude their female relatives; but we did not wish to imitate Oriental exclusiveness unnecessarily, and I found much to interest me in my intercourse with them. They always behaved to me with respectful and chivalrous kindness.

The Levantine ladies, who hide themselves from Moslems almost as scrupulously as the native Arabs do, were rather surprised, and they explained to me that it was quite contrary to custom for Moslems to see females out of their own families, and that the laws of their religion forbade them to do so. I took the first opportunity to make inquiry on the subject, and when two or three of the most intelligent and learned of our Moslem friends were assembled one evening at our house, I told them that I had an important question to ask them. I first reminded them that neither the customs of my country nor the voice of my conscience forbade me to see any of my fellow-creatures. On the contrary, I was taught to love every one, knowing that we are all of one family, the children of one God, and created by his will. Then I said, "Is there any law, which you regard as sacred and binding, forbidding you to see and converse with women out of your own individual families? If there is such a law, I will not cause you to disobey it, but will help you to keep it by hiding myself from you."

They seemed to be taken by surprise; but they clearly explained and proved to me that there is no law of the kind, and it is the law of custom only which immures the women in their harems. Mohammed Bek said that their women are now quite unfitted for society, and would not know how to conduct themselves in the presence of strangers. "If we gave them liberty they would not know how to use it. Their heads are made of wood. They are not like you. When you speak, we no longer remember that you are a girl; we think we are listening to a sheikh. To live in the world knowledge and wisdom are necessary. Our wives and daughters have neither wisdom nor knowledge. Give them wisdom, and we will give them liberty."

Satisfied on this point, I continued to see them, and I never had reason to regret it. I think that I gave them some new ideas on the capabilities and capacities of women, which may in time be turned to account.

Yassîn Agha, one of our most frequent guests, invited me to visit his family. I went with my brother. We were first received in a large vaulted room by the Agha and his sons and a few Moslem gentlemen, then the eldest son was desired to conduct me to the harem, that part of the house especially occupied by women. He led me across a court, and up an open stairway, into a large, handsome room paved with marble, where a group of women waited to welcome me. He introduced me to his grandmother, an aged-looking woman, almost blind, and to his own mother, and then he left me. They wore jackets and full trowsers made of common print. They led me into an inner apartment, where a younger wife of the Agha, gayly decked with embroidery, jewelry, and flowers, was seated with a number of children, slaves, and servants. The latter seemed to occupy almost the same position in the establishment as their mistresses, but some of them were very dirty, untidy, and ragged. In an open brazier in the middle of this room a charcoal fire was burning, and a little child sick with fever was on a mattress in the corner. The air was dry and hot, and I found it difficult to breathe, especially when they all crowded round me. My dress was examined with curiosity, and if I had not gently but firmly resisted, I think I should have been disrobed, so eager were they to see how my clothes were made and fastened. They patted me, stroked my hair, and called me all sorts of pet names.

They asked me if I were betrothed, and whether my brother
had a harem, and if he were fair and handsome. When I
took off my light kid gloves, one of the children began to
cry, saying, "Behold, see, the stranger is skinning her
hands." Lemonade and sweetmeats were handed to me,
and coffee was prepared by a black slave, who crouched
down by the charcoal fire. Narghilés and long pipes were
passed from one to another. The one which I smoked had
a very beautiful jeweled mouthpiece, sent up by the Agha
for my use. I explained to them that I had learned to
smoke in their country, and that in England ladies do not
smoke. They took me into a room well stocked with
lehaffs and mattresses, some of which were covered with
silk. They asked if I could work, and were surprised
when I answered that I could make all my clothes. They
told me that nearly all their dresses were made by tailors,
and that their mattresses, lehaffs, and divans, were covered
and made by upholsterers, so that they did very little
needle-work themselves. The eldest son, who had been
my guide, came to fetch me, and took me into a small
but lofty room, with palm fronds at least twelve feet long
in each corner, and dates hanging up in rich clusters from
the rafters.

I called afterward on Mohammed Bek. He had only
one wife, a pleasant young woman, who, with her infant
daughter, were under the especial duennaship of the Bek's
mother, one of the most dignified-looking Arab women I
ever saw.

The young wife, Miriam, was dressed in a dark cloth
jacket and pink cotton trowsers. She was very much tattooed. A row of blue dots encircled her large thick lips,
a star appeared on her forehead, and a little crescent on
her chin. Her eyebrows were strongly marked, and her
lashes very long. At her side, in her girdle, she had a
gold crescent-shaped box or case, embossed and chased. It
contained an inscription in Arabic characters, and she
regarded it as a potent charm.

Her little child had on a green silk skull-cap, to which were fastened coins, strings of pearls, and a blue bead to avert the effect of the glance of an "evil eye." Broad bands of silver, with tinkling bells attached to them, were fastened round her ankles, and she pattered about on the matted floor with her little naked feet to make them ring. She had on a tight green silk jacket, and short full Turkish trowsers, and a small red shawl for a girdle.

I liked these people very much, and often went to see them. One day when I called, about two years after my first visit, Miriam told me that she feared her husband was looking out for another wife. Some Moslem ladies, who had heard the rumor at the Turkish baths, had told her. She said, "I have lived for four years with the Bek and his mother, and I have been very happy, but I shall be happy no longer if he brings home a new bride. She will take his soul from me. Speak to him, O my sister, that he may not take another wife. He will listen to you, for your words are pearls and diamonds."

I ascertained afterward that the report was true, for Mohammed was negotiating a marriage with a girl of a tribe of the Metwalis; this was, however, soon afterward broken off, for the family or clan to which the Bek belonged became involved in a feud with the Metwalis, consequently the marriage could not take place. Mohammed had never seen the lady, so he was easily consoled, and Miriam rejoiced exceedingly.

In a third harem which I visited, I found four wives, who seemed to live very contentedly together. They were kindly treated and very much indulged, and were often allowed to go—*well guarded*—to the Turkish baths, and to visit other harems.

Their husband, Sheikh Abdallah, always had in his establishment the full allowance of four wives, and when one died the vacancy was soon filled. Though still in the prime of life, he had already had seven wives. I ascertained from them, by degrees, that they held supremacy in turn, for the space of a few days or a week. The honored one is said to be "holder of the keys," for during her temporary sway she is always in full dress—the mistress of the reception-room—and the favored one of the lord of the harem, while the rest attend to the cooking and household matters. This family seemed to be very well regulated, and I never saw any signs of ill-feeling between the wives, although the youngest and prettiest had no children, while the eldest, a lady of Nablûs, had three sons, and the two others, who came respectively from Saida and Damascus, had each a son and daughter.

The sheikh always sought for wives in various and far distant towns. After marriage the women rarely, if ever, came in contact with their relatives; thus, having no connections in Hâifa, they naturally sympathized with each other as strangers in a strange place. There were no old quarrels or jealousies to revive; on the contrary, there must have been subjects of novelty and interest to communicate. Perhaps this was one of the reasons why Abdallah's harem was more homelike and harmonious than any other which I visited.*

The chief room is long and narrow, with unglazed, wooden, latticed windows on three sides of it. A raised divan at the end of the room is regarded as the seat of honor, where the sheikh always sits. Narrow mattresses, carpeted and cushioned, are arranged on the floor close to the walls.

---

* It seems to me that Sheikh Abdallah thus carried out, in its most extreme sense, the spirit of the injunction of Moses, not to take a woman's sister to wife "to vex her in her lifetime."

Abdallah would not even run the risk of marrying any two members of one family, or even two girls from the same town or village. He was shrewd and clever, and understood the disadvantages of such unions. When Moses gave the above law he was legislating for a people who, like the Moslems, practiced polygamy and recognized it as lawful. He in his wisdom may not have approved of it, but he tried to mitigate its evils and make the best of it. He had no doubt often witnessed, as I have done, the quarrels, disputes, and jealousies which arise in harems where the several wives of one man are nearly related to each other. The more remote the connection or relationship among the women in a harem, the more chance there appears to be of peace within its walls.

I had known this family about three years, when, one day, as I sat in that room, surrounded by the four wives, their children and slaves, the sheikh himself was suddenly announced. All rose up at his coming. He took his seat by my side on the divan. None of the women ventured to sit in his presence till he had invited them to do so.

They all vied with each other to serve him. One placed a pillow for him cozily, another handed him sherbet, and the favored one had the especial privilege of preparing and lighting his pipe. He spoke very gently and kindly to them all, and fondled his children lovingly. He was dressed in in-door costume, and wore a long gown, called a kûmbaz, made of white goat's-hair, striped with white spun silk, and over it a bright-blue cloth pelisse, edged with fur, a very large white muslin turban, and yellow pointed slippers, without stockings.

I asked him if he had any books. He dispatched one of his little sons, with orders to bring to me all that were in the house. A slave soon appeared with a pile of dusty folios, consisting of manuscript copies of the Koran, illuminated profusely, and books of medicine and magic; but the favorite volume was brought by one of the wives. It was a thick, clumsy-looking quarto, and consisted of careful and detailed interpretations of dreams and omens of all kinds; in fact, it was a manuscript divination dictionary. The subjects were arranged in alphabetical order, beautifully written in large red letters, and the explanations were in black ink. The paper was so thick, yellow, and glossy that I at first mistook it for vellum. As the sheikh turned over the leaves of this book he said, "Lady, what was the dream of your last sleep?" I reflected an instant, and answered, "I was walking by the sea-shore, near the River Kishon, and was very tired, when suddenly a white horse, ready saddled, rose and stood before me, as if offering his services; so I mounted and rode on, as if I were flying, till I awoke." The women cried out, "It is a good dream!" And the sheikh looked in the dictionary for the words "white horse," and "sea-shore." After some consideration he assured me that my dream was a very good one, and that, though great dangers surrounded me, I should certainly escape from them. None of the women could read a single letter; but if any thing could induce them to learn, I think it would be their desire to read that book, every line of which they listened to most eagerly.

A tray of sweetmeats, nuts, fruit, and other dishes was brought in. The shcikh ate with me, and then retired; for none of the women would eat in his presence. I never saw an instance of an Arab woman eating with men except in families which had been strongly influenced by European society. These ladies were all very clever in making preserves, marmalade, and sweetmeats, and in preparing meat dishes, and seemed to be very devoted mothers. The children looked happy, and the elder sons were fine, intelligent youths.

In spite of the good-natured cheerfulness of the women, I felt that there was something wanting. Only the material part of their nature was developed, and developed so disproportionately, that the Moslems were right when they said that in their present state they are unfit for general society. In some of the harems the women live very unhappily, and are only like spies on each other. In some cases men who have two wives are obliged also to have two homes, that peace may be insured. The majority of Moslems do not practice polygamy.

Disagreements frequently arise from jealousy about offspring. The wife who has only daughters looks with hatred and envy on the mother rejoicing over an infant boy. I can fully realize the passionate despair of Hannah when provoked by Peninnah, and the muttered prayer and excitement which Eli mistook for the frenzy of drunkenness; and I can fancy I hear her at last triumphing and exulting over her son Samuel, in words of praise and prayer, inspired by the strongest feelings of her nature.

I expected to find very large families in those houses where there were two or more wives; but, as a rule, this was not the case. In the Jewish and Christian quarters the children are much more numerous than in the Moslem quarters. The Jews in Syria are permitted to take a second wife if the first has no hope of having any children.

Early in October, on a pleasant afternoon, I went with my brother into one of the fruit-gardens just outside Hâifa. We cautiously made our way, one by one, down a short, narrow lane of prickly pears, and passed a little mud and stone hut, the dwelling of the gardener and his family. They were Egyptians, who are considered much more skillful than Arabs in the cultivation of the ground. Fig-trees, pomegranates, almonds, elders, olives, palms, lemons, shaddocks—or, as they are called in Arabic, "lemûn helû," sweet lemons—and cucumbers of many kinds, flourished under his care. However, as every thing is sold in the market according to a tariff regulated by the Government, there is very little motive or inducement for emulation among gardeners, and no attempt is made to improve and perfect the delicious fruits and valuable vegetables of the country—quantity, without regard to quality, is the consideration of the Oriental cultivator.

Under an olive-tree, in the middle of the garden, on an old piece of matting, sat an aged Arab woman; her ragged white linen head-dress was arranged so as to shade her eyes, which were afflicted with ophthalmy. Her cotton dress was patched over and over again, and a heavy, striped abbai, or traveling cloak, was thrown over her feet. She was intently mumbling to herself, and slipping the beads of a black rosary rapidly through her long, thin fingers. Near to her was a little nook made of piled-up stones and earth, and covered with old matting. It was not much bigger than the hood of a bassinette, but it was evidently intended to shelter her head at night, for a rolled-up mattress and some heavy-wadded quilts were close to it. Old clothes were hanging on the tree above her, not for the sake of drying them, but the branch was her clothes-peg, and the tree her wardrobe. Two basins were behind the tree trunk, and the remains of a wood-fire between two blocks of stone. This was her kitchen. We greeted her with, "Peace be upon you;" but she gave us only gloomy answers, saying, "For me there is no peace," and still continued fingering her beads, without raising her head. She said an "evil eye" had looked upon her and had "destroyed the power" of her life.

A pleasant sound of falling water attracted us up to the large, square, raised, stone reservoir, round which, seated on a low parapet, a party of Arabs were smoking and chatting. Water was falling with some force into this pool, from a duct supplied by large earthenware jars, fixed with ropes, made of palm-fiber, to a large wheel. The wheel was kept in motion by a blindfolded mule, and as it turned round it dipped into a well, and the jars were filled with water, and in rising up again they emptied themselves into the duct, and so on again and again, as long as the mule kept up its monotonous round, urged on by a little barefooted boy, stick in hand. A hole in the lower part of the wall of the reservoir was every day unplugged for a certain time, and the water allowed to flow into the little channels or furrows which traversed the beds of vegetables and encircled the trees.

As we left the garden, a donkey, laden with the red shells or rinds of pomegranates, passed us. I was surprised to learn that the bright yellow dye used to stain leather is prepared from them.

We were walking toward the sands, through the burial ground. The sun had set. We had left behind us at some distance all the evening loungers about the town-gate, and all the smokers by the well-side and the garden, when we saw advancing toward us, in the twilight, a powerful-looking black man, girdled with sackcloth, carrying a staff, or rather the trunk of a slender tree, which still retained two or three of its forked branches. The man was tall, but his staff was high above him. He walked with an unsteady gait, and we soon recognized him as an African maniac, of whom some of the Europeans of Hâifa had complained to the Governor, because he walked in the streets quite naked; in consequence of this he had been turned out of town. We passed him, and then he followed close behind us, muttering and making strange noises. It was not very pleasant to have such an attendant. We turned sharply round and faced him, and then walked toward the town. He turned also, and preceded us. We were still among the tombs; and, in the rapidly-increasing darkness, it appeared the dreariest place imaginable—rocky and desolate, with tombs of all periods, some in the last stages of decay, falling and crumbling into strange shapes and heaps, others partially concealed by small, dark, evergreen oaks, and here and there was a newly-whitened sepulcher, which seemed to shine with a light of its own. The black man did not accompany us beyond this domain of death. When I looked back, and saw him standing there among the tombs, swaying himself and his scepter to and fro, I could not help thinking of the description, in the Gospel narrative, of that man who met Christ on the shores of the sea of Galilee, and "which had devils long time, and ware no clothes, neither abode in any house, but in the tombs."[*] I did not suppose that the poor African maniac was possessed of devils, but I thought that he might very likely be seized with the spirit of revenge; so I was glad to be out of his reach, and safe within the gates of the town.

* Luke viii, 27.

CHAPTER VI.

FROM HÂIFA TO NAZARETH.

On Saturday, October 13th, we made ready for a trip to Nazareth—Nâsirah—to meet Mr. Finn there. We started at about three o'clock in the afternoon, accompanied by our friend Saleh Sekhali, one kawass, and an Egyptian groom. We went out at the east gate, crossed the burial-ground, approached the Carmel range, and skirted the base of the hills, which are overgrown with low brushwood and evergreen oaks. We took a south-easterly direction, with the terraced slopes on our right hand, and a marshy plain on our left, all bright with lush-green grass, tall rushes, and reeds in full blossom.

We met strings of camels bringing grain from the Haurân, for the merchants in Hâifa and 'Akka. The peasants and camel-drivers were all fully armed, and seemed as ready for attack as for defense.

Presently we passed a more peaceful-looking party, consisting of a family belonging to the next village. First came a young girl, wearing a rather short open dress of old striped crimson silk, made like a very scanty dressing-gown, a long white shirt of very coarse heavy linen, and a shawl-girdle fastened low. A purple scarf sheltered her head and face—all but her large dark eyes, and fell over, her shoulders. She walked barefoot, and carried her yellow shoes in her hands. A woman with an infant son in her arms followed, riding on a large white donkey, which was urged on by a man who walked close behind. We exchanged greetings, and the strangers said to us, "May Allah lead you in the path that is straight!" In about forty minutes we reached the spring of Sa'adeh, which supplies one of the tributary streams of the Kishon. It gushes out of a deep, cavernous recess in the steep cliff, and forms a large, spreading, natural reservoir, where many kinds of ferns are fostered. Saleh told me that Arab poets call a stream "a daughter of the hills." He led the way where he knew there were firm stepping-stones, and we splashed through water, in some parts about two feet deep, guiding our horses between masses of rock and great stone bowlders, surrounded by tall trees and water-plants. Our progress was somewhat impeded by a number of goats and cattle, which were being led to the fountain.

Just beyond this we saw, high up on the hills on our right, a picturesque-looking Moslem village, called Kefr-esh-Sheik. On the flat roofs of its white stone huts there were little Summer-houses, made of tree branches, long palm fronds, and reeds. Most of the villagers in this district make these pleasant shelters in the Summer-time. It reminded me of the Jewish Feast of Tabernacles.

Busy groups were on the thrashing-floors. A man was winnowing a heap of wheat, by lifting up as much as he could at a time, and as he let it fall gradually, the wind carried away the chaff. We lingered a moment by the old stone well in the olive grove; near to it we saw a number of strong masculine-looking laughing girls. In a few minutes we came to the little village of Ain-jûr, with palm-trees and flourishing gardens round it. At this point we turned away from the hills, and made our way across the fertile plain.

A serpentine line of verdure marks the course of the Kishon. We approached it where it flows between steep banks of rich loamy soil, nearly fifteen feet high, bordered with fine oleanders, wild lupins, tall and blue, and St. John's wort, covered with golden flowers. There was not much water flowing, for there had not been any rain in Galilee for a long time; but the muddy bed, which at this spot is about twenty feet broad, seemed to me as if it would swallow us up.

I have seen this stream swollen and rapid, after heavy rains, when the Winter torrents of Galilee and Carmel flow into it; then it is a river "with waters to swim in, a river that can not be passed over;" and I can well imagine the hosts of Sisera, his chariots and horses, struggling there; and how "the River Kishon swept them away, that ancient river, the River Kishon." Judges v, 21. We crossed safely, and rode on, due east, to traverse some rounded hills, crowned with evergreen oaks, hawthorns, and syringas. I have seen them in the Spring-time full of blossom, when the ground which they shelter is carpeted with hyacinths, cyclamen, anemones, and narcissus. This is one of the most extensive oak woods in Galilee, the oak leaves are small and prickly, and the acorns large and long.

Here cheetahs are sometimes captured and killed—for the sake of their skins, which are made into saddle-cloths—foxes have their holes, and hyenas, cats, jackals, and wild boars abound. The town Arabs are by no means enthusiastic hunters. A Nimrod is rarely met with now, except among the European colonists.

In a little open glade we dismounted, and rested just outside the solitary tent of a peasant, while we took some refreshing fruit, then we hastened on again. These hills are renowned for echoes, which are called by Arabs, "the daughters of sound." My companions brought them forth, by firing their guns and shouting, and they made the forest ring with their songs; at its eastern extremity the trees grow so closely together, and the branches hang so low, that I had to ride cautiously, to avoid sharing the fate of Absalom. When we came out of the wood, we found ourselves on the brow of a high, steep, and terraced declivity. The smooth plain of Esdraelon Minor was immediately below us, one half of it shaded by the hills on which we stood, and the other half, as well as the opposite hills, were in bright sunlight. The little village of Nain was pointed out to me far away on the right.

We descended by a pleasant winding road, the trees

were more and more scattered, and at the foot of the hill only low brushwood grew.

We cantered across the plain, and ascended a low rounded hill, on which stood a village, literally formed of dust and ashes. The mud-hovels looked like dust-heaps, and their interiors were little better than dust-holes; but out of these abodes heaps of clothing crawled, scarcely looking like human beings, till they slowly rose, assuming forms of strange grace and dignity, and gazed at us with serious and untroubled eyes. We saw a group of old women leaning over a square hole dug in the ground. Saleh told me that this was the village oven. The bottom of it glowed with red heat. The fuel, composed of peat and dried dung,* was partially covered with stones, upon which thin flat loaves are thrown and quickly baked. When quite new, the bread thus prepared is crisp outside and rather soft within; but, when a day old, it is of the consistency of leather, and very indigestible. The women, in their dusky vails and dresses, crouching round that primitive oven, reminded me of the incantation scene in "Macbeth." The children of the place were beautiful, though bronzed by the sun, and smeared with dust and dirt. Some were clothed in rags of all colors, but the majority were quite naked.

We looked back across the plain; the sun had gone down behind the wooded hills, and red watch-fires gleamed here and there on the terraces and in the plain—guides and beacons for the shepherds and the *fellahîn*. Presently a party of wild-looking Arabs met us. Their leader was the son of a cavalry officer, who had just been dismissed from Turkish service. He and his followers were desperate fellows, noted for deeds of daring. They saluted us, and said that they had come on purpose to meet and escort us to Nazareth. This was quite an impromptu invention, for no one but Mr. Finn knew of our intention to go

---

* See Ezekiel iv, 15: "Lo! I have given thee cow's dung, and thou shalt prepare thy bread therewith."

to Nazareth; however, they turned and accompanied us. They looked very picturesque. Their large, heavy cloaks were made of camel's-hair, with broad brown and white stripes. On their heads they wore red and yellow kefias— fringed shawls—put on like hoods, and fastened round the crown with double ropes, made of camel's-hair. Their spears, adorned with ostrich-feathers, were twelve or thirteen feet long.

We paused at a spring, festooned with ferns and bordered with mossy stones, and alighted for a few minutes to water our horses. When Saleh was on the point of remounting, his mare suddenly started off, and soon disappeared in the dusky distance. Saleh was quite disconcerted; for the animal was a favorite one, and so docile that it was never considered necessary to tether her. She was accustomed to follow her master, and to obey his call like a dog. Saleh remembered that the village of which his mare was a native was about a quarter of an hour's distance from the spring, and this explained the cause of the flight. He immediately mounted a horse belonging to one of the Arabs and galloped away. He actually found his mare standing quietly in the court of the house in which she had been born, surrounded by her former owners, who were marveling greatly. Saleh rejoined us, and we soon entered the hill-country which encircles Nazareth. Our volunteer attendants rode now before and now behind, singing and shouting. Higher and higher we rose, meeting the fresh mountain air. It was so dark that I could only just perceive the figure immediately before me, and the loose white stones which clattered under my horse's feet, and the smooth slabs of rock over which he every now and then slipped and stumbled.

For about an hour I rode on silently, hardly knowing where I was going, but following in faith the steps of my leader. I was roused from a reverie by the words, "We are entering the olive-groves of Nazareth." I could just distinguish a range of hills, forming an amphitheater in the shape of a horseshoe, and the extent of the town could be traced by the lights gleaming from the windows of the houses which thickly dotted the valley below, and were grouped here and there on the hill-sides. The Arabs keep lamps burning in their rooms all night to chase away evil spirits. We descended abruptly between hedges of prickly pears, greeted by loudly-barking dogs, and inhaling a close, suffocating odor of dust and decayed vegetables. The word, "Hold your horse's head well up, for it is very steep here," prepared me now and then for a jerk down some rocky ledge or dusty declivity. At last we were safe in the valley; our escort disappeared; and we were led to the roomy but half-deserted house of Saleh, where he had resided till the death of his father, a few months previous, and where his brother and young sisters still lived. Two empty rooms were soon swept and garnished by men and boys, who brought a supply of matting, mattresses, cushions, and pillows from another part of the house, and we made ourselves at home. While we took supper, Saleh told me that his father, the head of a large family, had during his lifetime accumulated a considerable sum of money, which he kept in a secret place, probably buried. It was expected that he would some day tell his heirs where the treasure was concealed, but unhappily he was on a journey from Tiberias "when the Angel of Death met him." He was surrounded only by servants and strangers, to whom he could not intrust the important communication, and there was no time to send for his sons; so he died, and the secret died with him. Saleh, the eldest son, caused careful search to be made in and under the premises, but up to this time the property had not been found.

It is a very common practice, especially in the interior, to secrete jewels and gold in this way, and ancient deposits of great intrinsic value—and still greater interest as works of art and illustrations of history—are sometimes found.

The law of treasure-trove in Palestine, I believe, awards

one-third to the finder, one-third to the owner of the ground on which the property is found, and one-third to the Government.

There are certain men who spend nearly all their lives in seeking for—*kanûz*—hidden treasures. Some of them become maniacs, desert their families, and though they are often so poor that they beg their way from door to door, and from village to village, they believe themselves to be rich. There are others, who are called "*sahiri*"—necromancers—who seem to work systematically, and have a very curious method of prosecuting the search.

They select certain sensitive individuals, who are believed to have the power of seeing objects concealed in the earth, or elsewhere; but the faculty is only active when roused by the influence of necromantic ceremonies, which are understood by the professional treasure-seeker. He properly prepares the medium, and calls into full activity the visionary power; then, in obedience to his command, the hiding-places of treasures are said to be minutely described. On being restored to the normal state, the medium does not remember any of the revelations which may have been made. The practice of this art is considered "haram"—that is, *unlawful*, and is carried on secretly and not extensively. Those people of whom I made inquiries on the subject spoke with fear and trembling, and mysteriously whispered their explanations.

I knew an Arab family, of which all the female members are believed to be seers (clairvoyants?). They are all nervous and excitable to a high degree, and one of them is slightly deranged in intellect.*

Till a late hour visitors flocked in to see us, for our

---

* Does this system of the *Sahiri* throw any light on the history of the "Zahuris" of Spain, who were said to have the power of seeing into the recesses of the earth? The name is evidently of Eastern derivation, for "Zahur" is the Arabic for *appearing*.

In the first volume of "The Cradle of the Twin Giants, Science and History," by Rev. Henry Christmas, page 344, the following passages occur:

"Debrio, in his 'Disquisitiones Magicæ,' edition of Mayence, 1606, says there is a class of men in Spain who are called Zahuris. When he was staying at Madrid, arrival was soon known throughout the Christian quarter. First came Jirius el Yakûb, with his fat, burly figure, his crisp gray beard and twinkling eyes shining from under a large shawl turban. He is Mr. Finn's agent for Nazareth, and is very proud of his office, and of the few words of English which he can speak.

Saleh's pretty little sister, "Jalîly."—that is, "*the Glorious*"—led me to the room prepared for me. Her age was about eleven, and her face the fairest I had seen in Palestine. It was a pure oval, with a straight nose, small, well-defined lips, long dark lashes, and delicately-penciled eyebrows. The edges of her eyelids were strongly tinged with kohl, which gave strange power to large, melancholy gray eyes. Her finger-nails were slightly stained with henna, and her toe-nails deeply dyed. She wore a violet-colored muslin kerchief folded over her soft, brown hair, crossed under her chin, and tied in a bow at the top of her head. Her dress was green, edged with yellow braid, and open at the throat, showing a necklace of silver and coral ornaments.

(I think that green is a favorite color among Christian Arabs now, because, till lately, they were forbidden to wear it, for the Moslems regard it as their sacred color.)

I awoke, and rose early, for a half-opened door, which I had not noticed by the dim lamp of the previous night, attracted my attention. Just within it were three narrow steps, each higher than my knee. I climbed up, and turning sharply round, groped my way up three other steps, still more steep, and then stumbled against a low, cracked wooden door, which I unfastened with difficulty. When it burst open I found that it led to a terraced roof, to which there was no other access. The roof was high, and commanded a beautiful view of the town, with its mosque and

in 1575, a boy of that kind was there; these persons were said to be able to spy out what was concealed in the earth, subterraneous waters, metals, hidden treasure, or dead bodies. The thing was generally known, and its possibility believed in, not only by poets but by philosophers."

"We quote the following, concerning a lady, from the *Mercure de France*, of 1728: 'She perceives what is hid in the earth, distinguishing stones, sand, springs, to the depth of thirty or forty fathoms.'"

minarets, surrounded by tall, dark cypress-trees, and the convent buildings conspicuous in the Christian quarter. The mists were gradually passing away from the valley and floating up the hill-sides. The houses are of white limestone, square and flat-roofed; they look clean and cheerful. The ancient "city was built on a hill," but modern Nazareth, which is unwalled, has gradually crept into the valley, at the bottom of which all the newest and largest houses are erected.

Little Jalily was in an open court below with some women servants, who were making bread and chopping meat. She saw me, and ran up to greet me, saying, "May the day be white to you!" then she taught me the usual answer, "May it be to you as milk!"

It was Sunday. We went to the Latin Church of the Annunciation. We made our way through the nave, which is large and lofty. One side was crowded with men and boys bareheaded, and the other side occupied by women, kneeling on the marble pavement in rows. Their foreheads and the lower parts of their faces were quite concealed by folds of muslin and linen. As we passed by, they with one accord raised their heads for a moment, and their bright dark eyes flashed upon us from under their kohl-tinged lids like a gleam of lightning, then they bent their heads low and resumed their devotions.

The Latin Patriarch of Jerusalem was confirming a number of children. Mass was celebrated, with more than usual pomp, by some illustrious ecclesiastics and visitors from Rome. The organ was well touched by one of the monks, and the chanting was magnificent.

When this was over, we went down to see the Grotto of the Virgin. It is underground, just beneath the high altar. On the broad stone stairs leading to it, a troop of little Arab girls, belonging to the convent school, were seated. They looked full of animation and childish mischief, and the nuns or sisters of mercy, in whose charge they were, had great difficulty in keeping them in order. The children wore dressed in native costume. The nuns, who are very superior, lady-like French women, wore white caps, with broad plain muslin frills, and little black hoods over them, and the plainest of plain black stuff dresses. They looked very quaint, but cheerful and lovable. They are most persevering in their schemes for proselytizing and educating Arab girls. Some of their pupils speak a little French, but it is very difficult to secure the regular attendance of children at the schools. They are sad little truants.

One of the sisters is a careful doctor and skillful surgeon, and thus obtains great influence over the natives, to whom she distributes medicines supplied from France. A Hakîm—a doctor of medicine, male or female—can gain admittance and respect almost any where. A Romish missionary staff is never considered complete without a good physician.

The children, marshaled by the Sisters of Mercy, made way for us, and we went down to the Altar of the Virgin. It is of pure white alabaster, laboriously and elaborately carved, but badly designed, rococo. Sweet basil bloomed all round it, and tapers burned there brightly. Near it is a part of a granite column, said by a monkish tradition—which is indorsed by the Church—to be a fragment of the very room in which Mary stood when the angel Gabriel appeared to her. The room itself was conveyed by a miracle to Dalmatia, and afterward to Loretta, where thousands of pilgrims visit it! The kitchen of the Virgin is still shown under the church at Nazareth. Women now and then came down the steps and prostrated themselves, beating their breasts, and repeating Ave Marias, in Arabic, as rapidly as possible; then they kissed three spots indicated by ornament on the pavement under the altar. The walls of the church are hung with painted linen, which produces exactly the effect of fine old tapestry, and I did not discover that it was only imitation till I handled it. In the court-yard of the convent there are several fragments of ancient stone carving introduced in the modern walls.* We went to the Protestant Mission-House, and heard service in Arabic. Some pretty children and a few intelligent-looking men attended it. The pastor and school-teachers are Germans, but connected with the Anglican Church.

All the Latins of Nazareth were in their gayest dresses that day to do honor to the visit of their Patriarch. We met him walking with a little troop of monks and priests. He is a most remarkable-looking man, and wears a pale beard, at least half a yard long, parted in the middle. His broad-brimmed hat, nearly three-quarters of a yard in diameter, is trimmed with artificial colored flowers, and glossy green leaves of metallic luster. The people crowded round him to kiss his hands and to secure his blessing.

The usual dress of the men of Nazareth is bright and cheerful-looking, consisting of a sort of long dressing-gown, made of a mixture of silk and cotton, in patterns of very narrow stripes, commonly either red and purple, violet and yellow, green and blue, or purple and white. This is girdled with a shawl, or a broad leather belt, lined and stitched, with pockets and purses made in it. Red and yellow kefias—shawls with long knotted fringes—are worn in the town as turbans, but are generally put on like hoods for traveling.

The women, who are very handsome, but rather bold-looking, use a great deal of kohl for their eyelids; they tattoo their arms profusely and their faces slightly. Their head-dress is very peculiar; it is a tight-fitting cap, made of cloth or linen, with a thick, firmly-padded roll, one or two inches in diameter, round the front, just covering the highest part of the head, and fastened with strings, but not quite meeting under the chin. To this roll silver coins are sewed, as close together as it is possible to place them, except that a little space is left at the top

* They have been engraved in the "Builder"—No. 878—from drawings which I made in the year 1858.

of the head, and the coins fall, lapping one on the other, down each side of the face, and a little below the chin; at a distance it looks like a bonnet-front. Women wear coins as large as crowns or half-crowns; children generally have small ones, about the size of shillings. Muslin shawls or vails, of various colors or black, are folded across the forehead and over the lower part of the face; so that, out of doors, the eyes only are exposed. When in-doors, the lower folds are slipped below the chin; but the forehead is nearly always concealed, except by very young girls. They wear loose trowsers, white shirts, and long dresses, open entirely in front, made of striped cotton or Damascus silk, and girdled below the waist.

I went to Nazareth several times, and visited many of the Christian women in their homes. I found, generally, a great want of order and cleanliness among them. They are very proud of their town, and are constantly invoking "El Sit Miriam"—"the Lady Mary." Their faith in, and reverence for, relics is unbounded. In all their rooms I saw holy pictures, little images, and small crystal or glass cases of fragments of bones and rags. Rings are constantly worn as charms.

I asked a little child, who had once visited Hâifa, whether she preferred Hâifa and the beautiful sea, or Nâsirah. She answered directly, "Hâifa is not a holy place; but this town is holy; our Lady Mary lived here, and Christ, and Joseph." But although Nazareth is reckoned a holy place, it is by no means remarkable for its morality. In this respect it strikingly contrasts with Bethlehem, where the fathers and husbands are said to be severe and rigid disciplinarians, and where dishonor is punished with certain death. Nazareth had not a very good reputation in the time of Christ, and it does not appear to have improved.

I find that the younger girls are beginning to dispense with the coin head-dresses. They adopt, instead, the more simple red tarbûsh and mundîl. I expect that soon these curious and weighty ornaments will only be found in the smaller towns and villages of Galilee. Some silver anklets were shown to me, and described as "old-fashioned," but plain bracelets of silver, gold, or glass, are universally worn. I purchased one, formed of a twist of thick silver, with a very broad, clumsily-made, jeweled ring attached to it by a chain, also of wrought silver. The ring was intended to be worn on the fore-finger. One of my Nazarene friends told me that only the *fellahin* would wear any thing so barbarous and old-fashioned.

The change which is gradually being made here in the costume of the women does not depend on direct European or priestly influence, but simply on fashions introduced by settlers and visitors from other Oriental towns, especially Hâifa. The display in the bazars of jewelry and silk-tasseled caps from Stamboul, and colored muslin mundîls from European Turkey and Switzerland is accelerating the change. The supply creates a demand.

On Monday, the 15th, I called, with my brother and Saleh, on Luîs Khalîl, a wealthy native of Nazareth, who had lately built a handsome house of hewn stone. He had just returned from a trip to Marseilles, where he had been purchasing furniture for it. The terraces, courts, and corridors were tastefully bordered with beds of roses, pinks, and sweet basil, edged with broad stone copings. The floors were of inlaid marble, black and white. The surface of the walls of the inner courts was very much decorated with rudely-carved, round pateræ, of interlacing designs, in low relief. Over the doors and windows, and in other prominent positions, English-made *willow-pattern cheese-plates* were introduced, imbedded in stucco, as encaustic tiles might be. The owner of the house called my attention to this novel application of cheese-plates. He told me that he had himself designed the house and its decorations. The new European furniture was almost as singularly disposed of as the willow-pattern plates were. His unsophisticated wife and daughters marveled exceedingly at some of his purchases in Marseilles, and seemed rather more perplexed than pleased by them. His drawing-room, which was something like a French *salon*, with its mirrors and marble tables, was frescoed by a native of Nazareth, who had been tutored and employed by the Franciscan monks in church mural decoration. On the panels of the doors he had painted groups of flowers, very carefully and laboriously; but they did not produce a good effect.

Our host was the great man of his community after this trip to Marseilles, and, owing to his wealth and this famous journey, was for a time reckoned as a prophet, *even in his own country*. But, notwithstanding the comparative grandeur of his *salon*, those rooms of the house occupied by the women, and the cooking-places, were as untidy and inconvenient as the poorest establishments in the town. He was dressed in a suit of fine black cloth—full Turkish trowsers and tight jacket—a shawl girdle and polished boots—a small, red, cloth tarbûsh, with a muslin kerchief over it, fastened smoothly round his forehead. He wore a gold chain, as massive as an alderman's, outside his dress, and several rings on his fingers. His wife, however, retains her Nazareth costume intact, and evidently does not approve of innovations.

The Turkish Governor of the town called while we were there. He confidentially told my brother that the people of Nazareth were so proud and daring that he could do nothing with them.

We rode out presently, in a northerly direction, to meet Mr. Finn. Our host joined us, and a large party followed, including the Governor on a chestnut charger, decked with purple trappings adorned with mother-of-pearl. After a pleasant ride, we met the Consular party. By sunset their tents were pitched, and the English flag was waving over them in a pleasant olive-grove, just outside the town.

The next day Mr. Finn invited us to accompany him to Mount Tabor. We started at noon. It was oppressively hot. Gently, and almost silently, we rode toward the east, over hills sweet with wild thyme, and dark with thorny bushes—through valleys green with fennel, or rugged with rocks overgrown with gray lichens and amber-colored moss. Now and then we passed a clump of leafless bushes, every branch of which was covered with small, white, edible snails, which I mistook at first for buds. The only flowers I saw were the crane's-bill, goat's-beard, and small Indian pinks. Mount Tabor was full in view, like an irregular dark cone, rising above the other hills. In about an hour we entered a hilly and wooded district. The cool, pleasant shade of trees, and the songs of birds, roused and refreshed us, and, in groups of twos and threes, pleasantly chatting, we pursued our way. Mount Tabor, which had appeared to me to be gradually retreating as we advanced, was now quite out of sight; but after we had traversed some wood-crowned hills, and the dry beds of two or three Winter torrents, we saw it again, in all its beauty and grandeur. We hastened over a tree-covered slope, and down a fertile valley, and reached its base at about two o'clock. We gradually ascended an easy-winding path, pleasantly shaded, till we were about half-way up, when rocks and steep stone ledges, ancient masonry, and overhanging branches, obliged us to look cautiously before us, and to follow the steps of the leader carefully. Oaks—whence galls are procured—arbutus, pistacia vera, pistacia terebinthus—which yields what is called Venice turpentine—pistacia lentiscus—producing gum mastich—and locust-trees abound. They were wreathed with glossy-leaved creepers, but nearly every plant or shrub which I touched was armed with thorns as sharp as fine needles.

Looking down the steepest side, we could see the widespread wings of eagles as they hovered just below us, or swept rapidly through the air. Black and fawn-colored vultures appeared with their bright pinions perfectly poised and almost motionless, supporting them in steady downward flight in spiral circles. As they rose again, their wings were set in motion, and I felt the disturbance of the air now and then when they passed near to us. In trying to watch their circular sailing and heavenward wanderings I nearly reeled from my horse. They rose higher and higher, spirally, till they were quite indiscernible to the naked eye.

We alighted on the summit of the hill, at a quarter to three, on a smooth plateau surrounded by large masses of hewn stone and the foundations of strong walls. On one side there is an archway called "Bab el How-a," Gate of the Winds. On the other side we saw part of a ruined chapel and an altar in an apse, a limestone cave and a cistern hewn in the rock, and two or three patches of ground cultivated by a Russian hermit, named Erinna of Bucharest, who had lived on this mountain for fourteen years.

Once when I spent a long day here, with Colonel and the Honorable Mrs. Fred. Walpole, I took his portrait, and he told me the story of his life. His father, he said, was an extensive land proprietor in the Crimea, where he was born, but he went afterward to Bucharest. One night Erinna dreamed that an angel appeared to him and said, "Arise and go into the land which I will show you." This disturbed him very much, and all day the words were ringing in his ears. The next night the angel, in shining raiment, appeared again in a dream and repeated the words, led him through the air and showed him a mountain with a little cavern on its summit. On the third night the angel led him again to the mountain and told him that he was to dwell in the cavern. Erinna was so impressed by these dreams, or visions as he called them, that he took leave of his family, and for twenty years traveled in Russia, Greece, Egypt, and Syria, to seek for the mountain of his dream. At last he recognized the cave on Mount Tabor, and immediately took up his abode there, for he was convinced that it was the place indicated by the angel. He was then eighty-four years of age, and he said, "I thought I should soon die, but I am now heartier than ever, and yet I am nearly one hundred years old." One Winter's night, as he slept alone in his cave, he felt something soft and warm crouching by his side. He found it was a young leopard or panther: he gave it food and made friends with it, so that it would follow him about like a pet cat. For a long time Erinna and his four-footed favorite were the lions of Mount Tabor.

Erinna, like Robinson Crusoe, after years of solitude, found "his man Friday;" a fellow-countryman, a sturdy-looking, rather silent, middle-aged man, who volunteered to superintend the little field of wheat and barley, to cut wood for firing, and to fetch water from the rock cisterns. He called himself the hermit's servant, and hoped to inherit the hermitage, the sheepskin cap, the ragged mantle, and the reputation of Erinna.

The priests of Nazareth, especially the Latins, were very jealous of the influence of this anchorite, for he was regarded by Christian Arabs as a man of peculiar sanctity, and was supposed to enjoy the especial favor of God and his angels. Many people believed that he had the power of performing miracles, though he did not profess it. He told us that the Latins so strongly and perseveringly intrigued against him—representing him as a Russian spy—that he feared he should be banished from the country. He occasionally visited the sick at Nazareth and the neighboring villages: once he came to see us at Hâifa. He never tasted meat; his chief food was rice and oil, of which he purchased a store once a year. He kept a few goats for the sake of their milk; cultivated a little garden of herbs and vegetables; gathered wild fruit, and took "honey out of" the nests in "the rocks;" see Psalm lxxxi, 16. He made us some excellent coffee, of which he generally had a supply, chiefly for guests, that is, Christian pilgrims and travelers. He did not make the slightest attempt to render his cave clean or comfortable. Rude niches in the rocky walls served to hold his few books and a little red earthenware lamp. A mat of reeds, some heavy clothing and sheepskins on a stone ledge formed his bed. His companion, who belonged to the peasant class, occupied a cell close to it, which was used as the kitchen or cooking place. Two very rough delf dishes, two wooden bowls and spoons, and a metal stew-pan were to be seen there.

I asked Erinna if he had ever been married. He said that Mount Tabor was his only bride.

He and "his man Friday" assured me that they were very happy, and they looked so. They divided their days regularly, and worked, prayed, ate and slept systematically, but they seemed to think ablution unnecessary, and they wore the same clothes day and night. Erinna was ruddy and hearty, and though his bushy beard was quite white, he did not look as old as he reckons himself to be.*

The view from Mount Tabor is very extensive; it overlooks the plain of Esdraelon Proper, which is divided into squares and patches of cultivated land; it appeared from the distance like a rude mosaic, of every tint of orange, yellow, gray, green, brown, and lavender. Not a house, tent, or village could be seen to break its monotony, nor even a tree to cast a shadow; but the hills which surround it were clothed with woods, and dotted with towns, hamlets, and ruins. Mr. Finn said, "Fancy Barak with his 10,000 men upon this mountain; people that plain with the chariots, 'even 900 chariots of iron,' gathered together by Sisera, and see Sisera pursued by Barak unto Harosheth." He read the landscape round for me, pointing out the range of Carmel and the Mediterranean on the west—the hills of Gilboa and the villages of Jezreel, Endor, and Nain in the south—the hill-country beyond Jordan, and the mountains which encircle the Sea of Galilee on the east, and far away in the north Lebanon crowned with snow. Nearer to us we could see the Horns of Hattin—a rounded hill with two distinct mounds or peaks on its summit. This is called the Mount of Beatitudes, where tradition tells us that the Sermon of sermons was preached. After exploring the ruins and the

---

* Erinna died in 1859, much regretted by the peasants of the plain, and by the poor of Nazareth.

deep cisterns, we remounted. The sun had quite disappeared when we reached the foot of the hill. (On one occasion I walked down the steepest side of Tabor, with the help of a stout stick and a strong arm.)

The Rev. J. L. Porter says that Tabor rises 1,400 feet above the plain, and the plain is 500 feet above the level of the sea.

We had a pleasant ride back to Nazareth by moonlight. We spent the evening at the Consular encampment, and at a late hour walked up by lantern-light to Saleh's house.

The next morning I sat in the deep embrasure of a window, sketching, while my brother was busy in the midst of a group of Turkish Effendis and Christian scribes. They all carried inkhorns in their girdles, with cases attached to them to hold their reed pens. They sat on the floor and held single sheets of paper in their hands, and wrote without any desk or support. The points of reed pens are so delicate, that they would be easily fractured by pressure on a hard table or desk.

The population of Nazareth is computed by Dr. Robinson thus:

Moslems	680	
Greeks	1,040	who look to Russia as their protector.
Latins	480	Adherents of the Pope, and consequently French protégés.
Greek Catholics	520	
Maronites	400	

This gives a total of 3,120; but the most recent and careful inquirers assure me that this estimate is too low. They reckon the total at 4,000, and the Greek Church is said to be on the increase. I never met a Jew either in Nazareth or Bethlehem! There is a small Protestant congregation, which is rather fluctuating.

Khawadja Stephani, the son of the Greek Priest of Shefa 'Amer, came expressly to ask us and Saleh to return to Hâifa by way of his village, and to pass a night there at his house. We arranged to do so, and started soon after midday. We rode for some distance over rocky hills, where bees were busy among the blossoming herbs; across plains covered with tall thistles—their harsh stems, leaves, thorns, and spiny flowers were bright with a purple bloom, like that which we see on ripe plums, and from a distance a plain overgrown with them looked like a calm, blue lake. At about two we entered a garden inclosed by a low stone wall, situated at the bottom of a well-watered valley, where the lemon-trees were laden with green fruit, and pomegranates were plentiful. We dismounted and walked through the garden to the streamlet which traverses it, bordered with hawthorn, rose, and fruit-trees. Its banks, steep and grassy, were fragrant with mint and marjoram, and cresses grew along the edge of the water. Under a wide-spreading fig-tree, where tiny-leaved clover had made a smooth carpet, we spread our saddle-cloths in a half-circle, and took our seats. Soon a plentiful dinner was placed before us. We took it in primitive style, for we had neither forks nor spoons, and our only plates were thin Arab loaves, about a quarter of a yard in diameter and a quarter of an inch thick. Saleh made a drinking-cup for me of the large leaf of a water-plant, which he knew to be harmless. Each one of the party, as soon as he had eaten, rose and washed his hands at the stream, and then, selecting another tree for our shade, and a grassy bank for our divan, we rested, telling stories in turn, while the kawasses and servants made an end of the provisions.

In this garden I saw some remarkable double fig-trees, the trunks of which were twisted as perfectly and regularly as if they had been carved. I asked the gardener how he managed it. He said, "*Allah Karîm*"—"God is bountiful"—and then explained to me how tender saplings are planted side by side, and perseveringly entwined, or even plaited sometimes. He led me to one which he considered more perfect than the others. The twisted trunk was about half a yard in diameter; it rose six feet from the ground, as upright as a marble column, without any branches to break its perfect outline, and then spread out its crooked arms in all directions, clothed with green leaves—the largest which I had ever observed. This pleasant garden is near to the fountain which was the gathering-place of the Christian knights before the terrible battle of Hattin, and where the conqueror Saladin encamped after he had in that decisive conflict almost annihilated the Crusaders. Sephoris or Sefurieh is just opposite. It is a poor but interesting place. Jewish, heathen, and Christian ruins are to be found there, and tradition points to the house in which Anna, the mother of Mary, was born.

We mounted at half-past three, and followed the course of the stream. It flowed between orchards, gardens of cucumbers, and stubble-fields. All the horses and their riders seemed newly animated. They rode in circles, displaying feats of horsemanship, letting off their pistols while in full gallop; their long, loose, white Arab cloaks, made of goat's-hair, fluttered behind them, and the almost flying figures represented to my fancy the Templars of old on their fabled white-winged steeds. When the horses were well tired, the riders grouped together, and we rode through an oak-wood, talking of the Crusades. I found that our Arab friends were quite familiar with such names as Peter the Hermit and Richard Cœur de Lion. Oriental poets and historians call the latter "Ankitûr."

We soon came to an olive-grove, on a hill forming part of an extensive amphitheater, from the center of which rises a mount of conical form, and on it stands Shefa 'Amer, backed by a lofty castle, square and massive, looking almost as large as the village itself. The hill-sides, with the exception of the one which we descended, were clothed with evergreens; and the valleys for miles around were wooded with olive and other fruit-trees. We rode through a burial-ground, tastefully planted with shrubs, and passing an immense heap of dust, dirt, and rubbish—on the top of which a crowd of people had assembled to see us—we entered the village, and alighted at the house of Stephani. He led me up an open stone stairway, and along a covered terrace, into a long, lofty, cheerful room, with unglazed windows on three sides of it. One end of the room was furnished with Turkey carpets, narrow mattresses and cushions, which made a comfortable divan. The stuccoed walls were slightly frescoed with rudely-grotesque and droll designs of the most childish character.

Pipes and narghilés were ranged in a recess, and a handsome set of coffee-cups, with silver filagree holders, were on a low stand near the door. In a corner there was a broad, shallow, marble basin let into the floor, with a hole in the center to carry off water. It was the place of ablution, and three water-jars stood near to it.

This room was the "guest chamber," separated from the other part of the establishment.

Stephani said to me, "This is your house, rule over it as you will, command me and my family as your servants."

I was left to rest and to dress, and presently the gentlemen rejoined me.

Guests were coming and going all the evening. First arrived the stately Turkish Governor, a tall figure with a flat face, like a mask of shriveled parchment; in fact he resembled a Chinese mummy much more than a living Turk. He was intensely polite and complimentary, and confidentially complained to us of his poverty, and of the unprofitableness of his office. He was dressed in a suit of snuff-brown cloth, embroidered with gold, and a long sword hung at his side.

The father of Stephani, a very handsome old man with a patriarchal white beard, came and sat by me. He wore a long robe of coarse purple linen, and his turban was of the same color. He is the chief priest of the Greek community of Shefa 'Amer, and neighboring villages. His words were few, but his looks were expressive. He was evidently proud of his sons and of his little grandsons. At a sign from him, the latter came forward from the other end of the room to kiss my hands. They were clean, well-dressed, bright-looking boys. The room was full of visitors. Mattresses were spread all round against the walls, and there was not a space vacant, but not one woman came.

It grew dark, and the shutters were closed, when a tall, slender, brass candelabrum was brought in, and placed on the middle of the floor, at the upper end of the room. It supported a large oil lamp, with three wicks. Three long brass chains hung from it—one held a pair of lamp-scissors, another a long stout pin which is used to trim the wick, to the third an extinguisher was attached. At the lower end of the room, a large glazed lantern, with tin frame-work, stood on a low wooden stool—these lights shone on a strange and motley assembly. There was an Indian Jew there, with a very dark face and white beard, a dusky turban, and duskier robes. He came forward to claim brotherhood with us, for he was an English subject, and very proud of his nationality. He had journeyed from Hindoostan to see the city of Solomon, and to ascertain the state of the Jews in Palestine. He seemed to be a learned and enterprising man.

Isaac Shallom, a Jew of Aleppo, but a resident at Hâifa, brought me some soft, sweet, white almond paste, with pistachio nuts imbedded in it—a celebrated Aleppo sweetmeat. The Rabbi and chief members of the Jewish community of Shefa 'Amer were also present, with a few Moslems and Druzes, and a number of Christian Arabs. Arrack was handed round from time to time in the lower part of the room, and songs of praise were sung in honor of the chief guests. Saleh, who is no singer, but a very fluent speaker, said, "Ibrahim left his kindred, his home, and his country, he dwelt in a strange land among strangers, but he became mighty in the land, his family increased, his name became great. Even so may the name of Rogers be known throughout this country, may his children and his children's children dwell here in honor!" The idea was immediately taken up by the singers, and they improvised a song, the burden of which was, "May his children's children dwell here in honor!"

Some graceful compliments were paid to me, with prayers for my happiness. Then the singing, of which there was a great variety, became general. We heard Egyptian love-songs beautifully and plaintively sung by a gardener from the Nile, and a man of Bagdad gave us a curious ditty, jerking out his words at first, and by degrees toning them down into a languishing, drawling melody, in a minor key. The Arabs sang a great many monotonous songs; but one was very sweet—the chorus of it was, "O Beda-wiya." I think that this song would please English ears generally.

Isaac, the Jew of Aleppo, was asked to dance for me. The lantern was moved out of the way. He stood up at first very shyly, the Arabs sitting round, singing and clapping their hands, keeping time. He had on very full white drawers, a black jacket, yellow and white silk striped waistcoat, and a shawl sash. Round his red tarbûsh a blue mundîl was folded. He bent his head down and raised his arms above it. By degrees his feet and hands were in slow motion in harmony with the music, and his body swayed to and fro. Soon the songs grew louder, the clapping of hands quicker, and the movements of the dancer more decided, but they were as monotonous as the tunes which inspired them. During the whole of the dance he kept within a circle of about a yard in diameter; at last he spun round and retreated, hiding himself shamefacedly behind his friends.

Supper was announced, and many of the visitors retired. Servants brought in a round stand, about five inches in hight, and covered it with dishes. While this was being arranged, my brother begged to be allowed to fetch a certain man, named Habîb, to sup there. He had once been Stephani's chief friend, but a misunderstanding had arisen between them, consequently the two most influential Christian families in Shefa 'Amer lived as strangers to each other. Stephani readily consented to receive Habîb, who soon came, and the two long-divided friends embraced. They have lived in harmony ever since. Before eating, each one of us had water poured on our hands over the marble basin; for the Christian Arabs, as well as the Moslems, "and all the Jews, except they wash their hands, eat not." This is particularly necessary, considering that they do not use knives and forks; but each one "dips his hand into the dish" with his neighbor.

Stephani at first wished to serve us at supper, instead of sitting down with us, for it is the Arab custom for the host to wait on his guests as a servant. We overcame his scruples, and we ate together. Afterward, water was again poured on our hands—a servant stood by, holding native scented-soap and an embroidered towel—then we had coffee and narghilés.

An Arabic Bible published by the British and Foreign Bible Society—a Roman version, by the by—was brought in, and Saleh read aloud the Sermon on the Mount. Bible history is pretty well known in the Greek community; it is read in their churches in the vulgar tongue, and is not withheld from the laity. The bulk of the people, however, can not read. The few who can do so gladly obtain copies, but the Bible is rarely to be met with, except in those families of which one of the members is a priest or very studious, as Saleh, for instance.

The Greek priests must always be married men. Those of the villages and small towns are often very ignorant, and, as they rarely receive a systematic ecclesiastical training, their expositions and definitions of the articles and dogmas of their Church are very curious and conflicting. Their Bishops and higher clergy are generally foreigners, that is, native Greeks and Russians, and do not often learn Arabic, so they make little or no impression on the Syrian branch of their Church. The Latin clergy, on the other hand, are often quite unfamiliar with the Bible, and always strongly oppose its circulation, but are well grounded in matters of discipline and doctrinal points.

The two Churches vie with each other in circulating extraordinary traditions and legends of saints and martyrs, and they equally encourage pilgrimages to holy places and reliance on relics.

Soon after supper the room was cleared of all the smoking, turbaned, fezzed, and singing guests, slaves, and servants. My brother and Saleh went home with Habîb to sleep at his house. I was left alone in the large guest-chamber, where Stephani had caused a bed to be made for me. I opened one of the heavy shutters, to see my friends pass round on the side of the hill, five lanterns gleaming before them. I fastened the door with a stiff clumsy lock, the mechanism of which I did not in the least understand, and I soon discovered that I was a self-made prisoner, for I could not find out how to undo it again. I was obliged to resign myself to my fate, making sure I should be set free in the morning. I fell asleep on a soft, crimson silk pillow, under an embroidered lehaff, and did not wake till the sun shone on my face through the chinks of the ill-made shutters. I was up and dressed when Stephani knocked at the door, which he contrived to open. While the room was swept and garnished I went with him to take coffee at the house of Habîb. On my return to my quarters, the female members of the family, their neighbors, and the women-servants, came to look at me, but not till they were quite sure of finding me alone. They clustered shyly round the door, and I had to play the part of hostess and invite them to enter in. They were dressed in the same style as the women of Nazareth, and are quite as handsome, but more simple and modest-looking. Stephani's wife, a tall, dark-eyed woman, wore large heavy coins round her face, with a yellow mundîl folded across her forehead and tied at the back of her head; the open front of her red and white cotton dress was trimmed with a double frill, edged with braid. Her eldest daughter, a girl of ten, named Werdeh—

that is, Rosy—was very beautiful, with regular features, clear bronzed complexion, eyes brown and sparkling, the lids deeply tinged with kohl, and the hands and feet stained with henna. Her thick, dark hair was combed down over her high forehead, and cut straight across it just above her arched eyebrows. At the back her hair was allowed to grow long, and was plaited. She wore a head-dress of coins, for they are not yet going out of fashion in Shefa 'Amer. Her open dress was of white calico, ornamented in front profusely, with black, blue, and red braid. The sleeves were very long, and capable of concealing the hands entirely, but when the arms were raised the sleeves still hung down, for they were open as high as the elbow.

The room was soon crowded with women and girls. Their dresses, though various in point of texture and condition, were all of the same fashion—from the crimson and white striped silk dress of a young bride, to the ragged cotton garments worn by an aged servant, whose head-dress was stripped of all its coins. I was sketching Werdeh and her mother, when suddenly they, and all the rest, rose and scampered away, without saying a word, vailing themselves hastily. The entrance of the Turkish Governor and my brother, a minute afterward, explained their flight.

Little Daoud, the governor's son, came to see me. He wore an olive-colored cloth cloak, and a green muslin turban. His features were regular, but his face was very sallow. He tried to look dignified and composed while I took his portrait, but could not prevent a smile coming now and then. Saleh, and Stephani, with his father, joined us, and after lunch we went all together to the castle. On approaching it, I perceived that it was already falling to decay, although it was only built about 150 years ago. The lofty gates and archways are slightly decorated with fretted canopies, in the style of the Alhambra. A two-storied range of vaulted corridors and chambers surrounds an extensive court-yard. The ground-floor is well adapted for stabling, and would lodge about 500 horses. Tottering stone stairways led us to the upper floors. The pointed double windows, in deep embrasures in the outer walls, command magnificent views in all directions.

The west windows overlook the plain of Akka and the sea, with Mount Carmel and Hâifa in the background on the left. The north windows look toward Lebanon, with the city of Akka on the left, and the little town of Abilene in the foreground on the right, its tall white tower standing conspicuously in the midst of olive-trees and gardens. The banners of Richard I once waved there. The southern and eastern views are bounded by hills and mountains, rising one behind the other.

While petitioners for protection crowded round my brother, I wandered from hall to hall and from window to window, with Saleh for my cicerone. We climbed to the top of the embattled walls, and walked nearly all round the building; but the stones are falling, and allowed to remain where they fall, and scarcely any use seems to be made of the place.

As we left the castle, the governor asked me to go with him to see his wives. A glance from my brother told me that I might accept the invitation. Of course, none of the gentlemen could accompany me; so they walked homeward with Stephani, and the governor escorted me to his dreary-looking house. A gateway, through which a laden camel could easily pass, led us into an ill-paved guttered court, which was the only entrance to a square vaulted hall, with bare stone walls, and four unglazed windows quite out of reach. The floor was of earth, with smooth rock slabs here and there.

This was the governor's residence—his dining-room, withdrawing-room, nursery, stables, and kitchen all together! On one side, just within the door, a mule was feeding; a stone bench, hollowed out a little, was his manger; a patient ass stood by him. On the other side, a tethered horse was neighing; and on a heap of fodder, two dirty, delicate-looking children were kicking and crying out lustily. There was a sort of oven, or cooking-place, in one corner of the hall, and I could see the red glow of a charcoal fire. On the left hand there was a broad wooden platform, raised about two feet from the ground, with a low ornamental wooden railing at the edge of it. Here mattresses and lehaffs were piled up; I suppose it was the sleeping-place of the lord of the harem. We went straight across the hall, to a dais, in a broad, arched recess, just opposite to the door by which we had entered.' Two crooked stone steps led up to it, and two women—one old and the other young—stood there ready to receive me. They took my hands in theirs, and placed me on a cushioned seat on the matted floor.

The governor introduced me to the younger of the women, telling me that she was his wife, the mother of his little Daoud. She was perhaps twenty, rather tall and graceful-looking, with bright blue eyes and black hair, and a brilliant though dark complexion. She had used kohl and henna freely, and her chin and forehead were tattooed. I think that she was prepared for my coming, for she had on a fête-day dress. A blue cloth jacket, embroidered with gold, very open in front, exposed her tattooed chest, and a white spun silk shirt. Her full trowsers were of Aleppo silk, white and straw-colored. Her shallow red cloth cap was decorated with rows of gold coins, pearls, and everlasting flowers. A long purple tassel hung down behind, and a perforated, flat, crescent-shaped gilt ornament, about five inches wide, was fixed on the top of the head-dress. (Is this the "round tire" like the moon, referred to in Isaiah iii, 18?) Her long hair was plaited, and interwoven with black silk braid, to make it appear still longer. She told me that Shefa 'Amer was not a pleasant place to live in, and that she was quite a stranger there. I asked her what part of the country she came from. She said, "Neby-Daoud is the place of my birth, and the place I love." She referred to a cluster of buildings round the tomb of the Prophet David, or Neby-Daoud, just outside the walls of Jerusalem, by the Zion gate. She was happy to hear herself called Um Daoud, that is, "The Mother of David."

The governor interrupted her explanations, by telling her to make some lemonade for me. Close by the two steps of the dais stood a pair of high clogs, almost like stilts, made of inlaid dark wood and mother-of-pearl, with crimson leather straps. She fastened these on her henna-stained, naked feet—for the earth floor was very damp and dirty, and water rested here and there in little pools. Her husband followed her, and helped her to reach some green drinking-glasses from a niche in the wall. The other woman, who looked very old and careworn, remained by my side. When the young wife was out of hearing, I exclaimed, "How beautiful she is!" She agreed with me, and seemed to take a mother's pride and pleasure in her beauty. I did not know that the young wife was her rival; I fancied that she was her daughter, till she said, "Um Daoud is young, Um Daoud is happy; she is young, and is the mother of two sons;" (she pointed to a cradle hammock, suspended from the key-stone of the arch above us—in it a little swaddled figure was securely and gently swinging;) "but," she added, "I have no sons left, my sons are dead; and I am old, I am no longer handsome, *I am nothing, I am worthless.*" Then she explained to me that she had lived about twenty years with the governor before he took Um Daoud for his wife. I said to her, alluding to the little ones who had now crawled out of the fodder, "Whose children are they?" She said, "They are sons of the house"—that is, of the governor—and a slave, who stood near the oven, was their mother.

Presently Um Daoud returned with the lemonade. The governor himself brought me a tiny cup of coffee flavored with ambergris. Young Daoud now came in, and seemed delighted to find me there. He said, "Make my mother's face in your book," and, "Make my brother's face for me." The baby-boy was lifted out of the hammock; he was about six months old; his eyelids were black with kohl. I asked why kohl was used for a child so young. "It will strengthen the sight of his eyes, and make the lashes long and thick," said the elder woman.

I took leave of them, and found my kawass just outside the house waiting to take me to meet my brother at the Greek church. It is a modern building; silk hangings and gaudy pictures decorate the walls. The font is of marble; I think it is formed of an ancient Byzantine capital, hollowed out at the top. In a school adjoining the church a number of boys were noisily but monotonously intoning psalms, echoing the nasal twang of their teacher. I find that the Psalter is the chief class-book in Christian Arab schools, as the Koran is in Moslem schools. I have often seen boys with these books in their hands, who appear to be reading freely, when in reality they scarcely know their letters, but who repeat, parrot-like, large portions of them by heart.

We afterward went to the Jewish synagogue, where the chief rabbi received us. He showed me several copies of the Law and the Prophets, wrapped in crimson silk cases which are kept in a recess behind an embroidered curtain, or vail. In the middle of the building there was a high circular wooden platform, with seats of honor upon it. It was built so slightly that at first I thought it was only a temporary erection; but I found in all the synagogues which I visited raised central seats of equally slight construction.

The gentlemen then went for a ride. I declined doing so, hoping during their absence to see the women again; and Khawadja Stephani, at my request, sent his wife and children to me. They took me to see the lower part of the house; it was ill-arranged, untidy, and uncomfortable. They returned with me to my room. I made a few sketches, which amused them greatly. Soon such crowds of women came in that one of the men-servants of the house, who stood as guard or sentinel at my door, entered, and very unceremoniously drove about half of them out of the place, and they all withdrew when the gentlemen returned from their ride.

We spent the evening at the house of Habîb. A large party assembled to meet us in his spacious guest-chamber, and all the culinary skill of Shefa 'Amer had been employed in preparing a supper for us. Songs, complimentary speeches, and story-telling followed. I walked back to Stephani's house by the light of many lanterns, accompanied to my door by my brother and nearly all the guests.

At sunrise the next morning we were mounted and ready to start for Hâifa. Stephani, Habîb, and a large party joined us. Our Egyptian groom had charge of a beautiful Syrian gazelle-hound which had been given to my brother. We rode down into the valley and along a level road leading to a large fountain. A number of the village girls were already assembled there—some standing on the high stone platform surrounding the well, and others grouped round the base. In the distance we saw a procession of them, traversing, one by one, a narrow foot-path on the hill-side, with their replenished jars perfectly poised on their heads.

We turned out of the Akka road, and entered an extensive olive-grove. Picturesque groups of men, women, and children, in bright-colored garments, were busy among the trees, or hastening along the road. I had always seen the olive plantations so silent and deserted that it was quite a surprise to me. Saleh explained that it was the beginning of the olive harvest—the 19th of October—and all of these people had been hired to gather the fruit. The men beat the trees with long sticks, and the women and children pick up the berries.* We met a straggling group of figures, which looked so unnaturally tall and disproportionate that I could not make them out till I was

* "When thou beatest thine olive-tree thou shalt not go over the boughs again; it shall be for the stranger, the fatherless, and the widow." Deut. xxiv, 20.

told that they were Druze women. They wore tubular horns, from one to two feet in length, bound firmly on their foreheads, supporting heavy black or white vails, which almost shrouded the wearers, producing a very ungraceful outline. (Of these strange people I hope to speak more fully on a future occasion.) Presently we came to a rocky district, overgrown with dwarf oaks, thorns, and thistles, and then reached the fertile plain of Akka, traversed by the blue winding Kishon and its many tributaries.

The large fields of cotton had a very pretty effect, for they were in their full beauty. The bushes are about two feet high, the stems are reddish, the leaves are of the color of the maple in the Spring-time, the blossom looks as if it were made of butterflies' wings, white and spotted. When these white wings fall, a green bulb, in a triangular cup, is exposed; this grows to about an inch in diameter, and changes to a rich, glossy, chestnut color, and, gradually becoming harsh, splits into three parts, when soft downy cotton bursts from it. Saleh gathered a branch for me, including specimens of the plant in these three distinct stages. My brother told me that the Arabs do not cultivate the long-staple cotton—which is most valued in England—because it requires so much care in picking; for the pods must be gathered as soon as they ripen, and as they do not ripen all at once, the harvest necessarily extends over two or three weeks; whereas the short-staple cotton gives the cultivator very little trouble, for the pods are not injured by being left on the tree after they are ripe, and the harvest does not commence till nearly every pod is ready for picking; the consequence is that it is very soon over. This inferior cotton does very well for native use, and to fill the Arab mattresses, and lchaffs, or quilts; but it is not of much commercial value.

If the plain of Akka were cultivated with skill and energy it would yield abundantly. Under the present system the soil produces, in Winter, wheat, barley, beans, lentils, peas, and tobacco; and in the Summer-time cotton, sesame, millet, and many kinds of cucumbers. Poppy, mallows, and various herbs enliven it, while all the hills around are suitable for vineyards, olive-groves, and orchards. Flax, asparagus, gentian, scammony, and many other plants, valuable in medicine, grow wild there, and the marshes of the plain abound with kali, the ashes of which, mixed with olive or sesame oil, are converted into soap. The villages of this district are inhabited by Moslems, Christians, and Druzes, and a few Jews. They pay heavy taxes to the Government in wheat, barley, and money, and are bound to furnish camels, horses, or mules whenever the Pasha requires them.

We crossed a spring, round which tall reeds and short, soft grass grew. Thousands of edible snails were clinging to the stems of some straggling bushes. Wily, long-rooted marram-grass and sea-holly—eryngium maritimum—tamarisks, and willows bound the sandy soil, and kept it from drifting. We passed over some sand-hills, on which were a few scattered plants, with thick, downy, whitish leaves and yellow blossoms. Here we took leave of our Shefa 'Amer friends, and they returned to their olive-groves.

We were soon on the sea-shore. Two English merchant steamers were just entering the port of Hâifa. We cantered to the Kishon and crossed over it, by carefully keeping on the bar of sand which encircles the mouth of the river, sweeping out far into the sea. The water was above our horses' knees, and now and then an advancing wave covered us with spray.

We rode quickly along by the edge of the water, with the palm-grove and the fruit-gardens on our left hand, and the rippling waves on our right. We entered the town at a quarter to nine, just in time to receive two English merchant captains, at the Vice-Consulate, where poor Katrine, our *soi disant* mother, welcomed us with tears of joy, saying, "Praised be God! my children have returned to me in safety."

CHAPTER VII.

LIFE IN HÂIFA.

On Tuesday, October 23, 1855, a Turkish steamer from Constantinople entered the port of Hâifa, bringing a new Pasha for Akka, with his harem, and suite of thirty individuals, including an Armenian doctor. The chief people of Akka came to meet him, and our little town was in an unusual state of excitement. My brother went to welcome his Excellency, who afterward called at the Consulate with twelve attendants.

Newly-appointed Pashas may sometimes be persuaded into doing some good in their Pashalics; and, at the commencement of their reigns, choked-up fountains flow, broken cisterns are repaired, and aqueducts are kept in order, but only for a very little while. On the "new-broom" principle, the Consuls earnestly urged the new Pasha to give orders for the cleansing of the guttered streets of Hâifa, some of which were little better than open sewers, and in a dangerously-unwholesome state. They also advised the removal of the dust-heaps by the sea-shore, which had been allowed to grow into broad barricades, where vegetable refuse and all sorts of filth were thrown. The appeal was favorably heard, the work actually commenced immediately, and Hâifa underwent sweeping and scraping, probably for the first time in its existence. Men and boys ran hither and thither with baskets of rubbish. Beks and Consuls bustled about, giving orders, and the dust-heaps were by degrees shoveled into the sea.

The Europeans and the upper class of Arabs rejoiced at the prospect of living in a comparatively clean town, but the majority considered the reformation quite unnecessary, and grumblingly prophesied that some harm would come to Hâifa if such innovations were permitted.

Late on Thursday evening, Mohammed Bek came to the Consulate, lamenting the loss of a gold chain, with his signet ring on it. In the East more importance is attached to the impression of a seal than to a signature. Mohammed Bek feared that some improper use might be made of his ring by the finder, so a declaration of the loss was drawn up by Yusef Anton, the Governor's Secretary, signed by the Bek, and attested by my brother. Mohammed told us that he had missed his chain in the bazar, when surrounded by a crowd of boys, to whom he was giving instructions about the street-cleaning. It was a very fine night, and, half in joke, half in earnest, I offered to seek for the lost treasure. He took me at my word, and we went out all together. The town was perfectly still, the bazar was deserted, and as bright and clean as moonlight and the scavengers of Hâifa could make it; but, after all, I was not so fortunate as to find the ring.

As we returned homeward, the silence was suddenly broken by the wildly-wailing and shrieking voices of women, announcing that a death had just taken place. Their shrill, mournful cries rang in my ears all night.

On the following morning, October 26th, very early, I looked from the window, and saw a bier close to the door of a neighboring house. It was a painted wooden stand, about seven feet by two, raised slightly on four legs, with a low gallery round it, formed of uprights far apart, and two cross-bars. Two strong poles projected at each end from the corners. Above it a canopy was raised, made of freshly-gathered, elastic palm-branches. They were bent like half-hoops, and then interlaced and secured lengthways, with straight fronds. I sketched it, and presently I saw the dead body of a man, handsomely dressed, brought out and placed upon it. His face was covered with a shawl. Four men lifted the bier from the ground, and, resting the poles on their shoulders, bore it to the mosque. After a little while it was carried slowly along, passing the Consulate on its way to the Moslem burial-ground, preceded by about forty men, solemnly silent, and followed by at least fifty women and children shrieking wildly, singing, and screaming.

Between the palm-fronds I could plainly see the figure of the dead man. The head was foremost, and slightly raised. I could not help thinking that, if a voice endued with power to awaken the dead, would tell the mother and the widow not to weep, and order the bearers of the bier to stand still, and say to the dead man, "*Arise*," it would be in his fête-day dress that he would sit up under the canopy of palms, and begin to speak. See Luke vii, 11–15.

I made inquiry about the deceased, and found that he was a respectable Moslem, of about twenty-four years of age, and had left a wife and two children. He had died just before midnight, after a few hours' illness, so violent, that the Arab doctor pronounced it a case of cholera. There had been several very sudden deaths in Hâifa within a few weeks.

In the course of the day I became very ill. Frère Joseph, the Convent doctor, was sent for. He came and administered powerful doses of opium. The next day I was worse and very weak. He ordered emetics and bleeding, but I decidedly declined both, and dispensed with his attendance. My brother prescribed hot baths, and mustard and vinegar poultices, and I slept, but grew weaker and weaker. At three o'clock on Sunday morning, October 29th, he sent his kawass to Akka for a doctor, as a last resource. He wrote to the Pasha, and, ill as I was, I could not help laughing at the letter, on hearing it literally translated into English. It contained a request that his Excellency would allow his private doctor, the Armenian, to proceed to Hâifa to attend the "*girl brother* of the English Vice-Consul, who was attacked with a slight beauty, or prettiness." This is the polite Turkish form of alluding to illness, when woman is the subject of it.

Within a short time the doctor came with strict orders from the Pasha not to leave me till I was well. He spoke Italian fluently, as well as Turkish and Greek. He was full of persevering, quiet energy and good-will, which inspired me with confidence immediately. He administered small doses of castor oil, well mixed with sugar, water, gum arabic, and magnesia, in equal proportions, and prescribed linseed and mustard poultices. He prepared stiff, sweet starch, and some meal porridge with a little magnesia in it, and gave them to me in small quantities now and then, with lime-flower water to drink. He did not leave the house for three days and nights, and by Thursday, thanks to his skill and Katrîne's care, I was quite cured of my "slight prettiness," which was of a dangerous kind, and said to be cholera.

We met with great sympathy from our neighbors. On the evening when I first left my room a company of singers came on to the terrace to serenade me, improvising songs of rejoicing, and praying that I might soon "walk forth in the gardens, to breathe the air with strength and gladness of heart."

On the 1st of November I saw an immense number of swallows perched on the house-tops and on the ropes of the flagstaffs. I was told that they had been gathering there for several days. Before evening I saw them all assemble and take flight toward the south. They looked like a dusky cloud moving swiftly through the air.

Our friend, Saleh Sekhali, and his family, also migrated. They went to Nazareth, for they feared the cholera, and tried to persuade us to accompany them.

The most unhealthy period in Palestine is that which occurs after the falling of the first few autumnal showers,*

---

* The "early rain" spoken of in the Bible refers, I believe, to the *autumnal showers*, which are never very violent. They fall gently, and by degrees, and revive the parched and burnt-up earth after the Summer drought, and enable the peasants to sow wheat and barley. In Deuteronomy it is called the "first rain;" and Joel says, "Be glad and rejoice in the Lord your God, for he hath given you the *former rain* moderately."

The Winter rain usually falls heavily during November, December, and early in which usher in the rainy season, and it lasts till the rain falls regularly and in abundance. This interval does not generally exceed two or three weeks, but when it is prolonged—as in the year 1855, of which I am writing—fevers or other epidemics prevail.

On the 2d of November, a strong sirocco wind, hot, dry, and scorching, as if it came from a furnace, warped our books, and split and cracked our olive-wood furniture. We closed all the window-shutters on the eastern side of the rooms, but we could not exclude the fiery air.

There were four English merchant ships at anchor in the port, as well as several small Greek brigs. The masters complained, in no very gentle terms, of the injury done by the fierce hot wind to the woodwork and fittings of their vessels.

An English captain, on the point of embarking, came in, saying, "I hope you will give me a clean bill of health, Consul." "As clean as I can," he answered: "but I must state, '*Six deaths within six days—sudden, and reported cholera.*'"

After this the street-cleaning was for a time abandoned, and I noticed funeral processions almost daily, sometimes going from the mosque out at the east gate to the Moslem burial-ground, sometimes from the Greek or Latin churches slowly walking toward the Christian cemeteries through the west gate. Moslems are always carried to the grave in the open bier, head foremost, and buried in ordinary costume. I shuddered the first time that I saw a body thus committed to the earth, it looked so much like being buried alive.

<sub>January; and then it ceases till March or April, when Spring showers are eagerly looked for and welcomed, for they give strength and vigor to the ripening crops. This is the "latter rain;" for it is written, "The Lord your God will cause to come down for you the *latter rain* in the first month," which is the month called in Hebrew "Abib," or "the month of young ears of corn," and corresponds with the end of March and the beginning of April.

"Behold the husbandman waiteth for the precious fruit of the earth and hath long patience for it, till he receive the *early* and the *latter rain*."

In the Summer-time, that is, from May till September, no rain is ever seen in Palestine.</sub>

The upper classes of Christians are generally interred in coffins. The coffin is usually borne by four or six men, preceded by priests walking under canopies, and surrounded by crowds of people, chanting, bearing embroidered banners and a large cross, and sometimes accompanied by surpliced boys, swinging incense. At a little distance a troop of women follow, singing and screaming wildly; for the priests in vain put their veto on the attendance of female mourners.

There was not one case of cholera in the Jewish community.

Deaths were most frequent in the crowded Moslem quarter, but the Moslems did not seem to suffer much from fear. Perhaps their reliance on the doctrine of fatalism made them calm and apparently resigned. On the other hand, among the Christians, a demoralizing panic quickly spread.

By degrees nearly all the Europeans went up to the Convent, where they established a strict quarantine. Many of the Arabs went to Nazareth and Shefa 'Amer. Altogether, above a thousand people fled, and the Christian quarter looked quite deserted. It was remarked that there was only one hat left in the town—that is, only one Frank— alluding to my brother, who remained at his post endeavoring to reanimate the people. He went from house to house, giving advice and simple medicines, and, as he was not quite convinced that the epidemic was cholera, he examined two or three bodies immediately after death. Their appearance confirmed the current report.

The Arab word for cholera, or the pest, is "Howa-el-Asfar," which signifies "the yellow wind." Flags proclaiming quarantine are *yellow;* is it possible that the color was selected on account of this name? The Arabs told me that the worst cases of cholera occurred at the change of the moon, and that people who were attacked then never recovered! The women seldom left their houses, except to follow funerals; and the men grew more and more dispirited. Even our little tailor, Suleiman Shefa Amery, the merriest of the merry, the drollest of the droll, was at last infected with the general fear. His springing, self-satisfied step became slow and cautious, and his voice was subdued to a whisper. He had been in the habit of coming to the Vice-Consulate, now and then, to show me his work—embroidered jackets and trowsers for the *trousseau* of a bride, or a tobacco-pouch for a Bek. He was one of my many self-constituted teachers, and was at the same time profoundly respectful and deferential, and yet amusingly impertinent. He was the *beau ideal* of an Oriental tailor, and looked as if he had just walked out of one of the pages of the "Arabian Nights' Entertainment"—good-looking, and quick in every movement. He was always ready, unasked, to do a service—light a pipe, trim a lamp, pick up a pencil, smooth the pillows and cushions of the divan, fetch a glass of water, or proffer an opinion. He looked with a quick and critical eye on every one's costume, and valued each article of apparel unhesitatingly, as if speaking half to himself and half to the wearer.

I used to learn a greater number of Arabic words from him in an hour than from any one else in a day. He could neither read nor write, but his memory was acute. He remembered perfectly the promiscuous vocabulary which he taught me. He used to ask me, each time he came, the words he had told me on previous occasions; and at every successful answer from me he glanced round the room, expecting a look of approbation for himself, and one for his pupil.

He showed me how to do all sorts of Syrian needlework. He made very beautiful designs for embroidery, chiefly conventional foliage. He first stiffens the cloth or silk, by sewing thick paper at the back of it; then, with a piece of hard, white native soap, rubbed to a fine point, he draws, with a firm hand, a few graceful lines and intersecting circles within any given space. He completes the design, in the course of working it, with gold thread, and he never by any chance makes two patterns precisely alike. He seemed thoroughly to enjoy his work; but now even he was changed—his brave, self-confident spirit had left him. He no longer took delight in his needle or gold thread. He told me, regretfully, that some of his best embroidery was in the burial-ground; for men and women, Moslems and Christians, are often shrouded in their bridal robes or fête-day dresses. Suleiman was one of the few Arabs who seemed to think this was a very great pity.

When costly garments are buried, the grave is generally watched for some time, for fear it should be rifled.

Suleiman fled for a short time to Shefa 'Amer, his native place, and happily escaped cholera.

One day we rode up to the Convent. Two hundred of the people of Hâifa had taken refuge there. The gardens, which had before looked so quiet and monastic, were enlivened by little groups of Arabs, smoking under the trees, or strolling about. All the rooms were occupied. The French Consul came to meet us, but carefully avoided contact, and led the way to the reception-room, where pastiles were burning. His wife and children came to see us, but remained at a distance. They said that, while people were dying of cholera in Hâifa, they, the voluntary exiles, were almost expiring of *ennui* and fear on Mount Carmel.

By degrees, the health of Hâifa somewhat improved, and a large proportion of cholera cases were cured. Powdered charcoal, made of bread burnt in an open crucible, was taken by many people as a preventive; and, as far as I could judge, it seemed to be effectual. A teaspoonful, or less, in a cup of sugarless coffee, was the usual daily dose.

On November 14th, we went for a trip in the interior, with Colonel and the Hon. Mrs. Walpole. He claimed my brother's aid in seeking for Winter-quarters for his regiment. He kindly invited me to go too; so, accompanied by his Bashi-Bazouks, and furnished with a circular letter of recommendation from the Pasha to all the governors in his pashalic, we went to Shefa 'Amer, Nazareth, round the

Lake of Tiberias, and along the valley of the Jordan, up to the Anti-Lebanon, exploring all the old castles and ruins; but we did not come very much in contact with the natives. The interest of the tour is chiefly archæological and architectural, so I will pass it over here. We returned to Hâifa on the 10th of December.

M. Zifo, the Prussian Consul, called to welcome us. He said that he was the "only hat in town," and he was detained by business, much against his inclination, for cholera and typhus-fever prevailed. All the people were praying for rain. For three days after our return, there was not one death in the town, and some of the refugees came from the Convent. The French Consul was one of the first arrivals. Unhappily, his youngest daughter, the pet and plaything of the family, who used to lisp out Arabic and French so prettily, was immediately attacked with cholera, and died after twelve hours' suffering.

On the 15th the panic was revived; but a curious circumstance suddenly restored tranquillity to the minds of the Arabs. On the night of Sunday, the 16th of December, a woman dreamed that she saw four malignant imps. Each one held a stone, with an inscription on it, in his hand. She said to them, "What do you want? Why are you here to trouble me?" They said, speaking as with one voice, "We have come to throw four stones." Then she said, "Hasten to throw your stones, and go in peace." One was thrown at her—the others flew in different directions. She told her dream the next day, and seemed very much alarmed. The imps of her dream were said, by the interpreters thereof, to be "*imps of the yellow wind.*" The majority of the people believed that there would be only four more deaths in Hâifa from cholera. On the 18th, fourteen individuals were attacked; but only two died, one of whom was the dreamer. On the 19th, there were two more deaths, the last which were reported. The people were reassured, and flocked back from 'Akka, Galilee, and Carmel. But the wished-for season of rain had not set in.

Provisions were dear, and milk was very unwholesome, on account of the scarcity of herbage.

Several ships from Yâfa had taken refuge in the port of Hâifa. The winds were so wild and contrary, that two ships were wrecked off 'Akka, and two boats lost in the bay. The west wind was so strong for a day or two, that it filled the mouth of the River Kishon with sand, so that it could be crossed easily on foot. Then suddenly the east wind rose, and swept the bar of sand quite away, so that the river was twelve feet deep at the usual place of fording, and consequently impassable.

At Christmas the rain came; but it was rain such as I had never seen, except in strange old pictures of the Deluge. The town was traversed in all directions by rapid streams of mud and water. Rain came in at the ill-made windows, and our shutters and doors were wrenched from their hinges by the wild wind. Fortunately, the house for which we had been waiting was now ready, and weather-tight; and we managed to move into it, during the short intervals between the torrents. I had to ride there, although it was only at a very short distance. Most of the Arabs went about barefooted, with the water far above their ankles.

During the wet season, there were about three days of nearly continual rain, and three days of sunshine, alternately.

Our new house, the rooms of which were built round a corridored court, was next door to the French Consulate. The Consul's wife—a Syrian lady—kindly initiated me by degrees into all the mysteries of Oriental housekeeping.

Furnishing was a very simple affair. In one of the large empty rooms a native Jewish upholsterer was set to work to take to pieces all the mattresses, cushions, and lehaffs. Then, with a little machine, he separated the cotton which had become hard and close; he tore it and combed it till it was transformed into a fleecy cloud. He quickly remade the mattresses, fitting them to the iron bedsteads and divans, and cleverly quilted a stock of coverlets—lehaffs. His naked feet were almost as busy as his fingers. They served him to hold his work. When he wanted to wind a skein of cotton he always fixed it on his long, pliant toes, and used them as pegs when he doubled and twisted the thread; in fact, in many ways he made them useful.

In the mean time an Arab carpenter was engaged in sawing planks and joining them together, ready to place on low trestles round the rooms. On the rude benches thus formed, mattresses, about a yard wide, and cushions, covered with chintz or Manchester prints, were arranged. Deep, full borders, sewed on to the outer edge of the mattresses, quite concealed the rough woodwork underneath. This is all the mystery of the grand Turkish divans. Two native Jewesses assisted me with the musketo and window curtains.

Reed mats, to cover the cemented and stone floors, were made for us at 'Akka according to measure. I furnished one little room as nearly in English style as I could under the circumstances, but the rest of the house was semi-Oriental. There were no fireplaces in any of the rooms. In the kitchen there was a row of cooking-stoves fit for stewing and baking; similar, probably, to "the oven and ranges for pots," referred to in Leviticus xi, 35.

There was a good well in the corner of the court, and a little bell tinkled merrily every time the bucket was in motion. The former occupants of the house were Arabs, and they had left for my benefit a fine *henna-tree*—lawsonia. It is very like the privet, but the blossom is more yellow and delicate, and the scent is rather oppressive. The green leaves—which produce the dye—are dried, crumbled to a fine powder, and carefully preserved.

The stocking of the storeroom was the next consideration. It soon contained provisions for the Winter. A case of maccaroni, a basket of Egyptian rice, and two sacks of wheat, one of which I sent to be ground by millstones moved by cattle. Afterward I had the meal sifted at the house, the smeed was set apart for white bread, etc., and the remainder was stored for making Arab loaves for the servants.

The large terra-cotta jars, glazed inside, and rough without, ranged round the room, often made me think of Ali Baba and the forty thieves. One held the smeed, another held flour, another bran, a fourth oil, and some rather smaller ones contained olives and goats'-milk cheese preserved in oil, and a store of cooking butter. Oranges and lemons garnished the shelves. Dried figs strung on thin cord, and pomegranates tied one by one to ropes, hung in festoons from the rafters, and the bundles of dried herbs of Carmel smelled sweetly.

My kind neighbor taught me how to add to my stores at the right seasons, to make fruit preserves, to concentrate the essence of tomatoes, and to convert wheat into starch— by steeping it in water, straining it, and drying it in the sun—for making sweet dishes, as well as for the laundry. The Arabs do not starch or iron their clothes, so I had a little difficulty at first in procuring help in the "getting up" of fine linen. However, an Arab youth, who had once lived with a semi-European tailor, and professed to know how to handle an iron, though he acknowledged that starching was a mystery to him, volunteered assistance, and did his best. Subsequently a young Arab girl in our service was taught the art by an Abyssinian slave, the servant of a European neighbor, and she became very skillful.

Arabs only use starch for making a sort of blancmange, and they shrink from the idea of stiffening linen with it, for they have a strong respect for wheat in any shape. If a morsel of bread fall to the ground, an Arab will gather it up with his right hand, kiss it, touch his forehead with it, and place it in a recess or on a wall, where the fowls of the air may find it, for they say, "We must not tread under foot the gift of God." I have seen this reverence exhibited constantly, by all classes of the people, by masters, servants, and even by little children, Moslems, and Christians.

DEATH OF IBRAHÎM.

I was so busy that I had no time to feel my strange isolation. The mornings were devoted to household arrangements and lessons in Arabic. Visitors and visiting often occupied me after midday, and in fine weather I enjoyed a ride or a stroll with my brother before sunset, and pleasant evenings with him and his friends. When we were at last alone together we used to compare notes of our several occupations, observations, and adventures of the day. His long residence in the East enabled him to explain some of the intricacies and seeming contradictions in the characters of the Arabs, and to guide me in my intercourse with them. In outline during the Winter one day nearly resembled another, but the details were always pleasantly varied.

Ibrahîm Sekhali, my brother's secretary—and also my writing-master—an energetic, clever young man of the Greek Church, went to 'Akka like many others to avoid cholera. 'Akka was over-crowded, and small-pox broke out. Poor Ibrahîm caught it, and died suddenly on the 16th of January, 1856. His death threw a gloom over Hâifa, for he was a general favorite among Christians and Moslems.

On the 17th, early in the morning, Khalîl Sekhali, the father of Ibrahîm, called on us. He was a very stout, tall, robust-looking man, and wore a long robe or open pelisse, and a large white turban. His features were regular, and his beard long and white. He looked grand in his grief, and his lamentations for his dead son were solemn and dignified. He, with my brother and the chief people of our town, went toward 'Akka to join the funeral *cortége*, for it was arranged that the body should be brought to Hâifa for burial. All the horses and donkeys were in requisition, and nearly all the shops were closed.

I walked out to witness the wailing of the widow and her companions. They were outside the East Gate, near to the burial-ground. About fifty or sixty vailed women surrounded the chief mourners. I was led almost unconsciously by little Katrîne Sekhali through the crowd to an open space in the midst. In the center of this space the widow, young and beautiful, kneeled on the ground. She was unvailed. Her head was only covered by a little red-cloth cap. Her long hair was unbraided, and fell over her green-velvet, gold-embroidered jacket. She swayed her body to and fro, tossed her head back, raised her hands as if passionately pleading, then threw herself forward with her face to the ground, but suddenly started to her feet, and, with her dark eyes uplifted, and her arms raised above her head, she commenced shrieking wildly, and all the women joined in the piercing cry. Presently she fell down as if exhausted, and there was silence for a moment. Then a few of the women in the inner circle rose, threw off their vails, and danced round her, singing and making a rattling, tremulous sound from the throat, while the rest of the women joined in chorus. Professional mourners kept up the excitement by demonstrations of violent grief, and the professional singers improvised appropriate songs. This lasted for three or four hours, and the crowd gradually grew larger. I made my way through it with difficulty, for some of the women had worked themselves into fits of frenzy and hysterics.

I observed that the men who passed by kept quite aloof from this group of mourners, and made no attempt to look upon the unvailed widow. My kawass stood afar off, waiting for me. On emerging from the crowd, I could see the funeral *cortége* approaching along the sands. I was informed by a forerunner that the body of Ibrahîm had been interred in the 'Akka burial-ground, as it was considered dangerous to convey it so far as Hâifa. When the procession was near to the town, I went up on to the low roof of the custom-house to see it pass. First came the kawasses of some of the Consuls, carrying their long, silver-headed sticks or poles draped with black; then a large party of young men, dressed in various colors, solemnly silent, walking four abreast. At a little distance from these, Ibrahîm's horse, without a rider, was led by two men slowly and carefully. Some of poor Ibrahîm's well-remembered garments were on the saddle.

The three brothers of Ibrahîm followed in a line; then came his nephews and cousins, among whom was our friend Saleh, all looking thoughtful and sad. The next mourner was the mother. She sat cross-legged on a horse, supported by two men. Her face was vailed, but her drooping head expressed her grief—she had lost her favorite son. My brother, who had a great respect both for her and the deceased, rode by her side. Mohammed Bek followed, on a splendid white horse, surrounded by a group of Moslems; then came the 'Akka mourners, headed by the Giammal family, all on foot. Last of all, the father, looking heartbroken, rode slowly toward his bereaved home.

When all the men were out of sight, the company of women entered the gates, shrieking and singing. My kawass retreated hastily, and a young Greek of Scio, who was by my side, said, "You can remain here to see them pass, but it would not be proper for me to do so—men do not watch processions of female mourners;" and he retired.

First came a group of dancers, only slightly vailed, making slow and graceful movements, and waving scarfs and kerchiefs, pausing now and then in strange attitudes, resting for a quarter of a minute at a time like statues, and then singing and shrieking wildly, all the company joining in the chorus. The young widow walked alone, followed by two attendants who carried the orphan children. This group was surrounded at a little distance by the nearest female relatives of Ibrahîm. An irregular crowd of women and girls closed the procession, loudly echoing the songs of the leaders. Thus they went slowly through the town; and there was loud wailing and mourning in the house of Sekhali for seven days. But to the silent grief of the mother there was no limit. She lived next door to the Consulate, and I often saw her. She was completely changed. Her firm step had suddenly become faltering, and her head drooped. She seldom spoke, and her only words were words of lamentation and despair. Little Katrîne, the daughter of our friend Saleh, touchingly described her great grief, saying, "I think our aunt will die. She has no thought but for Ibrahîm. She does not wish to see any one but Ibrahîm. Always she is kissing his coat, his cap, and his gun. Always her face is wet with tears, and she will not be comforted. She can not eat, and at night she is awake; only a little in the daytime she falls asleep, tired of crying and of folding and unfolding all his clothes. No one can make her glad now."

Little Katrîne's fears were realized. The mother of Ibrahîm died on the 13th of February, fretting to the last for her dead son. I attended her funeral the next day. At an early hour I saw the procession form. Men carrying banners, embroidered with sacred emblems and monograms, led the way. Then came the Greek priests. One of them bore a large gilt wooden cross. The body was in a dark coffin, on which three white crosses were conspicuous. It was supported by six men. The male mourners were headed by the widower and his three sons. The women followed afar off. A large number of people lined the road all the way to the church, and fell in with the funeral *cortége* as it passed.

The bell was tolling as I entered the church. I went up into the women's gallery, which is very high, and opposite to the altar. I was led to the front of it, where a block of wood was given to me for a seat. The women, all vailed and in white sheets, sat around on the matted floor. I looked down into the church, through a sloping wooden lattice, at an angle of about twenty degrees with the ceiling, and so arranged that a view of what was going on below could only be obtained by leaning forward over this lattice, and with the face nearly close to it. Thus positioned, I could see easily.

The chancel was already crowded. A few European gentlemen, in dark clothes, looked conspicuous among the

Arabs in their many-colored garments. The chief female mourners, shrouded in white, were grouped all together on one side. The coffin, raised on high trestles, stood in the center. A narrow space was left round it. A priest stood at its head, slowly swinging a censer, while two others chanted psalms, and read the service monotonously and mutteringly. The people responded loudly.

Wax-candles were distributed by the younger members of the Sekhali family to every one present. There were about three hundred, and a strange effect was produced when all the candles, as well as the tapers fixed round the coffin, were lighted. Some looked pale and spirit-like in the sunshine; others were obscured in clouds of incense; while the rest illuminated dark corners, made darker by the dense crowd.

Khalil Sekhali, the widower, and his three sons, sat together in a conspicuous position near the door of the sacristy. Every one else was standing. In obedience to a signal from the chief-priest, an opening was made in the crowd toward them. After a few minutes of perfect silence, the widower walked unobstructed into the center of the church. He placed his hands solemnly on the coffin, pressed his broad forehead on to the head of it, pronounced a blessing, kissed a little Byzantine picture of Christ which was placed there, and then returned to his seat, bending his head low. After another silent pause the three sons followed his example; and all the nearest relatives came forward to kiss the picture. After the youngest child of the family had been lifted up to take this farewell, the rest of the congregation crowded round, and with less emotion and more haste performed the same ceremony.

By degrees all but the chief mourners withdrew, and then I went down into the church with the women. One by one they kissed the picture, muttering a short prayer for the repose of the soul of the deceased. Presently the procession re-formed, and went out at the West Gate to the Greek burial-ground; the women followed afar off, singing and crying wildly. And again for many days there was mourning in the house of Sekhali.

But the widower did not reject consolation. About a year afterward he sent messengers to Nazareth to seek for a wife for him, and when all was rightly arranged he went there to be affianced. But a monetary difficulty arose, and the contract was annulled. Another bride was sought and quickly chosen, for Khalîl said that he was determined not to be disappointed, nor to be a laughing-stock in Hâifa. He was after all actually betrothed on the very day first fixed for the ceremony, and the marriage took place soon after.

The bridegroom was about seventy and the bride seventeen! I called to welcome the young wife to Hâifa. She was very good-looking, but quite of the peasant class. She had a bright face; the forehead and chin were tattooed; her eyebrows were naturally black and well arched, and her eyelashes were long, so that no kohl was necessary. This peculiarity is expressed, in Arabic, in one word, "Khâlâ." Her countenance was ruddy, and the women said of her, "The wife of Khalîl is fair; roses grow upon her cheeks; she does not buy her roses in the bazar." This is also said of the women of Shefa 'Amer, who are generally bright and healthy in appearance, and use rouge but rarely. Khalîl was comforted. His three sons and their wives, with their little ones, dwelt with him under the same roof, and there was rejoicing in the house when a son was born to him in his old age.

Elias Sekhali, the eldest son of Khalîl, was studious, thoughtful, clear-headed, and logical, and universally liked by Christians and Moslems. He was employed in the French Consulate. He came very often to see us, and was eager to obtain information about the English Constitution, and the progress of civilization generally. He always had some amusing story or impressive parable to tell me when he found me alone. Many of them were original. I carefully chronicled all. He often spoke to me on the subject of the government of Syria. He said that there was no opportunity for the people to rise out of their present condition, while they are ruled by officers who have no sympathy with them, no love for the country, and no object but to enrich themselves.

The Arabs, under the present system of irregular taxation, do not attempt to cultivate the land as they would do if they were encouraged and protected by the Government. In many parts of the country a man will not run the risk of improving his estate. He will not plant new olive-trees, nor extend his orchards and vineyards, nor employ many laborers, for fear of exciting the rapacity of the Governor of his district; for if a man is supposed to be rich, excuses are readily invented to impoverish him; debts are coined, or false accusations are made against him, and he is thrown into prison till he pays the supposed debt or a large fine. In one particular instance the Governor of a certain Moslem village, having exceeded even the usual bounds of exaction, a united complaint was made to the Pasha by the indignant villagers. The Pasha, for the sake of appearances, immediately appointed a new Governor. He tried and imprisoned the offender for a few days; but soon made arrangements with him and set him free, after having accepted as a bribe a large proportion of the property which the Ex-Governor had so unjustly obtained!

I have heard of many similar transactions, and sometimes the actors have been well known to me, so that I have had an opportunity of hearing both sides of the story. Nearly all the Turks with whom I came in contact seemed to glory in successful intrigue, and were generally shrewd and clever. They had little or no sympathy with the Arabs, and apparently no true patriotism. There are very few Turks in Palestine, except civil officers and their *employés*, military officers, and soldiers. They are looked upon always as foreigners.

Pashas and Governors do not remain long or for any fixed time in one place. Wherever they go they, with few exceptions, "tread upon the poor, and take from them burdens of wheat; they afflict the just, and take a bribe." They naturally favor the Moslems; but money is their chief consideration. They not only injure the people whom they are appointed to protect, but they rob the Government which they are employed to serve. If appointments were given, with appropriate salaries, to men of honor and energy, fitted for office, instead of being sold to speculators, there would be hope for Syria. Crime would be punished and innocence protected in spite of patronage and piasters.

Elias severely felt the disadvantageous position of his countrymen. They live in a land overrun by Bedouins, where there is no security for property, and no encouragement for agriculturists; where there are no roads and very few modern books; where offices are purchased, laws tampered with, justice disregarded, and industry and commercial enterprise checked. I could not help sympathizing with him, especially as I by degrees became better acquainted with the capabilities of the Arab mind, and the wonderful fertility of the country. Under more favorable circumstances and better cultivation each would flourish. Elias admitted that oppression had demoralized the people to a lamentable extent. Their powers and talents were misapplied, their ingenuity and inventive faculties were displayed in artful cunning and clever intrigue. Their powers of endurance and self-sacrifice had grown into seeming apathy and indifference, their love of poetry and of the marvelous had been trifled with by teachers of strange doctrines and conflicting traditions, and their imaginations were incumbered with wild superstitions.

When Elias spoke thus despondingly, no such man as Fuad Pasha had been in Syria to inspire the hope of a better state of things. Elias was always ready to answer patiently and carefully my many questions. During nearly three years I was in the habit of seeing him frequently. In August, 1858, he went to Beirût on business. He was not well when he left home, and on Wednesday, the 1st of September, news was brought to Hâifa that he was dead, and had been buried at Beirût. This was a new and terrible affliction for the Sekhali family, for Elias was looked up to as the ruler and manager of the house. Khalîl, the aged father, felt the loss acutely, and the widow was quite prostrated. Grief bewildered and almost stupefied her—she could not even weep. "Call for the mourning women, that they may come; and for such as are skillful in lamentation, that they may come; and let them make haste, and take up a wailing for us, that our eyes may run down with tears, and our eyelids gush out with waters." And again there were seven days of weeping in the house of Sekhali. See Jeremiah ix, 17, 18.

I joined the mourners on the third day. As soon as I entered the house, I heard the minstrels and the loud cries of the people. See Matthew ix, 23. I was led into a large, long room. Women were sitting on the floor in rows on two sides of it. An open space was left down the middle to the end of the room, where the widow sat apart, with her two youngest children lying at her feet. Her hair was disheveled, and she wore no covering on her head. Her eyelids were swollen with weeping, and her face pale with watching. She looked as if she had suddenly grown old. Her dress was rent and disordered. She had not rested or changed her garments since she heard the tidings of her husband's death. She kissed me passionately, and said, "Weep for me, he is dead;" and then, pointing to her children, she said, "Weep for them, they are fatherless." I sat near to her. One of her children, who was about three years old, crept into my lap, and whispered, "My father is dead." Then he closed his eyes, and pressed his chubby little fingers tightly over them, saying, "My father is dead like this—he is in the dark."

The wailing, which had been slightly interrupted at my

entrance, was renewed with vigor. The assembled women were all in their gayest dresses—soft crimson silk with white stripes on it prevailing. There were many women from Nazareth and Shefa 'Amer and other villages. They had uncovered their heads and unbraided their hair. They looked dreadfully excited. Their eyes were red with weeping and watching. The air of the room was close and heated, for the widow and chief mourners had remained there for three days and two nights without rest, receiving guests who came to mourn with them. The room was always filled, for as soon as one set of people left another set came in. During my visit there were seventy-three mourners present, without reckoning the children who glided in and out.

Three rows of women sat on the matted floor on the right-hand side, facing three rows on the left. They were all clapping their hands or striking their bosoms in time with the monotonous melody which they murmured.

Presently an especial lamentation was commenced, to which I was invited to respond. I was still seated at the end of the room, near to the widow. The women on my left hand, led by a celebrated professional mourner, sang these words with vigor and energy:

> "We saw him, in the midst of the company of riders,
> Riding bravely on his horse, the horse he loved!"

Then the women on the opposite side of the room answered in a lower and more plaintive key, beating their breasts mournfully:

> "Alas! no more shall we see him
> In the midst of the company of riders,
> Riding bravely on his horse, the horse he loved."

Then the first singers sang:

> "We saw him in the garden, the pleasant garden,
> With his companions, and his children, the children he loved."

Then the second singers answered:

> "Alas! no more shall we see him
> In the garden, the pleasant garden,
> With his companions, and his children, the children he loved."

Chorus of all the women, singing softly:

> "His children and his servants blessed him!
> His home was the shelter of happiness!
> Peace be upon him!"

First singers—loudly and with animation

> "We saw him giving food to the hungry,
> And clothing to the naked."

Second singers—softly and plaintive:

> "Alas! no more shall we see him
> Give food to the hungry,
> And garments to the naked!"

First singers:

> "We saw him give help and succor to the aged
> And good counsel to the young."

Second singers:

> "Alas! no more shall we see him
> Give help and succor to the aged,
> And good counsel to the young."

Chorus of all the women, singing softly

> "He suffered not the stranger to sleep in the streets:
> He opened his door to the wayfarer.
> Peace be upon him!"

After this, they started to their feet, and shrieked as loudly as they could, making a rattling noise in their throats for three or four minutes. The widow kneeled, swaying her body backward and forward, and feebly joined in the wild cry.

Some of the women reseated themselves on the floor quite exhausted, some retired, and a number of guests from 'Akka came in and took the vacant places. A minstrel woman began slowly beating a tambourine, and all the company clapped their hands in measure with it, singing, "Alas for him! alas for him! He was brave, he was good, alas for him!" Then three women rose, with naked swords in their hands, and stood at two or three yards' distance from each other. They began dancing with slow and graceful movements, with their swords at first held low and their heads drooping. Each dancer kept within a circle of about a yard in diameter. By degrees the tambourine and the clapping of the hands and the songs grew louder, the steps of the dancers were quickened. They threw back their heads, and gazed upward passionately, as if they would look into the very heavens. They flourished their uplifted swords, and as their movements became more wild and excited, the bright steel flashed and bright eyes seemed to grow brighter. As one by one the dancers sank overcome with fatigue, others rose to replace them. Thus passed seven days and nights. Professional mourners were in constant attendance to keep up the excitement, and dances and dirges succeeded each other, with intervals of wild and hysterical weeping and shrieking. I remained about two hours in the room, and occasionally I watched from a window which overlooked it. I could see that the leader had a powerful influence over all present. A certain tone of her wild wailing voice drew tears from the eyes and produced hysterical emotion in some cases.

There are girls who have a morbid taste for the excitement thus produced, and are celebrated for the facility with which they fall into fits of uncontrollable weeping. The real mourners and the amateur actresses in these scenes are usually ill afterward, but the professional assistants do not appear to suffer from the fatigue or excitement, and they do not lose their self-control for a moment.

Poor Khalîl Sekhali never quite recovered the shock caused by this death. It became an epoch from which to reckon events throughout the district, where Elias had been so well known and so much respected. It was usual to say, "Such an event occurred before or after the death of Elias." And there was a saying current in Hâifa to the effect that "the men of the Sekhali family die always among strangers and away from home." But I suppose that the spell is broken now, for Khalîl, the old man, died in his own house, in January, 1860. I was not in Hâifa at the time, but I was informed that Khalîl had been staying at 'Akka and was very ill there. On his way back to Hâifa, in a very weak state, while riding along the sands, he was thrown from his horse, and so much injured that he was carried home, and died in three days. My brother went to the funeral, and in a letter to me he spoke of it thus:

"I never in this neighborhood saw a funeral so numerously attended. The church, as well as the court without, was completely crowded. Seven priests—four of whom had come from a considerable distance for the purpose—chanted the appointed psalms, and the burial service was performed as usual. After the Epistle, Gospel, and Absolution had been read, the chief priest said to the congregation, 'Dear brethren and children, Khalîl Sekhali was a man who lived very long in this world. He has had a great deal of business, and has been in communication with a great number of people. It is possible that in certain transactions he may have given cause for offense. Some people may have felt themselves insulted, some may have been grieved or offended, either with or without reason. This now is the time for pardon, and I hereby beseech you all present, and by the blessing of God I implore you all, to pardon him fully, to forgive him all offenses as you hope to be forgiven.' The whole congregation then answered, 'May God pardon him!'"

This ceremony of asking pardon of the living for the dead is observed in a slight degree at all burials among the Greeks, but it is not generally so emphatically expressed or so enlarged upon as in the case of Khalîl. He was a man of great influence. He was the founder of the Greek Church in Hâifa; and the only good houses in the town belonged to him or to members of his family.

CHAPTER VIII.

LIFE IN HÂIFA.

THE history of the Sekhali family has led me away from my own. I will return to the time when we hastened into our new house on account of the commencement of the Winter rains—Christmas, 1855.

On the 30th of December, after three days and nights of almost incessant rain, a bright, sunshiny afternoon tempted us out. We passed through the west gate, and the sudden change which had taken place in the appearance of the country surprised me exceedingly. The ground, which had lately looked so brown and parched, cracked into fissures by the Summer heat, was now carpeted with vividly-green grass and tiny leaves. Many large slabs of rock which had before been concealed by earth were now laid bare. The tombs in the Greek and Latin cemeteries, the broad stone thrashing-floors on the sloping plain, the masses of rock around and on the terraced hill-sides, washed by the recent torrents, looked brightly white.

We climbed the castle hill just behind Hâifa. White, yellow, and purple crocuses were growing round the roots of the trees, under the shelter of rocks, and in the midst of leafless thorn-bushes;* while the glossy-green leaves of flags, arums, squills, and cyclamen were unfolding and shooting up every-where.

We looked down on to the town. Thousands of birds, chiefly sparrows, were on the house-tops. The flat roofs are composed of massive beams of wood, crossed by planks, poles, and brushwood, overspread with earth and small stones, rolled firm and smooth. In preparation for the

---
* "The lily among thorns." Song of Solomon ii, 2.

Winter rains, the roofs had all been newly covered with mortar made of earth—brought from the common or uninclosed land of the hills—well mixed with straw. The newly-disturbed earth, rich in bulbs, and grass, and wild-flower seeds, had naturally attracted the birds, and as I watched them pecking and twittering there, I felt the significancy of the expression in the Psalms, which refers to the "sparrow on the house-top."

On the 30th of January, soon after sunrise, several little boys came with large bunches of the "narojus;" that is, the yellow narcissus, a favorite flower of the Arabs. The boys asked for "backshîsh," and said, "We have brought these flowers because they are called by the name of the Consul." Then I understood why many Arabs, especially children, called us "Narojus," instead of Rogers. In the afternoon I went on to the hills, where narcissus and wild hyacinths were growing in profusion. Goats were leaping and skipping from rock to rock, and enjoying the plentiful pasture. I looked down on the town. Its appearance was perfectly changed. Out of the lately-made roofs of earth fresh green grass had sprung, so that every house-top looked like a grass-plat; and on some of them lambs and kids were feeding.

But these grass-grown roofs are rarely sound enough to keep out the rain. We often heard our neighbors complaining of water pouring in torrents into their rooms, and I have sometimes been roused in the night by an unexpected sprinkling. Patches of fresh earth are added from time to time, and the roofs are rolled occasionally with a heavy stone, like a common garden-roller. One is usually kept on the top of each house, or block of houses.

When I went out, on the 11th of February, I saw laborers busy in the plain, at the foot of the Carmel Hills. Large patches of land were being plowed. The rich brown earth was thrown up by clumsy-looking plowshares, dragged by oxen. Boys were employed in gathering out stones from tracts of land, round which men were building low rough stone walls. New hedges of prickly pears were being planted round gardens and orchards, thus: a stone wall about a quarter of a yard high is made, and then quite covered with earth. Along the top of the bank thus formed portions of the cactus stems are planted, about a foot apart. These stems are green and broad, and so flat and jointed that they look like large rounded leaves joined together. In some places the rain had washed away the earth, and I could see the roots shooting out from the edges of the stems. The growth of the species of the cactus — *Opuntia* — is so rapid that a bank thus planted becomes, in the course of one season, a very formidable hedge. Its blossom is yellow, and it yields the pleasant, cooling fruit called "prickly pear," or "Indian fig." The Arabs call it "*subber*"—that is, "*patience*"—on account of the care and patience required in gathering and peeling it; for it is covered with spines and fine stinging hairs, and the plant is armed every-where with large sharp thorns. In spite of this the camel feeds on it freely. Even in the driest seasons the stems are juicy, and, when pierced, moisture oozes out plentifully. It is the natural home of the cochineal insect; but the cultivation of this valuable article of commerce is unfortunately neglected in Palestine.

The blossoming arum, the blue iris, squills, and daffodils were growing so abundantly in the burial-ground, that the sides of the tombs were quite concealed. On the unplowed land of the plain, and on the hill-sides, I found anemones, ranunculuses, marigolds, ground-ivy, cyclamen, and many other wild flowers.

The thorn-bushes, which during the Summer and Autumn had been so dark and bare, were clothed with delicate green sprays of finely-serrated leaves, which almost hid the sharp, cruel-looking thorns. They were sprinkled with little round buds—when they opened, they threw out silky tufts of crimson, crowned with golden-colored powder. The seed vessel is round, and divided into four quarters. At first it is almost white, but gradually becomes pink. At the apex there is a little green tuft, in the shape of a Greek cross. When the seed is quite ripe, it is about half an inch in diameter, and of a deep, shining, red color.

I have been told that it was of this thorn that the wreath was made, which once crowned the head of Christ. It may be so. I have never seen a plant of which so beautiful, and at the same time so cruel, a crown could be composed. This thorn is the *Poterium spinosum*. About Easter, it is seen in all its beauty, the leaves glossy and full-grown, the fruit or seed-vessels brilliantly red, like drops of blood, and the thorns sharper and stronger than at any other time. No plant or bush is so common on the hills of Judea, Galilee, and Carmel as this. It is used extensively for fuel, especially for the bakers' ovens, and "the crackling of thorns under a pot" may often be heard in Palestine.

The gardens and orchards looked very beautiful. Almond-trees were full of blossom. Lemon and shaddock trees were laden with fruit. The Winter rains were over; "flowers appeared on the earth, the time of the singing of birds had come, and the voice of the turtle was heard in the land." And again the appearance of the town of Hâifa was perfectly changed. The last few days of warmth and uninterrupted sunshine had quite withered and burned up all "the grass on the house-tops," so that there was not a green spot left. Boys and girls were gathering the short yellow hay; but there was very little of it, for the grass had not had time to grow up fully, or put forth its seed; and the harvest on the house-tops was mere child's play, "wherewith the mower filleth not his hand, nor he that bindeth sheaves his bosom." Psalm cxxix, 6–8.

On the 19th of February, early in the morning, a young Bedouin brought me a large wooden bowl full of clotted cream, and announced the coming of four men of his tribe. While he spoke, they entered. They were rejoicing, on account of the abundance of milk which their flocks yielded now that they were at pasture on the Carmel range. They were very dark, and wore long, white, cotton shirts with wide sleeves, and loose, heavy, camel's-hair cloaks. They seemed to be rather taken by surprise by the looking-glass, in which they could see themselves at full length. The one who seemed to be the chief of the party invited me to visit him, with the Consul, at his tents, at an hour's distance from Hâifa. In answer to my questions, he told me that there were several women at the encampment, and that they were busy making stores of cooking butter. The cream is shaken in goats' skins, and afterward boiled. When the milk and whey are completely extracted, the butter will keep good for a very long time. At this season the markets are always well supplied by the peasantry and the Bedouins together, and during the Spring housekeepers refill their butter-jars with a store for the Summer and Autumn. One of these Bedouins carried a lance, about twelve feet long. At the top of it there were two round tufts of black ostrich feathers, about one foot apart. The upper tuft was fringed with little white feathers. Between the tufts, strips of scarlet cloth were twisted. The lance was so heavy that I could not lift it. It was of wood, with a metal barb. All the men wore large red and yellow silk striped kefias—that is, fringed shawls—on their heads, fastened round the crown with a thick rope, and put on like hoods. They all had high, pointed, red-leather boots, which, however, they took off at the door. One man displayed a heavy silver ring on his finger. A name was roughly engraved on it. The wearer said, "Salute the Consul; may Allah keep all sorrow far from him!" Then he and his followers went away.

I had just dismissed the bearer of the bowl of cream with a backshîsh, when two little girls of the Sekhali family came to me, saying, "O Miriam, peace be upon you! We have thought you must be sad and lonely, now that the Consul is away from Hâifa. May he return to you soon, and in safety!" I invited my friendly little neighbors to take off their izzars—the white sheets in which they were enveloped—and to remain with me to breakfast. They wore dark cotton trowsers, made very full and long, and cloth jackets, closely fitting and fastened up to the throat. Their mundîls, or bright-colored muslin kerchiefs, were put on like shawls over the head, crossed under the chin, and the ends tied on the top of the head. Their hair was braided, and hung in long plaits over their shoulders. Their finger-nails and toe-nails were rosy with henna-dye. They left their yellow shoes at the entrance of the room. They were very much interested in turning out the contents of my work-box, and in looking through books of pictures, about which they asked many questions, and made curious comments, not only teaching me, unconsciously, Arabic words, but showing me the spirit of Oriental ideas. They were amused to hear about English children, and laughed heartily when I told them that in England a few camels are kept as curiosities, in a beautiful garden. They could not understand how we could live in a land where there are no camels to carry burdens. I tried to explain to them the use of carts and railed roads; but, as they had never seen a wheeled carriage of any kind, it was very difficult to convey the idea, even with the help of pictures. They were very clever, quick children; and, though only eight and nine years old, they could already make bread, and prepare many simple dishes. They were surprised that I had not been taught how to cook. It is the chief point in the education of an Arab girl.

While I was occupied with my amusing little guests, our Egyptian groom Mohammed arrived, leading a beautiful white mare, and bringing a letter from my brother, inviting me to go immediately to Shefa 'Amer—about three hours' distance—to meet him there, and to return with him to Hâifa the next day. The children said, "We are glad you will to-day see the Consul; but we are sorry you are going away from us; go in peace." I was soon ready, and mounted on the white mare. Her long mane and tail were deeply dyed with henna—bright orange color. It is said to be a preventive of disease. A large glass bead of sapphire blue hung from the neck of the animal. I asked the groom what it was for. He said, "It will avert the effect of a glance from an evil eye. This mare is so beautiful that she is in danger of being looked at with admiration and envy by those who have power to destroy her and her rider even by a look." He said he durst not suffer me to ride such an animal without this precaution. Many of my friends, Moslems and Christians, walked by my side as far as the gate, and "Go in peace, and return to us in safety," rang in my ears as I rode along the sands, attended only by our trustworthy groom Mohammed, and under the protection of the sapphire bead. I asked him if my want of confidence in the charm would destroy its efficacy. He answered solemnly, "*Its power can not be destroyed, praised be Allah!*" It was noon. The sun shone, but not too fiercely. The wind blew, but not too roughly; and the waves rippled round the feet of the mare, and of Mohammed's sturdy little donkey. We crossed the Kishon cautiously and safely on the bar far out at sea. The river was rather deep and dangerous that day.

We turned away from the shore and traversed the drifted sand-hills, where tall trees and shrubs were half buried; but grass was springing up plentifully where the land was firmer, and the rain rested here and there in quiet pools, bordered by the iris, blue and yellow, rank grass and blossoming reeds. Advancing a little further into the plain, we came to a perfect paradise of flowers. The ground for a mile or more in every direction was completely carpeted with anemones—scarlet, crimson, white, blue, purple, pink, and lilac—with patches of clover and mallows here and there, and buttercups and cyclamen. I had never seen such wealth of wild flowers, or such vivid coloring, and there seemed to be no one to enjoy it. We were quite out of sight of human beings and human habitations. The only building to be seen was the dome over the fountain of

Jethro, a retreat for ablution and for prayer, with a few troughs round it for watering cattle. It is just half-way between Hâifa and Shefa 'Amer. I paused for a moment to enjoy the scene and the silence. My mare began cropping the thickly-growing mallows. Mohammed exclaimed, "Ya Sittee, cows thrive on mallows, but to running horses they bring death." As we rode on again, I asked Mohammed if his parents still lived in Egypt. He replied, "God knows! It is more than twenty years since I left my mother. She was a widow, peace be upon her! and I have never heard of her since. It is too late now. No letter would reach her, for she is poor and unknown in the land. When the poor leave their parents, they leave them forever. That is the reason why mothers weep and refuse to be comforted when their sons go away from their homes. Letters can be carried for the rich, and for people who are known." He was surprised to hear that in England all houses are named or numbered, and that letters directed to the poorest people in the country are taken as much care of as those addressed to the most wealthy.

Mohammed had lost the use of one eye. In answer to my inquiry, he told me that his mother had purposely destroyed the sight, by the application of poisonous leaves when he was young, to render him unfit for service in the army, for he was her only son. This practice was very common in Egypt till Ibrahîm Pasha put an effectual stop to it by ordering a regiment to be formed entirely of one-eyed men, and every one who had lost the sight of an eye, either by accident or design, was compelled to join it. Mohammed, among others, was enrolled, and this Cyclopean regiment became the most formidable in Egyptian service.* We passed between large fields where wheat and barley

* I could not understand what sort of leaves Mohammed referred to, but they were gathered from a shrub which grows in gardens on the banks of the Nile. On homeopathic principles I suppose that this eye-destroying leaf should also have the power of renovating injured sight. Several Arabs—Christians—confessed to me, that when they were school-boys, they resorted to all sorts of schemes in order to avoid attending school. They used sometimes to rub their eyelids with freshly-gathered fig-leaves, and the milky juice which exudes from them soon causes the

were springing up vigorously, and over fallow ground garnished with blossoming weeds. Now and then we overtook a land tortoise, leisurely making its way across the country. They are very common in the plains of Palestine. Mohammed told me that Christians of the East eat them, especially in Lent, and the peasants catch and carry them to market-towns in great numbers. I afterward heard this confirmed, but I never saw the dish any where.

When we reached the hill country I could scarcely recognize the valleys and the hill-sides, which I had traversed in October, and again in November. Every thing was changed and beautified by Spring. There was no bare earth to be seen, it was all concealed by vividly-green vegetation. The periwinkle was conspicuous, and in the hollows of the white rocks and between the stones tiny flowers were flourishing. The evergreen oaks were garlanded with wild clematis, and a creeper with lilac bell-like blossoms traveled from tree to tree in graceful festoons. The "pastures on the hills were clothed with flocks, and the valleys were covered with corn." Here we saw some human beings, the first we had met on our way. There was a very old man, with a long staff in his hand, sitting under a tree. He rose up when he saw us coming. He wore over his long shirt a short pelisse made of sheep-skin, and an old shawl head-dress. Some youths came forward as we approached. They were bronzed and weather-beaten. They had nothing on but long coarse cotton shirts, girdled with leather belts. Long clumsy-looking guns were slung over their shoulders. Their heads were hooded in old red and yellow shawls. The herds and flocks upon the hills were in their care. The old man raised his hand to his forehead as we went by, and said, "God direct you." One of the

eyelids to swell so much, that they can scarcely be opened for two or three days, but no perceptible injury is done to the eye. When fig-leaves are not to be found, they used stinging nettles instead! The boys said that they cheerfully suffered this self-inflicted pain for a few days, for the sake of the holiday which necessarily accompanied it, and the temporary escape from the monotonous duties of school, and the thick stick of the schoolmaster. However, where Arab boys are kindly and intelligently taught, they learn eagerly and make wonderfully rapid progress.

young shepherds was sitting on a rock playing on a short flute, made of a reed. He placed the end of it in his mouth, and produced soft but clear musical sounds. I could detect only five notes. Mohammed pointed out a black tent, made of camel's-hair cloth and branches, pitched under a large terrebinth-tree. It was no doubt the portable home of the herdsmen. Here we were met by an African horseman, as black as ebony. He was dressed entirely in white and crimson, and was riding at full gallop. He paused to greet us, and said to Mohammed, "The English Consul is near at hand. He is coming forth to meet his sister, but my eyes have seen her first. I will hasten to give him joy, and tell him that she is well and on her way." Mohammed answered, "Go in peace. Blessed is the bearer of good tidings." We were soon in the olive-groves of Shefa 'Amer, and there to my delight I met my brother. Saleh, Habîb, and Stephani joined us. They handed blossoming almond branches to me, in token of welcome. We rode up the steep hill on which the town stands, and alighted at the house of Habîb. He led me into his guest-chamber, a large, eight-windowed, square room. On two sides of it mattresses were placed on the floor, covered with Turkey-carpets, and cushions cased in silk and satin were leaning against the walls. On one side a handsome carpet was spread, with a small silk-covered square mattress, and pillows arranged for one person only. This he said was intended for me. Egyptian matting covered the rest of the floor, and in one corner was a raised bed-stand, with muslin musketo-curtains. We went out on to the broad terrace, which overlooks the sea and the plain, and rested there, exchanging news.

I reported the visit of the Bedouins. My brother explained to me how the townspeople, the villagers, and the peasantry dread the approach of these wanderers with their flocks and herds, for, he said, "They not only spoil the pasture-land, but the crops are endangered. There will be no real safety for cultivators and agriculturists in Palestine till these incursions are put a stop to. The Bedouins come from beyond Jordan, every year, just after the Winter rains are over, when the grain is springing up, so that people do not venture to cultivate more land than they hope to be able to protect. That is one reason why there are so many waste places in the country, and why some portions of the most fertile plains are abandoned by the peasants of Palestine, and only cultivated by wandering tribes, who pitch their tents in a favorable spot, plow, sow, and reap, and then perhaps recross the Jordan, and return no more till the following Spring." According to the third and sixth verses of the sixth chapter of Judges, these wanderers used to commit just such depredations in Palestine three thousand years ago, and at the very same season. "When Israel had sown, then the Amalekites, the Midianites, and the children of the East (that is, from beyond Jordan) came up against them; they destroyed the increase of the earth and left no sustenance for Israel; they came with their cattle and their tents, and they and their camels were without number, and Israel was greatly impoverished." This is one of the chief causes of the present poverty of the country.

When the sun went down we entered the guest-chamber. Large lanterns were lighted and placed on two small stools in the middle of the room. The Governor, Abu Daoud, and his little son, arrived to greet me. Soon afterward Salihh Agha came, in his large scarlet cloak, edged with gold-lace and embroidery. His dark face was deeply shaded by his lilac and silver shawl, worn like a hood, bound round his head by a thick white cord of camel's-hair. His eyelids were kohl-tinged, and he looked rather fierce, on the whole. He and his brother, the celebrated Akîel Agha, are the most powerful and formidable people in the Pashalic of 'Akka. They came originally from Morocco, and are now in the service of the Turkish Government. They have three or four hundred armed horsemen under their command. They may be regarded as the mounted patrols of the hills and plains of Galilee; for it is their duty to keep the roads clear that people may travel in safety. To a considerable extent they succeed; and, thanks to their energy, highway robbery and murders are rare; but they can not of course keep all the wanderers out of the country. Over some tribes Akîel Agha has great influence, but with the Kurds and other hostile hordes he sometimes comes into collision, and warfare ensues, and then all the tribes friendly or in alliance with him naturally come to his assistance. Notwithstanding these outbreaks, it is certain that without the Agha's somewhat irregular guard affairs in the Pashalic of 'Akka would be very much worse, and traveling would be attended with more danger.

Akîel Agha's regiment is a motley crew, formed of desperate men from all parts of the country, reminding one of the four hundred over whom David made himself a captain—1 Samuel xxii, 2. They are distinguished by the name of "Hawara," and are, in fact, a tolerated tribe of marauders, empowered by the Government to keep other tribes in check.

Salihh Agha told me that he had served on the Danube for a short time during the previous year, but he did not like to be so far away from his children. His tents were now pitched at Abilene, about three miles from Shefa 'Amer. He sent his lieutenant to fetch his youngest son for me to see, though it was a dark night and long past sunset. Supper was announced, and we were conducted to another room. Water was poured over our hands as we entered; then we, seven in number, sat on the matted floor, round a circular tray, raised about six inches from the ground, and literally crowded with food. A very long, narrow towel was placed in front of the guests, and reached all round, resting on our knees, and its fringed ends met and crossed where I was invited to take my seat. There were six round dishes of heaped-up rice, boiled in butter; six dishes of boiled wheat, mixed with minced meat and spices; a few plates of fowls and lamb, and bowls of lebbeny or sour cream, and a good supply of sweet cream, cheese, olives, and salad. A cake of bread was placed before each person. As soon as Salihh Agha was seated, he began eating silently and—as it seemed to me—voraciously, quite in Bedouin style, making pellets of the hot rice or wheat in the palm of his hand, and with a skillful jerk tossing them into his mouth. He divided the fowls with his fingers, and did me the honor to pass the most delicate morsels to me. At this rate the contents of the dishes soon disappeared; for all the gentlemen followed the example of Salihh Agha, and as, one by one, they were satisfied, they rose and washed their hands. We then returned to the large room, where many visitors had assembled. Coffee and pipes were served. Songs were sung in praise of the Agha, and of the Vice-Consul, and other guests. The songs which called forth the greatest energy were descriptions of contending armies and of the chase. Arrack was handed round to the singers, but none of the Bedouins partook of it. Little Nimr, the son of the Agha, arrived. He was about seven years old. He came bounding into the room, and was soon wrapped in the folds of his father's scarlet cloak, and covered with kisses and caresses. I was struck by the change in the somewhat stern aspect of Salihh Agha. He was full of tenderness and demonstrative affection for his little son—an ugly boy, but of that piquant description of ugliness which is sometimes so attractive. The lieutenant wished him to go and have supper with him; but he said archly, "Did I come here to have supper or to see the English Sit?"—that is, *the lady*. He came and nestled by my side; took my hands in his; felt my dress, and said it was nice and soft. He showed in every action that he was accustomed to be noticed very much, and to be lovingly treated.

Wrestling was proposed, and Nimr immediately challenged Elias, the son of Stephani, a slightly-made, very pretty boy, also about seven, who deliberately took off his

little brown braided and hooded pelisse, while Nimr threw
down his loose camel's-hair cloak. They each wore scarlet
cloth jackets, with hanging sleeves like the hussars', wide-
sleeved, long white cotton shirts, and very full scarlet
trowsers. They took off the latter and their shoes. Little
Nimr—that is, *the Tiger*—looked proudly impatient. Young
Elias, quietly in earnest, made a spring on Nimr and threw
him down. The men clapped their hands and shouted.
The wrestling was carried on for nearly half an hour.
Elias was, almost in every instance, the victor. At last
Nimr, with a mortified look, after many falls, ran to his
father and hid himself in the folds of the scarlet cloak.
Elias looked quite calm and unexcited by his success.
He sat quietly by my side.

I find that wrestling is a very common exercise in the
Bedouin tents. Salihh Agha's elder boys, of fifteen and
sixteen years of age, were present. They behaved with
great deference and respect to their father, and did not
sit, or take coffee, or smoke in his presence without his
permission; but since that time the eldest son has distinguished himself in warfare, and has killed an enemy
of his tribe with his own hand; so he now enjoys the
dignity and privileges of manhood, and equality with his
father.

The room was cleared of the numerous guests at an
early hour, and then the wife of Habîb—my host—and
four women came to see me. One of them offered to
sleep in the guest-chamber with me, thinking I should
be frightened. The Arabs are very timid at night, and
always congregate together to sleep, and burn lamps to
drive away evil spirits when under a roof. They were
surprised that I could dare to sleep in darkness and
alone.

The next morning Habîb's wife came tapping at my
door early, and with curiosity examined my garments.
The room would soon have been full of women to assist
and inspect my toilet, if I had not decidedly expressed

a wish to dress before I received visitors; so only my hostess remained. She afterward led me to her room on the ground-floor. It was spacious, but very low. Beds, bedding, and carpets were piled up on a raised stone bench on one side, and on the other cooking utensils, dishes, jars, and stores were arranged. At the end of the room, opposite the door, a carpet was spread, and there I was invited to sit down to breakfast. In a corner a woman was preparing meat for cooking, and a large charcoal brazier stood near the door, where a girl was roasting coffee-berries. This room was evidently the parlor, bedroom, and kitchen, all in one. A charcoal-cellar and the stables occupied the other part of the ground-floor.

The mother of my host was busy superintending the baking of the loaves she had made that morning; so I went to the baking-house at the end of the street to see her. Stacks of wood, tree-branches, and thorn-bushes were piled up just outside the entrance to it. I peeped inside the low, stone building. It was like a furnace. The flat loaves were placed on large sheets of iron, which were heated from beneath by a glowing and crackling wood fire. Several women, whose faces, all but the kohl-stained eyes, were vailed, were waiting to take their cakes of bread in to be baked. They held them on round trays made of wicker-work and straw. A poor little boy, who looked very hungry, came with only one small loaf, and watched anxiously for his turn.

A white, semi-transparent lizard ran out from between the stones by the door. I stooped forward to examine it. The women around shrieked out exclamations of horror and disgust. In answer to my questions, they said, "Ya sittee, that is an evil reptile, he crawls over bread or other food, and breathes his poisonous breath upon it, so that he who eats that corrupted food may die, or be as one smitten with leprosy." Mohammed, our Egyptian groom, who approached at the moment, leading the white mare, said, "God preserve us! The words of the women are true words."

I hastened to prepare for riding. A gazelle hunt had been arranged for that day by Salihh Agha, and he had invited us to accompany him. The kawass and grooms and the Agha's people had charge of some fine gazelle-hounds. We met the rest of the party down by the fountain. Three of them were on foot leading boar-hounds. They soon left us, and entered the hill country of Carmel to seek for boars. Little Nimr was riding with the lieutenant on a chestnut horse, whose pedigree they say could be traced back to the time of Solomon. His defense against fascination was a white shell, called *wadat*, fastened to a cord hung round his neck.

We were joined by Habîb and Stephani, and our friend and fellow-townsman Saleh Sekhali. The latter said to me, "You must take notice to-day, ya sittee Miriam, of the great difference between the vision of people who live in towns and of those who live in the open country in tents." I soon had an example of this, for Salihh Agha scanned the horizon, and he and his people discerned in the distance a horse at full gallop. Before we townspeople could distinguish that the horse had a rider, Salihh Agha could describe his dress and even his features, though he was a stranger to him. His words were entirely verified when the rider came within the range of our vision. I congratulated Salihh Agha on the possession of such a faculty, and told him how much it astonished me. He said, "You also have a power which is a marvel to me. I have seen the writing in your book, [he referred to the note-book which I invariably carried and frequently used;] the strokes and figures in it are so fine and small and so close together that it made my eyes ache to look at them." The Agha could not even read or write his own language. Saleh Sekhali remarked, "The good gifts of Allah are divided; praised be Allah!" One of the Bedouins said, "Men who live in towns accustom their eyes to look only from one street to another and from one wall to another, but we who live in tents see to the ends of the earth.

When I am within walls I am as one struck blind, or as if a vail were held before my eyes. There is no space for sight within the towns."

We rode on quietly along the base of the hills among low brushwood, thistles, and flourishing thorns. The grooms had great difficulty in keeping the hounds in, so violently did they struggle to escape. We traversed a well-watered valley, where the mallow was growing extensively, to the hight of one or two feet, with lilac, pink, and silvery gray blossoms, and large, thick leaves. Men and boys were busy cutting it and rapidly filling their baskets. This plant is very much used by the Arabs medicinally. They make poultices of the leaves to allay irritation and inflammation. Lotions are prepared from them also. "Khubazi" is the Arabic word for mallows, and the little, flat, round seed-vessels, so well known to English children as "*cheeses*," are by the Arabs called "Khubiz," that is, "*loaves*," for the Arab bread is always flat and round.

While Stephani was explaining this to me, I saw five gazelles leaping one after another from a thicket of thistles. They disappeared behind some juniper-trees. We directed the attention of the now scattered huntsmen to the spot. They came galloping recklessly over bushes and rocks. The dogs were set free and soon started the gazelles. I rested in my saddle with Saleh Sekhali by my side, watching the graceful bounds of the startled animals, the racing and leaping of the hounds, and the skillful maneuvers of the horsemen. They missed the gazelles, but they succeeded in capturing four fine hares. Then there was a start in another direction, where a troop of antlered gazelles had been seen. I followed in the rear with the lieutenant and his little charge, Nimr, and from a distance we observed the chase for some time. Then we rode across the plain between cultivated fields and gardens of wild flowers. We paused at the fountain of Jethro, which had been fixed upon as the place for meeting after the hunt. There we found the Agha's people preparing dinner. They had dug two broad, shallow pits, in the ground, in which they had made fires of wood and thorns. In one a lamb was being baked whole, and over the other a caldron of rice was boiling.

In a short time the whole party was assembled. The panting dogs rolled themselves in the grass, the horsemen dismounted, and with difficulty the frisky and loudly-neighing horses were tethered. Some were fastened to iron stakes or pins driven in the ground. Grooms and horsemen generally carry them when they journey in places where there are no trees or rocks to which to bind the animals. All the men, however, had not been equally provident. Heavy stones were sought for and halters fastened to them, but not quite securely. The consequence was that two horses escaped and galloped away. I could not help being amused with the chase after these runaways, through marshes and tangled masses of vegetation. I preferred it to the pursuit of the swift-footed, poor little frightened gazelles, whose escape gratified me more than their capture did. The horses were caught at last, together, by the banks of a stream. When we reassembled we took our seats in the shade of the dome of the fountain, with acres of wild flowers round us. Dinner was ready. Two men brought the lamb on a large metal dish or tray; two others carried a mountain of rice, yellow with butter. Boys arrived with bowls of sweet clotted cream and new milk, and dishes of lebbeny. These provisions were arranged on a carpet of clover and mallows and grass. We washed our hands, the servants pouring water over them from earthenware jars. Large Bedouin cloaks and saddle-cloths were spread for us, and we gathered round the smoking and savory fare.

Each one of the Arabs on preparing to touch food uttered the words, "In the name of God the most Bountiful." The lamb was soon skillfully dissected by Saleh with his hunting-knife. A servant handed a flat, thin, large, leathcry loaf to each of us. The lamb was stuffed with rice and minced meat, almonds, raisins, walnuts, and spice. Salihh Agha placed some on my flat loaf, which served me as a plate, and he gave me a lump of meat in my hands. He had separated it from the bone with his short hunting-dagger. The Arabs cook their meat so thoroughly that it is very tender and easily pulled and torn to pieces.

The men made deep depressions in the pyramidal mountain of rice—but each one carefully helped himself from that part of the dish which was nearest to him, and did not, if he could avoid it, disturb the rice near to the hole made in it by his neighbor, except when by way of courtesy he placed a delicate morsel of meat into it now and then. A roasted hare was added to the feast and soon distributed. The cream was eaten voraciously by dipping pieces of bent bread into it and scooping it up as with a spoon, so the spoon and its contents disappeared together. Scarcely a word was spoken by the Arabs during the meal. One by one they retired, saying, "God be praised," and went to the fountain to wash their hands and mouths, uttering an invocation to Allah.

We afterward rested for a short time, and pipes and coffee were handed round. I took the opportunity of putting the Agha, his little son, and his attendant, Khalil, into my sketch-book. The latter seemed rather alarmed when he saw what I had done, and begged of me not to show his portrait in certain districts, for a price was set upon his head, and men sought after him to kill him. In the mean time, the servants and people so far emptied the large metal trays or dishes, that I could plainly see the Arabic sentences engraved on them—extracts from the Koran, and words of praise and prayer. Then most of the men covered their faces and slept, while I wandered about gathering and pressing specimens of all the flowers I could find, little Nimr good-naturedly helping me. Besides the ranunculus and anemone and others equally familiar, I met with many flowers which were strange to me. One was pink, and shaped very like a primrose, with pointed, succulent leaves growing in pairs up the stem. Pressure always changed the color of the flower from pink to blue. This plant would be a welcome addition to our gardens in England, where I have never yet found it. I made a drawing of the dome over the pleasant fountain, and when the sleepers woke they said, "Mashallah, the English girl takes no rest—God gives her strength." We took leave of the Agha and his people and our Shefa 'Amer friends, and rode with Saleh and our servants toward Hâifa, carrying one gazelle and two hares. We saw many groups of horses and camels grazing under the care of the Agha's men on the uncultivated portions of the plain. Tortoises met us and paused as if alarmed. They looked about them for an instant and then drew their heads under their horny shields. Hundreds of small birds fluttered out of the tall grass, disturbed by our approach, and flocks of wild ducks and geese now and then flew across the plain toward the marshes, and sea-gulls flapped their wings above us. We crossed the drifted sand-hills, and cantered along the smooth sea-shore toward the Kishon. Men were standing on its banks, throwing large floating nets, assisted by boys in a little boat in the middle of the river. The fishes of the Kishon are rather small, but abundant, and delicate in flavor.

There were seven ships off Hâifa—Greek, French, and Turkish. The sun was low when we went, one after the other, over the sand-bar. We hastened onward by the water's edge, letting our horses' feet just touch the fringe of the sparkling waves, startling hundreds of small white and sand-colored crabs. Their black eyes are fixed on the points of movable pinnacles, which are thrust out from the round eye-sockets, and stand upright. They scampered hither and thither nimbly, to get out of our way. Their rapidly-moving forms were repeated on the shining wet sands, till shape and shadow were lost under the coming wave. I have often caught and examined these curious little crabs. They are always very light in color—white or sandy—and they vary from one to three inches in length. I think that they must be of the kind called "Cancer Volans." They make holes in the sand, near the sea, and seem very timid when disturbed. They sometimes, however, resent interference. I have seen our gazelle-hound, "Rishch," amuse himself by running after them, tormenting them as a cat does a mouse, or peering into their burrows. When they had an opportunity, they used to cling to his long, delicate nose or lip, and he had some difficulty in shaking them off; but I never saw him destroy or injure one in any way. Fishermen use these crabs for bait, and make traps for them in the sand, in imitation of their burrows.

There were many friends to greet us as we entered the gate of Hâifa; for it was the hour of sunset, when people flock into town after an evening stroll. There was the Mutsellim, surrounded by his suite, walking slowly, with his silver and coral rosary in his hand, and his pipe-bearer by his side. A little group of Jews were there too, some wearing broad-brimmed hats and long gabardines, others with dark shawl-turbans and short cloth or silk pelisses lined with fur. Apart from these were companies of quite unrecognizable women, shrouded in white sheets from head to foot. They looked like moving pillars, for they took such short steps, scarcely lifting their feet from the ground, that their progress should be called gliding instead of walking. Even their little children seemed unnaturally demure and stately.

Short, sturdy-looking oxen, fat sheep, with long, broad, heavy tails, and black, glossy-haired goats, led by the herdsmen, were returning from the pleasant but unprotected pastures to seek shelter within the town walls for the night. The Christians were at the same time entering in at the opposite gate; for they almost always walk toward the western hills and plains—perhaps because their cemeteries are west of the town; while the Moslems prefer the eastern suburbs, where they bury their dead.

The call to prayer was echoing clearly through the town from the balcony of the crescent-crowned minaret, while the vesper-bell was ringing from the little belfry of the Latin church. Some of the people paused from their work, or stood still in the streets, to cross themselves, and to mutter an "Ave Maria" in Arabic; while the rest were declaring, "There is no God but God, and Mohammed is his prophet."

On Sunday my brother always read the Church service in Arabic, in the drawing-room of the Consulate, at nine o'clock. When British vessels were in port, we had service at eleven, with such of the captains and sailors as could attend; and English travelers who were passing through the country occasionally joined us. Saleh Sekhali was invariably present at the Arabic service, and no one was excluded from it. We generally mustered about six or seven. People came perhaps the more readily because they were not pressed or even invited to come. Curiosity induced many to pay one or more visits. The Arabs, and especially the Christian Arabs, could not understand how we could have religion without a *Priest;* solemnity without an *Altar;* how we could worship without a *Church;* or realize the presence of God without the elevation of the *Host.* They were always quietly and earnestly attentive while listening to portions of the Old and New Testament. After prayers, Saleh Sekhali often read by request several chapters, selecting some history or essay complete in itself. Women of the Greek or Latin Churches came occasionally, and remained unvailed when only Christians were present; but if a Moslem was announced they retreated immediately. The Moslems always expressed themselves much pleased with the service, on account of its simplicity and reverential character. I find that, besides the Koran, they regard *al Tora,* the Pentateuch; *a' Zabûr,* the Psalms; *a' Nabiyeh,* the Prophets; and *al Anjîli,* the New Testament, as holy or inspired books. Those who receive any one of these are to be tolerated.

The new Governor, Saleh Bek Abd-ul-Hady, an Arab, came now and then. He said that if there were an English college in the country, he would immediately send his boys to it. Many of our neighbors wished to send their little girls for a few hours every day to my care; but I could not undertake the charge; though, whenever I had time to spare, I encouraged children to come to the house—the only condition being that they should be clean and neat.

Moslem boys do not generally play with Christians, and even the Christian children are divided among themselves. Those belonging to the Greek Church have their street games apart from those who belong to the Latin Church, and they only unite to persecute the poor little Jews.

A gentle-looking little girl, of about six years of age, whose father was a much-respected European and mother an Arab, surprised me very much one day by saying, in Arabic, without any provocation, and with a gesture of scorn, to a Jewish workman, "Go, thou Jew, and be crucified!" The child, naturally good-natured and affectionate, shuddered when she partially understood how cruel and unjust her words had been. By my wish she begged pardon of the Jew; and then, by her own impulse, and to his great wonder, kissed his hands, while tears stood in her eyes.

It was with the hope of checking, as far as I could, this spirit of hatred, intolerance, and persecution, that I encouraged the little ones of Hâifa to meet together in my room. I prepared entertainments for them, played with them, told them stories about England, showed them pictures, avoiding reference to their various creeds. By making them happy together, I hoped that they would learn unconsciously to love one another.

I used sometimes to leave the children to amuse themselves alone, while I retreated to the end of the room, whence I could see and hear all that was going on, without throwing any check on their natural impulses. At such times, I have heard girls of seven and eight years of age, and even younger ones, discussing the comparative value of the wardrobes and jewels of the ladies of Hâifa. One child would say, "Sit Hafîfi has the largest pearls and emeralds," and, "Such a one has the greatest number of diamonds," and "Um Elia has the handsomest dresses and embroidered jackets." They could tell how many coins the women from Nazareth, who lived in Hâifa, had on their head-dresses.

On Sunday, February 24th, a Moslem, of considerable influence and learning, asked permission to attend the Morning Service. We welcomed him, and he, Prayer-book in hand, followed every word attentively, evincing unusual interest, *or curiosity*. He even abandoned his amber rosary for the time. Directly after prayers, however, the beads were to be seen again, rapidly slipping through his well-shaped, carefully-trimmed fingers. A Moslem does not appear at ease till he has a pipe in one hand and a chaplet in the other.

When the Christians had gone, I said to him, "Will your Excellency tell me the use of the rosary? Is it simply a toy, or is it a help to reckon prayer or praise?"

Without showing the slightest unwillingness, he explained its use, saying, "The attributes or characteristic excellencies of God are manifold; but there are ninety-nine which should be learned, and remembered continually, by all men. These rosaries consist of ninety-nine, or thirty-three beads, on which to reckon the attributes, thus"—he took the chaplet out of my hands, and, while passing bead after bead through his fingers, said, with unusual slowness and solemnity: "God the Creator—God the Preserver—God the most Bountiful—God the Deliverer—God the Eternal—God the Ever-present—God the All-seeing—God the most Merciful—God the All-powerful—God the King of Kings"—and so on, till the chaplet had passed three times through his hands; for it consisted of only thirty-three large egg-shaped beads of clouded amber. When he found how much pleased I was, he took pains to teach me the attributes.

I said to him, "Now that your Excellency has made me understand the solemn and beautiful words of the rosary, I shall be always sorry to hear them said quickly and thoughtlessly." He answered, "You are right, O my sister. God is to be approached with reverence." But I could perceive that he found it much more difficult to repeat the attributes *leisurely*, than to utter them, as usual, *rapidly*. After a pause, he said, "To every man who is not hateful or erring, one of these Divine attributes especially belongs, and influences his life." The date of the birth of an individual, in conjunction with his name, properly reckoned, discovers the particular attribute. As an example, he calculated mine, and always afterward called me "*Miriam the Intercessor*." I asked my Moslem teacher in what sense the word "Intercessor" was used as an attribute of God. He regarded it simply as mercy and goodness, and readiness to pardon. Another Moslem told me, one day, that it implied mercy pleading with justice. He acknowledged to me that he did not regard fasts, and forms, and ceremonies as important. He thought that doing our duty to man, and giving thanks to God, were all-sufficient. But he added, "If I did not keep the fasts and feasts, and perform certain ablutions and prayers three times a day, my voice would not be heard in the Medjlis—that is, the Council—and I should lose all my influence." He assured me that there were many enlightened men who felt as he did on the subject, but they hid the thoughts of their hearts.

My brother scarcely ever spoke to Moslems about their religion, and warned me to be cautious how I did so; consequently, I never introduced the subject, directly or indirectly, except when I found myself with any one of superior intelligence and judgment, and then only carefully, and *as an inquirer—never as a teacher or proselytizer*.

I invariably met with good-natured, if not satisfactory, answers, and gained some interesting information. I was satisfied that I did not give offense by the fact that my society was most sought for by those whom I had thus questioned — probably on account of the novelty of the circumstance.

In the afternoon all the Europeans then in Hâifa assembled, and walked in procession to the Latin church, to witness the christening of Jules, the infant son of the French Consul. Kawasses led the way. The child was placed on a crimson silk pillow, and carried by the nurse, Helwé, an old woman of Nazareth. The father, Mons. Aumann, conducted me. He said that there had never before been such a procession of Europeans through those narrow and crooked streets. It was formed of Consuls, and captains whose ships were in port, monks from Mount Carmel, and merchants of Hâifa, and two elderly Greek ladies, with large black lace shawls folded over their red cloth caps. The godmother was of Greek birth, but she wore an Arab costume, and was shrouded in a white sheet. We entered the little square church. Near to the highly and gaudily-decorated altar a number of bareheaded men—Arabs—were prostrating themselves, or beating their breasts. Behind them a group of women and girls, almost shrouded in white sheets, kneeled languidly, with mother-of-pearl rosaries in their henna-stained hands. Their many-colored mundîls—muslin vails—were thrown back over their heads, and bright, everlasting flowers, and jewels, and brighter eyes, in dark settings of kohl, were exposed. The men — Arabs — carefully avoided looking toward the women; but some of the latter seemed to expect to attract the admiration of the less scrupulous Europeans, and were not disappointed. On a table near to the font sacred oil and salt, and other necessaries for the ceremony of christening, were arranged on a white embroidered cloth. The parish priest read the baptismal service in Latin, but the little hero of the day somewhat disturbed and disconcerted him by screaming lustily. He strongly objected to the taste of the salt, and to the application of the water to his head, and of the oil to his chest. It was a relief to every one present, especially to the priest, when the ceremony was over, and the "newly-made little Christian"—as they all called him—was comforted in the arms of his nurse. We returned to the French Consulate. There was a large gathering in the marble-paved *salon*, where the happy mother received the congratulations of her neighbors, for Judas was her only son. It was quite a fête-day in Hâifa, especially among the Latins. Oranges boiled in sugar and spice, lemons cut up and preserved in honey, all sorts of Oriental confectionery made of sweetened starch and gums, and French *bonbons* and *liqueurs*, were distributed.

I took leave of the assembled guests, and strolled with my brother out at the West Gate. The declining sun was brightening the green slopes, the trees, and white rocks of the Carmel range. A small pink flower had sprung up plentifully in the stony places of the plain. Each blossom was in the form of a foliated Greek cross, and the small green leaves were heart-shaped. We sat on the mossy trunk and in the lengthening shade of a large locust-tree, discussing the events of the day, enjoying the scene and the silence; for we had wandered quite out of sight of the town. We were in the midst of a grove of fig, locust, and olive-trees. The ground was carpeted with wild flowers; the hills, fragrant with aromatic herbs, rose behind us; and the broad sea, red with the rays of the setting sun, was before us.

Our *tête-à-tête* was interrupted by the approach of our kawass, who came to announce the arrival of a special messenger from Jerusalem. The messenger himself soon appeared. He was a tall, powerful-looking African, very black and bony, clad simply in a coarse, unbleached cotton shirt, girdled with a leather strap. A large white turban protected his head and shaded his face. His wide, pliant feet were bare. He had walked all the way from Jerusalem in three days, and was the bearer of important dispatches from Her Britannic Majesty's Consul, Mr. Finn. He drew the packet from his bosom, and kissed my brother's hands as he presented it, and then stood resting on his long, thick staff.

I found that the letters contained directions for my brother to proceed immediately to Nablûs, to report the state of affairs there, and to ascertain the true cause or causes of the disturbances in the town and in the mountain districts around. A letter from Mrs. Finn advised and invited me to accompany him as far as Nablûs; that an escort might meet me there to take me on to Jerusalem to spend Easter with her. Rumors had reached Hâifa every day for some time past of skirmishes, and even pitched battles, between the supporters of Mahmoud Bek Abd-ul-Hady, the newly-appointed Governor of Nablûs, and the partisans of his predecessor in office. A tour through the Jebel Nablûs district was in consequence considered rather hazardous, and rain would be sure to set in in a day or two. However, I consented to go, on the condition that my brother would promise to travel exactly as if he were alone, both with regard to the selection of the route and of the halting-places, and the length of each day's journey. This settled, he proved to me that he understood I was in earnest by saying, "Then we will start at sunrise to-morrow, for that is what I should do if I were going alone."

This was a sudden change in our plans. Till past midnight I was busy packing portmanteaus, and providing for the safety of the house and furniture for an indefinite period, and guarding against the intrusion of rats and mice, moth and rust.

In the mean time my brother was in his office, in earnest consultation with his agent and our Governor, Saleh Bek. The latter asked to see me. I went to him, and he said, "My sister, you have a brave heart. You are going on a difficult journey, but you have no reason to fear any one, for you have no enemies. After a day or two you will reach my town—Arrabeh—and there you will find rest, and my wives and my children will welcome you, for they are still there. I have prepared to receive them here, and have sent for them several times, but they have not courage to travel, now that war has broken out. If you reach Arrabeh in safety, and they see you, perhaps their hearts will be made strong. God be with you and protect you! May you find rest at Arrabeh, and peace whithersoever you go!"

CHAPTER IX.

FROM HÂIFA TO ARRABEH.

AFTER a few hours of perfect rest, I rose before the sun, on Monday, the 25th of February. Katrîne, who had begged to accompany us, had packed up her bundle of clothes, and was rejoicing at the thought of spending the Festival of Easter at Jerusalem, for she was an earnest devotee. She had newly dressed her eyes with kohl for the occasion. I told her of the difficulties of the journey. She assured me that she had no fear, for she had made a pilgrimage to the Chapel of the Madonna on Mount Carmel, and wore round her neck a potent charm, which she had obtained there, believing it would preserve her from all danger. It was a scapulary, that is, a rudely-printed picture of the Virgin and Child, on a piece of linen, one or two inches square, said to be a portion of the smock which the blessed Virgin left on Mount Carmel when she graciously appeared in a vision to one of the monks of old. This smock must have been a very large one, for it furnishes an unlimited number of scapularies, which are sold by thousands to pilgrims from all parts of Europe. All the native Christians of Hâifa wear them, and most of the Europeans do also. I only know two or three exceptions. Some scapularies are enshrined in crystal lockets, or adorned with spangles and beads. Others are simply bound or lined with silk, or embroidered at the edges. Once, when I was ill, poor Katrîne put one secretly round my neck while I slept; and now, in preparation for the journey, she tried to induce me to avail myself of its protection.

The court was crowded with well-wishers, who came to say, "God be with you," and to express their regrets at our departure. The general impression was, that we were going on a perilous expedition. Town Arabs, especially the Christians, are generally rather timid, and being somewhat deliberate in their movements, they were wondering at the rapidity of ours. All articles of value were deposited at the French Consulate, the perishable stores were distributed, and very soon after sunrise we were mounted and ready to start. A guide, fully armed, furnished by our governor, with our kawass, Hadj Dervish, led the way. I followed, with my brother, and the French Consul's Arab secretary, who had begged to join us. Then came the muleteer, with the luggage and canteen, Mohammed, our Egyptian groom, Katrine, shrouded in a large camel's-hair cloak and mounted on horseback, and the tall African messenger on foot. We had advised him to rest a day or two at Hâifa, but he declared that he was not tired, and he said that riding would be more fatiguing to him than walking, for he was not accustomed to it.

When we had taken leave of our friends at the gate of the town, and had passed the Moslem cemetery, Katrine had disappeared. On inquiry, I heard that, in spite of her scapulary, her courage had failed her, and she had turned back, saying to the groom, that she thought it would rain, so she would go home again! Our agent, who was riding with us a short distance on our way—receiving final instructions—undertook to protect her during our absence.

The hills around were capped with black clouds, and before we had passed the gardens of Hâifa a heavy shower commenced. We drew our hooded cloaks over our heads, and rode on regardless of it. When we reached the rocky spring of Sa'âdeh, the rain-clouds suddenly traveled away in all directions, leaving a bright bit of deep-blue sky just above us; but on the mountains and over the sea the rain still fell—dark heavy curtains seemed to be hanging from the heavens, and they were torn and swayed by the changeful breezes. The spring among the rocks and reeds had considerably increased in force and extent since I had seen it in December. We crossed it cautiously and in safety. Many a tree had been torn up by the roots by the Winter torrents. Large stone bowlders, which a short time before were firmly imbedded in the earth, had been undermined, and stood tottering on the hill-side, as if ready to fall on us. The rain-refreshed grass and trees and flowers glistened in the gleams of sunlight, and filled the air with sweet odors.

We left the Nazareth road and took a south-easterly direction, along the borders of the almost dry bed of a branch of the Kishon. We entered the "Wady-el-Milh," the Valley of Salt. Among other wild flowers on the wayside, I recognized with strange delight patches of "crimson-tipped" daisies. It was midday. We were beginning to feel hungry, and told the guide to pause at the nearest spring, that we might alight and eat. We met a few camels grazing on mallows and clover. They were branded with marks which told us that they did not belong to the peasantry. "These camels proclaim that Bedouins are in the neighborhood. We will seek them out, and take our dinner with them to-day, for wherever we find them, we shall also find a fountain of good water," said my brother.

When we had rounded the next hill, we saw a number of square black tents, high up among the rocks and trees on the opposite side of the valley. We crossed the deep and stony river-bed, and scrambled up the pathless hillside, over the rocks and tangled brushwood. A group of Bedouins, in their large, heavy, white and brown cloaks, and red and yellow fringed shawl head-dresses, came leaping down to meet us, and to guide and welcome us to their encampment, in the midst of which we dismounted. There were fifteen tents altogether. We were led toward the sheikh's tent, which, like all the rest, was formed of very coarse black and brown "*curtains of goats' hair*,"* supported by slender trunks of trees and strong reeds from the banks of the Jordan. A rude palisading, of inter-

---
* See Exod. xxxv, 26; xxxvi, 14.

woven branches, divided the tent into two parts. In the lesser compartment some kids and lambs were guarded, and a group of women hastily retired from the other part, that it might be prepared for us. A little, half-naked, bronzed Bedouin boy swept the floor of earth with the leafy branches of a "box" tree. A weather-beaten old woman, in tattered garments, but with large silver bracelets on her shriveled arms, came forward and spread a rug or carpet for us. It was made of very coarse wool, and looked something like crochet-work, or close knitting, and was evidently of Bedouin manufacture. We were soon seated on it, and the sheikh and a number of men, smoking long pipes, took their seats opposite to us, in a half-circle, on the ground just outside the open front of the tent, thus completely inclosing us. There were between sixty and seventy people altogether in the encampment. They had large flocks of sheep and goats under their care; and, as we anticipated, they were near to a "fountain of sweet water."

The sheikh wished to have a kid killed for us. We declined, as we were in haste; but though we were provided with bread, my brother explained to me that etiquette obliged us to partake of theirs, and he said, "Go and find the women, it will be a good opportunity for you to see the process of Bedouin bread-making." I went to the other end of the encampment—the glow of a red fire between the trees guided me. Two women were skillfully stirring and spreading burning embers on the ground with their hands, as freely as if fire had no power to hurt them. Another was kneading some paste. The rest of the women and girls came crowding round me caressingly and wonderingly. They stroked my face and hair, and especially marveled at my closely-fitting kid gloves, which I put off and on for their amusement. They exclaimed repeatedly, "O, work of God!" One of the elder women said, "Where are you going, O my daughter?" I answered, "O my mother, I am going to '*El Kuds*' 'The Holy'"— that is, Jerusalem. Then she said, as if by way of explanation to the others, "They are pilgrims. God preserve them!" The women were all of a dark-bronze color. Their faces, and arms, and necks were tattooed and stained with henna, red and orange color. Their rather thick but well-shaped lips were *perfectly blue*, indigo having been carefully pricked into them in little spots close together; it produced a very unpleasing effect. The edges of their eyelids were blackened with soot. Their only garments were wide, loose, coarse cotton shirts, open at the bosom; some were black, others blue and brown. Over their heads black woolen shawls, edged with bright-colored stripes, were tastefully and simply worn. Many of the women were decked with clumsily-wrought silver bracelets and finger and ear-rings. None of them wore shoes. The dirty, tawny children were all nearly naked; but their heads were covered with white quilted skull-caps or red tar-bûshes, to which shells and beads were fastened—amulets to protect the wearers from harm.

A young mother, more intelligent-looking than her companions, came forward and saluted me gently. She, unlike the rest, wore a crimson shawl on her head, and the edges of her long blue shirt were embroidered round the sleeves and round the neck and bosom with coarse thread, wrought in quaint patterns, such as we see on very old-fashioned samplers in cross-stitch. She proudly showed me her little swaddled son. The complexion of his face was surprisingly fair; in fact, it was of a deathly whiteness. This, I was told, is usually the case in infancy among the Bedouins. I took the unyielding, stiffened, mummy-like little figure in my arms. His swaddling-clothes were of coarse indigo-colored cotton, bound round symmetrically with narrow strips of crimson leather, such as I had seen entwined about the Bedouin spears. The mother evidently had considerable taste in the arts of adornment, and in every respect she was superior-looking to the rest. In the mean time the bread was being made. A brisk wood-fire was kindled in the open air, on a small circular hearth, formed of smooth round pebbles, spread evenly and close together. When this primitive hearth was sufficiently heated, the embers were carefully removed, and well-kneaded paste, flattened out by the hand, was thrown on to the hot stones, and quickly covered with the burning ashes. In this way several large cakes of unleavened bread were soon made ready.

I returned to the tent. Our canteen and provisions had been unpacked, much to the amusement of the men, who were especially pleased with the knives, and forks, and spoons. Wooden bowls of cream and milk were brought, and the flat cakes of bread were served quite hot. They were about half an inch in thickness, and had received the impression of the pebbles of which the hearth was composed. This most likely was the same sort of bread which Sarah of old made for the strangers, in obedience to Abraham's desire, when he said, "Make ready quickly three measures of fine meal, knead it, and make cakes *upon the hearth.*"

The women stood in a group at a little distance looking on while we cut up our cold roast chicken. They had never seen people eat with knives and forks before. It must have appeared very barbarous to them. They laughed shyly, and hid their faces with the ends of their shawl head-dresses when they were noticed, and suddenly they disappeared altogether, as if in obedience to a given signal. I made a sketch of Kasîm, the handsomest and most stately-looking of the men. He blushed like a girl when he saw his face in my book. He expressed great curiosity about our intended movements, and was very communicative. The other men asked no questions — neither did they seem willing to answer any, except in the usual words "*Yâllem Allah*"—"God knows."

After a final cup of coffee had been passed round we remounted, and went on our way at about two o'clock, riding over hills covered with wild thyme, and through valleys where grain sown by the Bedouins was springing up; but it was thirsting for rain. We rose high on to the Carmel range, overlooking the plain of Esdraelon, and sometimes catching glimpses of the great sea on our right. We rode for a considerable distance without seeing any towns, or villages, or even tents, or the slightest indication of a road or track; so that I could fancy that I was traveling in an uninhabited country, except when we saw a long string of camels laden with charcoal, or a line of donkeys carrying such large burdens of thorns and brushwood that they looked just like hedges moving briskly along. They were evidently conveying fuel from a well-wooded district to towns and villages in the treeless plains. We were in a part of Palestine rarely, if ever, trodden by strangers, where the peculiarities of Eastern traveling are more apparent than in the more frequented roads. We discovered that our guide, who had been directed to conduct us toward Arrabeh, had misled us, and was taking us by a circuitous and unmarked route in order to avoid passing near to certain villages, where his life would have been in danger, for a price was set upon his head by his enemies in that district. He led us into the fertile plains west of the Carmel range.

Rain began to fall in torrents. Mohammed, our groom, threw a large Arab cloak over me, saying, "May Allah preserve you, O lady, while he is blessing the fields." Thus pleasantly reminded, I could no longer feel sorry to see the pouring rain, but rode on rejoicing for the sake of the sweet Spring flowers and the broad fields of wheat and barley.

For two or three hours we had not seen a building of any kind, not even a ruined khan in a valley, nor a watchtower on the hill-sides. At last we passed a small walled town, built on a low rounded hill, the eastern slope of which was dotted with white grave-stones. Olive-trees, fruit gardens, and plowed land encircled it. In a quarter of an hour we came to a little village, where the rude dwellings were crowded closely together, as if for safety, and flocks and herds fed in the neighborhood, guarded by shepherds fully armed. The rain ceased, and the sun shone out for a few minutes, with a red glow, over a waving field of wheat, and then went down. We desired the guide to halt at the next village. We rode on southward, and in about twenty minutes reached a place called "Khubeizeh," on account of the abundance of mallows growing wild in the neighborhood. A barricade of mud surrounded the village. The houses were so low that even I could not have stood upright in any one of them. Some were merely hollow cones of earth, others were square and roofed with brushwood. Some were like burrows, scarcely above the ground, and all were desperately dirty. The narrow streets, or paths between the houses, were mud and slime and standing water. The wretched-looking inhabitants followed us about or peeped at us from their miserable abodes, and a troop of dogs barked in loud chorus as we traversed the village in all directions. We found no spot suitable for a halting-place, so we hastened onward and soon arrived at Mehûf, a crowded hamlet, quite as uninviting as Khubeizeh.

The guide assured us that we should find safe shelter at Kefr Kâra, a Moslem village about three miles further south. No Christians inhabit any of the villages in this district. We decided to go on, although it was already very dark. Red, blinking watchfires could be seen here and there on the hills around, and rain began to fall as we rode across the plain as quickly as the darkness would let us. We sent our kawass on before, to announce our approach to the sheikh of Kefr Kâra. When we arrived he was at the entrance of the village, attended by a lantern-bearer, ready to receive us, and he said, "Welcome, and be at rest, we are your servants, all that we have is yours."

We found Kefr Kâra larger and rather superior to the other villages. There was only one stone house in it, however, and to that we were immediately conducted. We gladly dismounted at the open door, within which we could see the glow and smoke of a large wood fire. I found that the house consisted of only one very lofty room, about eighteen feet square. The roof of heavy beams and tree-branches, blackened with smoke, was supported by two wide-spreading arches. The walls were of roughly-hewn blocks of stone, not plastered in any way. Just within the door, a donkey and a yoke of oxen stood. I soon perceived that rather more than one-third of the room was set apart for cattle, where the floor, which was on a level with the street, was of earth, and partly strewed with fodder. We were led up two stone steps on to a dais, twenty-two inches high, where fragments of old mats and carpets were spread, and where three venerable-looking old men—one of whom was quite blind—sat smoking. They rose and welcomed us, and then resumed their pipes in silence. They wore large white turbans and dark robes. Their long beards were bushy and gray. Their feet were naked, for they had left their red shoes by the steps leading on to the dais. The sheikh took down some mats and cushions from a recess in the wall, and arranged them for us on the floor. In the mean time, the mule was led in and unladen, and our two horses were unsaddled and lodged in the lower part of the room! The sheikh asked us to allow his oxen to remain there, as it was likely to be a wet night. My brother consented, but desired that no others should be brought in, and that shelter should be found elsewhere for the horses of our servants and attendants. Nearly in the middle of the raised floor, the large fire made of piled-up wood and thorns, and resinous evergreen shrubs, was burning briskly. The deep troughs, or mangers, about three feet by one, were hollowed out of the broad stone coping at the edge of the dais. Mohammed, our groom, filled these troughs with barley, and our tired animals enjoyed their evening meal.

While our supper was in course of preparation, the sheikh, at my request, took me to see his wives. He led me out into the darkness. A little lantern, which he carried, partially lighted the muddy streets, and was reflected in many a pool of standing water. My guide paused in front of an irregular building of mud and stone, and, without saying a word by way of introduction, left me alone at the threshold of the wide-open door. Just within it I saw a group of harsh-voiced, loudly-talking women standing in front of an immense wood fire, which was burning on a raised floor, about three feet high. They were evidently entertaining another group of women, who sat on the dais round the fire, silently and eagerly listening. The leaping flames lighted up their large dark eyes, their long glistening teeth, and the silver coins of their head-dresses. I stood for a moment watching them, before I claimed their attention. There was no outlet for the smoke, except a hole over the door; so it was rather difficult, at first, to distinguish the shape of the room. There were curiously-irregular projections, and niches, and recesses, where mattresses were piled up, and jars and cooking utensils were arranged. The walls were of baked mud or clay, blackened with smoke.

When I announced myself, some of the young girls uttered exclamations of wonder and fear, imagining me to be a spirit; but the elder women silenced them, and welcomed me calmly and kindly, without showing any signs of surprise, though I was afterward assured that I was the first Afranjî—that is, European—lady who had ever paid a visit to Kefr Kâra.

The women who stood below lifted me on to the dais, the roof over which was so low that I could only just stand upright. I sat down with the group round the fire, and took off my hat and hooded cloak, and one of the women undertook to dry them. They were all exceedingly astonished that I only kept my head covered when out of doors—heads are never uncovered in the East, except as a sign of deep mourning. The women were dark, dirty, and rather haggard-looking, but dignified in their manners and movements. The girls were strong and handsome, but their well-shaped mouths and lower jaws were disproportionately large. They all wore head-dresses of silver coins, like the women of Nazareth, with the addition of three or seven chains of silver links and coins, hanging from the end of the head-dress on each side, in the same way that unfastened bonnet-strings hang. Their dresses were of dark indigo-colored cotton, very thick and coarse, open at the front, like loose pelisses, girdled and worn over white shirts and dark cotton trowsers. Their arms and faces were tattooed with spots and stars, their eyebrows were blackened with a thick pigment, and their eyelids stained with soot. Many of them wore silver bracelets. The ragged and half-naked tawny children were agile and rapid in their movements, observant, and mischievous. The young girls were soon satisfied that I was not a spirit, and they became very demonstrative and caressing, and were full of curiosity. One of them took a flaming brand from the fire, and held it near to my face, that she and the rest might see me more plainly. A very old woman, who seemed to have authority over them, rebuked them, saying, "Be silent, O foolish ones! if the stranger had a hundred tongues she could not answer all your questions; and do you not see that the poor child is tired? Let her rest in peace." Then they made coffee for me; and while I was taking it, a boy, better dressed than the others, came bounding in, exclaiming, "Where is the white lady? The Afranjî will not eat till she comes." So I rose and followed him into the street, where the sheikh awaited me with the lantern.

I returned to the house. My brother had caused the wood fire to be removed, for the smoke almost suffocated us. A small red-clay lamp stood in a niche in the wall, and the lantern was placed in a recess near to the door. Our supper of grilled chickens, hot bread, and sweet cream, was spread for us on the floor of the dais. At the same time a large wooden bowl of dried peas boiled in oil, and a dish of lebbany, or sour milk, and cakes of bread, were brought for our attendants and servants, who were grouped together with the horses in the lower part of the room.

After we had eaten, a number of the villagers came to see us. They all smoked their pipes, and drank their coffee, almost in silence, with the exception of the old blind man, who asked many questions. He, as if privileged by his blindness, begged me to put my hand in his, and then told me to tell him what I was like, that he might see me in his thoughts. He said, "Are you young, or are you old? Your voice is soft, like the voice of a little child; but your words are wise."

By degrees our silent guests left us. Last of all, the gentle old blind man, led by the sheikh, went away, wishing us rest and peace. The latter promised that he would send us some pillows and mattresses to sleep on. No women had visited us.

Just as we were wondering what sort of bedding we should have that night, to my great surprise and delight, the Arab-Jewish upholsterer, who had worked for me at Hâifa, made his appearance, carrying a nice new mattress, quilt, and red-silk pillow. He was a peddler upholsterer, but his head-quarters were at Hâifa. He had been engaged at Kefr Kâra making a stock of lehaffs and mattresses for an approaching wedding. As soon as he heard of my arrival, he insisted on bringing one of the new mattresses for me. He spread it in a corner of the dais. Then he brought another for my brother, and a third for the French Consul's secretary, and did all that he could to make us comfortable.

I was so tired, that I was glad to lie down directly, on the sheetless mattress, resting my head on the red-silk pillow. I covered my face with a handkerchief, and tried to forget where I was; remaining resolutely still, notwithstanding the attacks of a multitude of fleas. I had often encountered large assemblies of these lively little tormentors, but their numbers were as nothing in comparison with the fleas of Kefr Kâra.

A large cat, walking gently and cautiously over my head, startled me out of a dreamy and restless sleep. I roused myself and looked about. It was midnight. The lamp was still burning, and by its dim light I could make out the strange groups around. The first object upon which my eyes fell was the tall African messenger. He was on the opposite side of the dais, standing upright, leaning his back against the wall. His arms were folded, his eyes were wide open and staring. He looked immovable as a statue. His white turban, and the shining light of his eyes, made his head appear the most conspicuous object in the room. My brother was soundly sleeping on a mattress not far from me, and beyond him the Arab secretary, quite concealed under heavy quilts, was loudly snoring. The armed guide and our kawass, rolled up in their cloaks and carpets, were lying on the edge of the dais, their saddle-bags and saddle-cloths serving as pillows. The muleteer, resting on the luggage, and our groom, Mohammed, on a heap of fodder, were just below, with the tethered horses. The air of the room was heated and oppressive, and dense with tobacco smoke. There was no window, but over the closed door there were five small round holes. There were two deep, arched recesses in the walls for mattresses, cushions, and jars. In a recess in the lower part of the room the saddles and horse-trappings of our little party were piled up. In the stone wall, close to my resting-place, was the trap-door of a corn granary. I could hear rats and mice within, nibbling and scratching, and the gray cat again and again returned to post herself on my pillow. I sat up. My horse started out of his sleep, neighed and shook himself—walking as far as his halter would let him, disturbing the repose of all the rest, and especially of the donkey.

The groom rose, trimmed the lamp, spoke a few comforting words to his favorite horse, then rolled himself up in his camel's-hair cloak, and crouched down on the heap of fodder. In a little while there was silence and sleep all around again. But I was sleepless. The mysterious-looking figure of the black man completely fascinated me;

I could not long together keep my eyes turned away from him; he did not move a muscle or blink his great shining eyes. I could not decide whether he was asleep or awake, though I looked at him till I was almost mesmerized. I rested my head on my pillow, full of thought. Suddenly the idea entered my mind that it must have been in such a house as this that Christ was born, and in a manger, such as I saw before me, that he was cradled. It was Winter-time when, in obedience to the decree of Cæsar Augustus, Joseph the carpenter, of the house and lineage of David, went up from Galilee, out of the city of Nazareth, into Judea, unto the city of David, which is called Bethlehem, to be taxed or enrolled with Mary, his espoused wife.

I imagined Joseph anxiously seeking shelter and rest for her after her long journey. All the guest-chambers were already filled, and there was no room in the inn— that is, there was no room for them in the "house of rest for wayfarers"—"*the place of unlading.*" The raised floor was crowded with strangers, who had, like them, come to be taxed. But Joseph and Mary may have taken refuge from the cold in the lower part of the room. In imagination I could see them, half-hidden by the cattle, and warmed by the blazing fire of wood and crackling thorns burning on the raised floor close by. "And so it was, that while they were there the days were accomplished that she should be delivered; and she brought forth her first-born Son, and wrapped him in swaddling-clothes, and laid him in a manger." The manger was very likely close by her side, hollowed out at the edge of the dais, and filled with soft Winter fodder. I raised my head and looked at one of the mangers, and I felt how natural it was to use it as a cradle for a newly-born infant. Its size, its shape, its soft bed of fodder, its nearness to the warm fire, always burning on the dais in mid-winter, would immediately suggest the idea to an Eastern mother. I fell asleep, picturing to myself the whole scene—"the babe, wrapped in swaddling-clothes," "*lying in a manger*," Joseph and Mary joyfully watching over him, and the strangers and shepherds pronouncing blessings and congratulations.

When I awoke in the early morning, the level rays of the sun were streaming in at the wide-open door. The black man had gone. The Vice-Consul was sitting up on his mattress, performing his toilet under difficulties—his kawass acting as valet. The dragoman beyond was shaking the long purple silk tassel of his red tarbûsh into shape. The horses and other animals had been led away; and crowds of people stood at the door looking in. I kept quietly concealed under my quilt till my brother and all the men had disappeared; then some women came, bringing water to pour over my hands. At my request they closed the door, and the five round holes above it admitted daylight and a number of silvery-winged doves. They came one after the other, fluttered once round the room near to the rafters, and then flew away again in regular order. The women were exceedingly interested with the contents of my dressing-case, and wished to make experiments with them, but to this I decidedly objected. They had never heard of such a thing as a tooth-brush; yet their teeth—which reminded me of the teeth of wild animals, especially of the feline race—were as bright, regular, and healthy-looking as possible. Perhaps one of the causes of this is, that they invariably wash and cleanse their mouths thoroughly immediately after every meal.* Almost all Orientals adopt this excellent custom; but by the Moslems it is regarded as a religious and obligatory ceremony, and the act is accompanied by an ejaculatory prayer for purity. I had necessarily slept in my clothes. I shook myself into order as well as I could, and resumed my riding-habit, while the women rolled up the mattresses and lehaffs, and carried them away. Then I

---

* Is this custom indirectly alluded to in Amos iv, 6, where it is written: "I have given you cleanness of teeth and want of bread in all your places?"

was led to the house which I had visited on the previous evening. The hostess wore a striped silk red and purple pelisse, or open dress, instead of the cotton one in which I had seen her before. She received me very cordially, and would not allow any intruders to enter, while I had some new milk, bread, and coffee, and made notes of my night-thoughts. It was rumored that the manuscript book which I carried contained talismanic directions for seeking treasures. It had a patent lock and key, and a book thus guarded had never before been seen there.

In the mean time, my brother was breakfasting with the sheikh elsewhere, gleaning valuable information, and planning the day's journey. We afterward met in the large room—of which I made a rough sketch and measurements. It had been swept, and the dais was garnished with reed matting and cushions, and two old fringed carpets, about the size of ordinary hearth-rugs. We sat down together, and consulted our maps—Robinson's and a French one. As regarded that district, they proved very contradictory, and did not assist us much.*

At eight o'clock, our horses and attendants were ready. We mounted, and rode slowly. We were surrounded and followed by a great number of the villagers. The sheikh was in earnest conversation with my brother. The old blind man walked by my side, with his hand resting on the neck of my horse, which was carefully led by the wandering Jew upholsterer along the uneven and crooked streets. We paused when we came to the thrashing-floor, outside the village, and there took leave of our Kefr Kâra friends. The blind man pressed my hand to his lips and to his forehead, saying, "May Allah preserve you, O my daughter, and keep you from all harm!" With blessings and pleasant words ringing in our ears, we cantered quickly over a broad cultivated plain, across a stony river-bed, and then

---

* Even on the chart illustrating Murray's delightful Handbook, Kefr Kâra and Khubeizeh are not marked. But on a map in the *Weekly Dispatch Atlas*, Khubeizeh, and the villages in its neighborhood, may be found, and they appear to me to be quite correctly placed.

rose on to a range of hills, dark with evergreen oaks, and carpeted with wild flowers. We rode eastward, overlooking plains and valleys. The black man was still with us. I was informed that he was an inveterate opium-eater, and always slept in a standing or sitting posture, with his eyes wide open.

In half an hour, we came to a little, crowded, mud and stone village, at the edge of a wood. Here we dismissed our guide, for we could not depend upon him. He had enemies in the district, and traveled in fear. We alighted. A carpet was spread for us on a grassy and shady slope, just above a thrashing-floor, and there we took pipes and coffee with the sheikh. The elders and chief men of the village, in their great camel's-hair cloaks and white turbans, sat on the ground in a half circle opposite to us. They were fully armed. After the usual greetings and compliments, they eagerly asked for "khubber," that is, news, saying, "Whence do you come, O my lord, and what tidings do you bring?" They were all very active and energetic-looking, communicative, and inquiring. They differed in these respects from the Bedouins we had met in the Valley of Salt, and from the villagers of Kefr Kûra.

I asked my brother how this striking contrast could be accounted for. He said, "This valley is in a very lonely, unprotected, and fertile spot. It is on the confines of the Jebel Nablûs, a district which is very frequently disturbed, as at present, by civil war. The inhabitants are obliged to be constantly on the alert, and prepared for any emergency. This, perhaps, gives them that look of activity and intelligence which is common to all people who are habitually exposed to great dangers, and who energetically but cautiously prepare to meet them." An animated exchange of news took place. The young men and boys stood in little groups around, while the elders smoked and talked by turns.

Just beyond the village, there were some ragged black hair tents among the trees. They belonged to a party of gipsy tinkers and blacksmiths, who journey from village to village, just as their brethren do in the lonely parts of England; committing depredations in the farm-yards, and sometimes breaking into houses. These gipsies came out of their tents to look at us. Their complexions were very dark. The men had rather a sullen and stern expression of countenance, and were clothed in sackcloth, girdled with leather straps. Black shawls were fastened on their heads with ropes made of camel's-hair, in Bedouin style. The women and girls seemed hardy, bold, and daring, but good-natured. Their features were strongly marked. They approached and examined me with curiosity, and expressed surprise that I traveled without any female attendants. In their greetings I observed that they did not utter the name of *Allah*, though it is generally the first word on the lips of an Arab woman. The women wore long, heavy, dark, ungirdled shirts, made of coarse wool—not unlike the shapeless gowns provided for female bathers at English watering-places. They had no other garment, except a shawl or kerchief tied over their heads, from under which their straggling unbraided black hair escaped. Broad silver armlets adorned their tattooed arms, and clumsy cabalistic rings were displayed on some of the swarthy hands, to protect the wearers from harm.

The boys were naked, or nearly so. They tried to attract my notice by vigorously turning summersaults, walking on their heads, and suspending themselves from high tree-branches by their pliant feet.

These gipsies, besides attending to their tinkering, perform most astounding feats of jugglery, gymnastics, and magic. When they visit towns or large villages, they are gladly engaged by the inhabitants to tell fortunes, interpret dreams and dark sayings, and to give entertainments in private houses or in the market-places.

I have several times seen companies of this mysterious race of people in Hâifa, and have witnessed their exhibitions of necromancy, or rather sleight-of-hand, by torch-light in the open air. Among other performances, they call a boy out of the midst of the crowd. Then, *to all appearance*, they cut him into six pieces! After a few minutes of intense excitement and suspense of the lookers-on, the separated portions of the body are reunited, and the restored boy jumps up and runs away. The Arabs generally, and especially of the lower classes, firmly believe in the occult power of the gipsies. They are hated and feared, yet patronized and encouraged to a remarkable degree. These people speak Arabic, but they also have a language peculiar to themselves. The late learned Dr. Duff told us that the language of the gipsies in India, of which he had made a vocabulary, was somewhat similar to it, and many words were identical. These people are very mischievous, and when they are in the neighborhood, it is necessary to look well after the fowls, lambs, and kids, and to set a double watch in the orchards and vineyards, and the gardens of cucumbers.

The village sheikh provided us with a guide to conduct us to Arrabeh, and we remounted. The gipsy women could not understand how I could ride with both my feet on the same side of the horse. They said, "The hills round about Arrabeh are very steep, my lady; you will fall from your horse if you sit like that."

We rode for a short distance southward, with the Great Sea now and then visible on our right hand. Then we turned abruptly eastward, and pursued our way for about two miles in single file, in a narrow path, under the shade of trees. The glossy-leaved evergreen oak and the hawthorn were the most conspicuous. Cyclamen, ferns, mazereons, mosses, and lichens grew on and round the rocks in the deep shade; while here and there in sunny glades wide-open ranunculi, anemones, dandelions, and daisies appeared. Some of the tree branches were covered with gall-berries. We lingered to examine the ruins of an ancient town, of which no tradition even is left. There were large beveled blocks of stone foundations of walls, small tesseræ, and other traces of human art, extending for about half a mile along the hill-side. We did not see any sculptures or inscriptions. Our guide could not tell us any thing about the place. He said it was called "El Khirbeh," "The Ruin." A shepherd whom we saw seated on the edge or parapet of an ancient cistern gave us the same unsatisfactory answer. We descended into a broad plain, where thorns and thistles flourished. Lilies of the valley, the first I had seen, and a great variety of the orchis tribe grew among them. The gnat and bee orchis were beautifully developed. Hundreds of tiny birds were disturbed by our approach, and flew out of their nests in the low bushes, chirruping and singing. We gathered wild thyme, and gladly ate it with the bread which we had brought from Hâifa, for the morning air had sharpened our appetites. Lizards ran over the white rocks, and a hare now and then darted across our path.

As we rode onward my brother carefully explained to me the difficulties attending the government of the Jebel Nablûs district, which we were then approaching. He said, "The town of Nablûs, the seat of government, contains about twelve thousand inhabitants. Of these only three hundred are Christians, fifty are Jews, and nearly two hundred are Samaritans. The rest are Moslems of the most fierce and fanatical class.

"In the surrounding mountains there are four great factions always at enmity with each other. They are, first, the *Abdul Hady* family, whose head-quarters are at Arrabeh; and, second, the *Jerrars*, who possess a fortress at Senûr. They each sprang from the peasantry, and have a large number of followers in almost every village in the district. Third. The *Tokan* tribe, which has great influence among kindred tribes in the eastern desert. Fourth. The *Rayan*, who are of Bedouin origin, and very powerful; they congregate west of Nablûs. From one of these great rival factions, the governor of Nablûs is generally chosen, and duly appointed by the Pasha of Jerusalem.

"When a governor, for some offense, or through inability to satisfy the rapacity of the effendis, and other followers of the pasha, is put out of office, some member of a rival faction immediately repairs to head-quarters. With large sums of money, and presents, he buys the good-will of the pasha's secretaries and chief councilors, and through their mediation and influence succeeds to the governorship. As soon as he is installed in office he uses all means in his power, just or unjust, to recover with interest the money which he had dispensed in bribes. He levies impositions on the poor and unprotected, and plunders with impunity all who dare not or can not resist his power. It devolves upon him to appoint the sheikhs of all the villages in the district. Those who were already in office under his predecessor are allowed to remain if they make sufficient and appropriate presents to him at the time of his accession. If they neglect to do this the offices are given to those who make larger offers.

"This state of affairs has lasted for many years, and in the year 1851 five hundred people were killed and as many wounded in a conflict between these rival factions. The consequence was that a decree was made that none of either family should ever again fill any important office in Jebel Nablûs. But," continued my brother, "this decree has been disregarded, and the Abdul Hady family has succeeded in ingratiating itself with the Government; Mahmoud Bek Abdul Hady is chief Governor of Nablûs; his cousin, Saleh Bek—whose brother, Mohammed Bek, reigns at Arrabeh, the stronghold of the family—is Governor of Hâifa. On account of the present rebellion of the people against Mahmoud Bek, the chief Governor, Kamîl Pasha has encamped at Nablûs with a large body of cavalry, but he is in great difficulty. He is surrounded by intriguing councilors, who do not scruple to take bribes, and bind themselves to factions. My mission just now is simply to watch carefully, and report to Mr. Finn all that is going on, and to find out, if possible, the real position of affairs, without interfering or taking any part in them. In this you may be able to help me a little by quietly observing the state of the towns; for we shall probably be apart from each other in Arrabeh and Senûr. The fact of your being my fellow-traveler will perhaps induce people to receive us into their strongholds the more readily and unsuspectingly."

Thus informed, I felt a greatly-increased interest in the expedition. We were still riding in the plain, but thorns and thistles had given place to fields of wheat and barley, and plowed land. The sun was shining overhead, but rain was falling on the terraced hills before us, where olive-groves and blossoming fruit-trees flourished. As we approached them we felt the heavy drops, and were soon in the midst of a shower. We rode quickly through it, and descended into a narrow valley, at the end of which, on a rocky hill, brightened by a gleam of sunshine, we could see the town of Arrabeh, with its embattled walls and towers. After a very difficult ascent over smooth slabs of rock and loose stones, like a steep and irregular stairway, we reached Arrabeh. It was past mid-day, and rain poured down in torrents as we entered its great iron-bound, well-guarded gates. This is one of the best-walled towns in Palestine, but is almost unknown to travelers, being out of the usual route. It is not even mentioned in Murray's Hand-Book, but is marked on his map.

The houses all looked like small castles; they are square, and with parapets round their flat, terraced roofs. We went direct to the residence of Mohammed Bek Abdul Hady, the Governor of the town. His house, like all Moslem town-houses, was divided into two distinct parts; the men occupying one part, called the divan, and the ladies living in the other, which is called the harem. The ground-floor was occupied by horses and soldiers, and there our attendants and servants were lodged. We mounted an uncovered stone staircase, crossed a large court-yard, and entered the divan—a vaulted chamber, with wide, arched windows on three sides, commanding views of the valley and the town-gate. The deep, low window-seats were cushioned and carpeted. Here no ladies ever appear; I was told afterward that I was the only woman who had ever crossed its threshold. We found that the Governor himself was absent, but we were very courteously received by his relations; and they said, kissing our hands, "This house is your house, and we are at your service." They expressed great surprise to see us on a journey while the country was so disturbed. They said that every day there were skirmishes in the neighborhood, and at least one hundred and fifty people had been killed within a few days. Flocks were stolen, and camels were constantly waylaid and robbed of their burdens. A battle had been fought on the previous day, near to Arrabeh, and many lives were sacrificed. The sons and nephews of the Governor told us about it. They were engaged in the fight. One boy of about sixteen years of age showed us how he threw himself on the ground and pretended to be dead, and thus escaped a death-blow. He exhibited his spear stained with blood, and his pistols, of which he was very proud. They were of English manufacture.

The younger sons, about ten and eleven years of age, were told to conduct me to the harem. They carefully led me over terraced roofs, through courts, and halls, and passages, till we reached the female quarter. I was taken to a large vaulted room, with whitewashed walls and stone floors, lighted only from the wide-open door; for, as glass casements are not used, the wooden window-shutters were closed to keep out the rain. My young guides, Selim and Saïd, ran before me, and cried out exultingly, "An English girl! an English girl! come! see!" I entered, and in a moment was surrounded by a little crowd of women, dressed in very brilliant costumes. They were of various complexions—from the dark Abyssinian slave-girls in crimson and silver, to the olive and bronze-colored Arabs in violet and gold.

They pounced upon me as if I were a new toy for them; they kissed me one after the other, and stroked my face. They had never seen a European, and told me that no daughter of the Franks had ever entered their town before. They said, "Be welcome, O sister from a far country; this house is yours, and we are your servants." Then they asked me with whom, and how, and whence I had come. The ladies wore full, long trowsers, made of colored silk; short, tight jackets, made of cloth or velvet, embroidered with gold; and flowers and jewels in their head-dresses. The servants wore cotton suits, and the slaves red cloth. They wondered to see my plain, long, dark riding-dress and hat. I told them that I wished to change my clothes, as they were wet.

The boys went to order my portmanteau to be brought to the precincts of the harem, and then two slaves fetched it. As soon as I had unlocked it, the ladies, servants, and children, one and all, began examining its contents. In a minute or two it was actually almost empty. Mantles, morning and evening-dresses, night-gowns, and collars were passing from hand to hand; and, as the uses of them were not known, they were put on in all sorts of fantastic ways. One of the girls took a little lace-collar, and placed it tastefully on her forehead. She thought that it was part of a head-dress. I was very much amused, but was obliged to put a stop to their mischief by telling them to put every thing back into the box; they did so directly. I had already discovered that Arab women are like children; they almost always submit immediately to gentle but unhesitating firmness.

Then I dressed in the same room; for they said that they had not any other for their use. I fancy it was because they wished to see all my clothes, and how I put them on; theirs being so very different from ours. They told me that I wore too many dresses at the same time. They wear only a shirt of thin cotton or crape, made high to the throat, open at the bosom, and with long, wide sleeves; very full trowsers, drawn in and tied round the waist and below the knee, but falling in graceful folds nearly to the ground; and an open, short jacket, with a shawl tied round the waist like a sash or girdle. They kindly sent away my wet garments to be dried at the oven, and made a comfortable seat of cushions for me on the floor. One lady made some sweet sherbet of pomegranates, and handed it to me. A second brought me coffee in a little china cup without any handle, held in another one, exactly of the shape and size of a common egg-cup, made of prettily-embossed and chased silver.

Then Sit Habîbî sat by my side smoking a nargihlé, and in answer to my questions she told me that she was the eldest wife of Mohammed Bek, the Governor of Arrabeh, and she pointed out to me two other ladies who were also his wives. Then, at my request, she introduced to me the three wives of Saleh Bek, the Governor of Hâifa. They were very much astonished when I told them that I knew their husband, Saleh Bek, very well, and brought messages from him. They could not understand it, as they never had heard of a woman seeing any men except her own relations. A Moslem lady may not even see her future husband till the wedding-day. One of the wives asked me rather suspiciously if Saleh Bek had established a harem at Hâifa. I soon reassured and satisfied them on that point. They all showed much curiosity respecting English people. Werdeh, which means rosy, said, "Is your brother handsome and strong? Is he fair to look upon? Are all the people of your country white?" And one said, "Why do you travel about without your women?"

While I was answering these questions I was taking notice of the room. It was rather low and long, the floor was nearly concealed by fine matting. On the side opposite to the door a narrow mattress was spread, it was covered with a strip of soft carpet, like stair-carpeting. Cushions and pillows cased in Oriental silks, placed on the mattress, were leaning against the wall, and thus a sort of low sofa was formed, and on the middle of this I was seated, surrounded by the ladies. Opposite to us on each side of the door there were similar seats or divans, where several women and girls were sitting smoking. At the end of the room, on my left hand, there were two very large wooden chests, painted bright red and garnished with brass locks and hinges of pretty design. Behind them was a wide, deep, arched recess in the wall, where mattresses and wadded quilts were piled up one on the other. Mirrors from Constantinople, in gilt frames, were hanging on each side of this recess. On my right hand, at the other end of the room, black slaves and servants sat on a rug, taking care of some infants and young children who were crying and quarreling. They were keeping up a continual buzzing chatter, and every now and then bursting out into little shrieks and exclamations. The floor of the room was raised about six inches above the level of the court without, except a square space just within the door, where the women put off their high clogs or shoes before they entered.

Werdeh and Habîbî sat by me, stroking my hair and face caressingly. They wondered that I wore no headdress or ornament in my hair. The youngest wife of Saleh Bek of Hâifa, named Helweh, which signifies sweetness, sat close by the open door in a graceful attitude. She was only sixteen, and looked so pretty, and bright, and merry, that I opened my sketch-book and took her portrait. When the women saw what I was doing, they were very much astonished, for they had never seen any one draw a face or any thing else; indeed, it is contrary to the law of the Moslem religion to do so. They cried out, "O work of Allah! There is the face of Helweh! There are her eyes looking at us, and there is the coin of gold on her neck, and her hand holds the narghilé. O, wonderful!" Then Helweh came shyly to see the drawing, and she asked me if I drew her because she was the prettiest. I told her that I should like to draw any one who would sit near to the door, where the sunlight was streaming in. Then the others took the same seat in turn, and I made two more sketches, but Helweh was by far the prettiest. She had a sweet voice, which is rather unusual among Arab women, and was simple and frank in her manners. She wore yellow silk trowsers, ornamented at the sides with black silk braid. Her yellow pointed slippers were turned up at the toes. She wore no stockings. Her black velvet jacket was embroidered beautifully with gold thread, and a purple, red, and green shawl, twisted round her waist rather low, served for a girdle. A wide collar of gold coins encircled her throat, and a little, shallow, red cloth cap was arranged coquettishly on one side of her well-shaped head. A long tassel, springing from perforated gold balls, hung from it. Her hair, intertwined with silk braid, was divided into nine plaits and fell straight over her shoulders. Little jewels and pearls were fastened to it. Round her head, over her red cloth cap, or tarbûsh, she wore strings of pearls and coins and diamond and emerald sprays, and little bunches of red, yellow, and violet everlasting flowers, which grow wild on the hills in Palestine. She had large, dark eyes. The eyebrows were painted thickly, and the eyelids edged with kohl. She had spots of blue dye on her chest and on her chin, and a blue star tattooed on her forehead. The women were all thus ornamented, more or less, and they very much wished to paint and tattoo me in the same way.

I wrote down in my book the names of all the women and their children and servants in Arabic, and a description of their dresses in English. I found that Helweh was born at Kefr Kâra, and she told me how all the villages near to it were called. I explained the use of my map, and how by looking at it I could tell the direction of Senûr and other towns. Then they cried out more and more, "O work of God!" for they had never heard that it was possible for a woman to learn to read or write. They knew that men could do so, and their own sons went to a day-school at the Mosque, where a learned dervish taught them to intone the Koran and to write a little. But the women believed that boys possessed some peculiar faculty which enabled them to study and to understand the mystery of unspoken words. Even Selim and Saïd, my little guides, were surprised, and said, "Mashallah! the stranger knows the writing of our language."

At about three o'clock, which they call the ninth hour, some black women, almost hidden in white sheets, brought in dinner. The first woman carried a little low wooden stand, inlaid with ivory and mother-of-pearl. She put it down on the floor opposite to me. Then another woman placed on it an old, round, heavy metal tray, engraved with sentences in Arabic from the Koran. A large towel, embroidered with gold thread, was handed to me. After these preparations I was glad to see something to eat, for I was very hungry. The tray was soon quite covered with the following dishes: a small metal dish of fried eggs—a wooden bowl of lebbany, or sour milk—a bowl of sweet cream made of goat's milk—a dish of very stiff starch, like *blanc mange*, sweetened with rose-leaf candy, with almonds and pistachio nuts chopped up in it—a large dish of rice boiled in butter, with little pieces of fried mutton all over the top—and a plate of walnuts, dried fruits, sugared almonds and lemon-peel.

A black slave girl, with short scarlet cloth trowsers and scarlet jacket, silver necklace, armlets and anklets, stood by me, holding a silver saucer in her hand, filled with water, ready for me to drink whenever I wished for it. There was not a knife nor even a spoon to be seen, and I could find no plate for my especial use. I washed my hands and was invited to take up the food from any of the dishes, with a piece of a large flat loaf, very much like leather. They soon perceived that I was not much accustomed to that mode of eating, so they brought me a large wooden cooking spoon, at which the little ones laughed heartily. I wished the ladies to eat with me, but they would not. They allowed Selim and Saïd to do so, how-over, and they soon twisted their flat loaves into the shape of spoons, and helped themselves to milk and eggs, but the meat and rice they took up neatly in their hands. The ladies stood round all the while, to see that I had every thing I required.

When I had eaten, the tray was moved into the middle of the room, and a large metal basin with a perforated cover was placed before me. On the top of it was a cake of native soap—stamped with a sign commonly called "Solomon's seal"—and as I rubbed my hands with it, water was poured over them, from a curious silver jug, something like an old-fashioned coffee-pot, with a long, thin, curved spout. One continuous stream ran over my hands, and disappeared through the cover of the basin. The embroidered towel was handed to me again, with some water to rinse my mouth.

The three wives of the Governor and the three wives of his brother Saleh Bek, with their children, then sat down on the matted floor round the tray, and dipping their hands together into the various dishes, they soon finished the simple meal. Two or three more dishes of rice were brought in. Each woman rose as soon as she was satisfied, had water poured over her hands, and washed her mouth. Afterward strong coffee without milk or sugar was passed round. The servants and slaves then assembled at the tray, and ate with astonishing speed and voracity, and quickly all traces of dinner were cleared away.

Chibouques—pipes with red earthenware bowls and long tubes made of cherry-stick or jasmine, with ebony mouth-pieces—were handed to the elderly ladies, and two or three narghilés to the others, who took them in turn. After Helweh had smoked for a few minutes, she inclined her head gracefully, placed one hand on her bosom, touched her forehead with the pliant tube, and then handed it to the lady sitting next to her, who happened to be the second wife of her own husband, Saleh Bek. Thus it was transferred from one smoker to another, even to the handmaidens, with the words, "May it give you pleasure!" This ceremonious politeness is strictly observed among the Moslems, even between the nearest relations. The prescribed forms of greeting in habitual use appear to me to have the effect of keeping comparative peace and harmony in the harems.

A very beautiful narghilé was prepared especially for me. It was at least half a yard high. The glass vase or bottle was clear as crystal, and well cut. It was filled with water, in which rose-leaves were floating. At the top of the long-necked vase was a well-chased solid silver bowl, holding the burning charcoal and Persian tumbac. The pliable snake-like tube or hose connected with it was covered with red velvet and bound with gold wire. It was about four yards long. The mouthpiece was of amber, set with rubies and turquoise. The smoke passed through the water, bubbling and disturbing the red-rose leaves, and then traveled up the long tube. Thus the fragrant fumes of the tumbac were cooled and purified before they reached my lips.

I observed that there was a little whispering and consultation going on among the women, and then Helweh came and sat by me and said, "Are you married?" I said, "No," and they answered, "Why then have you left your father and mother? are they not kind to you?" I told them how good they were, and how my mother taught me to speak and read and write my own language, and the languages of other people. I tried to make them understand how English parents educate their children.

Werdeh said, "It is much better to marry and to stay at home than to travel about the country. The dangers are great now in this time of war, and the women should stay at home."

Sit Sâra said, "Werdeh has spoken wisely. Why do you not marry?"

I answered, "Ya sitta, there are no men of my country here. How can I marry?"

Sâra then said, "You speak our language like a stranger,

but you speak it sweetly. An Arab would take you. Why do you not marry an Arab?"

I replied—very much amused—"My mother is not here to find a husband for me. How can I marry?" I thought that this answer would settle the question at once in their estimation; but Sit Sâra said, "I will be your mother, and bring you to a husband. My brother is a Cadi, a great Judge of Nablûs. He looks for a wife. He has only three. He will love you because you are white."

I answered, laughingly, "Thank you, O my mother! what preparations must I make, and when must I be ready?"

Sit Sâra considered for a moment, and then said, "How many camels has your father got?"

I replied, "My father has no camels. In my country there are only three or four living camels kept as curiosities, in a house in a beautiful garden, with servants to watch over them and take care of them. We have a few stuffed camels also, in a large glass house." At this they all laughed loudly, and cried, "O most marvelous!"

Sâra continued, "Are your father's olive-trees new and fruitful?" "My father has no olive-trees." At this they were still more surprised. Sâra said, "Your father has gold. He will give you of his gold, and precious stones, and a red box, full of clothes and towels, some silk cushions, a red wooden cradle, and much soap. My brother has great wealth, and he will give camels to your father for your portion, and gold coins."

I found that they thought that I was in earnest. They all clapped their hands, and one of the women sang a song of rejoicing, thus:

> O Lady Miriam, child of a far-off land
> Dwell with us and we shall have joy!
> You shall be cherished above all the women
> In the house of my brother!
> You shall be his queen and his chief delight!
> For your face is like the moon,
> And your words are precious as pearls!
> O Lady Miriam, child of a far-off land,
> Dwell with us and we shall have joy!"

Then all the women rose and stood in a circle, forming a chain by slipping their hands into each other's girdles. They first moved slowly and gently round, in a measured step and to a monotonous tune, which they sang, while the servants and children, seated on the floor, were beating time by clapping their hands. They sang thus:

> "Let us dance; let us sing;
> He is looking from the lattice.
> He will throw to us showers of silver;
> He will throw to us showers of gold!
> Let us dance, let us sing:
> Faster, faster; louder, louder!
> Let him hear our mingling voices;
> Let him hear our twinkling footsteps.
> Let us dance, let us sing;
> Faster, faster; louder, louder!
> He will throw to us showers of silver;
> He will throw to us showers of gold!"

They sang this over and over again, and the dance gradually quickened till it became very animated, but the dancers always kept in step. At last they sat down quite tired. While they rested I told them how I passed my time at Hâifa, and I tried to give them an idea of my home in London, and how it was quite possible to live there, without camels or olive-trees. They asked me if the people ever danced in England. They were very much shocked when they heard that men and women danced at the same time and together.

At sunset little Selim told me my brother wished to speak to me. He led me to him. He was in the vaulted chamber, with several Effendis and Moslem gentlemen, who asked me if I did not feel afraid to travel in a country where the people were fighting and plundering each other. I said, "I am not afraid, your excellencies, for I have found that all in this land are kind to the stranger." Then they said, "May Allah make a straight path for you!"

Supper was brought into the divan for the gentlemen, so I returned to the harem. It was cheerfully brightened by little red clay lamps, placed in niches in the walls, and a large lantern stood on a low stool in the middle of the room. The women were wondering how I could dare to go to the men's quarter of the house. I explained to them that it was the custom in England for men and women to meet together constantly, and that we walked, or rode, or drove abroad unvailed. They were exceedingly surprised. I added, "We are governed by a Sultana, named 'Nassirah,' (Victoria,) a lady so much loved and respected by her subjects, that when she appears in the streets, or public places, the people cry aloud for joy, and shout, 'God save the Sultana!' Then her face is bright with pleasure, and she looks graciously around, bowing her head to rich and to poor alike. And on certain days the nobles, and the learned men and her officers, are allowed to kiss her hand." They cried, "O most wonderful!" and Sâra said, "Is your Sultana a girl?" I answered, "No, she is married, but the Prince, her husband, takes no part in the government." A sudden light seemed to break in upon them, and I found that I had unwittingly given them the idea that the women of England rule and take the lead in every thing, and are superior to the men. I could not entirely remove this impression, for they said, "Your Sultana could not keep the scepter in her hand, if she were not stronger and wiser than the men." One of the women said, "Can your brother, the Consul, write?" I tried to give them a more favorable opinion of my countrymen, but I do not think I succeeded very well, for they still seemed to fancy that women were their superiors.

Supper was brought for me in the same order as dinner, except that we had, in addition, a large dish filled with little green sausages. They were made of minced meat and rice, rolled up in leaves, dressed in butter. They were very nice. Asmé, a beautiful girl about eight years of age—the eldest daughter of Saleh Bek—and Selim, ate with me. The ladies stood in attendance. I described how English people sit on chairs, round a high table, and eat from separate plates, using knives, and forks, and spoons; and how men and women eat together. They cried out, "O, wonderful!" For they had never heard of a woman eating in the presence of a man—not even with her husband or father.

After supper they talked about the war. They told me how much they feared for their two eldest sons, who, though only fifteen or sixteen, went constantly to engage in the skirmishes in the mountains. These boys had often been slightly wounded, and every day their mothers expected to hear of one of them being killed. Then they sang a song about the Governor, Mohammed Bek, who was absent from Arrabeh, and they sang thus:

> "May our enemies perish before him;
> May the arm of our prince be strong;
> May he be mighty in the battle-field;
> May his enemies perish before him:
>   That our shepherds may pasture
>   Their flocks in peace,
>   And our camels carry
>   Their burdens in safety
> May our enemies perish before our prince,
>   Our prince and our protector!
> May he return to us with joy,
>   With great joy, and as a conqueror!
> And all the dwellers in the mountains
>   Shall tremble before him!"*

Then the black slaves danced, each one standing alone, a little apart from the others. They moved their arms above their heads slowly and gracefully, bending the body forward gradually; then suddenly they raised their heads, and rose to their extreme hight, with their hands high. Their limbs seemed very supple and pliant, and I think they enjoyed dancing very much; but it was not a pretty or lively dance. They sang about a beautiful Bedawî girl *with teeth like lightning.* I sang English songs at their request, and showed them a few of the measures and figures of our Western dances. They were most pleased

---

* Arab songs are very difficult for foreigners to understand. I could make out little more than the subject and spirit of the above while the women were singing them. Helweh, at my request, explained the words in simple language, assisted by signs; and a year afterward, when she was my neighbor at Haifa, she helped me to understand them sufficiently to enable me thus to render them into English.

with the Spanish waltz, which I danced slowly, with imaginary partners. They clapped their hands, beating time while I sang.

After this I was very tired, and I asked Sit Sâra to let me sleep. She said, "Let us walk out on the terrace. The rain is over; the stars are shining. Let us walk out, O my daughter! and the room shall be made ready." So we strolled on the terrace of the harem with Helweh. There were red watch-fires on the hills around. By looking through the round holes in the parapets we could see people in the streets below us, with servants carrying lanterns before them. Bright stars shone in the deep-purple night sky.

I was led across the court into a square room, and introduced to the fourth and youngest wife of the Governor of Arrabeh. I had not even heard of her before. She was surrounded by her women and attendants, and was sitting on a mattress propped up by pillows and cushions, and partly covered by a silk embroidered lehaff. Her head-dress was adorned with jewels, and roses, and everlasting flowers; and her violet velvet jacket was richly embroidered. Her cheeks were highly rouged, and her eyebrows painted. Her eyelids were newly dressed with kohl and her hands with henna. She lifted a little swaddled figure from under some heavy coverings, and handed it to me. It was her first-born son; he was seven days old, and his father had not yet seen him. The mother had hoped and prepared for the pleasure of placing her boy in his arms that night, but he had not returned to Arrabeh. A week is usually allowed to elapse before a Moslem father sees his new-born child or its mother, and the eighth day is generally kept as a day of rejoicing and congratulation. Professional singing women are hired for the occasion.

Coffee was made for me, and a narghilé prepared; but I did not linger long with the young Moslem mother and her infant son, for the room was so overheated that I could scarcely breathe. A large open brazier, filled with glowing charcoal, stood near the door, and the air and every thing in the place seemed to be impregnated with an oppressive odor of musk. Even the coffee and the fumes of the narghilé were strongly flavored with it. I was very glad to be in the fresh air again on the starlit terrace.

When we went back into the large room, I found that it had been nicely swept. In one corner, five mattresses were placed, one on the top of the other, with a red silk pillow, and a silk embroidered wadded quilt, lined with calico, arranged nicely as a bed for me. I rejoiced inwardly, thinking that I was to have the room to myself. But very soon I was undeceived, for seven other beds were spread on the floor, each formed of a single mattress only, with a quilted coverlid and pillow. (If a Moslem wishes to pay great honor to a guest, several mattresses are piled up for him or her to sleep upon, and these gradations of respect are curiously observed. Five is rather a high figure, but I have known my brother to have seven spread for him.)

I found that all the ladies, and children, and servants, and slaves, were to sleep in the same room with me! Two narrow hammocks, each about a yard long, were taken from a recess, and, fastened to ropes, suspended from iron rings in the ceiling. The hammocks were oblong frames, made of the strong stems of palm fronds, with coarse canvas stretched over them. To these, two swaddled and screaming children were securely bound. Ropes, made of palm-fiber, were fastened to the corners, and united and plaited together, about one yard above, and then fixed to strong ropes hanging from the ceiling. The four corner ropes formed a tent-like frame-work to support a piece of muslin for a musketo curtain.

When I began to undress, the women watched me with curiosity, and when I put on my nightgown they were exceedingly astonished, and exclaimed, "Where are you going? What are you going to do?" and, "Why is your dress white?"

They made no change in their dress for sleeping, and there they were, in their bright-colored clothes, ready for bed in a minute. But they stood round me till I said, "Good-night!" They all kissed me, wishing me good dreams. Then I kneeled down, and presently, without speaking to them again, I got into bed, and turned my face toward the wall, thinking over the strange day I had spent. I tried to compose myself for sleep, though I heard the women whispering together.

When my head had rested for about five minutes on the soft red silk pillow, I felt a hand stroking my forehead, and heard a voice saying, very gently, "Ya Habîbi!" that is, "O beloved!" But I would not answer directly, as I did not wish to be roused unnecessarily. I waited for a little while, and my face was touched again. I felt a kiss on my forehead, and the voice said, "Miriam, speak to us. Speak, Miriam, darling!" I could not resist any longer, so I turned round and saw Helweh, Saleh Bek's prettiest wife, leaning over me. I said, "What is it, Sweetness? what can I do for you?" She answered, "What did you do just now, when you kneeled down and covered your face with your hands?" I sat up, and said very solemnly, "I spoke to God, Helweh!" "What did you say to him?" said Helweh. I replied, "I wish to sleep. God never sleeps. I have asked him to watch over me, and that I may fall asleep, remembering that he never sleeps, and wake up remembering his presence. I am very weak, God is all-powerful. I have asked him to strengthen me with his strength."

By this time all the ladies were sitting round me on my bed, and the slaves came and stood near. I told them that I did not know their language well enough to explain to them all I had thought and said. But, as I had learned the Lord's Prayer by heart in Arabic, I repeated it to them, sentence by sentence, slowly. When I began thus, "Our Father who art in heaven," Helweh directly said, "You told me that your father was in

London." I replied, "I have two fathers, Helweh: one in London, who does not know that I am here, and can not know till I write and tell him; and a Heavenly Father, who is with me always—who is here now, and sees and hears us. He is your Father also. He teaches us to know good from evil if we listen to him and obey him." For a moment there was perfect silence. They all looked startled, and as if they felt that they were in the presence of some unseen power. Then Helweh said, "What more did you say?" I continued the Lord's Prayer; and when I came to the words, "Give us day by day our daily bread," they said, "Can not you make your bread yourself?" The passage, "Forgive us our trespasses as we forgive those who trespass against us," is particularly forcible in the Arabic language, and one of the elder women, who was rather severe and relentless-looking, on hearing it said, "Are you obliged to say that every day?" As if she thought that sometimes it would be difficult to do so. They said, "Are you a Moslem?" I answered, "I am not called a Moslem; but I am your sister, made by the same God, who is the one only God, the God of all, my Father and your Father." They asked me if I knew the Koran, and were surprised to hear that I had read it. They handed a rosary to me, saying, "Do you know that?" I repeated a few of the most striking and comprehensive attributes very carefully and slowly. Then they cried out, "Mashallah"—"The English girl is a true believer;" and the impressionable, sensitive-looking Abyssinian slave-girls said, with one accord, "She is indeed an angel!"

Moslems, both men and women, have the name of "Allah" constantly on their lips; but they do not appear to realize the presence and power of God, or to be conscious of spiritual communion with him. Their common greetings and salutations are touching and beautiful words of prayer and thanksgiving, varied with poetic feeling and Oriental sentiment, to suit any occasions. But their greetings, after all, seem to me only to express politeness, respect, kindness, good-will, or affection, as the case may be. Even as the old English "*God be with you!*" has lost its full significance—and more, it has even lost its sound, clipped as it is into a commonplace "*good-by.*" The Moslem ejaculations before and after eating, and during the performance of ablutions, though beautiful and appropriate, are now merely like exclamations of self-congratulation, without reference to any superior or unseen power. And the regular daily prayers so scrupulously said by men, though generally neglected by women, are reduced to ceremonial forms; while the words uttered are, in many instances, sublime and magnificent.

If this my notion be correct, it will explain why these women were so startled, when, in answer to Helweh's question, I said simply and earnestly, "*I spoke to God.*" This took them by surprise, and gave them the idea that I believed that my words were really heard. Whereas, if I had answered in commonplace language, such as, "*I was saying* my prayers," or "I was *at* my devotions," probably they would not have been impressed in the same way; though they might have wondered that a Franji should pray at all to their God. One of the women remarked, that no people, except Moslems, ever prayed to the one true God.

After talking with them for some time, and answering, as clearly as I could, their earnest, shrewd, and child-like questions, I said "good-night" once more. So they kissed me, and smoothed my pillow. But though I was fatigued bodily, my mind was so thoroughly roused and interested, that I could not immediately sleep. I watched the women resting under bright-colored quilts, with their heads on low, silken pillows. The lantern on the stool in the middle of the room lighted up the coins and jewels on their headdresses. Now and then, one of the infants cried, and its mother or a slave rose to quiet it; and it was fed without being taken from its hammock. The mother stood upright while the slave inclined the hammock toward her for a few minutes. Then there was silence again. The room was very close and warm, and the faces of some of the sleepers were flushed. At last I slept also.

When I awoke in the morning I found that all the beds had been cleared away. Helweh and Sit Sâra stood by mine, as if they had been watching for me to wake. A number of boys almost blocked up the doorway, where the sunlight was streaming in. Servants and slaves were chattering, and piling up the mattresses in the recess. Little children were quarreling. The boys alone were silent. A black girl was sitting on the floor, pounding some freshly-roasted coffee-berries in a marble mortar. Their fragrant aroma filled the room. I think that the mortar was made out of an ancient capital. It was beautifully carved, like Roman work. Another girl was making a kind of porridge of bread, milk, sugar, and oil, for the children.

When Helweh perceived that I was awake she called out to the boys to clear the doorway; and a group of women, shrouded in white sheets, who had been waiting in the court outside, entered. They were neighbors, who had been paying visits of congratulation to the young mother whom I had seen on the previous night. They had been invited to come in "to hear the English girl speak to God."

My garments were examined with curiosity, and I had very much more assistance than I required in making my toilette. When I was dressed Helweh said, "Now, Miriam, darling, will you speak to God, that the women, our neighbors, may hear?"

So I kneeled down, saying, "God, the one true God, is the Creator and Father of all; and those who seek him truly shall surely find him." Then, in a few simple words, I prayed that he would keep us in continual remembrance of him. That we might feel his presence; and that he would write his law in our hearts, and lead us to seek earnestly to understand and to obey his will concerning us. That we might be inspired to love him more and more, with a trustful and reverential love, and live in harmony with all people.

After a pause I said, "Will you say Amen to that prayer?" They hesitated, till Helweh exclaimed, "Amîn, Amîn!" and then the others echoed it.

Sâra said, "Speak yet again, my daughter. Speak about the *bread*." So I repeated the Lord's Prayer, explaining it—as I understand it—sentence by sentence, at their request. They asked me some very curious and suggestive questions, and they prayed that I would stay with them always. But while I was taking coffee, and hot bread and cream, one of the boys brought me a note from my brother, to tell me that he would be ready to start in half an hour, and that I was to go to him in the divan as soon as possible. So Sâra brought me my cloak and habit, which had been nicely dried and smoothed. With regret I took leave of my warm-hearted friends of the harem. They said, "Go in peace," and "Return to us again, O Miriam, beloved!"

CHAPTER X.

FROM ARRABEH TO NABLÛS.

ALL the little boys went with me into the divan, where my brother sat, surrounded by effendis and young men of the Abdul Hady family. He had dismissed the guide who had conducted us to Arrabeh, and decided to travel without one. We were safer alone. It might have compromised us to have in our party any one who had been engaged in the late skirmishes, or who belonged to a faction.

It was pouring with rain when we started; but the sun shone now and then, tracing vivid rainbows in the clouds. The undulating highlands which we traversed reminded me of the Sussex downs; while beyond them bare rocks and rugged slopes appeared. Far away on the right, the Mediterranean could be seen, between grayish-blue hills. Occasionally we passed quite an English-looking bank of grass and wild flowers; and wherever the poterium spinosum grew, it sheltered the sweetwilliam, the Chinese pink, and the forget-me-not. We rode over a large, well-cultivated plain, and met two horsemen, who courteously exchanged salutations with us, and then said, "What is the news?" and "Whence do you come?"

Rain fell heavily, as we rode on to a steep ridge, which commanded a view of the fortress of Senûr. It stands on the summit of a seemingly-inaccessible hill, of conical form. The road down the southern side of the ridge was so very difficult and dangerous for horses, that we, and even the Arabs, dismounted, and the animals were unwillingly dragged or urged along. We made our way cautiously, stepping, and sliding, and leaping by turns over the loosened stones and smooth slabs of rock; sometimes walking in the midst of a water-course, with the shallow but increasing stream rushing round our feet. We paused for a minute or two in a narrow valley, and stood in the shelter of a low, deserted hut, made of tree-branches and stones. Then, with difficulty, we mounted the hill, and reached Senûr. The inhabitants will not willingly make the approach to their town more easy while the country is subject to civil war.

We found the gates of the town closed; but, after a parley with the sentinels, we were admitted. It was just midday. I was tired, giddy, and wet. We were led into a large, vaulted, smoke-blackened hall, on the ground-floor of the castle. About fifty men rose, wrapped their heavy cloaks around them, and left the place as we entered. A carpet was spread for us in a deep, wide window-seat. I poured the water from the brim of my hat, and gladly threw off my cloak, and took a cup of hot coffee. In the mean time, another resting-place was made ready for us. Ibrahim Jerrar and his brother, the chiefs of the town, conducted us across the castle-yard, up a steep, uncovered stone stairway, into an open court. As we crossed the threshold of a vaulted chamber, in the highest part of the castle, they said, "Be welcome, and take your rest." Mats, and carpets, and cushions had been newly spread on the ground. The window of this room commanded a view of a small fertile plain, almost inclosed by hills, but which could be easily approached from the south-west by a narrow valley or pass. In time of war its dark vista is always carefully watched by the people of Senûr.

A lunch of bread, fried eggs, goat's-milk cheese, and olives was brought in, and placed on a round wooden tray raised a few inches from the ground. Serving men poured water over our hands. When lunch was cleared away, and coffee and pipes went round, an earnest conversation commenced between the Jerrars and my brother, while three or four men sat by, silently smoking and listening. I rested apart from them on a cushioned carpet, watching the animated group. I had never in the East seen any men so tall, well-proportioned, and handsome as the two Jerrars. Their large, loose, white and brown cloaks hung in graceful folds, and their red and yellow silk shawl head-dresses shaded bright, clear countenances, with classically-regular, yet very expressive features. My brother said to me in English, "If you have an opportunity, by all means take the likeness of our host, Ibrahîm. He is the most celebrated man in this district, both as regards courage, daring, and energy; and his family for many generations have been renowned for strength, vigor, and manly beauty. But," he added, "do not let him or any of the others see you sketching him, for he is quite as superstitious as he is handsome."

The men were all so earnestly engaged in smoking, talking, or listening, that, by writing and drawing by turns, I succeeded in securing the portrait without exciting observation.

Ibrahîm Jerrar took me to his harem. It was in the most central and secure part of the castle, and consisted of three rooms, opening into a square court. He introduced me to his three wives, and gave them directions to welcome me as a sister, and then left me with them, while he conducted my brother over the town. The women greeted me and stared at me with unconcealed wonder. They were more simple, frank, and innocent-looking than any Arab women I had seen. They were young and rather fair, stout and ruddy, and cheerful and bright as happy children. They belonged to the peasant class. Their long, open dresses, or pelisses, were of soft crimson and white striped silk. Large silver coins encircled their faces, and a row of small gold coins crossed their foreheads, like a fillet, to bind down their thick black hair, which was cut short in front and combed straight down, meeting their arched eyebrows, quite hiding their foreheads. Their eyes were large and clear, their eyelids were edged with kohl, and their chins and chests were dotted with tattooed stars.

They and their children, and their white-washed matted room, looked fresh, and clean, and pleasant.

I found that the handsomest, healthiest, and strongest girls are always sought for as brides for the Jerrars—that the health, strength, and beauty of which they are so proud, may be perpetuated in the family. I never heard of a Jerrar who could read or write, or even sign his name. On the other hand, many of the men of the Abdul Hady family are well educated, and set a high value on *book* learning; and the ladies of Arrabeh are somewhat polished, and look very different to the simple rustic women of Senûr. I made a sketch of the head of one of the wives while I tried to lead them into conversation, but I could not "bring them out." When I spoke they only looked wonderingly at me, laughed shyly at each other, or uttered some set phrase embodying a compliment or a prayer.

While I was resting and smoking a narghilé which they had prepared for me, I was suddenly called to rejoin my brother. I found that the young man who was set to watch the south-western approach to Senûr, had just given notice that he could see a body of Turkish cavalry issuing from the narrow valley into the plain below. Ibrahîm Jerrar told us that he knew that they were sent by Kamîl Pasha to search the town—to see if there were any Bedouins concealed there, ready to assist the people of Senûr in case of a siege. He added decidedly, "I have given my word of honor that there are no Bedouins within these walls. We are all peasants. *No one shall live to pass through these gates, who attempts to enter with an armed force, to examine the town.*"

My brother reasoned with him. Ibrahîm declared that he would receive the commander of the approaching party peacefully, and with honor and courtesy, *if he came alone;* but if *he approached with his soldiers the gates would be closed against him.* The hurrying to and fro in the narrow streets showed that preparations for resistance were being made. My brother said to me, " I am perfectly satisfied that there are no Bedouins in the town. Have you courage to go down with me alone into the plain, that I may speak to the cavalry officer, and prevent if possible a useless and unequal conflict?" I did not hesitate for an instant. So we mounted, and, as quickly as we could, we rode down the hill, quite unattended, while the people on the embattled walls and house-tops, and at the guarded gate, watched and directed us, wishing us "Godspeed." We were soon nearly half-way across the plain, and there encountered the advancing soldiers. When we were within speaking distance, we stopped suddenly, facing them. They were on the point of dividing to pass on each side of us, but my brother held up his hand energetically, and said, speaking as one having authority, "*Halt!*" and immediately they stood still. Then he called to the colonel, saying he desired to speak with him, and, keeping up his attitude of assumed authority, said, "O Colonel! you are going to Senûr in the name of his Excellency Kamîl Pasha. The answer to the message of which you are the bearer will be '*No.*' Go yourself quietly and peaceably, and obtain that answer from the town. But if you allow your men to advance one step nearer to it, you will be answerable for the consequences."

The Colonel unhesitatingly prepared to obey, leaving his little detachment in the plain, with orders to await his return. We rode slowly backward and forward among the wondering Turkish soldiers, who galloped round and round us, performing feats of horsemanship for our amusement. A black man, who seemed to be the Colonel's especial attendant, played on a triangle, and made fantastic movements with his turbaned head.

The detachment consisted of only seventy horsemen, and they would soon have been sacrificed if they had come into collision with the men of Senûr, and no object would have been gained. After a short delay, the Colonel returned quite satisfied, and rejoined his men. At the same time our servants and attendants came down to us with the luggage, and we pursued our journey toward Nablûs, which is about fifteen miles due south of Senûr. We were preceded by the soldiers. We rode for a little while in company with the Colonel, who told us that Kamîl Pasha had determined to destroy Senûr, and had offered a reward of thirty thousand piasters for the head of Ibrahîm Jerrar. When we reached the entrance to the narrow valley, our military escort took leave of us, and we soon lost sight of the soldiers. They galloped along one after the other recklessly, over rocks and brushwood, spurring their horses with the edges of their shovel-shaped stirrups.

These incidents, from the moment when "the young man who kept the watch" first perceived the horsemen issuing from the narrow valley, till they took leave of us, did not occupy half an hour, though it seemed a much longer space of time.

My brother explained to me that he had no real authority to interfere as he had done in this case. He acted not officially, but individually, feeling that principles of humanity, and our somewhat critical position, justified him. It was singular that we had been the well received guests of the heads of the two great rival factions of the district, within a few hours, and had thus gained much important information.

Hills and valleys, rain and sunshine, checkered our way till, at about sunset, we reached the olive-groves of Nablûs. Although I was wet, and cold, and tired, all my energy and delight returned when the beautiful valley between Mount Ebal and Mount Gerizim, and the well-built town of Nablûs were in sight, with glimpses of the distant sea, where the sun was going down. I was surprised to see a quantity of mistletoe on the olive-trees. The great gates, which were on the point of being closed, were thrown back for us, and we rode through dark arcades and narrow streets to the house of Ody Azam, the British Consul's agent. There we were comfortably entertained, for our host, who could speak a little English, was accustomed to receive European travelers. His house, indeed, was a kind of hotel, and his wife and niece quickly made ready their most cozy room for me. Our arrival was soon announced, and visitors thronged the large divan all the evening, for my brother was well known in Nablûs. Priest Amran, of the Samaritan community, came, speaking with earnest gratitude of the kindness of the English people, and of the English Government.

Kamîl Pasha—who had been my host at Hebron—sent an Effendi to convey his salutations to us, and a number of Turkish officials followed. I knew the Effendi very well. He was a Christian, and the first of his creed who had been raised to the rank of Effendi in the Jerusalem Council. I said to him, "Tell me, O most honorable, is it true that his Excellency Kamîl Pasha has offered a reward of thirty thousand piasters for the head of Ibrahîm, the chief of Senûr?" He answered, "Even so, most excellent lady!" I then said, "Will your honor salute the Pasha in my name, and inform him that I have the head of the chief, Ibrahîm Jerrar, in my possession?" The guests who were present stared, and even my brother was taken by surprise. The Effendi said, "Are you throwing dust in our eyes? Is my lady laughing at the Pasha's beard?" I said again, "Let his excellency know that I have in my possession a head which he desires to obtain." I spoke in a seemingly-serious tone, and would give no further explanation. The people were evidently as much amused as they were puzzled.

The next morning, after a perfect rest, I rose and was called into the divan, where the Effendi awaited me. Kamîl Pasha had sent him to greet me, and had authorized him to receive from my hands the head of the rebel chief. I said, "Where is the purse of piasters, O your honor?" He replied, "The piasters are not with me, O my lady!" I answered, "Then I can not give you the head." So he went away and presently returned with the Pasha's page, who carried a large round tray of hot canâfi, a sweetmeat made of vermicelli, baked with butter, sugar, almonds, walnuts, and spices. The Pasha had ordered it to be brought to me. A number of people whose curiosity had been excited came to see the issue, and to partake of their favorite dish.

The Effendi graciously placed the dish before me, and, after a general washing of hands, all present partook of it. I was asked if I would inform them where the head was. I said, "It is in my portmanteau in the opposite room." Then the Effendi said, "Will you show it to us, O gracious lady?" A glance from my brother induced me to comply, so I fetched the drawing, and the men, on seeing it, cried out immediately, "Ibrahîm!" "It is Ibrahîm Jerrar!" "It is Ibrahîm of Senûr!" "O work of God!" The gravest and most stately-looking of our guests seemed thoroughly to enjoy the joke. They went away to explain the mystery to Kamîl Pasha, who afterward called to see me and the portrait, which he asked me to allow him to keep. I said, "With pleasure, your excellency, if you will consent to regard it as the *real head* and *the only head* of Ibrahîm Jerrar, and act accordingly." His excellency laughingly declined to do this, so I have kept my sketch, which he, however, seemed rather unwilling to part with. He examined it carefully, and held it in his hand for a long time, but I would not alter my conditions. However, another drawing which he selected from my folio, I gave to him. He and his suite went away apparently very much amused.

We found Nablûs and its neighborhood in a very unsettled state. It was exceedingly difficult to convey letters from this district. Postmen were constantly waylaid and robbed. My brother, who was directed to write every second day to Her Britannic Majesty's Consul at Jerusalem, employed special messengers. They were several times attacked, and were severely beaten when they attempted to preserve the dispatches and letters intrusted to their care.

This is always the case in Syria during civil war. Intriguing officers, and the leaders of contending factions, do not like their proceedings to be reported to head-quarters, and they generally endeavor to mislead the European Consuls. My brother spent several hours every day at Kamîl Pasha's encampment, and accompanied his excellency when he visited the neighboring villages.

In the mean time I was rarely left alone. I was visited at all hours by Moslems, Christians, and Samaritans; the latter people interested me greatly. Priest Amran, a cheerful, shrewd-looking, well-informed man, between forty and fifty years of age, used to hear me read Arabic every morning. He gave me an interesting account of his little community, whose numbers amounted to only one hundred and ninety-six.* He said that there was great difficulty sometimes in arranging suitable marriages among them, for they never intermarry with strangers. The priest is always consulted on the subject; and as he or his aged father, Selâmeh, alone have power to celebrate a marriage, none can take place without their consent. He said, "At the present moment the marriageable men are more numerous than the marriageable girls. Our girls are all young, and I am very much troubled about it."

As an instance, he explained to me that Yakûb esh Shellabi, whose visit to England may be remembered by some of my readers, had been betrothed to Zora while she was yet a child. Yakûb was in England when Zora was marriageable; Amran did not permit her to wait for him, but married her to Habîb, a widower, who had one little girl, named Anithe. She was seven years old, and was to be given to Yakûb in the place of Zora, who was now her step-mother. He said, "This marriage has caused me great anxiety and much trouble."

Another man, who was only thirty, and for whom a girl could not be found, had married a widow fifty years of age, and he was now trying to persuade Priest Amran to allow him to put her away, that he might be betrothed to the priest's daughter, who was about eleven. He said,

---

* According to Wilson's account, they numbered one hundred and fifty in the year 1843.

"Nearly all our girls are promised before they can speak, and are married when they are eleven or twelve."

Priest Amran took me one day to the Samaritan quarter. It is an irregular cluster of two-storied houses, in the most crowded part of the town. We passed through white-washed passages, and ascended a crooked, uncovered, steep stone stairway, leading into an open court, where a large, glossy-leaved lemon-tree grew close to an arched door, through which we passed, after "putting off" our shoes. I found that I was in the synagogue. It is a simple, unadorned, vaulted building, in rather a dilapidated state. Amran introduced me to the chief priest, his aged father, "Selâmeh"—he who, in 1808, corresponded with Baron de Sacy. He received me very courteously. After a short conversation about Yakûb esh Shellabi, he said, "I am very old, but I shall die in peace, thanking God that he has let me live to see my people under the protection of the English Government." He said this in allusion to the fact that Lord Clarendon had sent instructions to the Consuls resident in Palestine, expressing the interest which Her Britannic Majesty's Government takes in the Samaritans, and directing them to afford, in case of need, such protection as may be proper toward Turkish subjects. His Excellency Lord Stratford de Redcliffe had also been instructed to use his good offices with the Porte in favor of the Samaritan community. A mat was spread on the stone floor, and there I rested, listening to the slowly and earnestly-uttered words of the aged priest. He wore a loose blue cloth robe, lined with crimson, over a yellow and red-striped satin kumbaz, which is made like a dressing-gown. His large turban and his long beard were white.

He directed my attention to the vail of the temple. It was a square curtain of white damask linen, ornamented with *appliqué* work; that is, pieces of red, purple, and green linen were sewed on to it, forming a beautiful pattern of conventional ornament. He supposed it to be six or seven hundred years old, but I imagine that it is the work of the sixteenth century. After I had copied the design of the vail carefully Priest Amran drew it aside, and revealed a deep recess, where the rolls of the law are kept. Then his father rose, and with trembling hands brought out the celebrated copy of the Tora or Pentateuch, which is said to have been written by Abishua, the son of Phinehas, the son of Eleazar, who was the son of Aaron. It is kept in a cylindrical silver-gilt case, which opens on two sets of hinges, and on its red satin cover Hebrew inscriptions are embroidered with gold thread. At my request Selâmeh sat down for a little while, holding it in his hands, that I might sketch it and him. When he had carefully returned this precious roll to its place, he showed me several later copies of the Pentateuch—some in the Samaritan, others in the Arabic character; a printed collection of psalms or hymns; several commentaries on the law of different periods; a history of the community from the Exodus to the time of Mohammed; and a very curious manuscript, called the Book of Joshua, which begins with an account of the journeyings of the company of spies who were sent into the promised land by Moses, and concludes with fabulous stories of the life of Alexander. This seems to be rather a favorite book. It is written in Arabic, but the proper names and certain words are in the Samaritan characters. It is said to be of Syriac and not of Hebrew origin. I brought a copy of this remarkable work to England.

A number of the neighbors came into the synagogue to see me, and to invite me to their houses, and fair little children crowded round. I took leave of the aged Priest Selâmeh, and he gave me his patriarchal blessing. Then I went with Priest Amran to call on Habîb and his wife Zora, who had been the betrothed of Yakûb esh Shęllabi. I was led into a large, low, but very airy room, with raised divans, nicely carpeted and cushioned, on two sides of it. Mats and rugs on the stone floor made the place look comfortable, and a red brass-hinged box, a rudely-carved red cradle, ornamental corner cupboards, and painted wooden shelves, with rows of green drinking-glasses ranged upon them, relieved the whitewashed walls.

Habîb, to whom I had been previously introduced, welcomed me with courteous gravity. His pretty little motherless daughter, Anithe, came forward promptly to greet me; but Zora, the young wife, seemed unwilling to appear. Priest Amran told me that she was purposely hiding. Habîb went out into the court of the house, and when he reëntered his wife followed him with seeming reluctance; she looked embarrassed and sad, and returned my salutations sullenly. She was rather handsome, and was decked as a bride; she wore full trowsers and a tight jacket. Her chest was very much exposed, and painted or tattooed bright-blue; her gold necklace or collar was large and massive, and several coins were attached to it; her head-dress was adorned with red and yellow everlasting flowers, and folds of blue crape; her hands and feet, which were naked, were so delicately and artistically stained with henna, that she looked as if she had fine lace mittens and sandals on. She made me some lemonade, while Anithe brought me a narghilé.

Many women came in; among them was Yakûb esh Shellabi's mother. She said impetuously, "How long shall I wait for my son Yakûb and not see him? Why does he stay so long away from his country and his people? Why did you leave him in England, O lady? I shall die and never see him again." I answered, "Be comforted; your son will return to you and give you joy." Zora seemed troubled at the mention of his name, and left the room; but Habîb smiled a smile of self-congratulation, and asked if I thought that Yakûb would return in time to claim his little daughter. The child evidently quite understood how affairs had been arranged, but did not display the slightest interest or emotion. While the other girls and women who were present asked with curiosity and volubility all sorts of questions about Yakûb, and were highly amused with the account I gave them of his reception in England, little Anithe maintained a quiet and dignified reserve, which I suppose, according to Samaritan etiquette, was very praiseworthy and becoming.

Zora did not reënter the room; but when I passed through the court, on my way to the house of a neighbor, I saw her with her mother engaged in cooking. She had been crying, and on seeing me she hastily ran into a storeroom and disappeared. Amran said, "She is not quite reconciled yet to the new arrangement; but her husband is good and well off, and she will soon be happy."

I visited three other houses, all of the same character as Habîb's, but his was the most comfortably furnished. On the whole, I was very favorably impressed with the appearance of the Samaritan community. The men were generally handsome, tall, healthy-looking, and intelligent, but very few of them could read or write. The women are modest, and the children very pretty and thoughtful, yet full of life and activity. I am told that the Samaritans live to a great age, and generally escape the epidemics which break out occasionally in Nablûs. Perhaps this is owing to the simplicity of their lives, and their scrupulous cleanliness. They observe the ceremonial laws of Moses with fidelity. Three times a year they go in solemn procession to the summit of Gerizim, repeating portions of the law as they ascend, and they still proudly proclaim to pilgrims and travelers, "Our fathers worshiped in this mountain." The mountain is now called "Jebel-el-Tor."

They do not receive any part of the Bible, except the Pentateuch. They say that the other books are forgeries, and they regard the seventeenth chapter of the Second Book of Kings as a cruel calumny, originating with their enemies the Jews. The Jews, on the other hand, declare that this portion of the Bible is rejected by the Samaritans, simply because it records their true history and testifies against them.

The Samaritans declare themselves to be children of

Manasseh and Ephraim, and their priest is said to be lineally descended from a branch of the tribe of Levi, by whom their services have been conducted throughout all generations. Priest Amran explained this to me, and then said, "Alas, I have no son! I have no son to whom to teach the holy language, no son to assist me in the services, no son to inherit the priesthood. God forbid that I should be the last of my race, and leave my people without a priest!"

It was a cause of bitter sorrow to the Samaritans when, some time ago, the last male representative of the Aaronic family died; for he was the last of their hereditary high-priests—the last to offer sacrifices for them. They are obliged now to limit their ministrations to such services as may legally be performed by Priest Amran and his father, who represent the tribe of Levi, of whom it is written, that the Lord spoke unto Moses, saying, "Present them before Aaron the priest, that they may minister unto him. And they shall keep his charge, and the charge of the whole congregation, before the tabernacle of the congregation, to do the service of the tabernacle." (See Num. iii, 5, etc.) And again it is written, that God spoke unto Moses, and said, "Thou shalt put upon Aaron the holy garments, and anoint him and sanctify him; and thou shalt anoint his sons, and their anointing shall surely be an everlasting priesthood throughout all generations." And unto Aaron God said, "Ye shall keep the charge of the sanctuary, and the charge of the altar; and thy brethren the Levites [such as Amran and his father] shall keep the charge of all the tabernacle: only they shall not come nigh the vessels of the sanctuary and the altar, that neither they, nor ye also, die." (See Num. xviii.)

With these verses before me, and knowing the character of the Samaritans, their belief in the true descent of their priests, their implicit faith in the Divine inspiration of the Tora, and their consequent reliance on the efficacy of ceremonial services, I can well imagine their desolation when they buried the last of the anointed sons of Aaron, and were left without a high-priest to minister for them. With the house of Aaron the celebration of the highest offices of their religion ceased. No sacrifices can be offered now, and there is no one "to make atonement for the people."

During the days of unleavened bread the Samaritans live in tents, on the mountain near to the ruins of their ancient temple. "On the fifteenth day of the first month," the whole congregation, men, women, and children, except such as are ceremonially unclean, being assembled, the priest stands forth on a mound, and reads, in a most solemn and impressive voice, the animated description of the Exodus.

In a trench, ten feet long by two feet wide, previously prepared by laborers, a fire is kindled, and two caldrons of water are placed over it. A round pit is dug, in the form of a well; and it is heated to serve as an oven. Then lambs are brought, in sufficiency for the whole community. Seven is now the usual number. At sunset, seven men, in white dresses, take each a lamb before him, and at the utterance of a particular word in the service appointed for the day, all seven lambs are slain at the same instant. Every member of the congregation then dips his hand in the blood of the dying victims, and besmears his forehead with it. Boiling water from the caldrons is poured over the fleece, which causes the wool to leave the skin without much difficulty. It is plucked off with great nicety. The bodies of the lambs are examined, lest there be any blemish. The right shoulder and the hamstrings are cut off and thrown on the heap of offal to be burnt with the wool. The seven bodies are then spitted, and forced into the hot bake oven. A trelliswork is then placed over the top of the oven, which is covered with grass and mud, to keep in all the heat. A few hours after sunset they are withdrawn, and the Samaritans, each "with his loins girt and a staff in his hand," eat hastily and greedily of the food thus prepared. The scraps of meat, wool, and bone are carefully sought for, and burnt on the heap, that not a morsel may remain. My brother has twice been present at the celebration of the Feast of the Passover, and from him I obtained the above description.

The Feast of Tabernacles is also kept "in this mountain." It happens in the early part of the Autumn, when tent-life is very pleasant and refreshing. The people "take the branches of goodly trees," such as the evergreen oak and the arbutus, and they "make booths," roofing them with interlacing willows, pliant palm fronds, and boughs of the glossy-leaved citron and lemon trees, with the green fruit hanging from them in clusters. For seven days the people dwell there, rejoicing and giving thanks to God.

Sometimes the Samaritans, to their great distress, have been obliged to celebrate their festivals elsewhere, and in secret, owing to the fanaticism and persecuting spirit of the Moslems of Nablûs. But Priest Amran said, "Now that the English word has been spoken for us, we shall no longer fear; and, notwithstanding the civil war, the Paschal lamb will this year be slain on the mountain where our fathers worshiped. The time is near at hand, O lady! tarry with us till the Passover, and we will make a pleasant tent for you on the mountain, that you, with the Consul, may witness the celebration of the festival and eat of our unleavened bread."

Most of the Samaritan women came to see me in my private room at the hotel. Yakûb esh Shellabi's sister, a fine girl—very like her brother—came several times, and Zora grew somewhat sociable. I could plainly see, by her manners and by her few words, that she was angry with herself and with her absent betrothed, and still more angry that she had not been permitted to await his return. She even seemed imbittered against the English people, as if they had lured Yakûb away from her, and I did not wonder that this marriage had given Priest Amran "much trouble." The women do not hide their faces from men of their own community, but they vail themselves closely in the streets and in the presence of strangers.

They were generally very simply dressed, in trowsers and jackets of Manchester prints and colored muslin headkerchiefs and vails. When out of doors, they shrouded themselves in large white cotton sheets, and, though the former were faded and the latter patched, their poorest garments looked clean. I saw very little jewelry, except on the head-dresses of the most recently-married women. They nearly all, however, wore glass bracelets; and some of the children had anklets, made of tinkling silver bells. The girls had a few small coins sewed to the edges of their red tarbûshes, just in front.

The Samaritans seem really to represent one family. The people look to the hereditary priest as their father and divinely-appointed guide, and he apparently knows the history and character of every member of the community. He is king, magistrate, physician, teacher, counselor, and friend of all. It struck me very forcibly that the Samaritans are not animated with any religious emotion or feeling, though they certainly venerate their theological system and all that is connected with it, especially the site of the ancient temple on the mountain where their fathers worshiped. They attach great importance to ceremonial and especially to sanitary laws relating to marriage, to food, and to ablutions. They observe the Sabbath-day strictly, in a material sense, but without the slightest sign of spiritual devotion. Their services are noisy and seemingly irreverent.

They do not avoid friendly or commercial intercourse with strangers, though they will not intermarry with them. The few native Protestants in Nablûs are on a very intimate footing with the Samaritans; and native Greek Christians, and many Moslems, are on good terms with them. But their Jewish neighbors do not like them at all. They accuse them of heresy and even of idolatry, and avoid them as much as possible, saying that they are worshipers of pigeons! This is a very anciently-founded calumny. The Samaritans, on the other hand, declare that the Jews neglect the Law of Moses, and have departed from purity of life and worship, and follow the Talmud. They date their separation from the Jews from the time of Eli the priest, whom they regard as a usurper, for he was not of the priestly family of Eleazar, but a descendant of Ithamar, the fourth son of Aaron.

In 1842 the Samaritans were cruelly persecuted because they would not embrace the Moslem faith, and the Mohammedan Ulemas threatened to murder the whole of their community, on the plea that they had no religion, not even believing in one of the five inspired books, which are: 1. Law of Moses; 2. New Testament; 3. The Psalms; 4. The Prophets; and 5. The Koran. A sect which acknowledges the inspiration of any one of these five books is legally tolerated by the Mohammedans. This being known to the Samaritans, they endeavored to prove their belief in the Pentateuch; but the Mohammedans, not being acquainted with the holy language and characters in which it was written, disbelieved them. They then applied to the Chief Rabbi of the Jews in Jerusalem—a recognized representative and head of the Jewish faith—who gave them a written declaration, certifying, "That the Samaritan people is a branch of the children of Israel, who acknowledge the truth of the Tora"—that is, the Pentateuch. This document, accompanied with presents, put an end to the persecution for a time. I mention this merely to show in what light the Samaritans are regarded by the superior and learned Jews.

Those who knew Yakûb esh Shellabi in England will perhaps like to hear something about him. He is the only Samaritan who ever traveled so far west. He returned to his people in the Autumn of 1856, and soon reaccustomed himself to the simple yet active life of the Samaritans. He advised Priest Amran to establish a school, and oblige all the children of the community, both girls and boys, to attend it regularly, that all of the rising generation might be taught to read and write Arabic, and to cast accounts. Yakûb much regretted that he was unable to do either, and was too old to learn. I am told that this school has been established, and is called the Shellabi School, in memory of Yakûb's visit to England, where he had learned to set a very high value on book-learning.

He did not, after all, marry little Anithe. She was not old enough to be his bride immediately on his return, and another arrangement was consequently made, as the following curious specimen of Oriental correspondence will show. It was a reply to an inquiry concerning Yakûb, and is a true and literal translation of a letter from Priest Amran to E. T. Rogers, Esq., Her Britannic Majesty's Vice-Consul, Hâifa:

"To the perfection of energy, the most virtuous, and unsubornable, the presence of the most praiseworthy brother Khawadja Rogers, the illustrious. May God Almighty lengthen his days! Amen.

"After heart-felt prayers for your preservation, I beg to inform you that I was honored by your bountiful letter, dated the 17th of June, of Western calculation, collectively with Daûd Tannus,* and we read with pleasure of your preservation, and we thanked the Almighty, who hath vouchsafed that you should think of us. Your sweet slip [a postscript] which was inclosed in said letter I have read. I find that you ask me whether Yakûb esh Shellabi is married or not. My Lord, he has been married ever since last year to a very pretty partner, who is exceedingly good. Her name is Shemsch [Sunny]; and last Thursday, the first day of Western July, she gave birth to a male child, who resembles the moon, and they have called his name Emîn [Faithful]. Please God that this may happen in like manner to you. I have given you this glad tidings, which is all that is necessary in petitioning you to honor me by

* The principal member of the native Protestant congregation in Nablûs.

letting me know all that I can do to serve you, and God lengthen your days! My Lord, your petitioner, [signed and sealed,] Amran, the Priest. Written in Nablûs, 9th July, Western year, 1858."

Another child has been born to Yakûb, and I have heard him speak proudly, lovingly, and tenderly of his little ones, and of his young wife Shemseh, and of the flourishing Samaritan day-school.

A few days after my arrival in Nablûs, I was sitting in the divan at the hotel, with a little company of Samaritans, Greek priests, and Protestant Arabs, when a very poor Moslem woman forced her way into the room, notwithstanding that the kawass and servants at the door endeavored to prevent her entrance. She cried out, "Make way! I must speak to the English lady, the Consul's sister." I said, "Let her speak."

She was almost shrouded in an old blue-and-white check linen sheet, of native manufacture. She was very aged, and tottered across the room to me, and then partly drew aside her thick cotton vail, and kissed my head and my hands violently and impetuously, beseeching me to intercede for her son, who had been imprisoned for insulting and striking our kawass in the bazar.

She said, "I am a widow, and the offender is my only son, my sole support. Speak for him, for my sake. Speak for him, for the sake of the mother of your brother. Speak for him, that he may be set free!"

She kneeled down, and tried to kiss my feet, and embraced my knees imploringly. I raised her up, saying, "Go now in peace. I will speak to the Consul about your son."

She went away rejoicing, and cried aloud, "The gates of the prison are thrown open! The offender, my son, is already free; for the English word is spoken!"

I made inquiries about the prisoner, and, for my "word's sake," my brother applied for his release, and before sunset he was free.

He came in the evening, with his mother, to thank me; for he had heard that I had spoken a good word for him. He had been flogged, but looked very submissive, and well pleased at his unexpected and sudden release. When the doors of a Turkish prison are closed, they are not readily opened, except with a golden key; and this man knew that his friends were too poor to offer an efficient bribe.

He said to me, "O my protectress, in memory of your intercession, I will seek occasion at all times to render service to you, and, for your sake, to all English people." I replied, "Take care of your mother, and try to live peaceably with all men."

They went away, murmuring blessings. When, a few weeks afterward, the Protestants of Nablûs were cruelly attacked by the Moslems, this man proved himself a stanch friend to them. For Protestants are regarded as English *protégés*, even as the Latins are looked upon as French, and the Greeks as Russian subjects.

I had some very interesting conversations with the Arab schoolmaster of the little community of Protestants at Nablûs. He is a native of Nazareth, about thirty years of age, the uncle of our coffee-boy and pipe-bearer, Yusef, described in a former chapter. He was educated at the Diocesan School, Jerusalem, and there learned to speak English pretty freely. His foreign accent, peculiar idioms, and Orientally-constructed phrases, amused me exceedingly. He seemed delighted to have an opportunity of talking English. He was very anxious to be made acquainted with the rules of domestic life in England, and especially the customs and laws relating to betrothals, weddings, divorces, and the settlement of property. I satisfied him on these points as well as I could, and he, in return, gave me an account of his marriage. I will repeat it, as nearly as possible, in his own words, which I noted down on Sunday, March 2d, the day on which he related it to me.

"I shall make you see how, in this country, marriages

are made. Perhaps your English customs are not quite
good in this matter, and our customs also are not good.
It is better that we take from you a little, and that you
also take some teachings from us. I went, four years ago,
to Nâsirah, my town, for my espousals. All knew that
I went to look for a girl. I had no father; I had no
mother. I went to the house of my aunt, the sister of
my father, and said, 'O my aunt! seek for me a girl,
that I may be espoused quickly.' And she said, 'Be at
rest, O my son! I know a good girl for you; I shall
speak for her.' Then my heart was heavy, because I
must not seek and see her for myself; and I said, 'O my
aunt! how can I do this thing and not see her? Perhaps
her eyes are bad; perhaps she has manners not good. I
must see her. Hide me that I may see her.' My aunt
was much afraid; but she loved me, and she said, 'Make
your heart strong; *I will cheat her for you.*'

"So she went out and sought for the girl she wished to
take for my wife. She was the child of our neighbor;
and when she found her she said, 'My daughter, I seek
you. Come with me to my house. Let us work together.
I have a thing to show you.' Then I stood where she
must come that way. Her face had no vail. She did
not know that I was hid. She was a little while working
and talking with my aunt. I saw that she was beautiful
and fair; she was eleven of age. She spoke well and
softly, and her words were good words; and my heart
went out of myself to her. In a little while she came
by where I stood, and she saw that I was looking on
her with power. Then her face came very red, and she
ran home very fast to her mother, and my aunt also went
to her. And the girl cried and said, 'O mother! they
cheat me—they cheat me!' Her mother gave her comfort,
and said, 'Be at rest, O my daughter! Now that he has
seen you, he will wish you for his wife; he will take you.'
But the girl was full of anger, and said again, 'It is not
good that they cheat me.'

"My aunt came to me, and told me of her anger and her grief, and said, 'It is better not to speak any more of this, and we will find another girl.' But my heart had gone forth to this one, and I could not think for another. So I went to the Greek priest and told him the whole matter. And then the priest went to the father of the girl, but the father said, 'Not so; I have two larger girls; they must not be left; they must make their espousals before this little one.' Then I said to the priest, 'Speak for me again, that I may have that little one.' So the father made a writing, and I put my seal on it, and agreed to give him much silks, and cottons, and soap for this daughter—more of all these things than he would make me give for the larger daughters; for he knew my heart was gone out from me. I saw her again, for not quite one minute, when the espousals were made and witnessed. Then my aunt made a room ready for me in her house, and many men came to eat with me there a good feast. And many women went to eat with the girl in the house of her father, and danced before her, and sang songs of rejoicing. And all people knew that we were espoused; but I might not see her again.

"Then I went to Nablûs. And, after a year, four men, with horses, went for me from this town to Nâsirah, and they brought her, and then immediately we were married."

He introduced his young wife and her infant son to me. She was very bright and cheerful-looking, with a high color, and dark, clear eyes. She said that Nâsirah was a much better town than Nablûs for Christians to dwell in.

The Protestant congregation of Nablûs was founded by Dr. Bowen, the late lamented Bishop of Sierra Leone. He established a loom there, and gave the people an opportunity of working. He paid them for their labor, taught them many useful arts, and afterward, by degrees, gave them religious instruction. He was a great favorite with all classes, and many of the Greek Catholics declared themselves Protestants.

Since Dr. Bowen's departure, the community has been very fluctuating, and sometimes quite dispersed. When I attended their service in the school-room, there were about twenty men and thirty boys present. A dozen women sat in an adjoining room, looking in and listening at an open arched window. They were all closely vailed. The service was well conducted by Michael Kawarre, a native teacher. The Gospel was read by a boy, only twelve years of age, in a clear though very monotonous voice. The responses were made most energetically.

M. Zeller, a German, had recently been appointed by Bishop Gobat to take charge of the community, and he was eagerly studying Arabic, that he might commence his missionary labors. He kindly left his lonely study, now and then, to explore Nablûs and its neighborhood with me.

One morning we walked through the stony, arched, narrow, tortuous streets, out at the nearest gate, and rose on to the raised road or terrace, which nearly encircles the town. He led me to the hill beyond the burial-ground, whence I could see the whole extent of Nablûs, with its mosques and minarets, its irregular groups of houses, with domes and terraced roofs, its dark archways and colonnades, and the gardens of lemons and oranges around. Then we climbed a steep and stony path, to see an ancient fountain and a reservoir formed of a sarcophagus, where closely-vailed women were washing their tattered garments. A group of men were leisurely building up the broken stone wall of the water-course. They were working with clumsy-looking tools, and each man had a gun slung over his shoulder.

We followed the course of the duct, which conveys water from the fountain along the terraces round the town. The stones of the aqueduct were moss-grown, and between them bright juicy leaves of the most vivid green had sprung up. At short intervals there were square apertures, through which we could see the running limpid water, in a frame-work of maiden-hair and other ferns, and white and lilac blossoms. We came to a large square ancient pool, or reservoir, well filled and in good repair, near to the governor's new residence, which is the handsomest dwelling-house I had seen in Palestine. It is built of well-hewn fine limestone, and enriched with marble pavements, columns, and arches. Mahmoud Bek Abdul Hady designed it himself.

We reëntered the town, and paused before the portal of the mosque. It was originally the entrance to a Christian church, as the design plainly shows. The clustered columns, the richly-foliated and varied capitals, the deep, dental, and zigzag moldings of the pointed arch, are of Siculo-Norman character. While we were carefully examining the details, signs were made to us—rather roughly—by some of the guardians of the mosque, that we were approaching too near to their place of worship, and lingering there too long; so we retired, and traversed the bazars. The shops were well stocked, and busy with buyers and sellers. There were small arcades especially devoted to the sale of tobacco; others were filled with the refreshing odor of green lemons, oranges, citrons, and shaddocks. The bazars for vegetables and prepared food were rather difficult to pass through; they were thronged with Turkish soldiers from the Pasha's camp, who were seeking their midday rations. Some of them were carrying large metal dishes, containing a medley of chopped vegetables, or deep earthenware plates, filled with pease-pudding, garnished with slices of lemon floating in oil; others hurried through the crowd with bowls of steaming soup before them, which very effectually cleared the way. There seemed to be no friendly feeling between the soldiers and the townspeople. Angry voices and loud cries surrounded us, and in several cases blows were exchanged before a bargain was settled. The long, narrow bazar where dried fruits, olives, rice, butter, and cheese were sold, led us to the entrance of an important mosque, the exterior of which is rich in relics of Christian art of the twelfth century. After pausing before it for a few minutes, we made our way down a street almost blocked up by camels, and thence passed into the principal bazar, the finest arcade in Palestine. It is rather wider and much more lofty than the Lowther Arcade, and about five or six times as long. Here European goods are displayed, such as Manchester prints, Sheffield cutlery, beads, and French bijouterie, very small mirrors, Bohemian glass-bottles for narghilés, Swiss headkerchiefs, in imitation of the Constantinople mundîls, crockery-ware, and china coffee-cups. But the brightest shops are those in which Damascus and Aleppo silks, and embroidered jackets and tarbûshes from Stamboul, appear, with stores of Turkish pipes, amber rosaries, and bracelets from Hebron. On the low shop-counters the turbaned salesmen squat in the midst of the gay wares, and they smoke and gossip, stroke their beards, and finger their rosaries from early in the morning till sunset.

An opening in the middle of this arcade led us into an extensive khan, well planned, but so out of repair as to be almost useless. It is an uncovered square space, inclosed by a two-storied range of buildings. The ground-floor is well adapted for lodging camels and other beasts of burden, but the upper chambers are so dilapidated that they afford but little shelter. We mounted a broken stone stairway, and with difficulty reached the terraced roof, which commands a good view of the town.

When we reëntered the arcade, we heard ourselves unexpectedly addressed by name, and, turning round, we saw Ody Azam, my host, in his little shop, selling pens, pencils, and paper, and Birmingham wares. He said that the Arabs wondered how it was that I could walk freely and unvailed in public places, adding, "Our women do not enter the bazars; it would be a shame for them."

The chief productions of Nablûs are cotton, olive-oil, and soap. The latter is made in large quantities, and sold throughout Palestine; it is grayish-white and makes a good lather. The oil of Nablûs is famous for its clearness and purity. The neighborhood is rich in vineyards and fig-gardens, and all "precious fruits brought forth by the sun." The people are much attached to their town, and are very proud of it. They seem to think there is no place in the world to equal it.

When I returned to the hotel I found a turbaned stranger waiting to see the Vice-Consul. He introduced himself to me as Sheikh Mûssa. He wore a loose olive-colored cloth robe, bordered with sable fur, and a purple and drab striped satin under-dress, and purple cloth pelisse. He said he had heard that I could make faces on paper, and that, if I liked, I might take his portrait, on the condition that I would tell the Consul at Jerusalem that he had not interfered in the late intrigues. I answered, "I should like to take your portrait; but how can I tell that which I do not know, and how can I know that you have taken no part in these troubles?" "Nevertheless," he replied, "take my portrait, and show it to the Consul, Mr. Finn, and I shall find favor with him." He sat for an hour, with his rosary and pipe in his hands, most patiently, and then went away.

Shortly afterward Mahmoud Bek Abdul Hady, the Governor, came in with my brother. The former, whom I had seen several times, asked me many questions about my visit to his relations at Arrabeh. I showed him the sketches I had made there. He invited me to go to his new house, saying that his wives had expressed a wish to see me; but he added, "If you take their portraits, you must promise not to show them to any one in this country. You may show them in England to your friends and to the Queen, but it would be a shame for me that men in this land should see the faces of my women." I gave my promise, and he said, "It is well; the English word is spoken. Come at sunset and you shall find welcome." He said, "Do you like Arrabeh or Senûr better?" I said, "I found greater pleasure at Arrabeh, and I hope very much to see again the friends who received me there so kindly." He said, "God be praised that Arrabeh has found favor with you!"

Then he went away, and at sunset my brother accompanied me to his house. Two kawasses and lantern-bearers led the way. We were conducted into a vast open court, paved with marble, and the governor came out to meet us, and led me into the divan, or reception-hall, where a number of Moslem gentlemen were assembled. They rose from the raised divans, which were ranged on three sides of the room, and stood still till my brother and myself had taken the places prepared for us on the chief divan. The governor arranged an embroidered cushion for me, and sat by my side, and then said to the standing guests, "Itfuddal!"— a word of wide significance, corresponding with the Italian "*favorisca*," and meaning, in this instance, "*Be seated.*"

The room was very lofty. The white walls were ornamented with blue arabesque borders, painted in fresco. The arched windows and large doorway were of Saracenic form. A part of the floor was raised a few inches, to form a dais, and was spread with handsome carpets, and in the center stood a tall brass candelabrum supporting an oil lamp. In the lower part of the room a number of servants waited. They were the attendants and lantern-bearers of the several guests. Richly-dressed Abyssinian slaves handed round the coffee, flavored with ambergris, and others carried silver trays of sweetmeats. A costly narghilé, the mouthpiece of which was set with diamonds and sapphires, was brought for me.

I had expected to be conducted only to the harem, and was rather taken by surprise on being ushered into the midst of this company. I did not venture, in the presence of men, to speak to Mahmoud Bek about his wives, for it is not considered delicate to do so, and my brother could on no account allude to the object of my visit. I waited impatiently for a long time, hoping that a messenger would come for me.

In the mean time an interesting discussion on civilization

and life in towns and villages and tents was carried on. Our host showed us a plan for the completion of his house, and asked my advice about the interior decorations and details. He had evidently a strong natural taste and talent for architectural construction, and was a good judge of building materials. He told me that he could judge whether stone was of a durable nature or not, by its taste. I have often seen an Arab touch newly-quarried stone with the tip of his tongue, and I suppose that he could by this means ascertain its quality. There are some fine quarries in Palestine, but the stone generally preferred by builders is that which is brought from the ruins of some ancient building, and which has already stood the test of centuries.

More than an hour passed, and still I had no summons to the harem. I said to Mahmoud softly, "I came to-night in consequence of your especial invitation;" he answered, "I am greatly honored by your presence, O my lady! you have given me great pleasure, and I have profited by your words and your counsel—this room, which no woman has ever before entered, is yours."

A special messenger from the Pasha came to seek my brother, and we took leave of Mahmoud Bek. He attended us to the outer door with much deference and a great many compliments, but he did not make the slightest effort to detain me to visit his harem. I suppose he was afraid that I should "reveal the secrets of his prison-house," or on consideration he may have thought it actually dangerous for any of his ladies to have their portraits taken. It was rumored that he had recently married a very beautiful girl, and that in his establishment there were some fair young slaves from Constantinople. The fact was, I believe, I had answered his many questions about my sojourn at Arrabeh rather too unreservedly, and had unwisely showed him the portrait of his cousin Saleh's pretty wife Helweh. I was always on my guard afterward under similar circumstances. This governor, Mahmoud Bek, was an elderly man with a long gray beard. He was full of energy and enterprise, and appeared clever, penetrating, and shrewd, but obstinate and tyrannical, and was the head of a very troublesome faction.

The next morning Sheikh Mûssa came that I might finish his portrait. He said, "They are idiots and 'majnûni' who believe that a man is in danger of losing his soul if a resemblance of him be made on paper with lines of a pencil point—but it is not well to make him of wood or to carve him in stone." He added, "In this land there is much ignorance and folly, but we must hold our peace, for if we speak the thoughts of our hearts to fools they will say, 'It is your folly and not ours—we are wise—ye are fools who doubt our wisdom.' Thus the wise hold their peace, and the foolish ones of the earth are made proud and strong in their folly. Thus it is decreed."

The afternoon was especially bright and balmy, and my brother spared time to ride out with me in company with M. Zeller and a few Protestant Arabs. We passed out of the town at the east gate and went down the Nablûs valley in a south-easterly direction, with Mount Ebal on our left and Mount Gerizim, nearer to us, on our right; the former looked rather rugged and bare, but the latter was here and there clothed with trees and herbage. Pointing to a tree growing far above us, Ody Azam said, "That old olive-tree is the largest in the whole country; its trunk is so thick, that if four tall men joined hands, they could not entirely embrace it."

We crossed and recrossed winding streams and artificial water-courses, in the gardens and cultivated fields of the winding valley. After half an hour's ride we paused and alighted by an isolated and fallen granite column, half buried in the earth, at the foot of Mount Gerizim. Near to it was a pit, almost filled up with rubbish and earth, and encircled with large hewn stones—"Now, Jacob's well was there." My brother drew my attention to it, saying, "It was to show you this choked-up fountain that I brought you here to-day; for Jews, Samaritans, Christians, and

Moslems all agree in associating the name of the Patriarch Jacob with this spot. To Christians it is especially interesting as the scene of Christ's interview with the woman of Samaria, when 'He being wearied with his journey *from Judea* sat thus by the well *at midday* while his disciples went *up the valley* into the city to buy meat.' And we are now sitting under the shadow of Gerizim, of which the woman spoke when she said, 'Sir, our fathers worshiped in this mountain; and ye say, that in Jerusalem is the place where men ought to worship.' And from this well-side Christ's memorable answer was given—'God is a spirit, and they that worship him must worship him in spirit and in truth.'"

The outlines of the surrounding hills were sharply defined against a sky intensely blue; the large village called Tulluzah, supposed to be the ancient and "comely Tirzah," half-way up Mount Ebal, was pointed out to me. Its houses were scarcely distinguishable from the masses of rock and the great stone bowlders on the rugged slopes. Terraced vineyards and fine olive-groves nearly encircle the village and mark its limits.

Flourishing fruit gardens and groves skirt the base of the mountains, and groups of evergreen oaks stand here and there. The plain and the valley were vividly green with wheat and barley, beans and lentils. Bright wild flowers garnished the low stone walls or landmarks between them. It was the 5th of March, and we could consequently say, "There are yet two months and then cometh the harvest." It must have been earlier in the Spring when Christ beheld this landscape and said to his disciples, "Lift up your eyes and look upon the fields." He spoke figuratively—but these very fields suggested the figure.

Though quite half an hour's walk from the town, this well must have been a favorite place of resort of the children of Israel, from the time when he gave it to them, and drank thereof himself, and his children, and his cattle. When the woman of Samaria said to Christ, "Sir, the well is deep," she spoke truly. It is a circular shaft cut out of the solid rock, and when it was measured a few years ago it was found to be seventy-five feet deep, and yet the true bottom of the well was not then reached on account of the accumulation of mud. Yakûb esh Shellabi, when a boy, was let down into this well, and I have often heard him describe his descent. An account of it was published in a little book called, "Notices of the Modern Samaritans, illustrated by incidents in the life of Yakûb esh Shellabi, gathered from him and translated by Mr. E. T. Rogers"— my brother. I will give the extract which records the circumstance, for I do not suppose that any one living has ever been down that well except Yakûb. He was exactly twelve years old at the time.

"In the year 1841, a Scotch gentleman, named Dr. Wilson, arrived in Nablûs, and made great inquiries for Jacob's Well, and having found out the exact spot, he hired ten strong men and myself to accompany him thither; and in passing through the bazar he purchased four camel ropes. I could not understand all this preparation, but on arriving at the mouth of the well I soon discovered the reason. It appeared that one of the Scotch missionaries* had some years ago dropped his Bible into the well, which Dr. Wilson was now so anxious to extricate. The men were soon set to work to remove the huge stones from the mouth of the well, and I was chosen, as being of light weight, to be lowered down for the search.

"I was much afraid at first; however, I consented, upon some consolatory words, and pecuniary persuasion, and a promise to take me to England made by Dr. Wilson. The rope was therefore tied round my waist, and I swung round—having no means of steadying myself—till I was quite giddy and faint from the impurity of the air. The four camel ropes were joined together, and still I had not reached the bottom; two shawls, which composed the turbans of two Samaritans who were with us, were then tied to the

* The Rev. Andrew Bonar, of Callace.

end of the rope, and by that means I alighted safely, but much frightened and overcome. The bottom of the well was muddy, but no water was there at this time, as the spring was dry. Dr. Wilson had given me two beautiful white candles and a small box of sticks. The sticks were for the purpose of making a light. This was the first introduction of lucifer matches into Nablûs. I had seen Dr. Wilson make use of one, up above in the open air, and was much surprised; but now, down in this dark place, upon striking the end of one against the rough side of the box, I was amazed at the report and ignition, and made up my mind not to waste any, but to keep the box carefully in my pocket, and I thought that this box alone would fully compensate for my trouble in coming down. I had been told to remove all the stones from the east, and to place them westward, and then to return them to their original position, and to place in the east those from the west; and in executing the latter command, I found a dirty little book, about six inches long by four inches broad, and three-quarters of an inch thick. Dr. Wilson shouted down from the mouth of the well several times, 'Have you found it?' The same answer, 'No,' was continued for some time; but now I did not exactly know how to answer. 'This could not be the book,' I thought, 'for the recovery of which he had expended so much labor and money; and yet it might be, if it were a book of necromancy for guiding him to hidden treasures.' When Dr. Wilson heard that I had found something, he caused me to be hauled up, and welcomed me and my treasure, which I felt almost ashamed to give him; yet he was much delighted, patting me on my back, and paying all the men as well as myself very handsomely.

"He wrapped the Bible in a handkerchief, and deposited it in his breast-pocket most carefully. It was currently believed that this was a book of necromancy, just as it had struck me in the well."

After lingering for some time by the well-side, we rode

across the fields to the center of the mouth of the valley, where, nearly due north of the well, there is a square space, surrounded by high, plastered, whitewashed stone walls. We dismounted, and, passing one by one through a narrow opening, we stood within the inclosure. In the center is a clumsy-looking tomb, about three feet high and six feet long. The top terminates in a bluntly-pointed ridge. At the head and at the foot a rude stone pillar, the same hight as the tomb, is set up on the floor. There are many niches in the walls for small lamps, and they are lighted during certain festivals, and by devotees on particular occasions. The walls are almost covered with inscriptions in Hebrew, Samaritan, and Arabic; some, which were deeply engraved, seem to have been written more than two hundred years ago. Modern European travelers, too, have left their names there. This is supposed to be the tomb of Joseph. It is recorded that when he was on his death-bed he exacted a promise from his sons that they would carry him into the land given to Abraham and his seed forever. So, when he died, "they embalmed him, and put him in a coffin in Egypt." And again it is written, "The bones of Joseph, which the children of Israel brought up out of Egypt, buried they in Shechem, in a parcel of ground which Jacob bought of the sons of Hamor, the father of Shechem, for an hundred pieces of silver: and it became the inheritance of the children of Joseph." A vine was trailing over the northern wall, and I gathered a few of its tender leaves and tendrils; and the wild campion, white and red, flourished round the tomb.

We then rode toward Nablûs up the middle of the valley. Clouds were gathering in the west over the sea, all tinged with ruddy golden light from the setting sun. A small tower on Mount Gerizim marks the spot where the Feast of the Passover is kept and the Paschal Lamb slain. As we approached the town we saw a large concourse of Moslem boys playing at hockey, or some similar game, on a broad, smooth plot of ground just outside the eastern gate; and while we paused to watch the skillful players we heard shouts, and screams, and war-cries from within the walls. We hastened in, and found that a sudden excitement had seized the Moslems in one quarter of the town. We inquired the cause, and were told by a Moslem that news had arrived that the surrounding villages were up in arms and preparing to attack Nablûs. This we found afterward was an impromptu fabrication to deceive us; the real cause of the uproar was a report that a Christian had killed, injured, or insulted a Moslem.

Fortunately the false impression was removed before any mischief was done; but the loud, angry voices of the groups of men, and even women, in the street, convinced me for the first time of the hazardous position of Christians when the fanaticism of the lower class of Moslems is fully roused. We rode unmolested through the gathering crowds, not suspecting that a general massacre of the Christians was actually then being proposed. We did not understand the facts of the case till we reached the hotel, when the tumult had quite subsided, in consequence of the discovery that it was a Christian and not a Moslem who had been slightly injured. I could see that a trifling provocation, real or imaginary, might at any moment lead to bloodshed; yet I did not entertain any fears for myself or for my brother. I felt perfectly safe there without well knowing why. A party of Moslem gentlemen spent the evening with us, and seemingly, though not avowedly, they did all in their power to remove any unfavorable impression which I might have received from witnessing the momentary excitement at sunset.

On the following day, the 6th of March, we called on Michael Kawarre, the native Protestant catechist and teacher. His brother was the Prussian Consular Agent, and their father, Samâan Kawarre, and his friends, received us very cordially, in a small but pretty vaulted chamber, with low, carpeted, and cushioned divans on three sides. A large shallow dish, containing at least two hundred bunches of freshly-gathered blue violets, stood on a low stool in the center of the matted floor, and filled the air with their pleasant odor. I expressed my admiration of these flowers to Samâan, and he said, "Lady, I will bring you a sweeter and more precious flower." He went away, and presently returned with his little granddaughter, Zahra, which signifies flower, held lovingly in his arms. She was a pretty child of about four years of age, but as serious and composed as a woman. She wore smooth, ruby-colored glass bracelets on her wrists, which had been put on many months before, and were now too small to pass over her chubby little hands.

These glass bracelets are often obliged to be carefully broken before they can be removed from the arms of young children, for they are simple rings of various colors, and made without any fastening.

I asked Zahra where the violets grew. She said, "They came up out of the ground under the lemon-trees, for the ladies. They come only now, they are not there always."

I said, "What do the ladies do with the violets?" "The ladies put them in their head-dresses, and are glad, because they have a sweet smell." But one of the guests said, "The little one has not yet learned that these flowers are dried in the sun, and then used for making tea for those who are sick of fever."

As we left the house, one said to us, "Come into the garden where the violets grow." We followed him, and went into a spacious inclosure, where lemon, citron, orange, and quince trees made a pleasant shade, and apple and almond trees were full of blossoms. The ground was completely carpeted with the clustering heart-shaped leaves of the violet, and sprinkled with its blue blossoms. I have seen them in our own wild-wood walks, crowding lovingly together in groups, or springing up round the trunks of ancient trees, but I never saw such a profusion of these sweet flowers as I did then in that Nablûs garden. We could not move a step without crushing the tender leaves beneath our feet. We were led into the center of the garden, where a very large square pool or reservoir had been made, with a stone parapet round it. On the south side there was a pleasant vaulted stone chamber, with a wide-spreading archway opening close on to the edge of the pool. Here carpets and cushions were spread, and coffee and pipes, sherbets, and fruit and flowers were brought for us.

This is the beau-ideal of Oriental afternoon enjoyment—a lulling narghilé in an arched recess, near to a pool or stream of sparkling water—in the midst of a fruit garden, carpeted with violets, in the Spring—and with white everlasting flowers in the Summer and Autumn. These delights are the chief subjects of many of the modern Arab songs and poems.

Before sunset we traversed the town from one end to the other, and went to the house of Daûd Tannûs, the chief member of the Protestant community in Nablûs, where we had been invited to dine. We were led up a crooked, open stone stairway, to an irregular uneven court, into which several rooms and a kitchen opened. In the latter the mistress of the house and women-servants were busy in the midst of savory odors. They stood in the wide doorway, half hiding their faces, and looking shyly at us as we passed to the guest-chamber. Monthly roses and carnations in full blossom, planted in large, broken, red-clay water-jars, turned upside down, stood on each side of the entrance steps. The room was large, though not lofty—raised divans covered with Manchester prints were on three sides of it, and a musketo-curtained bed on the other. Fifteen of our Nablûs friends were assembled there to meet us, and among them M. Zeller, but no women appeared.

While we were seated on the divan, one of the guests said to me in broken English, "Your friendship with your brother, the Consul, has already become a proverb in this city." "How so?" I inquired. He explained: "To-day I heard people angrily talking and crying near my house, and they made a great noise, and I rose and went to the door of my house, and a man named Yusef came that way, and I said, 'What was the reason of that noise?' and he replied, 'Only two women disputing and fighting; but they have now made peace, and they have sworn to each other a friendship like unto the friendship of the English Consul and his sister!'" I said, "Is it then in this land reckoned a strange thing that a brother and sister should be great friends?"

Another guest, a thoughtful and intelligent man, to whom my question was repeated in Arabic, replied, "People in this country are naturally surprised that you can journey with the Consul, share his pursuits and the dangers to which he may be exposed, and be really and truly his companion. It is a thing not understood here, where the education of men and women differs so greatly, and where brothers and sisters see but little of each other after their childhood, except when the father of a family dies—for then the eldest son becomes the guardian of his widowed mother and of his brothers and sisters. But the latter are married early, and then he has no more charge concerning them. Our women marvel greatly among themselves that you have left your country and your home to travel with the Consul, while your parents are yet living, and they conclude that you must have a strong friendship for each other."

And a third spoke and said, "Thou hast spoken truly, yet let it be known also to our English sister, that our women and girls rejoice greatly when they have many brothers, and it is their pride and delight to hear their friends say, 'Happy art thou, O sister of seven men; may they soon be married, and may you live to see their children's children!' And it is said that a woman sometimes regards the life of her brother as more precious than her own, or than that of her husband, or her son.

"When Ibrahîm Pasha, the son of Mehemet Ali, ruled in Palestine, he sent men into all the towns and villages to gather together a large army. Then a certain woman of Sefurieh sought Ibrahîm Pasha at 'Akka, and came into his presence, bowing herself before him, and said, 'O my lord, look with pity on thy servant, and hear my prayer. A little while ago there were three men in my house—my husband, my brother, and my eldest son. But now, behold, they all have been carried away to serve in your army, and I am left with my little ones without a protector; I pray you grant liberty to one of these men, that he may remain at home.'

"And Ibrahîm had pity on her, and said, 'O woman! do you ask for your husband, for your son, or for your brother?'

"She said, 'O my lord, give me my brother!' and he answered, 'How is this, O woman—do you prefer a brother to a husband or a son?'

"The woman, who was renowned for her wit and readiness of speech, replied in an impromptu rhyme:

> "'If it be God's will that my husband perish in your service,
> I am still a woman, and God may lead me to another husband.
> If on the battle-field my first-born son should fall,
> I have still my younger ones who will in God's time be like unto him.
> But, O my lord, if my only brother should be slain,
> I am without remedy—for my father is dead and my mother is old,
> And where should I look for another brother?'

"And Ibrahîm was much pleased with the words of the woman, and said, 'O woman! happy above many is thy brother; he shall be free for thy word's sake, and thy husband and son shall be free also.' Then the woman could not speak for joy and gladness. And Ibrahîm said, 'Go in peace—but let it not be known that I have spoken with you this day.'

"Then she arose and went her way to her village, trusting in the promise of the Pasha. After three days, her husband, and son, and brother returned to her, saying, 'We are free from service, by order of the Pasha, but this matter is a mystery to us.' And all the neighbors marveled greatly. But the woman held her peace, and this story did not become known till Ibrahîm's departure from 'Akka, after the overthrow of the Egyptian Government in Syria, in 1840."

Several similar anecdotes were related while preparations for dinner were being made. A large circular tray was brought in, and placed on a stand, raised about six inches from the matted floor, in the middle of the room. Our kawass, and the servants and attendants of the guests, acted as waiters. They bustled backward and forward across the court, from the door of the kitchen to the table, which was soon covered with steaming, yellow mounds of rice, crowned with limbs of fowls and morsels of lamb. A large wooden bowl—containing a medley of rice, minced mutton, raisins, pine-seeds, and butter—stood in the center, and was surrounded by plates of vegetables.

After water had been poured on our hands, we gathered round the board, and took our places, in Oriental fashion, on the floor. A damask napkin, about half a yard wide and ten yards long, was passed round in front of the assembled guests, and rested on their knees. Its gold-embroidered and fringed ends met where I was seated, between our host, Daûd Tannûs, and my brother. Flat cakes, or loaves of bread, were distributed, and we ate in primitive style, for neither knives, nor forks, nor spoons appeared. Deep impressions were soon made in the mounds of rice, and by degrees the dishes were carried away, and replaced by others, containing sweet starch and creams, stewed apricots, and preserves.

We left the table, one after another, and performed the customary ablutions in due order. When we had reseated ourselves on the divan, coffee and pipes were served, and lamps were lighted. The table was carried out into the open court, and two or three bowls of rice being added to the dishes we had left, the numerous attendants and servants of the house took their evening meal there together by lantern-light, forming a study for a Rembrandt.

I went into an adjoining room for a few minutes, to see

the ladies of the house, and the neighbors who were with them. They received me very kindly, but with a little shyness. One said to me, "I hope you have made a good dinner—we have nothing here fit to offer you—we are only simple people, and can not serve you as we should like to do." I said, "I very much enjoyed that which your hands—peace be upon them—prepared so nicely; but I should have enjoyed it still more if you, O my sisters, had eaten with us." They seemed quite amused at the idea, and some of them blushed and laughed heartily. One of the elder women said seriously, "It is not our custom, O my daughter, to eat with men—it would be a shame for us." And a young girl exclaimed, "O lady, the bread and meat would choke us, if we took it in the midst of a company of men." I took leave of the women, and returned to the divan, and at about eight o'clock the guests separated, for genuine Oriental dinner-parties are never late entertainments.

Daûd Tannûs gathered his finest roses and carnations for us, and we walked home through the narrow streets, attended by lantern-bearers and several friends.

In the mean time, preparations had been made for my journey to Jerusalem. The Consul, Mr. Finn, had sent his Hebrew dragoman and his head kawass to fetch me, that my brother might be free to follow Kamil Pasha, without anxiety, wherever he might go. It was expected that the Pasha would visit all the rebellious villages, and perhaps besiege some of them, in which case he might be absent from Nablûs for many days. Under these circumstances, I had no alternative, and immediately made ready for starting early on the morrow.

Till a late hour, friends and neighbors, of all sects and classes, came in to take leave of me, and to wish me a prosperous and safe journey. The Moslems especially marveled that I could venture to travel so far without my brother. They said, "May God make a straight path for you on his earth!"

CHAPTER XI.

FROM NABLÛS TO JERUSALEM.

I WOKE early on the following morning, Friday, March 7th, with an unusual sense of oppression and sudden fear, as if I had some very sad or difficult task to perform that day. The packed portmanteaus and the riding-habit, in readiness by my side, instantly brought to my recollection the plans for my journey to Jerusalem—a journey of about thirteen hours, and generally made in two stages, but which I had determined to accomplish in one, as there is not a good halting-place on the road, nor any village in which I should have been willing to seek a night's lodging unless in company with my brother, or in case of absolute necessity.

By the time I was thoroughly aroused my fears had vanished. Mohammed, our faithful Egyptian groom, came tapping at my door to ask for my luggage, and he said, "Be of good cheer, lady, may the day be white to you!" and the kawass of Ody Azam, who stood by the door, said, "If this day be dark to our lady, it will be darkened indeed unto many."

I breakfasted early, but it was half-past eight o'clock before the horses and riders were all ready. Then after taking leave of my good-natured hostess, I mounted and rode through the streets of Nablûs with a few friends, who had arranged to accompany me a short distance on the way. Priest Amran, the Samaritan, who walked by my side, with his hand on the neck of my good horse, exclaimed, "Passover is nigh at hand, and you will not be with us on the mountain—this will be a grief to us, for our hearts had been made glad with the thought that you would be with us, and now, behold, our hope is departed from us."

I told him how sincerely I regretted leaving Nablûs so soon. Then he pronounced a prayer and a blessing for me, and went his way.

A Christian of the Greek Catholic Church who was with us, and who had heard the words of Amran and my answer, said, "Rejoice, rather, O lady, that you are privileged to keep the festival of Easter in the Holy City, Jerusalem, that you may worship in the Church of the Sepulcher of our Lord. It is better for you to do so than to pass the Holy Week on 'this mountain' with Samaritans, who besmear their foreheads with blood, and believe not in the name of Christ and our Blessed Lady." I was strikingly reminded of Christ's words to the woman of Samaria: "The hour cometh when ye shall, neither in this mountain nor yet at Jerusalem, worship the Father." "God is a Spirit, and they that worship him, must worship him in spirit and in truth."

There had been rain during the night, and the stone houses of Nablûs, the white rocky terraces which bordered the fruit-gardens on the hill-sides, and the slabs of smooth stone in the plains, glistened like mirrors in the gleams of sunshine. The grass, the wild flowers, the fruit-trees, and the broad fields of wheat and barley were still wet with the recent shower, and looked vividly green where the quickly-traveling clouds overshadowed them.

We took the upper path over the spurs of Gerizim; it was rocky and stony, but bright with mezereons, vetches, and forget-me-nots. We met a number of soldiers and several large parties of horsemen. The traffic on the roads leading to Nablûs was greatly increased at that time, owing to the presence of Kamîl Pasha and his troops. The lower road, which is nearly in the middle of the plain, and passes near to Jacob's Well, was traversed by companies of peasants and strings of camels, donkeys laden with firewood, and women carrying bowls of milk or cream. I was assured that the scene was unusually animated for the time of the year, but the plain is more busy and cheerful-looking in harvest time.

We passed two small villages, the lawless-looking inhabitants of which came out to watch us as we went by, while their children shouted in chorus, and their dogs barked savagely. In about one hour and a half we came to Hawara, which is the third village on the way from Nablûs. It is a large, strongly-built place, though unwalled. Its houses are like little castles. The olive-trees and gardens around it were in flourishing order.

Near to this spot the upper and lower roads are united, and just where the two ways meet we paused, and my brother and my Nablûs friends took leave of me, and rode quickly away down the lower road in the plain, while I went on with my little escort, which consisted of three individuals.

Mr. Finn's head kawass, a clever and energetic Moslem, led the way. He wore a scarlet cloth jacket braided with gold, full white cotton trowsers, and a' red cloth tarbûsh. He carried a sword and pistols, and was mounted on a fine black horse, of which he was very proud.

Mohammed, our faithful Egyptian groom, who had charge of the luggage, was dressed in a long hooded drab cloth pelisse, made at Aleppo, and ornamented tastefully with broad black braid. He was riding on his indefatigable little donkey.

Simeon Rosenthal, the Hebrew dragoman of the British Consulate at Jerusalem, was the third. He was born of Jewish parents at Bucharest, but had embraced Christianity, and had lived in Jerusalem nearly thirty years. He spoke English pretty fluently, but with Oriental idioms; in fact, nearly every sentence which he uttered was like a quotation from the Bible. He was a stout, elderly man, with a ruddy face, bushy gray hair, and twinkling gray eyes. He was dressed in European clothes, but wore over them a large white abai or cloak made of goat's hair, and a broad-brimmed hat covered with white calico, and with white muslin wound round it and hanging down behind like a vail. He carried a brace of pistols, and to his care I was especially committed, though Mohammed, the groom, seemed to think that he was my more natural guardian, and he kept as near to me as his laden donkey and the uneven roads would let him. Sometimes he was almost wedged in between me and a projecting rock, or he came suddenly forward just under my horse's feet, or would follow me so closely that he was in danger of a kick. He was very good and attentive, and if he saw me look at a flower he would immediately jump down to gather it, though I never could teach him to bring me a stalk more than an inch long, and he rarely brought me the right flower.

I looked back now and then to see the last of my brother and his little party, as they rode toward the green valley of Nablûs. Simeon, who was by my side, said, "I pray you, Miss Rogers, do not look back any more. When you look back so, as if you had no heart to go on, it makes me think that you have no trust in me. I pray you look forward only." To reassure him, I cast no more longing looks behind, and, though I felt rather sad, I would not let it be perceived.

For about two hours we passed through a highly-cultivated district of hills and plains, dotted with villages, olive-groves, and orchards, and green fields where laborers were busy. Women, with their heads covered and their faces almost concealed with white linen or cotton vails, were gathering tares, bright wild flowers, and weeds among the corn. Some of them had infants slung on their shoulders, and in unsown tracts of land, girls were toiling at picking out the stones. Men were sitting in groups smoking and gossiping, while others were digging up the ground in gardens and orchards, and placing large stones round the trunks of old olive-trees. They looked up from their work to gaze at us with curiosity. Simeon overheard the criticisms of some passers-by. They were wondering who I might be, when one of them settled the question, very decidedly, by saying, "She is a foreigner belonging to the harem of Kamîl Pasha, and she is going to Jerusalem for safety, for there may be war in the neighborhood of Nablûs soon."

At a little after midday we rested for half an hour near to a well-side at the foot of a very steep hill. Cold fowls and bread and wine were spread for me, on a smooth block of stone. At one o'clock we started again, and attempted to ascend the hill, by one of the worst and most stony roads in the country. Simeon's clumsy saddle slipped down over the back of his horse; but he was fortunately able to save himself by clinging to the neck and mane of the animal, and then jumping to the ground. He directed the kawass to guide us by another road, even though it might be a longer one, saying to me, "I am afraid for you, for if any harm befall you, I shall not dare to see your brother's face again." I consented, though rather reluctantly, to take the longer and easier road.

The scenery had quite changed. We had left behind us the pleasant plains of Ephraim, and the cultivated gardens and terraced hill-sides; and, with the exception of one unusually-fine oak, which stands conspicuously near to the ruins of an ancient castle, on a high ridge, we did not see a tree for several miles. But the beautiful *poterium spinosum*, in full leaf and blossom, grew profusely wherever there was any earth on the stony hills. We passed down a wild and narrow glen. The cliffs on each side were steep and abrupt, pierced with caverns, and channeled with water-courses, and in the bottom of the valley there were large rocks of fantastic form, percolated by rain, and tinted red, gray, orange-color, and lavender, relieved by black and white. On the rock-ledges above us there were scanty crops of barley, wheat, and lentiles, and olive and fig trees appeared again in small groups. Flocks of goats and larger cattle were being led out to seek for pasture by rather desperate-looking herdsmen, well armed. I was informed that we were traversing a district celebrated, from time immemorial, for the lawless and daring character of its inhabitants. The pleasant sound of falling water attracted my attention. It was trickling down the side of the cliff, amid ferns, mosses, liverwort, and tiny wild-flowers with blue and yellow blossoms. It splashed into reservoirs, hollowed out one below the other in the native rock, at the foot of the cliff. This pretty water-fall is appropriately called "Ain-el-Haraami-yeh," or the "Fountain of the Robbers," for it is often the scene of violence, and travelers are frequently waylaid by bandits in this wild glen.

At three o'clock we were about half-way on our road to Jerusalem, at the entrance of "Wady-el-Tîn," that is, the "Valley of Figs." It is well named, for it is a long wide grove of trees. But it was then so early in the Spring that the fig-trees were not sufficiently advanced to be beautiful, and though some of them had "put forth their green figs," and on others a few tender leaves appeared, they were for the most part almost bare. They gave me the idea of a petrified leafless forest, for the tortuous trunks and branches were almost as white as the rocks and stones amid which they grew. This valley in the Summer-time is a lovely place, for then the large green leaves form a perfect shade, the ripe and abundant fruit cools the lips of the thirsty traveler, and the air is filled with a sweet odor exactly like that of the heliotrope. The road led us over an extensive plateau, where hollyhocks and anemones, and other bright blossoms, grew among thorns, while here and there patches of cultivated land appeared. On the hills around we could see solitary villages perched on rocky terraces, in the midst of orchards and vineyards.

The way was easy for the horses, and the sun had lost its power, so I urged the kawass to ride forward more quickly, and I followed him, cantering between the cornfields, and among the thorns and Spring flowers. But I soon found that Simeon could not keep up with us. I waited for him, and when he, almost out of breath, joined us, he said, "I am very sorry, but I have no power to run." So we proceeded more slowly, and did not reach "Beitîn" till six o'clock.

The shades of evening were deepening rapidly, and we did not pause to examine the extensive ruins on the ridge, but alighted in the valley close to the remains of an ancient cistern, formed of large, well-hewn stones. The bottom of it was covered with a bed of fine fresh grass, in the midst of which a stream of water flowed from fountains gushing out of the rock just above it. Scriptural topographists, ancient and modern, agree that this is the Bethel of the Bible. Abraham of old very likely drank of that fountain, and the handmaidens of Sarah may have lingered there day after day when they went down to draw water. There we rested for about half an hour, and took coffee.

The sun had gone down when we rose up to pursue our journey. We were more than three hours' distance from Jerusalem. The stars were shining brightly in a dark sky overhead, but all round the horizon a halo of pale light concealed them. The temperature changed very suddenly at sunset, and we were glad to put on hoods and cloaks. The kawass wrapped a brown camel's-hair abai around him, and in this dusky costume it was quite impossible to distinguish him on his black horse, as he rode on before me, through valleys or down steep slopes. Now and then, as we ascended a hill, or traversed high table-land, I could see the silhouette of his tarbûshed head against the sky, just above the horizon. I could not make out any of the objects around me except the white rocks in the midst of dark bushes and thorns, and now and then a smooth sheet of water, which reflected the stars, and looked very deep; but my leader splashed through it, and when I followed, I found that the water only wetted my horse's fetlocks, and was the result of the recent rain. Sometimes I could see a solitary tree in dark relief against a white cliff, or the outline of a village crowning a hill-top. I could not judge of distances correctly, and I was several times startled by dark objects, appearing to me to be gigantic and far away, but which I found were in reality insignificant in size, and so close to me as to be within reach of my riding-whip.

We were going on in single file, and I was immediately behind the kawass. I was so tired of trying in vain not to lose sight of him, that I said to Simeon, "Oblige me by riding forward, and I will follow you. Your white horse and white cloak can be seen even in this darkness, and I am tired of watching the kawass." He passed, and for a few moments rode before me, but suddenly stopped, halfway down a steep declivity, saying, "I am afraid for you. I can not let you ride, and I not see you. Not Jacob gave more anxious charge to his sons when they carried away Benjamin, than I have received concerning you, and how can I let you ride in these dangerous paths out of my sight? Let me follow you, I pray, and you keep close as you can to the kawass, and do not let your horse run—there are loose stones here, and smooth slabs of rock—let him go very gently." I yielded to his entreaty, and once more rode after the invisible leader. I trusted to my horse that he would keep in the right path, and I went on silently as if in a dream.

Suddenly my musings were interrupted. My horse started back on his hind-legs, for the kawass had turned abruptly round and had come to a standstill, and exclaimed, "Ma fî darb"—"There is no road!"

He explained that he had been out of the right track for about half an hour, and he had only just then discovered that we were approaching the brow of a steep cliff. His horse had nearly carried him over the edge. Mohammed began abusing him in very strong terms and sarcastic undertones, while Simeon seemed to be much alarmed and in great trouble.

We were on high table-land, and had reason to be thankful that we had not been dashed down into the dark defile below. I asked the kawass if he had any means of judging where we were. He said he knew we must be somewhere between Er-Ram—the ancient *Ramah*—and Tel-el-Fûl, which is by many Biblical topographists believed to be the ancient *Gibeah*.* He proposed to alight and to look for some signs by which he might recover the lost track and a practicable path leading to it. So he tethered his horse to a tree, and Simeon and Mohammed did the same, but I remained mounted. Mohammed handed a hookah to me, and I sat still, smoking, while the three men went in different directions to see if they could recognize any rock, tree, or streamlet, fountain or ruin which might give them a clew. I told them not to go out of sight of the light of my hookah, or out of each other's hearing.

It was with strange emotion that I rested there, in the darkness and alone.

I should have suffered, perhaps, more from fear, if the strangeness and peculiarity of my position had not excited my interest and wonder so completely as to rouse within me the spirit of love of adventure. The silence of night was broken at intervals by the crying and snarling voices of jackals, and the barking and yelling of wild dogs and hyenas.

Now and then I heard the men calling to each other, and the tethered animals would sometimes neigh and shake themselves, as if answering the voices of their respective masters; but my horse stood perfectly still, while I smoked, and thought, and looked up into the night-sky, where the stars appeared infinite in number, and now shone close down to the darkened horizon. I was almost overwhelmed with the multitude of new ideas and vivid scenes which passed

---

* When a "certain Levite" was traveling from Bethlehem home to Ephraim with his recovered "concubine," toward the close of the day he said to his servant, "Let us draw near to one of these places, to lodge all night in *Gibeah* or in *Ramah*; and the sun went down upon them when they were by Gibeah, and they turned aside thither to go in to lodge in Gibeah." And the city was destroyed and the people were scattered for the wrong they did to the travelers that night; and behold the flame of the city ascended up to heaven. Judges xix.

through my mind. "My spirit had climbed high," by reason of the very danger near, and "from the top of sense overlooked sense, to the significance and heart of things, rather than things themselves."*

In rather less than half an hour, though it seemed more to me, the joyful cry of "El-hâmdoulillah!" "El-hâmdoulillah!"—"Praised be God!"—was echoed from one side to another, and soon Simeon, who had not been far off, was by my side, and the other men rejoined me. They had found the right road, and a way to reach it; so we started again, following the kawass.

We had to go down a very difficult and dangerous declivity. My horse, usually very sure-footed, stumbled forward over a smooth slab of inclined rock and some loose stones. I was very nearly thrown over his head—the excellence of my hunting-saddle saved me; but I was so shaken and startled that I trembled from head to foot, and was obliged to pause for a few minutes. A hookah, the Oriental panacea, was brought to me. It was so very dark down in that valley that I could scarcely distinguish one of the men from the other as they gathered round me. I soon recovered my composure and courage to proceed. We splashed through a stream, and scrambled up a steep embankment, and crossed a stony wady before we regained the proper route.

I had desired the kawass to fasten a white handkerchief over his head as a beacon for me. We were going up a hill, and I was watching this mark, when suddenly a circle of light appeared near it, like a nimbus, and was accompanied by a clicking noise. I found that our leader was preparing a light for his narghilé by a method which I had never before seen adopted, although it is a very common one.

The moistened Persian tumbac, which is used in narghilés and hookahs, can only be smoked by means of a piece of red-hot or live charcoal. The lover of tumbac, when on a

* Mrs. Browning.

journey, always provides himself with a flint and steel, some tinder and prepared charcoal, and a little round wirework basket, about two inches in diameter, suspended by three chains, more or less ornamented with beads and silk tassels. When a pipe is required, a piece of tinder is lighted, and placed with some charcoal in the basket, which is whirled rapidly round and round. The charcoal soon becomes so thoroughly red-hot that it is ready to be placed on the moistened tumbac in the bowl of the pipe. This explained the mystery of the nimbus round the head of my guide.

As soon as we reached the hights of Tel-el-Fûl—the "Hill of Beans"—I could see, in the west, the well-remembered and marked outline of Neby Samuel, and in the far east the long, level line of the mountains of Moab, and southward, straight before us, I recognized the hills round about Jerusalem. Soon afterward, from the summit of Scopus, we perceived the dark minarets and domes of the Holy City and the Mount of Olives, where a light was burning in the little tower which was then called "Graham Castle."

It was half-past eleven when we stood by the crenellated walls of Jerusalem. The gates were closed, and there was death-like silence there, till the kawass knocked loudly against the west or Yâfa Gate. The sentinels within were roused, and they cried, "Who is there?" We explained, and then one of the sentinels said, "The gate was kept open till ten o'clock, but now the key is with the Governor." The Governor was living at the other end of the town; however, a messenger was immediately dispatched to him to ask for permission to admit us. Another messenger was sent to the Consulate to announce our safe arrival. We, in the mean time, tired and hungry, were shivering in the midnight air outside the gate, and twenty minutes elapsed before it was thrown open for us. Then I entered in with joy; for I felt at home there, and safe.

I hastened across the well-known Castle Square, and up the narrow passage, clattering over the uneven pavement, and drew up my horse at the entrance to the Consulate, where my kind friends—Mr. and Mrs. Finn—came out to welcome me. They led me, hooded and cloaked as I was, into their brilliantly-lighted drawing-room, where a *conversazione* of the "Jerusalem Literary Society" was being held. The rooms were quite English in character, and bright with lamps and well-arranged flowers, and filled with English guests, many of whom were recently-arrived travelers, strangers to me.

Large logs of wood were burning and crackling on the fire-dogs in the chimney-place. The whole presented a most striking contrast to the scenes and society by which I had been lately surrounded, and the delight I felt made me almost forget my fatigue. After the guests had gone we lingered for an hour by the fire in pleasant chat; and then for the first time I slept and found perfect rest and peace within the walls of Jerusalem. It was very pleasant when I woke in the morning to see the Consul's children round me, and to hear their English greetings, and their glad, familiar voices.

I found Jerusalem in the early Spring altogether different to Jerusalem in the hot Summer-time, when it had often appeared to me, literally, "a city of stone, in a land of iron, with a sky of brass," and when at midday all unsheltered places were quite deserted, and those people who could do so lived in tents in olive-groves in the valleys or on the hills round about Jerusalem. Now all was changed; the few open spaces within the city walls were green with grass, or patches of wheat and barley, and the whole of the mosque inclosure was like meadow-land sprinkled with flowers; the very walls were garnished with rough leaves, stonecrop, pellitory, and bright blossoms. Among them the bitter hyssop and bright-yellow henbane were pointed out to me, growing luxuriantly on the Tower of Hippicus, in the dry moat, and on all the most ancient buildings; while out of the cracks of the domes, and on the terraced roofs of many of the houses, straggling herbage sprang.

In the streets there was renewed activity; for already the Latin pilgrims were beginning to flock to Jerusalem that they might celebrate Easter at the Holy Sepulcher. English and American travelers were to be seen in the principal streets, sketching under difficulties in the midst of crowds of lookers-on, or making bad bargains with the turbaned salesmen in the bazars. Outside the town, too, the scenery had changed. Wherever the earth rested on the rocky hills verdure appeared, and the plains, and the cemeteries, and valleys were gay with flowers. Bulbous plants abounded, especially asphodels, and the hyacinth, squill, garlic, and star of Bethlehem. Every evening at sunset large companies of people, of all tribes and nations, might be seen entering the city gates, after having enjoyed their evening walk.

I made pleasant excursions in the neighborhood, and revisited many of the chief places in Jerusalem with parties of English travelers, and thus the time passed till March 18th, when to my delight my brother arrived soon after sunrise, in company with the Pasha and his troops. During the day a fierce hot sirocco wind prevailed, and threatened to scorch and destroy the crops. Before sunset we rode out with a large party to see the Jewish plantation, where newly-grafted olive-trees were putting forth new leaves, and apricot, and nectarine, and other fruit trees looked flourishing. But the fields of wheat and barley and the beds of vegetables thirsted for the "latter rain." The gardeners and farm-laborers had been praying for it for many days. They called our attention to a small group of dense black clouds which were then slowly rising out of the west, and one of them said, "Our hope is in those clouds." As we rode homeward a few large drops of rain reminded us of the gardener's words. During the night the west wind rose with unusual violence, shook the house to its foundations, and disturbed all the sleepers. The Arab servants, who rose and went from room to room to make the shutters and windows more secure, said, "It is well; this strong wind will bring rain. The cisterns will be filled with water, and the corn will grow. Praised be God!"

On the following morning, March 19th, torrents of rain and hail began to fall, and continued without intermission all day and during the night. On Thursday the storm was even more violent. The hailstones generally were as large as cherry-stones, but some were three or four times the size. At midday wide flakes of snow fell, but melted quickly.

On Good Friday, March 21st, the first sounds I heard on waking, were the joyful voices of the children. They knocked at my door, crying, "The Kedron is flowing! the Brook Kedron, you know! It is flowing; make haste and get up. See, here is some of the water!"

I found that the peasantry had entered the city at sunrise, in triumph, to announce the news. They had brought several goatskins and jars filled with the water. The bearers of good tidings are now, as of old, entitled to a backshîsh, so these peasants reaped a good harvest that morning in Jerusalem.

The storm continued, and did not cease for a moment till Saturday morning, and there was scarcely an upper chamber in Jerusalem which was uninjured by it. I was assured that three such days of rain had never been witnessed there at that season by any one living. Spring showers are generally of short duration, and quickly followed by sunshine. But this unexpected supply of water was very welcome, for the Winter rains had been less abundant than usual, and had not filled the pools, or "sent the springs into the valleys which run among the hills."

On Saturday afternoon the sun shone brightly on the rain-refreshed earth, and hundreds of people went out to look at the waters of the Brook Kedron. I rode with my brother out at the Yâfa Gate, and along the valley of Gihon. We made our way quickly down to En Rogel, the source of the stream. It is south-east of Jerusalem, and called by the Arabs "Bîr-Eyûb"—the Well of Job. We were surprised to find that not only had the spring below the well bubbled up as usual, but the force of the body of water was so great, that it had risen up and overflowed the ancient shaft, which is one hundred and twenty-five feet deep. A large concourse of people were already assembled there.

Groups of Moslems sat under the olive-trees, close to the stream, smoking narghilés, drinking coffee, playing with their rosaries, and looking supremely happy. Boys were going about selling sweetmeats and cakes, which they carried on round trays made of reeds. There were several rival purveyors of coffee and pipes. One would have thought that it was fair-day at En Rogel. All sorts of skins, jars of all shapes and sizes, and other vessels had been brought down to the stream, that they might be filled there. Women in white sheets sat in groups on the sun-dried rocks, apart from the men, enjoying pipes and sweetmeats, and children were swinging on ropes tied to the tree-branches. Many of the European residents of Jerusalem were strolling about with their little ones, and the newly-arrived English travelers watched the scene with evident interest and delight.

"Shall we follow the course of the Kedron, and see how far it goes?" said my brother. I readily assented. So we left the noisy but picturesque crowd, and made our way down the valley under the olive-trees — now splashing through the murmuring musical waters, where they passed between the low stone-wall boundaries of fruit and vegetable gardens—now rising on to the sloping hill-side, and returning to the stream whenever there was a practicable path in it, or near it. The rugged rocks around were garlanded with green, thorny creeping plants, and within the niches and in the caverns of the limestone cliffs masses of maiden-hair and other ferns appeared. It was very pleasant to observe the turnings and the windings of the new-born river, remembering that on the morning of the previous day only, it had sprung fresh and free from its source, to make itself a path in this valley, inviting all the little streamlets from the hills to flow with it. In one place, about a mile from En Rogel, it passed over broad, smooth slabs of time-polished red stone, then tumbled over a little ridge of rocks into a bed formed of small pebbles. Having gained renewed vigor by this fall, it rushed impetuously along a channel about five feet wide, made for it in the midst of a terraced olive-plantation. When thus confined, it was about one foot deep, but when freed from this artificial training, it spread itself over the wide rocky bed beyond, and only wetted our horses' fetlocks as we splashed through it. Sometimes the brook does not flow further than this olive-grove. At other times, when the Winter rains are abundant, it travels down "Wady er Raheb"—The Monk's Valley—to the Convent of Mar Saba; but its ancient destination was evidently the Dead Sea, into which it fell from the "Wady Nar"—The Valley of Fire.

We followed the course of the stream for nearly an hour, and still, to our surprise, it flowed rapidly; but as the sun was declining we gave up the chase, and retraced our steps. We overtook our friends, who were still lingering by the source of the stream.

A Moslem kawass of the British Consulate said to us, "This is the blessing of blessings. Who has ever told of the Kedron flowing in Adar? It comes in the Winter, and even early in Spring; but who has heard of its waters rising at this time? Yet," he added, "while we are rejoicing and giving thanks, there are men whose hearts are hardened by love of money, and who will be sorry to see these rivers of rain—for they have just bought up all the stores of wheat, thinking that the harvest would fail this year for lack of rain. May God destroy their house! Their hope was, that they might make themselves rich by the hunger of the poor." The setting sun warned us that we must hasten toward the city before the closing of the gates, and we rode home with a large and cheerful company.

Easter Sunday was unclouded, and the people of Jerusalem looked unusually animated, and in their gayest costumes. The Arabs of the Latin Church, as they met each other that morning, exchanged the customary greetings, "Christ is risen!"—" He is risen indeed!"

During Easter week, rain and sunshine succeeded each other, and every now and then we could see a bright but transient rainbow spanning the hills. Mr. Meshullam came to tell us that he and his family had been almost washed out of their little stone-house in the valley of Urtas. A spring had suddenly burst up in their dining-room, another in the stables, and a torrent of water rushing down the valley had carried large pieces of rock and stone over the vegetable and fruit gardens, doing considerable injury to the crops. Solomon's Pools, which, only a few days before, had been the safe and favorite play-grounds of Meshullam's children, were all quite filled in less than four hours. The little ones had been gathering cresses in the corners, at the bottom of the pools, just before the gushing of the springs.

On March 31st I was roused early, by the booming of cannons from the Tower of Hippicus, and I heard that news of the birth of an heir to the Imperial throne of France had just arrived.

Mons. Barrière, the French Consul, called in person to announce the happy event. Mr. Finn immediately caused preparations to be made for a *soirée* to celebrate it that very evening. I helped to deck the drawing-rooms with green garlands and wreaths of flowers, and about one hundred wax candles were fixed in the front windows. When they were lighted at sunset they produced a very pretty and, for the East, quite unique effect; for Her Britannic Majesty's Consulate was then next door to the Protestant church, and, unlike all other dwelling-houses in Jerusalem, it had an English façade. A great many cressets were flaming on the roof, and shone with fitful brightness on the group of kawasses and Abyssinian servants who were feeding and fanning them. Fire-works were skillfully displayed in the court-yard, to the delight of hundreds of spectators. A large party assembled at the Consulate. A number of English travelers came, and many of the European residents. In the course of the evening some Arab musicians were allowed to enter, to play and sing for the especial entertainment of the strangers present. Impromptu songs were sung in honor of the Imperial Prince.

Invitations had, in the mean time, been issued to all the members of the "*corps diplomatique*" to a *déjeûner à la fourchette*, to celebrate the birth of the Prince officially, at the French Consulate, on the following day, April 1st.

I went, in company with Mr. and Mrs. Finn and my brother. We were received by M. Barrière, the Consul, and Mad^{me} L.—*née* Leseppes—the sister of the then Consul-General for Syria. The Pasha and all the Consuls, in full uniform, were soon assembled, but no other ladies arrived.

As this was rather a singular *réunion*, I will describe it in detail. After we had taken coffee, his Excellency Kamîl Pasha conducted Mrs. Finn to the elegantly-spread table in the breakfast-room, and placed her on his left hand. I was at the same time led in, and seated on his right hand. Mad^{me} L. sat exactly opposite to the Pasha, and was supported by the English Consul and the Latin Patriarch. Then the Spanish Consul-General and the other European Consuls, Abbé Ratisbon and several other distinguished French ecclesiastics, Le Comte de Fontenoy, and M. Gilbert, the Pasha's secretary, took their seats, making altogether eighteen.

Turkish, French, Greek, and Italian culinary skill had been employed in preparing the entertainment. While we partook of it, an animated conversation was being carried on in French, with occasional Spanish, Turkish, Italian, and German expletives, but no English was spoken.

The English Consul proposed the first toast; it was for Abdul Medjid. M. Barrière answered it, and the Latin Patriarch made a graceful comment.

Then the Pasha rose, and, in florid Turkish, proposed the health of the Emperor's son and heir. Mons. G. interpreted this speech, and several other toasts followed. The alliance of Turkey, France, and England was especially alluded to by the Pasha, and the toast was very heartily responded to.

The gentlemen did not linger at the table, but led us immediately to the divan, where cigarettes and narghilés were distributed. When I saw that Mad^{me} L. took the former, I did not hesitate to take the latter. The Pasha good-naturedly alluded to my visit to Nablûs, and asked for the particulars of my journey to Jerusalem. Coffee and French motto bonbons were handed round, and there was no sign of breaking up the party for an hour or more. Then, one after another, we left.

On Saturday, April 5th, after having spent the day in the Mosque, with a large party of English people, I returned to the Consulate, and was startled to hear that reliable news had just arrived, that the Rev. S. Lyde, an English subject, had accidentally caused the death of a deaf and dumb man, a Moslem, as he was on the point of leaving Nablûs. The Moslems were revenging themselves on the Christian population, and the Protestants especially were the objects of their fury. Ody Azam's house, where we had lodged, had been attacked, as well as many others, and the Christian quarter was plundered.

A meeting of the Pasha and of some of the Consuls was immediately held. My brother volunteered to proceed to Nablûs to examine the state of affairs there, and to see what means could be devised for Mr. Lyde's safe conduct to Jerusalem. He went the next morning, long before sunrise, attended only by his kawass and groom. The Pasha and some of the Consuls had endeavored to persuade him to have a body of soldiers with him, and even tried to induce me to add my persuasions to theirs. But I instinctively felt, as he did, that he was more safe alone, than if he went with an *antagonistic and yet insufficient* force. Considerable anxiety was felt on his account, for it was thought to be a hazardous enterprise.

He arrived at Nablûs before the excitement was subdued. The people seemed to be taken by surprise, and to be calmed by his confidence in them. He found that Mr. Lyde had been kindly protected from the enraged populace by Mahmoud Bek Abdul Hady, in his new and beautiful house, which was actually besieged by the people, and considerably injured, because the Governor refused to yield the offender up to them. Mr. Lyde, seeing the mischief that was being done, made his will, wrote a few letters, and then begged the Governor to let him go out to the mob, that they might be appeased by his death. He said, "If they can not kill me, others will surely suffer." However, the Governor steadily persisted in protecting him, and detained him as his prisoner, saying, "Be at rest—I and my family, my servants and all my household, will risk our lives, rather than let yours be sacrificed." The disappointed crowd gathered menacingly round the building, and threw stones and fired at it for some time, and then went away to wreak their vengeance on the unoffending inhabitants of the Christian quarter.

The following extract, from a dispatch addressed to Mr. Finn by my brother, will show the persistent cruelty of the fanatics:

"I then went to the house of M. Zeller, where I found the lower rooms utterly pillaged, and the floors covered with broken china, leaves of books, maps, and papers of all descriptions, in fragments. Upstairs, I found the trunks, desks, boxes, a chest of drawers, etc., broken and destroyed. In fact, the populace left nothing undone that could possibly be effected toward the injury of the Christians. Fortunately, most of the Protestants were, and are still, away with the Bishop, otherwise they would certainly have been murdered." [This refers to Bishop Gobat, who was making a tour through his diocese, and had passed through Nablûs a few days before the outbreak.]

"Samâan Kawarre, father of the Prussian Agent, is killed. Hanna, servant of M. Zeller, is dangerously wounded, and despaired of. J. Tannûs and his wife, and several others, are badly wounded—besides eleven women, who are seriously injured by excessive fright," etc.

On the 10th, about midday, I was attracted to the window by sounds of prancing horses and tum-tums, and saw Mr. Lyde, in the midst of a little party of Turkish irregular cavalry. He alighted at the Consulate, a prisoner *en parole*. We all went out to meet and welcome him, and he gave us an account of the riots. He was very dejected. He said to me, "Mr. Rogers ran a greater risk on my account than my life is worth."

On Sunday, the 13th, my brother arrived. The riots were quelled, but the Christians felt less confidence than ever in their Moslem neighbors. Most of the Protestants had come to Jerusalem, and the rest were at Nazareth. My brother had brought with him the jeweled head-dresses, and necklaces of gold coins and pearls, belonging to some of the Christian women of Nablûs, and gave them into my care. He had been earnestly entreated to do so by their owners, of whom some had taken flight, and feared to carry their valuables with them—and others, who remained at home, felt that no hiding-place was safe while the town was so unsettled.

Mahmoud Bek Abdul Hady, the Governor, had certainly protected the Christians, during the outbreak, as far as he possibly could.

The indemnity of 55,000 piasters, adjudged to the injured Christians by the Porte, was not paid till two years afterward.

Mr. Lyde's trial, at Jerusalem, occupied a considerable time. He was eventually condemned to pay a certain sum, as "*blood-money*," to the heirs of the deceased man, who was a well-known and rather favorite character in Nablûs. He was deaf and dumb, and slightly deranged in intellect, and consequently was superstitiously respected by the Arabs, and was yet, at the same time, an object of their amusement. He was a professed beggar, and very importunate. It appeared that he stopped Mr. Lyde's horse, near tò the Nablûs Gate, and, by signs and gestures, besought alms, which were refused. When Mr. Lyde tried to pass on, the deceased caught hold of the end of a loaded pistol, which was in the holster of the saddle, and unfortunately cocked. Mr. Lyde, knowing the danger, endeavored to remove his hand. In doing so, the pistol went off, and the man was killed on the spot. Mr. Lyde was immediately surrounded, but he hastened to the Governor, and gave himself up as prisoner. [Mr. Lyde did not long survive this calamity. His mind became very seriously affected. He imagined himself to be the Redeemer of the world. A visit to England in 1858, however, dispelled the delusion; and he returned to his missionary work in the East, in apparently good health, but died, very much regretted, shortly afterward.]

By the 15th of April Jerusalem was thronged with people. The population was nearly doubled by the influx of Russian, Greek, and Armenian pilgrims, who had come to pass the Holy Week—old style—in the Holy City, to visit the neighboring shrines which they reverence, and to attend the Easter services in the Church of the Sepulcher. Every day added to the number of these earnest devotees. Most of them are poor people, who have saved a sufficient sum of money to enable them to perform the pilgrimage. They generally return home quite penniless, but happy in having realized the great object of all their struggles. There were, however, a few pilgrims who were distinguished by rank, office, or wealth, and who traveled with brilliant cavalcades.

On the 24th of April I was roused at three o'clock by the booming of cannons from the citadel. They flashed for an instant every few minutes, lighting up my room. Then there was silence and darkness, and I slept till seven, when another volley woke me, and I rose. Every one was busy, for Kamîl Pasha had issued a proclamation, ordering "all the people of Jerusalem to rejoice and be glad, and render thanks to God, and to illuminate their houses," in celebration of the announcement of peace between Russia and Turkey. The tinmen, and the dealers in "lamps, old and new," and the makers of lanterns, reaped a golden harvest that day. Contrivances for illuminating engaged every one. There was a great demand in the bazars for gilt wire and colored paper wherewith to incase wax-candles.

At noon a busy and merry little party of English girls assembled at the Consulate. Paper roses and carnations grew rapidly beneath our fingers, and were fastened to the tree-branches and boughs with which Hadj Ali, the Egyptian groom, supplied us. He brought us a donkey-load; but he had made his selection *without any sentiment*, and as he thought carrot-tops much more beautiful than olive-branches or laurels, he gathered the former in abundance. However, they made bright-green garlands, and had a pretty effect with our flowers, and no one could guess what they were. We had several visitors, who were much amused while we were making our garden grow. The Spanish Consul-General, the French Consul, and some English travelers came. The Pasha's Secretary, who peeped in several times, said he would report to Kamîl Pasha how thoroughly we were obeying the orders of the day.

The sun went down, and then by degrees the city was lighted up. Rings of light encircled the minarets and some of the domes. The Latin convent and Bishop Gobat's house were brilliant with flambeaus and cressets, and a flood of light streamed through the garlanded windows of the Consulate. Groups of white-sheeted women, and crowds of men and boys carrying torches and colored-paper lanterns, paraded the streets. About an hour after sunset a sham fight took place, under the direction of the chief commander of the troops. We went with a large party on to the roof of the offices to witness it. The Tower of Hippicus, occupied by the regulars, was besieged by the artillery and irregular Turkish troops. The city trembled with the booming of cannons, and the volleys of fire, and the thrilling sound of musketry. Large bonfires, and iron baskets filled with pitch and tar, were lighted in conspicuous places, so as to make it seem that some of the buildings had taken fire; and by their light we saw men scaling the walls, and to all appearance large masses of stone were hurled upon them. The cannons and battering-rams were dragged along, and troops were rushing incessantly across the Castle Square. We heard the cries and shouts of the soldiers. At last the tower was taken and victory proclaimed. The bugles, drums, fifes, and pipes, and tum-tums sounded. The whole affair was exceedingly well managed, and gave us a vivid idea of the actual sieges which Jerusalem has from time to time suffered. In Scriptural and other historic records descriptions or notices of no less than thirty-four distinct and successful sieges of the city may be found.

A large party assembled afterward at the English Consulate, including the Pasha and his suite, the commander of the Turkish troops, and several Consuls and travelers. Among the latter was Lord Abercrombie, who had only arrived a few hours before. He with his party had crossed the desert on their way from Cairo, and had been detained in quarantine for a few days at Hebron. They came in sight of Jerusalem at about midday, when the flashing of guns and the booming of cannons so much alarmed them that they were on the point of retreating to the coast for safety, thinking that the city was in a state of insurrection. However, when they were informed of the true cause of the firing, they eagerly proceeded on their way to join in the festivities.

On Saturday, April 26th, or Holy Saturday, the day preceding the Greek Easter, I visited the Church of the Holy Sepulcher, to witness what is said to be the miraculous kindling of the sacred fire over the tomb of Christ. After traversing a few winding and windowless streets, stony and irregular, and then almost deserted, we entered the busy bazar which leads to the church. Here all was bustle and confusion; buyers and sellers paused to watch the concourse of people hastening to the festivals. We passed under an archway, and found ourselves opposite the beautiful façade, with its double doorway and sculptured friezes. It was about half-past eleven. The square court was lined with Turkish soldiers. The surrounding terraces and house-tops were covered with women shrouded in white sheets, and forming picturesque groups, sitting and standing in the dazzling sunlight. Crowds of Greeks and Armenians were entering in at the door. I was met there by Mons. Lesselle, the *Cancelière* of the French Consulate, and with difficulty he led me into the church, and across the area of the rotunda, where all was confusion and excitement. The pilgrims were running and leaping in all directions, uttering wild cries, and a monotonous sort of chant. The noise was almost bewildering. With Mons. Lesselle's assistance I climbed up a steep platform, and then ascended a tottering staircase, which led to the Latin gallery on the north side of the rotunda.

One portion of it had been set apart for strangers, and I was glad to be safely placed there. It was like a large opera-box, with heavy but insecure railings in front, close to which chairs were occupied by a Dutch Baroness and her daughter, a monk, and the celebrated Abbé Ratisbon, an American lady and a Scottish lady, to all of whom I had been previously introduced. There were several Arab women seated on the matted floor in the back part of the box, smoking narghilés. Among them I recognized with pleasure the lady at whose house I had rested at Ramleh. After I had exchanged greetings with her I went forward, and took the seat in front prepared for me, and looked down on to the strange scene below. In the center of the extensive area of the Rotunda rises the carved and decorated marble shrine over what is supposed to be the tomb of Christ. The top of it was on a level with us. Wild-looking men, with their clothes disordered, and their caps and tarbûshes torn off—some with their long hair streaming, others with their shaven heads exposed—were performing a sort of gallopade round it. They jumped, they climbed on each other's shoulders, they tossed their arms into the air, dancing a frantic dance, that would have suited some Indian festival. Sometimes this revelry was arrested for a moment, only to commence in another form.

The actors, whose numbers had been continually augmenting, stood in groups, in little circles, tossing their heads and arms backward and forward to a monotonous cry, which grew louder and louder every minute, as the movements of heads and arms became more rapid. They kept this up till they looked mad with excitement, and they beat themselves and each other fearfully. Then they broke up the separate circles, and ran round and round the sepulcher again, with frightful rapidity, heedless of trampling one another under foot. Here and there a priest was giving himself up to the frenzy of the people, and, to gain a reputation for sanctity, he allowed himself to be most unceremoniously handled. His cap was torn off, and he himself was lifted up and carried in triumph round and round the shrine. The pilgrims believe that the fire would never come down on the tomb unless bands of the faithful thus encircled it.

In the mean time I had a pleasant chat with the Baroness. She had been six months on the Nile. She said, "My husband is dead, and I have no son; my daughter and I are alone in the world. We travel everywhere together, and alone; we have seen every people of Europe." The Abbé Ratisbon directed our attention to a change in the scenes going on below. The wild mob had been driven back to make room for the entrance of an orderly procession, formed of bishops and priests in gorgeous robes. They carried silk and gold-embroidered banners, and chanted with solemnity and great emotion a beautiful litany, while they walked three times slowly round the sepulcher. A path had been made for them by a body of Turkish soldiers, who lined the inner and outer circle of the rotunda. They behaved with praiseworthy impassiveness, and they actually looked like automata. But the impatient pilgrims came forward again, bursting wildly through the ranks. The procession of priests was broken, and soon disappeared altogether. The soldiers retired, and the people recommenced their frantic dance round and round the sepulcher with renewed energy. The Arab worshipers shouted from time to time:

> Christ, the Son of God, died for us!
> Christ, the Son of God, rose for us!
> This is the tomb of Christ our Savior!
> God preserve the Sultan!
> Christ, the Son of Mary, died for us!
> Christ, the Son of Mary, rose for us!
> This is the tomb of Christ our Savior!
> God preserve the Sultan!"

All the galleries, and even the niches in the square columns, were now occupied by lookers-on. Kamîl Pasha and his suite were in a box of the Latin gallery immediately above us. The French Consul, my brother, and several English travelers were also present. For about two hours the above scenes lasted. Then I observed a break in the crowd exactly opposite to an oval aperture which looked into the inclosure of the sepulcher. A priest in bright-yellow silk robes advanced toward it, and was welcomed with wild cries. He stooped forward, and thrust his head and shoulders and one arm through the hole, quite blocking it up. In this awkward posture he remained for a long time, and allowed himself to be beaten severely by the people who clustered round him.

There was a terrible struggle to try to gain a position commanding a view of this priest; for he it was who would distribute the sacred flame. He was, for the occasion, called the "Priest of the Holy Fire," and had paid a large sum of money for the privilege of receiving the sacred flame from the hands of the "Bishop of the Holy Fire," who was within the tomb, almost in a state of nudity. Every one in the area had either a torch or a taper ready to be lighted.

A pause of eager expectancy — a silence almost as exciting as the noise — was succeeded by a startling and tremendous shout, which shook the building to its foundation. A voice from within the sepulcher had proclaimed that the miraculous fire was kindled! The priest now drew forth his head from the hole, and held up a mass of fire, amid cries of thanksgiving and rejoicing from the multitude.

In less than a minute a hundred torches were burning brightly, and soon the light spread all round the Rotunda. We looked down upon the waving firebrands and flaming torches, held up by naked arms, outstretched exultingly — the men themselves could scarcely be seen through the sea of fire and smoke. At this juncture there appeared to be a very suspicious movement in the crowd. The Armenians and Greeks were evidently attacking each other angrily, and trying to extinguish each other's torches. One sect was jealous of the other. The sacred flame from heaven, as they called it, had been distributed unequally, and it was said that the priest of the fire had conveyed it to one party before the other, instead of giving it to them at the very same instant, according to the regular stipulations. This priority, real or pretended, was the pretext for a general fight. Every hand was raised in defense or offense. Flaming torches were tossed about recklessly, and clubs, kûrbages, and sticks were raised. The Turkish soldiers were recalled, but at first they only seemed to add to the general confusion. After about ten minutes' violent conflict, the Armenians succeeded in driving the Greeks into their church, which is on the eastern side of the Rotunda. The great brass gates were closed upon them, and for about five minutes there was comparative peace and silence.

The Pasha, with his suite, descended from the gallery above us, and was making his way across the area, when the Greeks suddenly burst out of their church, and before His Excellency could pass, another contest arose, more dangerous and exciting than the first.

Clubs and sticks were thrown down into the area to the Greeks, through the high windows looking from the terraced roof of their neighboring convent. The Armenians were so well provided with such weapons, some of which were spiked, that it was supposed that the outbreak was premeditated.

Wild cries and heavy blows resounded on all sides, without intermission. The Pasha himself was roughly handled, and he lost some of his decorations in the scuffle. The Commander of the Cavalry was thrown down, and several people high in authority were attacked by the infuriated mob. Large pieces of wood were hurled up against the galleries, where, to add to the confusion, most of the spectators were crying and screaming with fright. The door of our box was suddenly opened, and a number of women shrouded in white sheets were pushed in for safety—then the door was closed again.

We who were in front were in danger of falling into the area below, for the wooden railings were tottering and leaning outward at an angle of nearly forty-five degrees. I had great difficulty in keeping the Arab women from pressing forward, and thus pushing us over. They all seemed panic-stricken, and were sobbing convulsively. The Dutch Baroness was distracted with fear, not for herself, but for her only daughter, who, however, was perfectly self-possessed and calm, and tried to inspire those around her with courage. The monk and Abbé Ratisbon looked pale and terrified. The latter said to me, "It is not fear,

Mademoiselle, but indignation that excites me." The soldiers were endeavoring to clear the church, and it was expected that they would receive orders to fire on the obstinate fanatics, who, not content with injuring each other, began to attack the building itself. Pictures of saints and martyrs were destroyed by sharp-pointed sticks being thrust into them. The carved and gilt wooden vases, which ornamented the tawdry, cage-like covering of the tomb, were deliberately aimed at and knocked down; and two priests, who had intrepidly climbed on to the top, to try to preserve the crystal and silver lamps and other valuables there, were pelted piteously. As soon as the ornaments were displaced they were picked up, and used as missiles wherewith to assault the galleries. Many a large piece glanced close to us, who were near the front, but happily we escaped injury. The Scottish lady was so overcome with alarm that she fainted, and then at my urgent request the Arab women fell back as far as they could, to make room for her to recover herself, and to enable us to retreat a few inches from the railings in front of the box. The conflict became more and more furious. We saw terrible wounds inflicted, blood flowing from shaven heads, frightful gashes on uplifted faces, and people thrown down and trampled on. Screams, imprecations, and desperate prayers resounded. For more than a quarter of an hour this fierce fight lasted; then, by degrees, it abated, and the Turkish soldiers succeeded in driving out the chief of the combatants, not, however, without receiving some serious blows.

When the place was partially cleared, we saw that the marble pavement of the Rotunda was strewed with fragments of glass, silver chains, bits of carving, broken tapers, torches, and tarbûshes, and the entire surface shone with oil, which had streamed from the hundreds of lamps thrown down and crushed under foot. We were hoping that our friends were all safe, when to our relief they appeared crossing the area with the English travelers who had been present. They all looked pale and anxious, for they understood better than we did the dangers which had threatened us. They had greatly feared that the woodwork of the building would take fire, when escape from the galleries would have been almost impossible. They approached to assure us of our safety, and begged that we would wait quietly till they could come for us. The French Consul and the Commander of the Cavalry paused just below our box. They seemed very much excited; the former said, "I pray you, ladies, do not attempt to stir yet."

Some time elapsed before it was considered prudent to allow us to leave our retreat, for the fight was being carried on desperately in the court and streets outside the church. At last the French Consul, my brother, and several friends came for us, and we were led away. I found that the oil floating over the marble floor was at least a quarter of an inch deep. The Turkish soldiers still had possession of the building. They had behaved with great moderation during the whole of the riot, and apparently did all they could to prevent bloodshed. They had quite cleared the outer court when we crossed it, and were standing all round it with fixed bayonets. But the streets were obstructed by groups of quarrelsome people, and with difficulty the kawasses cleared a way for us. When we were safe at the Consulate, my brother returned to the Sepulcher, to see what damage had been done. He took, without opposition, from the hands of an Armenian, a heavy stick, five feet long and three inches in diameter, and he examined a great number which were armed with spikes.

The Pasha held a council immediately, and it was decided that the Greek and Armenian services should for the future be held at different hours, so that such disgraceful and dangerous collisions in the church might be avoided. It was ascertained that very few deaths had occurred, but some serious injuries had been inflicted.

I have conversed with many educated Greeks, both priests and laymen, on the nature of this ceremony, and I found that, without exception, they were heartily ashamed of it. Some of them plainly admitted that it was an imposture, others called it a pious fraud, but all agreed that it would not be advisable to disturb the faith of the mass of the people, who were thoroughly impressed by the belief that God himself descends, and with his glorious presence kindles the fire over the tomb every year on Holy Saturday. One Greek priest, a kind and earnest man, said to me, privately, "If it were possible, which is rather doubtful, to destroy the wide-spread and deep-rooted reliance on the reality and genuineness of this miracle, we should do more harm than good, for we should at the same time inevitably shake the faith of thousands; they would doubt all things, even the existence of God; they would abandon the Holy Church, and be left without any religion to guide them."

I could sympathize with him heartily, for his was a very difficult position. But I felt more strongly than ever what a mistake it is, *to try to support that which is believed to be the truth by that which is known to be false.*

Unhappily, the argument used by that amiable but fettered priest is a very common one. Religion has been so incumbered with forms and ceremonies, that the ceremonies are, by the mass of the people, mistaken for or confounded with the essence of religion.

Men fear to disturb them now, lest truth and error should fall at the same time, as if they thought that religion in its simplicity and purity could not stand alone.

When will truth be fully trusted and be permitted to triumph? When will people believe that truth is stronger and safer than trickery and wrong, and that there is always danger in teaching and supporting an error, but no danger in acknowledging one?

"Ye shall know the truth, and the truth shall make you free." John viii, 32.

"Clothe not the truth with vanity, neither conceal the truth against your own knowledge." Koran, ch. ii, Sale's Translation.

"The very essence of truth is plainness and brightness."—*Milton.*

"Great is the truth and stronger than all things; it liveth and conquereth for evermore; she is the strength, kingdom, power, and majesty of all ages. Blessed be the God of Truth."—*Zorobabel.*

Some people defended the celebration of the festival because it was an ancient custom; but, as Cyprian says,

"Custom without truth is but agedness of error."

Unfortunately, there is another powerful motive for keeping up this solemn jugglery. Large sums of money are spent in Palestine every year by the pilgrims, who come from all parts of Russia, Greece, and Turkey, and the people of Jerusalem, Bethlehem, and Nazareth naturally regard Easter as their harvest-time.

Priests, shopkeepers, relic-manufacturers, householders, owners of camels, horses, and other beasts of burden, would all more or less feel it, if the annual pilgrimages were to cease; and as the holy fire is the chief attraction, the temptation to encourage the delusion is very great.

Is this strange ceremony a relic of the services of the fire-worshipers of old? There are two or three Moslem shrines which are said to be miraculously illumined on certain days, and I am told that as early as the ninth century the Syrian Christians believed that an angel of God was appointed to light the lamps over the tomb of Christ on every Easter-eve.

CHAPTER XII.

DOMESTIC LIFE IN JERUSALEM.

About an hour before the sun went down, on Holy Saturday, we rode out of the city, glad to breathe the fresh air after the fatigue and excitement of the morning. We passed out of the Yâfa Gate, and went all round Jerusalem, close to the walls. I saw a number of poor peasant-girls coming out of the olive-grove opposite to the Damascus Gate. They wore tattered white cotton vails and homespun purple linen dresses. They were barefooted, but they all looked merry, and carried boughs of trees and flowers in their brown hands. One of the youngest had a branch of hawthorn, with glossy green leaves and several bunches of white blossom on it. It was the first bit of "May" I had seen, and, well pleased, I stopped my horse and asked the girl if she would give me a part of it. She looked up good-naturedly, and, seeing a rosebud fastened in my habit, she said, "Lady, if you will give me the flower which grows in your bosom, you shall have my hawthorn blossom." So we made the exchange.

On the 2d of May news reached us of serious skirmishes between the rival factions in the district of Jenin. The little mud-built village called "Khubeiseh," which we passed through on our way to Kefr Kûra, had been the scene of conflict, and many people whom we knew had been engaged in it.

On the 5th my brother started for Hâifa, by way of Nablûs and Jenin, and I was once more left with my kind friends at the Consulate, where I enjoyed leisure and excellent opportunities for sketching, studying, and observing all that was going on around me.

There was no more rain, and the sun was daily increasing in power. English travelers continued to arrive every few days, and I often had the pleasure of accompanying and guiding them in their "Walks about Jerusalem," and their excursions in the neighborhood.

Roses were abundant at this time. It was the season for making rose-water and conserves. The peasant-women brought basket-loads of roses into town every morning. Often at sunrise these women might be seen pausing on their way by a streamlet, to empty their baskets into the rippling water, literally making a bed of roses for the river. *Perhaps* they do this, as they say, only to wash their flowers, and to make them keep fresh and look as if wet with dew; but *I think* it is more probable that they wish to make their roses heavy, for they sell them in the market by weight.

On Wednesday, May 7th, a hot, oppressive, sirocco wind prevailed. Early in the afternoon I rode out with little Skander Finn and his cousin L. We went down into the valley of Hinnom, where hawthorns, covered with pink and white blossom, scented the air. The olive-trees were in flower, and the fig-trees green with fresh leaves. We passed the Aceldama, and reached En Rogel. There was no water in the rocky river-bed; however, it had not flowed in vain. The reservoirs were filled, and the parched earth revived. We went a little way down the valley, crossed the dry bed, and dismounted. We climbed half-way up the hill on the left-hand side, and reached a ledge or natural terrace in front of a steep cliff, which L. assured me was caverned, though no signs of a cavern could be seen. The ledge was so overgrown with tall thistles that it was difficult to find a footing; we beat these down, and found the door which they concealed. The top of the door was only slightly above the level of the terrace, which sloped abruptly down to it, like the entrance to an underground cellar, but without any steps. With the help of Hadj Ali and his stick, and by clinging to roots and weeds, we contrived to slide down and pass through the doorway, which I measured, and found it was four feet by seven, cut in the solid rock. After a minute or two we became accustomed to the sudden darkness, and could partially distinguish the objects around us. On the left side, just within the cavern, there was an immense pedestal, quite plain. We went down slipping and sliding, cautiously, one after the other, down deeper and deeper into the darkness, till we came to a column, about twelve feet in circumference, supporting a roof which appeared to me to be about twenty feet above us. The base of this column was far below the level of the door, but as it was nearly opposite to it, it caught on one side a little reflected light, and there maiden-hair grew luxuriantly, but the other sides of the pillar were only clothed with pale mosses and drooping fungus assuming grotesque forms. I removed a mass of maiden-hair to examine the nature of the native rock of which the pillar was formed. It was quite white, and crumbled easily beneath my touch.

In the mean time L. and Skander were exploring the distant recesses, and their spirit-like figures, gliding about in the darkness below, gave some idea of the depth and extent of the cavern. The floor, which was of loamy earth, continued to slope downward. There were three other massive columns; the farthest one, I should think, must be about thirty feet high. My guides warned me not to follow, for they had come to a large, though shallow, pool of water. The rain had streamed down the steep bank, and had made for itself a smooth channel to the bottom of the cavern, carpeting the way with rich soil from the surface of the terrace above. Water was trickling slowly down the walls and from the roof. Bats, disturbed by our approach, blundered against us now and then, and the damp, cold, deathlike atmosphere made us shiver. We climbed up again, and Hadj Ali helped us to reach the thistle-grown terrace in safety. We were gasping for a breath of fresh air, and rested for a minute or two blinking in the dazzling daylight and basking in the warm sunshine.

Then we scrambled over rugged rocks and through thickets of thorns and thistles till we came to a large recess in a steep white cliff. It was like a room, entirely open on one side, about eleven feet in hight, ten feet deep, and fourteen feet wide. It was, to all appearance, a natural excavation which had been partially squared by human art. In some places the ceiling looked as if it had once been coated with rough cement. The white walls were rather damp, and were garnished with maiden-hair of the finest kind I had ever seen, and many plants which love the shade were flourishing there. Out-of every crevice some delicate leaf or tendril crept. This cave was no doubt formerly inhabited by human beings; kings, priests, and prophets of old may have lodged here.

Skander had climbed higher up the hill, and now called to us, saying, "I have found a wonderful place up here—come and see." With difficulty we followed, and found him stretched flat on his face, peering into a dark opening, about one foot high and six feet broad, close to the ground; he said it was like a large fox-hole. I could not possibly enter this cave, but I stopped and looked in, and could see that there were some ancient sepulchers within; I counted four. They were, I believe, cut in the solid rock, and were ornamented with bold, effective moldings and bosses. This place seems to be worthy of careful exploration. The entrance is likely soon to be quite concealed by the stones and *débris* falling from above, and the tangled masses of vegetation near it. There is no tradition connected with it, and it is on that account, perhaps, that it is so rarely pointed out to travelers.

We mounted and rode homeward, looking toward the south-east corner of the Holy City. The sunlight was gleaming on the terraces just below it, and it tinged with an emerald luster the fields of barley there. On the right, above En Rogel, the ruins of Siloam appeared, and we could just see Absalom's Pillar.* As we rode round the

---

* It is this view which the lamented Mr. Sedden painted so faithfully. The picture is in the South Kensington Museum.

base of Mount Zion, Hadj Ali gathered a beautiful branch of a pomegranate-tree, covered with bright blossoms, the first I had seen that year.

We remembered that Ramadan, the month when the followers of Mohammed fast by day and feast by night, had commenced on the previous Sunday; so we hastened on, that Hadj Ali might prepare his evening meal, and be ready to eat it at the moment of the firing of the "*mogarib*," the signal gun at sunset—the sound so welcome to hungering and thirsty Moslems. Poor Hadj Ali had not taken food or even smoked a pipe since sunrise. This fast, which lasts for thirty days, is observed with extraordinary fidelity by people of all classes.*

On Thursday, May 28th, I was invited to visit the new schools for young Jewesses, established by Sir Moses Montefiore. The morning was bright and dazzling. We passed the barracks, and entered the street leading to the Armenian convent. The sun was almost vertical, and the polished stone pavement reflected back the heat and light. The high walls of the houses on each side scarcely cast a line of shadow: only the little casement windows jutting out here and there, and the bright flowers which climbed through the trellis-work, or hung from the roofs, traced fantastic and delicate shadows on the ground. Not a breath of air was stirring. It was midday, and no one was to be seen in the broad, unsheltered, silent street,

---

* In the second chapter of the Koran the rules for observing Ramadan are given thus:

"O true believers, a fast is ordained unto you, as it was ordained unto those before you, that ye may fear God.

"The month of Ramadan is the month of fasting, in which the Koran was sent down from heaven—a direction unto men, and declarations of direction, and the distinction between good and evil. Therefore let him among you who shall be dwelling at home in this month fast the *same month;* but he who shall be sick or on a journey shall fast the like number of other days. God would make this an ease unto you, that ye may fulfil the number of days, and glorify God for that he hath directed you, and that ye may give thanks. . . .

"It is lawful for you to eat and drink at night until ye can plainly distinguish a *white thread* from a *black thread* by the daybreak; then keep the fast until sunset."

According to Moslem divines there are three degrees of fasting. The first and second are strictly material; the third is the fasting of the heart from worldly cares, and the restraint of the thoughts, which must be concentrated on God.

where even the dogs were sleeping, as if overcome by the heat and light. We turned to the left and passed a walled-up archway, once the entrance to an ancient mosque. We skirted the back of the Armenian convent, and thus reached the Jewish quarter, and were very soon knocking at the school-house door, over which there was a well-engraved Hebrew inscription.

While we waited for admittance, I looked up at the windows. Two were square, unsheltered openings; a third jutted far out from the wall, and through its quaint and fanciful wooden lattice we could see bright and rare flowers; the fourth was a large, square oriel window, supported by a stone bracket, and protected by an iron balcony. A crowd of happy-looking children were peeping from it. One dark-eyed little creature had a red cloth tarbûsh on the back of her head, and a rose in her black hair. The others wore soft muslin kerchiefs of various colors, tied tastefully on their heads.

We entered the door, crossed a small court, and were led up an open staircase on to a terrace, the low, broad walls of which were converted into a garden. Flower-pots had been imbedded in the masonry, at regular distances, along the top of the parapets. Thus a sort of floral battlement was formed, and produced an excellent effect; for the plants were kept nearly all of the same size and hight. The rose-bushes, pinks, and cloves, in full flower, contrasted well with the dark-leaved myrtle, the cape jasmine, and the white walls.

We were politely received in this court by a Spanish Jewess, who conducted us into a light, cheerful room, containing animated groups of girls, varying in age from seven to fourteen, perhaps. I counted thirty-one children; but the full number usually assembled there was thirty-five. Eight forms and a double row of desks gave quite a European character to the room, and the raised, pulpit-like seat of the teacher indicated order and authority.

The girls were nearly all engaged at needle-work, and

our guide exhibited to us, with evident pride and pleasure, a considerable stock of wearing apparel, the result of one week's work in that room. The simple garments were very nicely made, considering that most of the little workers did not know how to sew six or seven months before. The mistress could not tell us what was done with the work when finished, as it passed from her hands at the end of each week. The children looked busy and bright. Some of them were singularly beautiful. One tall and stately girl of about fourteen was acting the part of monitor, and she answered our questions, in Arabic, with the utmost modesty and self-possession, and glided among her little pupils with native grace and dignity. All these children were natives of Palestine; they spoke Arabic, and wore the Arab costume. Their heads were, without exception, covered either with muslin kerchiefs, or with the simple red tarbûsh.

The windows of this room were large, and thrown wide open. They looked eastward, and commanded views of the whole extent of Olivet, and the misty Moab Mountains far away. The midday breeze sprang up suddenly, and slightly cooled the fiery air.

After lingering for a short time to enjoy the prospect, we were led to another room, equally large, light, and airy. Here we found about thirty children, under the care of two female teachers. One tiny little creature was learning a Hebrew lesson, and carefully spelling words of two letters. Another child of seven or eight was reading, with very little hesitation, some Scripture history. The other children were seated comfortably, and with perfect ease and freedom, yet without disorder, upon mats, or in the deep, carpeted window-seat. There I recognized the happy faces which I had seen from the street below. They looked up at me smiling, as much as to say, "We know you again; we saw you waiting at the door."

They were all at needle-work, and I could not help observing the extreme delicacy and beauty of their hands.

If, as it is said, this is a distinguishing feature of noble birth, then these young daughters of Israel are of princely race. Some of the little hands were stained with henna, and almost all the nails were tinted, and looked like the delicate, rose-colored shells we find on the sands on English shores.

The children were uniformly neat and clean, and there was a picturesque variety of costume there that struck us pleasantly, contrasting with our recollections of the ugly uniforms in some of our public schools at home and abroad. As we were retiring, a shy little creature summoned up courage to give me the rose from her hair, and then she peeped at me slyly between her tapering fingers.

These two rooms were set apart expressly for the children of parents belonging to the Sephardim Congregation, consisting of the Spanish and Portuguese Jews settled in Jerusalem.

We were now led down-stairs again to the open court, which we crossed; and, after ascending another stairway, we found ourselves in the school of the Ashekenazi Congregation, formed of German, Russian, and Polish Jews. Here there were fifteen children, and they all seemed to be under seven years of age. They were much more fair, though less beautiful, than those in the other rooms. They were sitting, very much at their ease, perched up on the sloping desks, with their little feet resting on the forms. How thoughtful and kind it was to allow them this freedom during the hot weather! There was not a sign of fatigue, or any expression of rebellion against restraint, in any of the young faces around us. There was activity of mind and rest of body, in a pure air.

The Jews of Jerusalem are especially careful not to allow their children to associate with Christians or Moslems; and they will not suffer them to stray away from home, or play in the streets, for fear they should learn bad habits, or be constrained or induced to be baptized into a Christian Church. Consequently, the little ones were confined nearly all day in the close, ill-ventilated, small rooms of the Jewish quarter, till this school was established. Here they assembled early in the morning, and, taking proper hours for rest, recreation, and for meals, returned home at sunset. Already a great improvement was observed in their appearance; they looked more healthy, and their lives were happier.

A little girl of five years of age, with pink cheeks, blue eyes, and hair almost white, was reading aloud from some Hebrew volume, and was evidently interested by it. I cautiously inquired whether she knew by heart all that fell so fluently from her lips. I was assured that I was listening to genuine reading.

We went down-stairs to the second German room, where most of the girls were between thirteen and fifteen years of age, and the rest younger. We heard two of the eldest read, with emphasis, several pages from the Life of Moses— a book written expressly for the use of women and children. It is a paraphrase of the Bible history of Moses, in a curious, harsh dialect, being a compound of Hebrew and German. It is printed in Hebrew characters, and embellished with quaint and curious wood-cuts, in the style of the followers of Albert Dürer.

In these two rooms fifty-five pupils generally muster.

The housekeeper, who had guided us from room to room, then led us to her own, and exhibited some shirts, which she and the elder pupils had been making to order. They were stitched and hem-stitched, and neatly finished off. She seemed delighted with our approval and praise; for this shirt-making was quite a new accomplishment, as the Jews of the East wear much more simple under-garments than these.

We took leave of her, and I returned to the Consulate, very tired. My friends went on to the Rothschild Schools, of which they afterward gave me a very favorable report.

When I was in Jerusalem, in 1859 I made inquiries

about these schools, especially the one established by Sir M. Montefiore, intending to visit it again. To my surprise and regret, I was told that it no longer existed; and I could not obtain any satisfactory account of it, or understand why it was broken up. I suppose that Oriental indifference to female education is the chief cause.

On the 13th of May, Mrs. Finn, in behalf of the "Jerusalem Agricultural Association," purchased a portion of the beautiful valley of Urtas. I witnessed the making and concluding of the bargain. Ten of the fiercest and wildest-looking Arabs I had seen were assembled in the office of the Consulate, with their chief, a tall, powerful man, called Sheikh Saph, whose family, local tradition says, has for ages been distinguished for the hight and strength of its men.*

Mrs. Finn came forward, and stood in the midst of the group of men, and said, "O Sheikh, do you agree to sell?" and Sheikh Saph answered, "I agree to sell, O my lady; do you agree to buy?" and Mrs. Finn replied, "I buy, O Sheikh." Then the purchase-deed, which had been already prepared, was read over, signed, and sealed; and one hundred and fifty sovereigns were counted slowly into the hands of the Sheikh. He received the gold with great gravity and seeming indifference; but his men looked on eagerly, with hawk-like eyes. After this, about a hundred coins, of small value, were thrown on the office-floor, according to custom, and were eagerly scrambled for by all present. Thus the exact sum paid for the ground could not be ascertained. This method of selling any thing, for a known and an unknown sum, is called "a sale by the uncounted group." When this precaution is neglected in dealing with Arab tribes, a purchaser may be obliged to yield up property to its original owner at any moment, for the amount of the purchase-money.

Sheikh Saph and his two chief followers were invited

---

* This is rather curious in connection with 2 Sam. xxi, 18: "Then Sibbechai the Hushathite slew Saph, which was of the sons of the giant."

into the drawing-room to take coffee. They made strong professions and promises of faith and good-will toward their "noble lady, Mrs. Finn," saying, that they would protect the property at the risk of their lives, and as if it were still their own. They went away evidently quite satisfied with the transaction.

On the 15th, Mr. and Mrs. Finn went to Urtâs, to stay there for a few days, for change of air, and to superintend the arrangements for inclosing and cultivating the recently-purchased land. I was invited to spend a day with them, in company with an English traveler, Mr. W., and Skander Finn. We started from the Consulate at sunrise, and rode quickly across the plain of Rephaim to Rachel's Sepulcher, and over the hills by Bethlehem. A well-mounted kawass led the way, and a mule carrying Debibu, the Abyssinian servant, and a tent, followed. We reached the pleasant valley in about two hours. It looked to me more beautiful than ever, with its rippling streams, its flourishing fruit-trees, and rose-bushes covered with flowers.

We found our friends waiting for us, seated at the wide entrance of a dry cave, in a white limestone rock, just above the new garden-ground. We went together up to Mr. Meshullam's cottage. His wife showed me a large sieve full of fine roses, which had been gathered before sunrise. We breakfasted in the rose-scented room, and then rested for a short time on the cushioned stone divan, under a large fig-tree, the thickly-growing leaves of which now afforded perfect shelter.

A ride was proposed, and we mounted. Mr. Finn led the way in a south-westerly direction, over a steep and pathless hill, which looked as if it had never been traversed except by wild goats and conies. When we commenced descending, we found it necessary to dismount; and, one after another, we led our horses, slipping and sliding, over large smooth inclined slabs of rock and loose stones, till we reached a broad level platform, where rich earth had rested, and formed a bed for wild flowers. Here we paused for those of our party who had prudently taken an easier route round the base of the hill. They presently overtook us, and we were reminded that Amos, the herdsman and prophet, who said, "Shall horses run upon the rock?" dwelt not far from here, and very likely he had often seen them stumbling or stepping cautiously over such hills as this. We rode all together up a narrow winding valley, where wild thyme and heath, and blue, yellow, red, and white salvias, grew abundantly among the gray rocks, which were half-covered with orange-colored lichen. The air was warm and fragrant.

At the head of the valley there was a rounded hill, crowned by a low clump of trees, which sheltered a white tent. The northern and western slopes were green with bearded barley. This lovely patch of cultivated land contrasted strangely with the wild hills around, where there was not any sign of human industry. Mr. Meshullam enjoyed our surprise, and then explained how he had cleared the land and sown it, and made a little garden on the top of the hill. The soil was very rich in quality, but rather thinly spread over the surface of the rock.*

There were higher hills rising beyond, and sheltering this retreat. We ascended gradually, till we reached the

* This ground has been greatly improved since, and when I visited it in 1859, I found that Peter, one of Mr. Meshullam's younger sons, a brave and enterprising young man, had, on his return from service in the Crimea, built a little stone house there, and inclosed a large portion of cleared land. He often lived on the hill for weeks together, his only companions being two or three native peasants, and his favorite dog, and a few other domestic animals. He adopted the Bedouin costume, and lived quite like an Arab, except during his occasional visits to Jerusalem and other towns. He has lived from childhood in Palestine, and his physical strength, quickness of action, and foresight have endeared him to the Arabs. He is known and respected by most of the Sheikhs in the district. He has more than once been requested to become the chief of a small tribe. He told me that he would have accepted the office gladly, if he could have done so without becoming a Mohammedan. He was dreaded by the doers of mischief for miles around. He found the neighborhood infested with wild boars, jackals, foxes, and other beasts of prey. He killed a great number, and very often succeeded in shooting hawks and eagles.

When His Royal Highness Prince Alfred was in Palestine, in the Spring of 1859, Mr. Peter Meshullam was one of his most constant companions on the inland journey from Jerusalem to Tiberias, and thence to Haifa, where the *Euryalus* was at anchor.

highest point in the range, which commanded a wide prospect in every direction.

Looking eastward, I at once recognized the Dead Sea, calm and blue, and the long line of the Moab Mountains beyond; but the rest of the view all around was to me, as well as to Mr. W., only a maze of white, gray, and brown hills, and dark valleys checkered with cloud-shadows, without any roads or landmarks.

Mr. Finn read the landscape round for us, and its features soon grew familiar to me. We were looking eastward, and he said, "That dark ravine to the right, in the range of rocks on this side of the Dead Sea, is the Valley of the Wilderness of Engeddi, where David 'dwelled in strongholds' during his exile. That peak, like an extinct volcano, which rises above the surrounding hills, is the Frank Mountain, called by the Arabs, '*Jebel Furidus*,' that is, the Lesser Paradise Mount. A little way to the right of it, on that terraced and rounded hill, are the ruins of Tekoa, where Amos guarded flocks and herds, and gathered wild figs, in the days of Uzziah, King of Judah, two years before the earthquake. We will go there some day, and look for a wise woman." Turning toward the north-east, he said, "Do you notice a depression in that long range? Look a little to the left of it, and you will distinguish the leaden roof of the Convent of Bethlehem, and then you can make out the surrounding buildings. Farther north is Mount Olivet; and, now that a black cloud is passing over Jerusalem, you can plainly see two tall minarets rising white and bright out of the city."

Many of the hills, especially in the south and east, were crowned with ruins, and showed signs of former cultivation, but now they were deserted. The stone walls of the ancient terraces were broken down, and the earth washed away, and, where vines and fig-trees once grew, thorns and thistles had sprung up—the whole land truly is made silent and desolate. We were overlooking a large portion of the division of the tribe of Judah. See Jer. vii, 34—"I will cause to cease from the cities of Judah the voice of mirth, and the voice of gladness, the voice of the bridegroom, and the voice of the bride: for the land shall be desolate." A string of camels and a few horsemen were hastening across the country, and now and then we caught sight of them. Here and there a few black tents were pitched and flocks were feeding, but there was nothing else to give life to the landscape.

The wind, which had been gradually rising, now blew so violently that we could scarcely stand against it. The cloud which had overshadowed Jerusalem was whirled far away, and unless we had known exactly where to look, and what to look for, we could not possibly have distinguished the hill on which the city stands from the rocky hills which encircle it. We were reminded of the words of Carlyle: "The eye only sees that which it brings with it the power of seeing." We rode down into the valley for shelter, but we were presently tempted to ascend the opposite hill, for we saw some square black tents among the low trees and bushes. We rode up to the encampment and dismounted, and were soon surrounded by a group of dusky Arabs. They had cultivated a little patch of ground with barley and beans, and a few wild olive-trees grew at the base of the hill. Their half-naked little children were playing with the goats, jumping from rock to rock and rolling on the ground; the elder ones were gathering wood for the fire. The women were attending to a caldron of rice, which was suspended gipsy-fashion over a wood-fire in the open air. They clustered round Mrs. Finn and me, examining us with curiosity, especially wondering at our gloves and boots. They all looked rather languid and fatigued—the effect probably of the daily fasting, for they were very rigid Moslems of Bethlehem origin. We asked them how long they intended to remain there? They replied, "We shall remain here till Ramadan is past."*

From the top of the hill the flash of the "mogarib," or

* See note, page 60.

sunset gun from the citadel at Jerusalem, could be seen, and, partly on that account, they had chosen the spot for their encampment. Besides this attraction, there was water near, and pasture for their flocks, and dwarf oak-trees, and resinous shrubs and thorns, which they cut down for fuel. The gum-cistus flourished there, and was covered with wide-open, delicate blossoms, white, pink, and lilac, which fell off when the flowers were gathered, and fluttered away in the breeze like butterflies.

We remounted and went by another route toward Urtâs, making our way along narrow wadys, and crossing ridges, where tall hollyhocks and the hibiscus abounded. Presently we came to a hill on which there were extensive and interesting ruins. We dismounted and scrambled up among rocks, hewed stones, and thistles, and thorn-bushes, which grew on the ancient terraces. When we reached the plateau on the top of the hill, Mr. Finn, who had previously explored the place, pointed out to us the foundation of a very large building, divided into compartments. The walls had been broken down, but in some parts they stood four feet high. They were built of very large, well-beveled blocks of stone, not joined together with mortar, but the interstices were filled up with finely-crushed stones. The ground was strewed with tesseræ about three-quarters of an inch square, with which all the inclosed spaces had evidently been paved.

From the style of the masonry and the general outline, Mr. Finn judged that this was a good example of Jewish workmanship of an early period, and as ancient as any existing in the country. The buildings must have covered a large space, and were apparently all connected with the central and principal one. The Arabs call this ruin the *"Dâr el Benât"*—that is, the house or "retreat of girls;" but they have no tale to tell about it. There is no historical notice or tradition of any Christian convent having existed here at any time; and there is not the slightest indication of Christian art in the general ground-plan.

The great beveled stones which are scattered all over the hill, and rest in heaps in the valley below, as if thrown down by an earthquake, are exactly like the stones of which Solomon's Pools and other ancient works are formed. Mr. Finn suggested that this was possibly one of the places of which Solomon spoke when he said, "I made me great works; I builded me houses." And the singular traditionary name, "Dar el Benât," which has clung to it, may signify that this was an establishment connected with Solomon's harem, which, it is said, contained "seven hundred wives and three hundred concubines."

I can imagine the time when the now fallen walls were standing, and inclosing cool chambers, columned corridors, terraces, courts, fountains, and gardens of citrons and roses; when the hill-sides were covered with vines, and the valley below was well watered, and brought forth all kinds of goodly fruits and fragrant spices. Gathered together there, I see in fancy "virgins without number;" agile and graceful mountaineers from the Lebanon; proud and stately daughters of Jerusalem; sweet, shy girls from the plains of Sharon; and the fairest of the fair maidens of Shunem; contrasting with the dark loveliness of the melancholy young African exiles, who wore "the shadowed livery of the burnished sun," and gloried in the tints he made them wear.*

Guarded by "valiant men of Israel," and surrounded by handmaidens and slaves, they were nursed here in luxury and splendor—decked with ornaments of gold, and silver, and precious stones—clothed with raiments of fine linen, and silk, and embroidered work—anointed with oil, and perfumed with sweet odors. Every art was employed that could add a new charm to beauty. I can hear their songs of rejoicing when the Winter rains passed away and the flowers appeared on the earth. I can see them early in

---

* "I am black but comely, O ye daughters of Jerusalem!"
SONG OF SOLOMON i, 5.

the morning in the vineyards, or on the stairs cut in the rock on the hill-side, going down into the garden of nuts, to see the fruits of the valley—to see whether the vine flourished and the pomegranate budded; and to this day, at every marriage festival in the country, their wild, picturesque, and passionate love-songs are echoed in a language very nearly allied to their own. On this subject I hope, on some future occasion, to speak more fully, in some notes on the Life and Times of Solomon, and his Song of Songs.

We lingered a long time among the ruins. I picked up a handful of tesseræ, and then went down to the valley. We found traces here and there of a rocky staircase, the joint work of nature and art. At the base of the hill wild pomegranates and the arbutus grew. Just as we were mounting I saw on the top of a seemingly-inaccessible heap of rocks and hewed stones a very fine honeysuckle. Mr. W. determined to gather it for us. He leaped across the deep dry bed of the Winter torrent, and climbed over the bushes and rocks, and soon returned in triumph with such a large, bright trophy of pink hollyhocks, at least five feet high, and long, trailing branches of the honey-suckle, that it frightened all the horses as he approached. We rode on, laden with flowers. The honeysuckle smelled very sweet; its blossoms were large, and of a pale-yellow color, shaded with white and pink.

We made our way quickly to Urtâs, and after dinner we sat for a short time under the fig-tree. The peasants came down from the ancient village above to look at us, and we took the opportunity of putting some of them into our sketch-books. Then we mounted, and had a delightful ride back to Jerusalem. It was long past sun-set when we reached the gates, but the keeper of the key had been detained to admit us.

Thus the Spring-time passed pleasantly. Day after day my attention and my interest had been excited by scenes and incidents which vividly illustrated the treasured records of the past, and threw new light for me on Hebrew chronicle and Gospel story. I had seen and entered into the spirit of human life in all its progressive stages. I had found shelter in the tents of lawless wanderers, and claimed sisterhood with Bedouin girls. I had lingered among more peaceful tribes, who dwell in patriarchal simplicity in stationary tents, surrounded by flocks and herds. I had lodged with the fellahîn, in their rude villages of mud and stone, encircled by orchards, gardens, fields of grain, and pasture-land, and had associated with the townspeople, the great men, the law-makers, and the governors of the land. In the mean time I had occasionally enjoyed the society of some of the most highly-cultivated and noble representatives of the civilized nations of Europe. I could find some meeting-point of sympathy with all, and I truly felt that "one touch of nature makes the whole world kin."

My desire to make my friends in England share my pleasures, and to enable them to see, as far as possible, a true reflex of all that I saw, led me to look carefully and earnestly on all things. I seemed to possess unusual strength and power of resisting fatigue, and acquired habits of ceaseless and minute observation. My pen and pencil were almost always in use. Friendly voices often said, "You are working too hard; you do not take sufficient rest;" or, "Unless you work with less intensity you will suffer sooner or later. In this country, at this season, it is absolutely necessary to have a little sleep or perfect repose at midday."

I did not take warning, and at last sleepless nights came, and were followed by weary days and loss of appetite, and my almost unnaturally-excited and overtaxed strength suddenly gave way. I remember one hot night, after in vain trying to sleep, I rose and sat in one of the eastern windows of the Consulate on Mount Zion, and watched for the rising of the sun over the Mount of Olives. I waited for a long time before there was any change in the cool gray sky or any colors on the dusky earth. Every thing was as still as death. Presently there was a pale, golden tinge in the east, and the dark mountains of Moab grew dim and shadowy in misty light; the brightness rose up into the heavens, which suddenly became orange, blue, and rose-colored. The tall date palm-trees, so black and so motionless a moment before, now stirred their green fronds gently, and the delicate yellow grasses on the house-tops and on the terraces quivered and shook as if just awakened out of sleep, and birds fluttered from their nests chirping and twittering in chorus; but it was some time before the sun appeared above Mount Olivet. That was on the 26th of May. Afterward I became weaker and weaker, taking no note of time; sometimes riding out very gently into an olive-grove to rest under the trees, while I idly watched the children at their play, or the flickering shadows of wide-winged birds, or the busy insects creeping in and out among the stones and the wild flowers. But there were days when I could not rise from my bed, and sometimes I thought that I should die there. For two or three days I was quite deaf through extreme weakness. The late Dr. Macgowan was unremitting in his attention, and I never shall forget the kindness of my nurses, of whom Mrs. Finn was the chief.

On the 18th of June Um Issa, one of the servants, came to my bedside, and said gently, in Arabic, "Be glad and rejoice, for now you will be well quickly. The Consul has come, God be praised!" From that time I began to recover, and the next day I rode up with my brother to Mr. Graham's little tower on Mount Olivet, and took up my abode there for a few weeks. It is a genuine Arab structure. On the ground-floor are stables and a kitchen; and a vaulted chamber above, with a broad window in a deep recess, serves as the sitting-room. A few stone steps lead to the flat roof, which forms a pleasant terrace, and is protected by a low wall, as are most of these flat roofs, and as they must have been anciently, in obedience to the law: "When thou buildest a new house, then thou shalt make a battlement for thy roof, that thou bring not blood upon thine house, if any man fall from thence." Deut. xxii, 8. From this terrace we had almost a bird's-eye view of Jerusalem. Looking down the slope of Olivet, sprinkled with trees and rugged with rocks, we saw the deep Valley of Jehoshaphat, which separated us from the city.

Mr. Graham and my brother went into the city every morning, and I used to sit in the window-seat sweeping the landscape with an excellent telescope, watching the worshipers in the mosque area, or gazing on the hills round about Jerusalem, till every one became as familiar to me as the face of a friend.

The olives and fig-trees around were flourishing, the pomegranates were in full leaf and blossom, and the fruit was beginning to form. The patches of wheat and barley on the terraces had been reaped, and thorns and thistles were springing up in the stubble-fields. My friends from the Consulate used to come sometimes to spend the midday hours with me, and my brother generally arrived in time for an evening stroll. This quiet life brought back my strength, and I could again use my pen and pencil with delight and with an untrembling hand; and, by taking regular hours of rest, I found that I could work and enjoy all pleasant sights and sounds without suffering any ill effects.

On Saturday I noticed that large companies of women gathered together on the slope of the opposite hill, below the St. Stephen's Gate. They sat in little groups under the olive-trees. They were all shrouded in white sheets, but many of them took off their mundîls, or muslin face-vails, thinking themselves quite out of sight of strangers—but I could distinguish their features through the telescope.

Ropes were fastened to the tree-branches, and the children began to swing with great glee. The women followed the example, and seemed thoroughly to enjoy the monotonous movement. By midday there were more than a hundred women assembled, besides groups of children, so restless that I could not count them, attended by unvailed Abyssinian servants.

Several black men came out of the St. Stephen's Gate, carrying provisions; they handed them to the female servants, and then went away directly. Soon a number of circular trays were placed in the shade and covered with simple food and sweetmeats. Water was poured from jars over the hands of the women, and then they sat on the ground round the well-filled dishes. They were not nearly so silent over their meal as men are. They lingered over it, and I could see that they were laughing and talking merrily. Then they washed their hands again, and took coffee and smoked narghilés while the servants had their dinner; and they all remained there, some sleeping and others chatting, under the trees, till an hour before sunset, when they vailed themselves closely and went into the city. It is a very common practice in the Summer-time to keep holiday thus.

On Friday, the 4th of July, the wind rose suddenly at midday, and was so violent that I was obliged to have all the casements closed, and even then the curtains were blown about and papers fluttered through the rooms, yet the heat was intense.

On Saturday, the 5th, I went with my brother, early in the afternoon, to the little village on the top of the central point of Olivet. We called at the house adjoining the mosque. We entered a court and mounted a steep stone stairway, and reached a broad terrace, with high, raised, stone divans on each side of the arched entrance to a large but low room. Carpets and cushions were quickly brought out and spread on the raised seats, and a handsome Moslem, the son of an effendi of some note in Jerusalem, who was staying up there for change of air, invited us to make ourselves at home.

In a few minutes, the master of the house, a fine, gray-bearded, turbaned sheikh, joined us. After we had taken sherbet, coffee, and a narghilé, he opened the door at the base of the minaret, and we groped our way up the winding stairs to the top, and then stood in the balcony, silent with delight at the wonderful prospect which presented itself. Looking eastward over the wilderness of bossy hills, we saw a large expanse of the Dead Sea, with the Moab Mountains beyond, stretching far away north and south. The sun shone magnificently, shedding a halo of glory on every object. In the foreground of the view a *wely*, or dome, stood on a rounded hill, which was covered with olive and fig trees. This is called the Dome of the Witnesses. Beyond this, there was no sign of life—all was desolate. But, looking westward, we could see Jerusalem stretched out like a map beneath us, and there were evidences of human skill and industry on almost all the hills.

While we were there, the *Cancellière* of the French Consulate and M. Gilbert joined us. The latter said that Kamîl Pasha had been to the castle to call on us, and, hearing where we were, had followed us. So we went down on to the terrace to meet him.

Our host asked me, in a low voice, if I would visit his harem, as his wives had expressed a wish to see me. With my brother's permission, I went. The old man led me through a court, and up on to a terraced roof, where an elderly woman, the wife of his youth, awaited me. He went away, and she said, "Welcome, O my daughter; we have heard of you, and have been longing to see you and speak with you." She took me into a little garden on the house-top, and two handsome women, with features of Egyptian character, came forward to greet me. They wondered that I ventured to remain in the lonely castle on the hill, and said, "We dare not live there. God has given courage to English girls." I then inquired how many English girls they had known. "We know you, and we have known one other only. She was a girl who lived in the castle for a long time with her father." I found that they referred to the daughter of Mr. Barclay, the author of the "City of the Great King." They asked after her with warm-hearted kindness.

Suddenly, while we were speaking, the two younger wives started up, and went to the other side of the garden, crouched down in the shadow of the wall, and made their way cautiously down to their rooms. I said, "What has disturbed you?" The old wife, who did not move, directed my attention to a window, or rather a small square opening, in a house not far off. A man was looking from it, evidently surprised to see a stranger there, for he lifted up some children to look at me. The old woman said, "Never mind, let us gather some flowers before we go down." There were dahlias, hollyhocks, balsams, scavias, African marigolds, everlastings, roses, sweet basil, and myrtles in full blossom. I made a bouquet of the three last, and the woman said, "Why have you passed all the other flowers to take these?" I said, "These are the flowers I love the best for their scent and for their beauty." She said, "Even as you love one flower better than another, so God loves one creature more than another. You are one of the favorites of God, and he protects you in all dangers."

She wore by her side a flat gold box, about four inches wide and six inches long, suspended by a double chain. It was engraved with sentences from the Koran, and she said that it contained a charm against the power of an evil eye, and against sorcery. I told her I never wore charms. She replied, "You do not require any—no one can hurt you."

We went down into the women's room. The two young wives were waiting for us at the wide-open door, and had prepared coffee and sweetmeats for me. The room was large and low, without any windows; there were small holes near the ceiling.

I saw several young children. They seemed very much neglected, and the flies were allowed to tease them terribly, clustering on the edges of their unwashed eyelids, and buzzing about their sugar-crusted lips.

The sun was going down, and the muezzin cried out from

the minaret close by, so I rejoined my brother; and we retired, to allow our Moslem friends to enjoy their evening meal. I went several times afterward, to sketch from the minaret, and to see the women.

On Sunday morning, July 6th, I sat alone in the window-seat of my home, on Mount Olivet, and watched the funeral of a Moslem woman. The procession issued from the St. Stephen's Gate. Some soldiers and other men carried the open bier. The body, covered with a sheet, was lying down flat, but the head was very much raised, and the face concealed by a mundîl. The open grave was close by the wayside. A number of men were grouped around it, and some women were watching from the slope above, wailing wildly, swaying their bodies to and fro, and throwing up their arms, as if pleading passionately. The clumsy bier was propped against a rock, and the dead body fell into an awkward sitting posture. Two men went down into the grave, and quite disappeared. The corpse was then removed from the bier, the sheet was taken off, and disclosed a figure just like an Egyptian mummy. It was handed, not very gently or reverently, to the men below, and then eight men held the sheet over the opening. After a minute or two the sheet was withdrawn, the men who had been covering up the body appeared above ground, and the grave was quickly closed. The crowd dispersed, and in a short time all was quiet again.

It was a very hot day, and I was quite alone, for I had been persuaded not to venture into the town to church. At about three o'clock, I saw a large body of irregular Turkish troops issuing from the St. Stephen's Gate. They rode in single file down into the valley, and then rose up the sides of Olivet, along the path toward the village above. They all carried guns, and most of them had long spears. They were dressed with no attention to uniformity, but nearly every one wore a red and yellow silk *kefia*, or fringed shawl head-dress. I counted fifty-two in the first detachment, but others followed in small parties, took the road along the valley, and disappeared behind the Garden of Gethsemane.

A little before sunset my brother returned, and, in answer to my questions about the soldiers, said, "They were on their way to Abu Dis, a village on the other side of the hill, which is now in arms against El Tûr, the village just above us. Several skirmishes have taken place during the last three days, and a few people have been killed on both sides. The Pasha is now determined to put a stop to the fighting. His Excellency has just now told me that he intends to encamp up here, and will have his tents pitched near to this tower." He did so, and shortly afterward his pretty green tents were to be seen under the olive-trees.

On Tuesday, July 8th, Mr. Graham and my brother returned from the town early and said, "Now put on something that clay will not spoil and rocks will not tear, and we will take you to explore the Tombs of the Prophets."

Having equipped myself accordingly, and provided wax candles, we rode up to the top of the hill through the little dusty village of El Tûr. We traversed the large cucumber gardens beyond it, and entered a fine mulberry orchard. A troop of half-naked little brown boys were up in the trees, gathering the ripe and abundant fruit and shouting merrily; while a few women, in purple linen dresses and white cotton vails, stood beneath with large trays and baskets made of reeds, which they were rapidly filling. We alighted under the trees. One woman, who seemed to have authority over all the rest, advanced to me and gave me some of the fruit. I had never tasted finer mulberries. Then, to my surprise, I was led to the mouth of a circular well, quite dry, and nearly filled up with dust and rubbish. We got down into this and crept through a hole in the side, and crawled along a winding and descending way on our hands and feet till we found ourselves in a circular chamber in which we could stand upright. It was about twenty-four feet in diameter, and in the middle about ten feet high. A little light came into it from a hole pierced through the solid rock above. Here we lighted our candles, and Mr. Graham drew my attention to three holes leading in different directions. He entered the central one, moving backward and pushing his way along on the ground. I crawled in head-foremost and much more easily. We were gradually descending, and presently came to a corridor which branched off in a curve on each side, forming part of a circle of which the chamber we had left seemed to be the center. This corridor was about ten feet high and six feet broad; it was vaulted and cemented, and the floor, of rock, was made level. There were a great number of chambers and niches in the walls, but there were no remains of coffins of any kind. From this gallery, which was only a quadrant, other passages branched off. We entered one which led us to a gallery of the same kind, but larger, and forming part of a more extended circle. Mr. Graham advised us not to venture into the passages which he had not previously explored, for they are rather puzzling, and the place is quite a maze to an unguided stranger. The outer quadrant is said to be 115 feet in length, and sixty feet distant from the circular chamber which is its center. The passages which lead to and unite the two quadrants are roughly hewn in the rock. Some of the narrowest ones look like natural fissures. The ground on which we walked or crawled was close, firm, and dry, and neither dusty nor sandy.

The atmosphere was chilly and yet oppressive. We made our way back to the mouth of the well, and were glad to see the sunshine through the green leaves of the mulberry-trees, and to breathe the fragrant air again.*

The range of Olivet is divided by slight depressions into three parts. On the northern hill the little tower which we occupied is the most conspicuous object. The central and highest elevation is crowned by the village El Tûr. On the southern hill there are no buildings, but the olive-trees are more numerous than on any other part of the range. We

---

* I went on another occasion down into this strange place, and found the walls quite wet, and the ground like damp clay.

mounted and rode southward, pausing under the trees on the brow of the hill. Looking toward Jerusalem we saw a large party of Bashi-Bazûks galloping up the hill and entering the city gates. The sun was going down. In a few minutes afterward we heard shouts and songs of triumph, and a troop of armed villagers made their appearance. There were about one hundred, and they marched in irregular order along the winding, rocky path just below us, close to Siloam. My brother said, "That is the little army which was sent forth by Siloam to take part in the fight up here."

As we returned to El Tûr, we were overtaken by a bright-looking peasant boy, singing lustily. He was riding on a little black donkey, which came leaping and dancing along as if he were as merry as his rider. The boy stopped his song and the donkey immediately stood still, as if it were an understood arrangement. We found they were pausing by the side of a well, and I also waited there to let my horse drink from the stone trough close by. An old man had just filled it from a goatskin. The boy told us that there had been a hard fight over the hill that day, and added, "Five souls were killed." However, it turned out that two of these souls were horses. We stopped in the village to speak to the old sheikh of the mosque. He said, "Good-night, and God's blessing be upon you, O my daughter!" I answered, "A hundred good-nights to you, O my father!" The moon was shining brightly when we reached the tower.

On the 18th of July I went into town to stay at the late Rev. J. Nicolayson's for a few days, that I might take leave of all my friends in Jerusalem and make preparations for starting for Hâifa. When all was in readiness, my tent was pitched at the Talibîyeh, where Mr. Finn had encamped again. Mr. Graham was on the eve of departure for England, much to the regret of the Jewish converts and even of the most steadfast Jews of Jerusalem, to whom he had shown unfailing kindness. Mrs. Finn and her coadjutors in the management of the Jewish Plantation, and Mr. Meshullam and his family, united in publicly testifying their sense of his kindness, by inviting the principal Israelitish Christians living in Jerusalem to spend Thursday, July 24th, at Urtâs, to meet him and his friends, among whom we were included.

By this time my readers know the road to the pleasant gardens of Urtâs. The scenery was slightly changed, for the corn was all reaped, and green millet was growing on the plains.

We reached the valley at an early hour. The little stone house could not accommodate one-half of the party, so we were conducted by Mr. Meshullam to a guest-chamber made ready for the occasion. It was the joint work of nature and art. Three sides of it were formed of the steep rugged rocks, like seaside cliffs; a fourth wall had been built up of hewn stone, and was furnished with a wide door, for this place was ordinarily used as a stable for cows, horses, and camels. It is about fifty feet by thirty. Two large fig-trees grew in the middle, and their leafy branches made an appropriate roof. Divans, cushions, and carpets had been spread on the ground, and over these, boughs and leaves of sweet lemon and citron were strewn. On the ledges of the brown and yellow rocks a few wild flowers grew, and one tall wild hollyhock stood proudly in a corner, covered with pink blossoms. Wild honeysuckles crept from the slope above, and festooned the rude walls. A table was arranged in the center, and breakfast was spread.

There were twenty-three Christian Israelites present, besides Mr. Graham and about a dozen of his friends, with Mr. and Mrs. Finn, and the Rev. J. Nicolayson. The latter, after breakfast, stood in the shade of a rock, and addressed the company present with affectionate and earnest gravity. The Rev. Mr. Hefter, an Israelite, then rose and spoke to his brethren, " and when they heard that he spake in the Hebrew tongue, they kept the more silence." Mr.

Nicolayson repeated to us in English some of Mr. Hefter's principal remarks. Then the Third Psalm was sung in Hebrew, in alternate solo and chorus, to a very ancient Oriental melody, which was sweetly echoed by the rocks and hills around—rocks and hills which had very likely been trodden by David himself. The bright wild goldfinches in the trees above us joined loudly in the song.

After this, the company separated into little groups. Some wandered to the vineyards, where the well-trained vines were laden heavily with fruit. Others went to see the spring, and we rested by the stream, enjoying the sound of the rippling water, which flowed along just outside the guest-chamber.

I induced a peasant-boy to let me take his portrait. He sat on a rock opposite to me, half in the sunlight and half in the shade. He wore a red and yellow shawl as a turban, and a coarse white linen shirt, with a red leather girdle. On his finger he displayed a large silver ring with a small blue stone in it, as a defense against evil eyes and necromantic arts.

Some Arab sheikhs from Hebron came to Urtâs to settle some business. They seemed very much surprised to see so many strangers there.

When the shadows began to lengthen, the guests assembled, and the table was spread with fowls, and various Italian and Eastern compositions. The chief dish was a fine lamb, stuffed with rice, raisins, pistachio-nuts, pine seeds, and spice, roasted entire, in a hole dug in the ground for the express purpose. The garden had furnished abundance of vegetables, and ears of maize or Indian corn, which were boiled whole. The great attraction of the dessert was a pyramid of ripe peaches, the "first-fruits" of the orchard.

Several appropriate and interesting speeches were made, and Mr. Graham, after speaking of the beauty of the valley in particular, and the natural fertility of the whole country, said, "Although there are so many waste places and desolate hills, they are not barren, they only want cultivation. Let us be of the same mind with Caleb, the son of Jephunneh, and Joshua, the son of Nun, who brought a good report of the land." Then all present, with one accord, answered, shouting, "It is a goodly land! It is a goodly land!"

Soon afterward we rode homeward, and the moon had risen when we reached the Talibîyeh.

CHAPTER XIII.

FROM JERUSALEM TO HÂIFA.

On Friday, July 25th, all was in readiness for our return to Hâifa by way of Yâfa. Khawadja Ody Azam, of Nablûs, had arranged to accompany us, and we started about one hour before sunset.

We hastened along the valleys and over the hills, now quite familiar to me, and reached Kyriat el Enab—commonly called Abu Ghôsh—at nine o'clock. Close to the village there is a large, smooth, circular platform of earth, slightly raised and surrounded by large stones and shrubs. A gigantic mulberry-tree stands in the center. Under its shade the chief men of the village assemble nearly every day. It is their council-chamber, their exchange, their lounging-place, and their play-ground. They smoke, they sleep, they play at draughts and other games, and transact all kinds of business there. This spot is the favorite camping-ground of travelers, and here we alighted. My brother led me over the stones on to the platform. Two or three lanterns were hanging from the tree-branches, and shone upon a little party of Moslems, who were seated in a circle just beneath. They rose on seeing us, and greeted us gravely. A large reed-mat, rolled up and leaning against the tree-trunk, was immediately put down for us.

Our arrival was made known to Hajj Mustafa Abu Ghôsh, the Governor. He sent us his greetings, with some melons, grapes, coffee, and a couple of wax candles. The latter, for want of candlesticks, we stuck in the ground. A white cloth spread over the mat served as our supper-table. The Moslems watched us in perfect silence while we chatted over our cold roast chickens.

The stars shone splendidly, and a very slight breeze stirred the leaves of the tree above us. In the mean time, our tents had been pitched. The Moslems went up to the village, and we retired to rest.

At five o'clock on the following morning we started again. We lunched in a fruit-garden at Kubâb, where prickly-pears were fine and abundant, and reached Ramleh at eleven o'clock. We rested during the heat of the day at the house which we had visited in August. A new drawing-room, or divan, had been built, and the white walls were bordered with blue arabesque designs, and hung with curious pictures, specimens of caligraphic art. Long histories were written in ornamental Arabic characters, arranged so as to represent animals, real and imaginary. There was a lion very carefully done. At a little distance it looked only like an ordinary quaint pen-and-ink drawing, though in reality every line consisted of part of a word. The Arabs very much admire these tedious, unartistic, and time-taking productions. Almost the only modern Arabic poetry which is published partakes of the same spirit of ingenious trifling; for the chief aim seems to be, to compose verses in which certain names and phrases are introduced intricately, in an acrostic form, with elaborate care, but without any true poetic feeling.

The real poetry of the country is unwritten. It is the every-day language of the people. They are all—more especially the Bedouins and the peasants—unconscious poets.

Their natural artistic feeling, and their sense of beauty and fitness, are shown in their costumes, which are always harmonious in color, and never embroidered except with pure and graceful designs. They show their skill and taste in the simple and appropriate forms of their home-made lamps, jars, dishes, stoves, and other articles of domestic use, which they model in clay and expose to the sun till they are thoroughly baked.

The windows of the new room commanded a fine view, the central object being the tall, Saracenic tower, for which

Ramleh is renowned. It was built early in the 14th century. There are fruit-gardens on each side of it, and the white domes of the houses appear between the green trees. In an open space in front a troop of tired camels were kneeling, and their drivers were sleeping in the shade of the rough stone garden-walls and hedges of cactus. The olive-groves and palm-trees of Ramleh, and the wide undulating plain of Judea could be seen beyond, and the picture was bounded by a range of blue and gray hills, which the sunny haze caused to appear more distant than they were in reality. I sketched this scene, while my good-natured hostess watched my pencil. She said, "Peace be upon your hands, O my daughter!" We mounted again at about five, rode quickly over the sandy plain, and at about an hour after sunset we reached the Yâfa Gardens, where the air was balmy, warm, and fragrant, and reminded us of the atmosphere of a well-kept English conservatory. We went straight to the Latin Convent by the seaside, and found that the suite of rooms belonging to the Patriarch of Jerusalem had been prepared for us, by his orders. A Spanish monk spent the evening with us, on the starlit terrace, looking over the Mediterranean.

The next morning, Sunday, we breakfasted with Dr. Kayat, the English Consul, and then accompanied him to the Mission House, where service was conducted by Mr. Krusé. I spent the remainder of the day there with his family. Mrs. Krusé had established a day-school for Arab girls. She told me that she found it difficult and rather discouraging work, not on account of deficiency of capacity in the children, but because the ideas which they imbibed unconsciously, and therefore perhaps the more deeply, in their homes, constantly counteracted the influence of the lessons which they learned at school. We sat for a long time in the cool of the evening among the flowers on the terrace, and watched the sun as it went down.

The next day my brother was busy at the Consulate. He settled by arbitration a rather serious and long-standing dispute between an English naturalized subject and an English protégé. The Arabs praised his judgment and tact loudly, and said, "He has done well and wisely. He has saved the lamb without leaving the wolf to suffer hunger." The disputants declared themselves content and reconciled.

At four o'clock we started to go by land up the coast to Hâifa. A large number of our friends walked with us as far as the town-gate, and then took leave of us, saying, "Go in peace," and "God direct you." The broad sandy road outside was, for the distance of a quarter of a mile, lined with people, sitting on very low stools, or half-reclining on mats. I do not know any place where there are so many well-dressed turbaned and tarbûshed loungers to be seen smoking, musing, gossiping, and playing with their rosaries, as outside the gate of the town of Yûfa just before sunset. In the same place a market is held in the early morning, and then there is a crowd as large, but much more motley, noisy, and busy.

We soon made our way to the shell-strewn shore. The sea was rolling toward us on our left hand, the white-crested waves washed over the half-buried skeletons of the many ships and boats which had been wrecked there, and threw under our horses' feet masses of sea-weed and large fragments of sponge. Little birds were running swiftly along the sands, and gulls were flapping their broad white wings above our heads. The cliffs on our right were very low, and here and there covered with thistles and shrubs. Sometimes we could see the inland country, the Plain of Sharon, bounded by the far-away hills of Judea. The sea margin is broad, and composed almost entirely of broken shells.

We were approaching a river called "Nahr el Aujêh." We saw some peasants who were ahead of us preparing to cross. They took off their clothes. One of the men made a tight bundle of his scanty clothing, and threw it with a bound safe on to the opposite bank. The others, less ven-

turesome, tied their wardrobes on the backs of t[
mules. Then they plunged into the stream, an[
their reluctant mules carefully, they walked thr
water, which was as high as their waists. The[
safe over and hastily dressing themselves, by the
reached the river-side. We found the stream v[
and even in the best fording-place it was at l[
feet deep. My horse was rather tall for an Ara[
carried me over so well that I did not get very w[
in leaping and scrambling out of the stream on to
we were all well sprinkled. The sunset was clou[
sky was shaded in imperceptible gradations, fro[
red, which merged into orange tints of every sl
palest was lost in a broad belt of delicate green,
blended with the blue above us.

A multitude of crabs were running from their s[
toward the sea, and oyster-catchers were busily s[
evening meal. The cliffs on our right hand were
siderably higher and steeper. They were formed
glomerate of shells and sand. In some places t[
was very narrow and rocky. The twilight deepened
and a thick mist rose from the ground, so that [
only see the upper parts of the figures moving b[
We met a long string of camels, swinging themselv[
along, and a group of Bedouins followed them
looked very strange and shadowy, partly concea[
partly magnified as they were by the mist. Our
moving steadily before us, appeared to be glidi[
without feet. We rode on quickly to El Haram, v[
reached by making our way through a curious win[
sure in the cliffs. It is an ancient water-course, wh[
serves for a road. A low rough wall of rock stand
center, and divides it into two natural causeways.

The groom alighted and led the way, groping a[
winding road with a large lantern in his hand.
as we reached the top of the high cliffs we were ou[
mist, and could see the silhouette of "El Haram [

Aleim "—" *the Sanctuary of Aly, the son of Aleim.*" This place consists of a few well-built stone houses, clustering round an ancient mosque. It is a very favorite retreat of Derwishes and Moslem saints. We were conducted through several court-yards and passages, then up a steep uncovered stone staircase, on to a wide terrace, where a party of Moslems were sitting round a little mountain of rice, and eating it quickly and silently by star and lantern light.

The sheikh of the village welcomed us, and invited us to enter the spacious and lofty guest-chamber, which opened on to the terrace. Little red earthenware lamps of antique form were lighted and placed in niches round the room, and then we could see that the roof was dome-shaped, the ceiling fluted, and the walls plastered and ornamented. But the whole surface was blackened with smoke from the wood-fires, which are always kept burning in the center of the floor in Winter-time.

There was nothing in this room except a few old reed-mats, which were spread all round near the walls. We had some of our tent furniture brought in, and after taking supper, making notes, and chatting with the sheikh over our coffee and narghilés, we walked for a short time on the starlit terrace, where our fellow-travelers and servants, rolled up in their cloaks and wadded quilts, were already in deep sleep. We rested for a few hours in the great guest-chamber, and when the muezzin sang from the little minaret close by, saying, "Awake, sleepers, it is better to pray than to sleep," we answered to the call, and then went on to the terrace.

The day was just beginning to dawn. It was three o'clock, and the loud shrill voice echoing from the court-yard below, reminded us that it was the first hour of "cock-crowing."* The moon had not long risen. She was in her last quarter, but looked very clear and bright.

After breakfasting, we mounted at four o'clock, and continued our journey northward along the coast, but at

* The second "cock-crowing" is at sunrise.

a little distance from the sea, which was quite concealed from us by a ridge of drifted sand-hills. We traversed a wild, undulating, sandy plain, uncultivated, uninhabited, treeless, unwatered, and quite unmarked by roads. There were patches of *poa bulbosa*, marram-grass, sea-holly, and thistles of many kinds, with pink, blue, and yellow blossoms. Our guide had to look very carefully about him so as to keep in the right direction, for there was no sign of a beaten track any where; but occasionally we were reminded that we were not the first travelers on that road, by the skeletons and bleached bones of camels and horses which we saw half-buried in the sand.

The sun, though not yet in sight, brightened all the Eastern sky, and showed the dark outlines of the distant hills. We watched for his coming. Presently half of the red globe appeared, and by degrees we saw the whole, just resting as it were upon the horizon. After a moment's pause he seemed to leap up into the sky. At the same instant, we with one accord pronounced the name of "Edwin Arnold," quoting his sweet song of the "Marriage of the Rhine and the Moselle," and we repeated the well-remembered words with new pleasure as we rode along. The sky was intensely blue, and the moon still shone high above us.

After sunrise, we met many droves of camels laden with melons. It was the time of the melon harvest. Every step we advanced, we found the land firmer and richer. The long fibrous roots of the marram-grass had bound the sands together, and made a bed for shrubs of many kinds, but all were thorny and prickly. A few evergreen oaks and thorny bushes enlivened the desert-like scene. We drew near to a narrow winding river. Its course was marked by tall, flowering reeds, which, in the distance, looked like miniature palm-trees, and it was bordered by thickets of oleanders, lupins, and St. John's-wort, all in full flower. We crossed this stream, which is called the "Nahr el Fulik," and noticed on our left hand extensive ruins of

an ancient city and fortress, which appeared to us to be
Roman. We made our way through a wild shrubbery,
formed chiefly of ilex, arbutus, hawthorns, and rue. Now
and then from the rising ground we had a wide view of
the sea, which was as yet only partially illuminated by the
sun. Lines of light traversed its smooth surface, gleaming
through the openings and breaks in the cliffs.

We had reached the melon-growing district, and a lively
picture of Arab life was before us. Up to the very edge of
the cliffs, all along the coast as far as we could see, there
were beds of various kinds of melons; and groups of dusky
peasants, in white shirts and white turbans, were busily
engaged gathering them, counting them, and building them
up in pyramids. Hundreds of camels were there too, some
walking away well laden, others kneeling down patiently,
while their panniers were being filled with the bulky fruit.
We passed several mud-built villages. White tents were
pitched in the midst of the gardens—I was told that they
were the tents of the tax-gatherers, who had come to claim
the tribute on the melon harvest.

We alighted in the midst of these scenes, near to the
flourishing village of Um Khalîd. It was half-past seven.
We rested for a little while under a large solitary tree.
Looking westward, we could see a broad strip of the now
sunlit Mediterranean beyond the melon-gardens, which are
by no means picturesque. The large rough melon-leaves lie
flat on the level ground, which looks as if it were strewed
with great green and yellow marbles, fit for giants to play
with. There were no hedges or trees to break the monotony of the view, but the busy laborers gave life to it. The
plots of ground are divided by furrowed lines, where thorns
and thistles flourished. I sketched the scene for the sake
of its singularity and simplicity. We wished to buy a few
melons, but the overseer of the laborers told us that we
might take as many as we liked, but he could not sell them
except by hundreds. After a refreshing rest, we remounted
and rode through miles and miles of melon-ground. Wher-

ever the land in this district was left uncultivated or fallow, the wild colocynth had sprung up plentifully. This fruit on an average was three inches in diameter, and firm and hard as a stone, with a smooth, green, white-and-yellow rind, marked like fine marble. We filled our saddle-bags with it, for it is only regarded by the Arabs as a weed. Squills, too, grow profusely, but are plowed up and destroyed.

We went down to the seaside, and found a pleasant strip of shade under the low cliffs, where there were mountains of melons waiting to be carried away in Arab boats, and the camels were coming and going quickly along the winding road from the cliff to the shore.

We watered our horses at a stream called Abu Zabura. It had not sufficient force to reach the sea, but formed a shallow lake not far from it.

We soon afterward caught sight of the picturesque ruins of Cæsarea, and alighted there at half-past ten, and rested in the shade of a large stone gateway. The horses were all unsaddled, and we made arrangements to remain there during the heat of the day. In a short time nearly all of our party were fast asleep. I tried to follow the example, but in vain; so I climbed up the cliff and looked about.

Not a human being was visible. Thorns and thistles grew among fallen columns and huge masses of masonry. The site of an ancient Christian church is marked by four massive buttresses, which stand erect and firm, though the walls they were intended to support fell long ago. The most important relic of ancient Cæsarea is the mole, which stands far out at sea, beaten by the waves, and fringed with surf. The large beveled stones and granite columns have fallen into strange and complicated disorder; but they seem to cling together, and to support each other in their desolation. I came down on to the sands again, and made a careful drawing of this remarkable ruin, stone by stone, while I sat exactly opposite to it, in the shelter of a short tunnel, which pierces the cliff in a sloping direction toward the sea. I supposed it to be part of an ancient sewer. I gathered some tall sea-poppies, with pale-yellow blossoms, which grew close to it, and picked up a few imperfect shells.

After taking some refreshments we mounted at half-past three, and continued our way along the sands. We could see in the broken cliffs the sections of the foundation of the outer walls of Cæsarea; three walls originally surrounded the city, each one at a considerable distance from the other. The beach was strewed with blocks of marble. Mounds of masonry resting on rocks, and festooned with sea-weed, stood there firmly, though continually washed by the waves.

We rode on quickly till we came to "Nhar Zurka"— "the River of Crocodiles." I have been told by many people that small crocodiles are found here even now. Tradition says that on the shores of this river there was once a colony of Egyptians. The colonists procured some young crocodiles from their beloved Nile, and succeeded in thoroughly establishing them here.

There is a fable, often told by the Arabs to this day, which gives another version of the history of the introduction of crocodiles into this river:

"Once upon a time, an old man and his two sons dwelt upon the banks of the river, and fed their flocks in the green pastures of the plain.

"And the old man died, leaving to his two sons his hidden treasure, and his flocks and herds.

"Now the younger son was industrious and prudent, and his wealth increased greatly.

"The elder one was idle and profligate, and he became poor. In his poverty he looked with jealous anger on the rich flocks and herds of his brother, and considered in his heart how he might destroy them. He journeyed to Egypt, and thence brought young crocodiles and placed them in the river. His hope was, that his brother's flocks would be devoured on going to drink, or while feeding on the banks.

"Now, a short time afterward, the young man went down to the river to wash himself, without taking thought of the danger which he in his wickedness had spread there.

"The crocodiles swiftly approached him, and seized upon him and destroyed him.

"Such was the will of God, and thus the wicked fall into the nets which they spread for their neighbors."

On the south side of the river stands an isolated stone building, now in ruins. We supposed it to have been an outpost of Cæsarea, and perhaps it marks the site of the city called by ancient geographers, "The City of Crocodiles."

We found the river rather difficult to ford, for it was deep, broad, and rapid, and there was no one near to guide us to the easiest fording-place. A few hours sometimes makes a vast difference in the character of the mouth of a river; the wind may entirely carry away the sand-bar, or change its position. Our kawass made many experiments before he found a safe path for us, which we traversed carefully, one after the other in single file, and landed on the opposite side very wet and chilly.

We soon came to a picturesque but dangerous and rocky bay, where small coasting-boats are often wrecked. Here Colonel the Hon. F. Walpole had a short time previously attacked a party of Arabs who were remorselessly plundering some half-drowned sailors, and pillaging their wrecked vessel. Some of the wreckers were taken to Yâfa as prisoners by the Colonel. We saw about fifty rice-baskets on the beach, relics of the freight of the vessel which he had protected.

In the year 1858 a little Arab craft—laden with rice and oranges, and carrying a Jewish family, consisting of a father and mother, and several children—was wrecked here in a fearful storm. The boat struck, and was split in half. One or two of the boatmen were saved; the passengers were all drowned or dashed to death on the rocks, with the exception of a boy about a year old, who was thrown by a high wave safely on to the shore, where a number of wreckers were assembled to watch the fate of the vessel. They took up the young child wonderingly. A small party of Bedouins, who were passing by at the time, offered to take charge of him, and bring him up as one of their own children, saying, "Do no harm to him, for it is the will of God that he should live." So the wreckers gave him up to them, and the little Hebrew boy was carried away I know not where. Some peasants who were on their way to Hâifa witnessed this singular transaction, and through them I heard of it. They said that the boy was fair, strong, and healthy, and they would themselves have taken him if the Bedouins had not done so. This boy has perhaps been nursed by a Bedouin mother, and will learn to live a wandering life in the land of his forefathers, in utter ignorance of his real origin. It would be very interesting, if it were possible to watch his career, to see how far he will retain his national characteristics, physical and moral, and what influence he will have on the little tribe with which he will no doubt at an early age incorporate himself by marriage. I should like to meet him when he has arrived at manhood, if I could be convinced of his identity.

Bedouins frequently name their children after some circumstance connected with their nativity, or some cotemporary event; but there is every reason to expect that this little Hebrew boy, like Moses, is called by a name having some allusion to his strange history. For instance, "Ebn el Bahr"—*Son of the Sea*, or "Minbahr"—*From the Sea*, would be natural Bedouin names for him. It would be difficult but not impossible, I think, to trace him out now. My first impulse, on hearing of the circumstance, was to try to recover the boy, and restore him to the Hebrew community, but it was not in my power to do so.

It was said that his parents were Algerine Jews, who were about to settle in Palestine. The wrecked vessel had conveyed them from Egypt to their untimely graves on the shores of the land which they so longed to see, but which their youngest child alone was permitted to reach in safety. He probably was the only one of the family who had not learned to love it, and to believe it to be the land which was promised to his forefather Abraham, and to his seed forever.

Perhaps the descendants of this little Hebrew boy will some day be a subject of discussion, and a puzzling ethnological enigma for scientific travelers.

Beyond the bay the sands were broad and smooth. I could see in the distance, straight before us, the well-remembered rocky islands, and the village of Tantûra, where, in September, we landed, "because the winds were contrary." When we had nearly reached this place we turned away from the seashore, and rode inland toward a little Moslem village, called Kefr Lamm. We approached it through a district in which fine building-stone abounds. We rode through ancient quarries, and over large, smooth slabs of rock, polished like marble. We looked into the arched recesses, and peered into large, artificial, gloomy caverns, where, perhaps, the stone-cutters of old used to eat and sleep. These quarries have evidently not been worked for centuries—not, perhaps, since Athlite and Dora were built. Large trees and shrubs had sprung up out of the earth which had fallen from above, or had been drifted by wind and rain into sheltered places in the bottom of the quarries.

The sheikh, and all the chief men of Kefr Lamm, came out to meet us, for we were expected, and were well known there. We rode through flourishing fields of Indian corn, millet, sesame, and tobacco, and alighted on the outskirts of the village, which consists of low houses, built of mud and stone. I found my tent, which had preceded me, already pitched amid little mountains of wheat and barley, near to an extensive thrashing-floor, where oxen were busy treading out the corn. Carpets and cushions were soon spread for us on rising ground, in the open air, and coffee and pipes were brought. The sheikh, and the priest, and the old men of the village sat opposite to us in a half-circle, while the young men were standing round, or resting on the heaps of wheat near.

We were not quite a mile from the shore, and were facing the sea and the setting sun. A long line of coast was in sight. The rocky islands and ruins of Tantûra—the ancient Dora—could be plainly seen, a little way to the south, and the tall tower of Athlite, or Castelum Pelegrinum, appeared far away in the north.

At the moment when the sun dropped down into the sea, the village priest rose, and stood in the middle of a large, smooth, and well-swept thrashing-floor, which was close by. He looked earnestly and solemnly toward the south, and sang, in a loud and sonorous voice, the call to evening prayer. There was no minaret or mosque in the village. The sheikh, and the elders who had gathered round us, immediately rose and assembled on the thrashing-floor, in a double row behind the priest, who thus looked truly like the leader of the little band. They echoed his words, and followed all his movements with precision, kneeling and bowing their faces to the ground, and uplifting their hands and rising to their feet with one accord. They were joined by the laborers from the other thrashing-floors and by our Moslem servants, but the younger men who had been talking with us hesitated at first to attend to the call to prayer. They looked at each other as if undecided what to do, and then at us, as if they were ashamed. We tried, by keeping perfectly still and silent, to make them understand that we did not expect or wish them to neglect their devotions on our account. Suddenly they rose altogether and ranged themselves in a row on the border of the thrashing-floor, and their strong voices blended with the voices of their fathers as they cried, "There is no God but God, and Mohammed is his Prophet."

No women came forward to pray, but I saw some standing afar off watching the assembly. The prayers occupied rather more than a quarter of an hour. I had never seen a service conducted with more solemnity, even within the sacred inclosure of the Sanctuary at Jerusalem.

Immediately afterward, supper was brought for us, and at the same time a wooden bowl—rather shallow, but about a yard in diameter, and filled with steaming rice boiled in butter—was placed on the ground at a little distance from us. Metal dishes containing meat, eggs, vegetables, and cream, were added to the feast, round which the sheikh, the priest, and the elders of the village assembled. They ate quickly and silently, dipping pieces of their thin leathery loaves into the dishes of fried eggs or into the cream— tearing the tender morsels of meat to pieces with their fingers—dipping their hands together into the mound of rice and skillfully and neatly taking it up in pellets. When they were satisfied, they retired one after the other to wash their hands and to light their pipes. Their places were quickly taken by the younger men and boys in turn, and, when they had all finished, the servants gathered round, eating from the same dishes, the simplest of which had been replenished during the repast. Several sets of Arabs silently swallowed their supper while we leisurely used our knives and forks. The fragments that remained after the feast were not carried away till all the men and boys of the village had eaten there, but the women ate elsewhere in private.

We had some fine green figs, the first I had tasted that year. We found all the fruits and vegetables in the plain of Dor, in a much more advanced state than those in the hill-country of Judea. After sitting in the open air till about nine I retired to my tent. My fellow-travelers, including my brother, wrapped themselves in cloaks, and slept on the hillocks of wheat. I rose at five, and from the door of my tent I watched the rising of the sun above the range of Carmel.

After taking some excellent milk and coffee, we started and rode through the well-cultivated fields, the fruit and vegetable gardens, and the neglected quarries north of Kefr

Lamm. We were soon by the seaside and in the road which we had traversed in September. We again looked with admiration on the ruins of Athlite, and passed through the ancient defile into the plain, across which the road formerly passed; many traces of it may still be seen. This plain was much more green and beautiful than when we had seen it before, and the fountain called "Ain Dustrei" was bordered with oleanders covered with pink blossoms. At about eight we paused by a spring, down on the sands, half-way between Athlite and the headland of Carmel. There is a square stone building over the spring with a deep trough or reservoir all round it. Here we alighted and breakfasted on fish and peasant bread, and then rode on quickly to Hâifa, which we reached at ten o'clock, July 30th, and the hearty welcome with which we were greeted gave us great pleasure.

Our friend Mohammed Bek was one of our first visitors, and he was soon followed by Saleh Bek Abdul Hady, the ex-governor, who told me that his wives whom I had visited at Arrabeh were established in Hâifa, and were longing to see me. There were some additions to the European colony, and when Signor Vegetti, the Dutch Vice-Consul, called, he informed us that he had obtained a piano. It was the first which had ever been introduced into Hâifa, and there was no one in the town, excepting myself, who knew how to touch it.

He invited all the Europeans to a soirée a few days after our arrival, that the new instrument might be inaugurated. I had previously tried it and consented to preside on the occasion, as there was no one else to do so.

There was quite a sensation in Hâifa that night, and the open space in front of the house was crowded with listeners, among whom were the new governor, Zachariah Agha, a Turk, Mohammed Bek, and all the chief Moslems. They called the next day on Signor Vegetti, begging him to invite me to meet them at his house, that they might see and hear me play. Then they came to my brother and requested him to induce me to go; so an evening was fixed upon, and we went. We found the Governor and about twenty Moslem gentlemen, in their richest embroidered costumes, assembled in the drawing-room, at the Dutch Vice-Consulate, where we were received by Signor Vegetti and his aged father and mother. The antechamber was crowded with servants and lantern-bearers.

The piano had been tried in turn by nearly all the guests, and they said, "We can not make it speak the same language which you cause it to speak, O lady!" I handed to them some pieces of music, saying, "Could you do so with the help of these?" It was very amusing to hear their exclamations, and to observe the surprise with which they watched my fingers, especially when they found that I looked all the while at the book before me. They are accustomed only to see small and portable musical instruments, and they wondered at my command over one so large. They said, "The laborers at harvest-time do not work so hard or move their hands so quickly." They seemed to be more struck with the rapidity with which the keys were touched than with the sounds which were produced, till I played their national anthem, "Abdul Medjid." Then they all seemed roused, and a clear-voiced singer, the Sims Reeves of Hâifa, came forward immediately and sang. The rest of the company joined in chorus. One of the Beks seemed to appreciate music so much that I told him that if he would buy a piano for his wife I would teach her the use of it. He said, "O my sister, our women are not capable of learning—their heads are made of wood—it would be as easy to teach donkeys as to teach them."

By degrees nearly every one in the town became familiar with the sounds of the piano, and it gave rise to many very pleasant soirées. This was the dawn of a new era in the history of the little European colony at Hâifa, and music and singing were cultivated with energy.

I was very busy in the mean time putting our house in order, after my long absence from it. Katrîne, my old servant, had returned to Bethlehem; so I trained a young girl of Haifa to take her place.

I had not time to visit the harem of Saleh Bek till August 11th, which was the first day of the Feast of Bairam, when all Moslems are to be seen in holiday costume. I went to the house attended by a kawass, who waited for me in the inner court while I was led up a crooked, uncovered, stone stairway to a small square court, and thence into a large and lofty but rather gloomy room. In a moment I was surrounded by my well-remembered friends of Arrabeh. The children came forward shyly, and Helweh led me to a cushioned seat on the floor, saying, "We have been longing to see you, O light of our eyes; let us see you often. You are not like us; you may come to us whenever your heart tells you to come, but we may not go to you. When we first came here, and found ourselves in a strange place, and heard that you were not yet arrived, our hearts sank within us."

The house which they occupied was in the castle square, and was not so comfortable or so well built as the one in which I had seen them at Arrabeh. Narrow mattresses were ranged all round the chief room of the harem where I was received, and the floor was covered with matting. The ceiling was vaulted, and all the windows which looked out on to public places were blocked up, so that the light only came from the door and window which opened to the half-covered private court. Mattresses, pillows, and wadded quilts were piled up in an arched recess, and a thin muslin curtain was drawn in front of it. Two red boxes and a red cradle stood at one end of the room, and a charcoal brazier with all the requisites for making coffee and preparing narghilés were close to the door. A large embroidered camel's-hair cloak, and a sword, gun, and spear, were hanging against the white cemented walls. Coffee flavored with ambergris, and delicate sherbet made of almonds and rose-leaves, were handed to me. The servants who were present were the same whom I had seen at Arrabeh.

Helweh, the youngest and prettiest of the three wives, looked much more womanly and sedate, though not less affectionate, than formerly. She wore very full, deep, rose-colored silk trowsers, and a tight jacket of violet and white striped Damascus satin, sprinkled with small bunches of flowers, and round her waist was a fine Cashmere shawl. The eldest wife was dressed in flowered silk, and her three young daughters—of whom the eldest, named Asmé, had grown very beautiful—wore violet-colored silk jackets, embroidered with silver-braid, and quite closed in front. Their trowsers were of light muslin, and made very full and long. They each wore little red-cloth Constantinople tarbûshes, put on coquettishly a little on one side. The other wife was busy with an infant boy of whom she seemed to be very proud.

While I was answering their many questions about my long journey, and receiving their commiserations because neither I nor my brother were yet married, the lord of the harem sent word that he would, with my permission, enter in to greet me. So he came. When he appeared the wives and the women-servants immediately rose and stood deferentially till he was seated; then, as they resumed their seats, they saluted him by touching their foreheads gracefully with their hands. In the mean time the children came forward and kissed his hands. He seemed to be very kind and gentle to all his family. He said to me, "I rejoice to see you here, O lady; I hope that you will often come, for where you are there is clearness and brightness."

His children unconsciously proved to me that they were accustomed to be caressed by him, for they clustered round him lovingly, and little Saîd was especially demonstrative. He said, coaxingly, "O my father, may I go to see the house of the English lady? it is her wish that I should go." Asmé, his eldest daughter, scarcely spoke a word, and sat sedately still and impassive; and the face which a few minutes before had seemed to be so beautiful with vivacity and cheerfulness looked quite unattractive.

It seems to me to be a part of Oriental etiquette for the elder children to preserve a kind of grave decorum in the presence of a father; the younger children alone are free to show their natural feelings, and demonstrative affection is regarded as childish and undignified.

The wives did not look quite at their ease, perhaps because it was the first time that they had ever seen their husband in the presence of a stranger, but they trimmed his pipe and waited on him with assiduity. The servants and slaves were standing near to the door, whispering together, and appeared very much amused.

Saleh Bek informed me that he was about to send two of his sons, aged fifteen and sixteen, to the Latin college at Antûra, a French establishment, not far from Beirût. He said that if there had been an English college in the country, where as good an education could have been obtained, he should have chosen it in preference. While we were talking an Arab lady was announced, so Saleh Bek immediately rose, and, hastily taking leave of me, retreated. The lady kept her face closely vailed as she passed him in the court. When she came into the room the eldest wife rose, and, kindly welcoming her, assisted her to take off her white sheet and colored-muslin vail, which she handed to a slave to fold up. I found that the newly-arrived guest was Um Selim, who had left Yâfa to reside in Hâifa near to us. She had come to the harem to meet me there. After the usual greetings had been exchanged, an animated conversation was carried on by two of the wives and Um Selim. They spoke so rapidly and vehemently that I could scarcely understand a word. In the mean time Helweh, who was by my side, explained to me in simple words, gently spoken, the subjects of the conversation and the causes of the occasional bursts of laughter.

After inviting the children to come and see me on a certain day, I took leave and went with Um Selim down into the court, where the kawass awaited me. We passed the open door of the divan or reception-room for men. It was filled with visitors. The son of Yassîn Agha, on seeing me go by, came out and asked to be allowed to lead me to his house that I might visit his mother. I did so, and afterward went to three other harems.

On the second day of the feast I visited some of the poorer Moslem families in the back streets of the town. Following the kawass, I made my way with Um Selim through dirty narrow lanes, with gutters running down the middle of them.

We paused at the house of a Moslem who was in my brother's employ, and who had very recently married a poor gardener's daughter. We went through an arched doorway into a square ill-paved court-yard, where a tent or booth of palm-branches and evergreen shrubs had been made. An old mat was spread within it, and we were invited to sit down there. The young wife was rather shy and not at all prepossessing in appearance. Her wide mouth and large glistening teeth were made to appear still more prominent by the row of blue spots round the edge of her thick lips. Her eyes were dark with kohl, and her chest painted and exposed. She seemed to be kept completely in awe by an elderly woman—I think it was her mother-in-law—who played the part of hostess and acted as guardian to the young wife, who did not appear to be very comfortable nor accustomed to her new life. She had never seen her husband till her marriage-day, not quite a month before. The "honeymoon" is not understood among the Moslems; they have, I believe, no word or idea answering to it.

After we had taken a tiny cup of strong coffee without sugar, the elder woman took us to see the house, which consisted of one room only, which opened into the court. It was large, lofty, and windowless, and looked like a barn, and the door was large enough to admit a laden camel. This room served as parlor, kitchen, and bedroom, except in bright weather, when the tent of tree-branches was used. I was very much surprised to see an old Italian print, representing Moses holding the tables of the Law, nailed against the smoke-blackened wall, and ostrich eggs and ornamented lamps suspended from the ceiling. I asked the woman what the eggs were for. She said, "They will keep darkness and sorrow far from us;" but she did not know whence the picture came, or what it was for, and seemed surprised when I told her that it represented "Neby Mûssa," the prophet Moses.

A few days afterward, when Saleh Bek Abdul Hady called, he saw a set of chessmen on our table. He eagerly inquired if we could play, adding, "I have not had a game at chess since the time of Ibrahîm Pasha. I used to play with his officers at 'Akka." When he found that I understood the game he exclaimed, "El-hâmdou lillah! [*praised be God!*] I will come every day to play with you!" I said, "Excuse me, that would be too often; I have not time to play every day." However, we spent an afternoon at chess about once a fortnight, and I found that I had a skillful and careful antagonist. He was the only Arab in Hâifa who could play chess.

His children, especially the boys, frequently came to our house, and were soon quite at home there. They and their young cousins from Arrabeh, who sometimes came on a visit to Hâifa, were very intelligent and inquiring, and picked up, almost unconsciously, a great deal of information from our illustrated books.

The three little girls came sometimes, but were always accompanied by an old female servant—or duenna—to prevent them from being seen by strangers. These visits were only made when it was known that my brother was out of town. The women came once to see me, by special permission, but the doors of the Consulate were guarded by their own servants all the while they were there. I went to see them as often as I could, and was always heartily welcomed. Except on fête-days, they were generally dressed in jackets and trowsers made of Manchester prints or muslins.

I found that the senior wife, who had evidently once been very handsome, formerly belonged to a wealthy Turk, and had been presented to Saleh Bek, in her youth, as a reward for some special service. She had been brought up in great privacy, in a harem in Constantinople, and was thence conveyed to her new home at Arrabeh, where she was at first very unhappy, for she was a complete stranger there, and spoke only Turkish. Fortunately for her, Saleh Bek understood it, and she, by degrees, acquired the Arabic language. Though she had come from a great city, she had seen so little of it, that she knew no more of the world and its history than her new companions in Arrabeh, and hardly so much perhaps as the wives, concubines, and servants which Saleh Bek afterward took from the little villages in the neighborhood. The seclusion in which Moslem girls are kept is more or less strict, in accordance with their rank or position—the poor having unavoidably more liberty than the wealthy.

Helweh, who came from the little village of Kefr Kâra, seemed to possess more natural quickness of comprehension than any of the other women.

They had long before heard Christians spoken of, but in terms so vague that they hardly regarded them as fellow-creatures; but now that they lived in the little sea-coast town of Hâifa, where there was a mixed population, including Moslems, Jews, and Christians of distinctly various sects, and people of many nations, they were by degrees receiving new impressions, and ideas which probably would not have entered their minds if they had continued to live in the interior, and in such an exclusively Moslem district as the Jebel Nablûs.

They had already become acquainted with a few of their neighbors, and were constantly hearing of something which was to them new and strange. Whenever I visited them, I found that they had some wonder to relate to me, or some story to tell, which had reached them either through female servants, or Christian or Jewish guests, or the professional singing women, or, more often still, through the gossiping attendants at the Turkish baths; stories which were almost always entirely misunderstood, and which gave rise to false yet strong impressions. It was an interesting study for me to watch the constructions which they put on the circumstances, manners, customs, and forms of worship, of which they heard, but which they could not comprehend or realize. I found it almost as difficult to help them to understand the ways that were not as their ways, and the thoughts that were not as their thoughts, as it would be to describe the nature and effect of light and color to a man blind from his birth.

Helweh, especially, used to ask me suggestive questions about religion. She often said, "Why are not all people of one religion? Why are they not all Moslems? it would be much better."

She always seemed to forget that I was not a Moslem. She sometimes appealed to me, with touching confidence, asking me to tell her what it was right to do under particular circumstances. Instead of deciding for her, I used to try to awaken in her mind some principle by which she might judge rightly for herself.

I often found appropriate and ready answers, by adopting the very words of Christ, conveying the simplest and most comprehensive of those lessons of love which were taught long ago in this land, and listened to by people as uninstructed and eager as Helweh herself, and by Scribes and Pharisees who were put to silence by words addressed not to any particular sect, but to all the world.

These women who thus questioned me made me think more earnestly and carefully than I had ever thought before, and they unconsciously helped me to understand the natural progress and growth of ideas. I could, by identifying myself with them, partially imagine the absence of all those thoughts, feelings, and conceptions which had grown with my growth and strengthened with my strength, till they seemed almost to be a part of my mind.

But this interesting harem was not my only school. I mingled at the same time with European and native Christians, and especially with the Sekhali family, and with devout Jews, who kindly helped me to understand all the laws, and the fasts, and the feasts which they observed. The Oriental Christians are unhappily very bitter in their hatred of the Jews. They generally treat them with great contempt, and make a merit of avoiding association with them; but they agree with the Moslems in admitting that the Jews throughout the East are, as a body, remarkable for the purity of their lives, the simplicity of their manners, and the strictness with which they observe their religious services. They are, however, notorious for the quarrels which take place among themselves, and for the noisy disputes which sometimes arise between the representatives of the different congregations or communities. The Jewesses, especially of the Ashekenazi communities, are renowned for their domestic virtue and industry.

On October 5th my brother started for Beirût on business. I remained at Hâifa, and then more than ever I found how very kind and thoughtful my neighbors of all classes were; especially I thank the French Consul, M. Aumann, and his family, for the friendly and active sympathy which made me feel that I was not alone, although there was no one in the town who could speak an English word to me.

Nearly all the Moslem ladies of Hâifa took the opportunity for visiting me then, and the Governor and the members of the town council called several times to see if they could serve me in any way.

On the 10th of October, early in the morning, a boat was lost in a whirlpool within sight of Hâifa. The day was very sultry, and in the evening the sea was perfectly calm, and the air heavy. After spending a few hours with the French Consul and his family, in their moonlit and marble-paved court, I went home, and notwithstanding the almost suffocating heat, I slept soundly, till I was roused by a deep murmuring sound, which was like subterranean thunder, and I felt my bed trembling beneath me. At first I thought a wind storm had risen, but that was impossible, for the muslin musketo curtains were not more agitated than my brass bedstead, which rocked from east to west. I was very soon satisfied that I was for the first time in my life experiencing a shock of earthquake. I rose immediately. The room was bright with moonlight, which streamed through the rattling Venetian shutters. I opened the window. The moon was nearly full; and, just above the range of Carmel, it was as red as the sun appears to be when seen through an English fog. The ground trembled violently three distinct times, the second shock being the strongest. There were heavy storm-clouds resting over Hâifa, their western edges were tinged with the lurid light of the red moon. My maid-servant was sleeping soundly. I walked out into the open court of the house. The two kawasses were rolled up in their wadded quilts on their mattresses in the arched corridor, and seemed undisturbed. A storm of thunder and lightning followed, and I walked through the house from room to room, watching the progress of the storm and the breaking up of the clouds.

The next morning, early, the Governor, several of the vice-consuls, and many Arab friends, called to hear if I had been disturbed and alarmed by the earthquake. Those who lived near the mosque told me that they had taken the precaution of moving out of their houses in the night, for the minaret rocked so violently, that every one who watched it expected that it would fall. Happily no accident of consequence occurred—a few old walls only were cracked and shaken. Mons. A. told me that during the shock he had observed that the sea was violently agitated, and covered with foam, though there was no wind.

The Arabs were all in great consternation, for they regarded this convulsion of nature as an ill omen. For several subsequent days nothing else was talked of. The shocks had been strongly felt at 'Akka, Sûr, and Saida, and slightly in the interior.

All my visitors had some story to tell me about former earthquakes, and especially about the terrible one which occurred in 1837, when Safed and Tiberias were destroyed, and when Hâifa was for three days almost deserted, and people lived outside in the open air, not venturing to enter their houses, the shocks being so frequent. The heavens, they said, were dark at midday, and the sea had a strange red tinge. Some people went so far as to declare that "its waters were turned into blood," and all agreed that it lost its saline flavor, and had rather a sweet taste.

On the 22d of October there were steady showers of rain during the day, and in the evening I watched one of the grandest thunder-storms I had ever seen; it was followed by a wild storm of wind and rain, which lasted all night. Soon after sunrise the wind ceased, and there was a great calm; but the streets of Hâifa were like canals, and some of the old walls, which had been damaged by the earthquake, were quite broken down. In the gardens many of the finest trees had been uprooted or stripped of their branches: the pliant palm-trees seem best calculated to resist the fury of these equinoctial gales.

I spent the afternoon of the 23d of October with the young widow of Îbrahîm Sekhali. She was still mourning bitterly over her loss. I tried to excite her interest, and succeeded in gaining her attention by telling her about the home of my childhood and my school-days. She seemed for a while to forget her own troubles, in wondering how I could leave my parents and my country, and having left them, how I could consent to stay alone in a town where there were none of my "*own people.*"

We were thus talking, when her black slave, who was sitting on a mat at needle-work in the sunshine close to the open door, suddenly rose, and, kissing my hands, said, "There is joy for you! there is joy!—your brother, the Consul, has even now arrived. I hear the sounds of many voices in your court." She was right; for at the same moment we saw the flag hoisted, and as I hastened away she said, "This is your reward; God has brought happiness to you, even as you have to-day spoken pleasant words to the mother of fatherless children."

In another minute I was with my brother. He was accompanied by a Turkish gentleman, who had traveled with him from Beirût, and who had just received the appointment of Governor of Hâifa. His son, a nice boy of about ten years of age, was with him. They dined with us, and the little Turk found it rather difficult to manage a knife and fork. The father asked me if I would undertake to civilize him. They were complete strangers in the town, so they remained at our house for two or three days.

On the 25th, Zachariah Agha, the ex-Governor, called to take leave of me, and then the new Governor established himself at the castle. He told me he did not think that he should send for his wives, as he could not tell how long he should be allowed to remain in office at Hâifa.

Some wealthy Moslems have a home, and a wife or two, in each of the villages or towns where their public or private business obliges them to reside for any length of time during the year.

A few days after my brother's return I observed that nearly all the shops of Hâifa were closed, and the streets and market-places were almost deserted. On inquiry I learned that "the day of ill luck" had arrived, a day on which Moslems will not, on any account, make bargains or transact business. This dreaded day is the first Wednesday in the month of Safar, the second month of the Mohammedan year. (In 1856, the year of which I am writing, it fell on October 29th.) The Moslems will not, if they can possibly avoid it, even speak or think on any subject of importance, and they generally remain in-doors on this ill-omened day.

Mohammed Bek came to the Consulate at midday, asking me to be his guardian, and to allow him to remain in my presence till sunset, pretending that he thought that no evil spirits could approach him there.

I was told by a "true believer" that bad angels have, on that particular day, full power to carry out all the mischief which they may have plotted during the year. In Constantinople all the public offices are closed, in consequence of the prevalence of this impression!

On Thursday, the 4th of December, the Feast of "Sainte Barbe" was celebrated by all the Christians of the Latin Church at Hâifa. I went early in the morning to see Madame Aumann. I found her planting grains of wheat, barley, and millet, and seeds of lentils and grass, in plates and ornamental saucers and large shells. She merely covered the grain or seeds with water, and then ranged the dishes in the sun. "This," she said, "is always done on the fête-day of Ste. Barbe, and by Christmas-day the grass and the grain will have grown." But she did not know what it was intended to signify.

She invited us to meet all the Europeans at the French Consulate that night, and we went. We found every one full of fun and merriment, and one of the guests, a Mons. Jullien, who had lately arrived from Algiers, and had served in the army there, appeared with mock solemnity, in a scarlet robe and white cardinal cape, in the character of the priest of Ste. Barbe. To my surprise, the most devout Catholics present did not seem to be shocked. I asked one lady, whom I knew to be very earnest in the performance of what she believed to be her religious duties, if it gave her pain to see such mockery, but she simply said, "It is custom; there is no harm in it."

When we were all assembled, we were led into a room, in the center of which was a low stool, on which was a very large dish made of wood. It was filled with wheat, boiled in honey or sugar, and mixed with pomegranate seeds. Over the surface sweetmeats and bleached nuts were sprinkled, and round the edge of the dish twelve tapers were burning, and a flag was stuck in the middle.

Before we partook of these sweets, the *soi-disant* priest chanted a litany in an unknown tongue, which neither he nor any one present understood. After this mummery was over, Madame Aumann fetched a smooth, silver, blunt-pointed pin, about three inches long and the eighth of an inch thick, with an ornamental head. She then burned some sweet gum and frankincense in the flame of a little antique lamp, and held the pin in the flame till it had become quite black; then, after waiting till the pin had cooled, she inserted it dextrously between her half-closed eyelids, and rubbed it backward and forward, as if really "*rending her eyes*," as Jeremiah expresses it,* till she had produced the effect so much admired by Orientals. She handed the little instrument round, and nearly every one of her guests followed her example. It was astonishing how the appearance and expression of all the faces, especially of the fairest ones, were altered immediately. I scarcely recognized my brother, who certainly would not have submitted to this adornment if he had not believed that he could wash it off immediately; but to his dismay it was many days before the black tinge disappeared, and then only after persevering and frequent rubbing. Hélâny, one of the female servants, took the lamp and the frankincense which Madame A. had used, and held a white earthenware plate over the flame. She thus collected a quantity of soot. The soot thus prepared is mixed with antimony, and kept in little ornamental bottles, ready to be used in the manner described on page 113.

The Europeans, especially the semi-Europeans, strictly avoid those customs which they regard as peculiar to the Arabs, but at the feast of Ste. Barbe they seem to tolerate that which at other times they most condemn.

No one could give me the slightest reason for this fantasia, or tell me any thing of its history or origin, or what Ste. Barbe had to do with the germination of grain, the dish of sweets, and the twelve candles, which I suppose

* Jeremiah iv, 30.

represented the twelve apostles. Even the village curé, of whom I made inquiries the next day, could not give me any information. He said, "It is a custom peculiar to the Eastern Christians." The Greeks kept it much in the same style on the 16th of December.

On referring to Butler's "Lives of the Saints," I find it is recorded, under the head of December 4th, that Saint Barbara was a holy virgin and martyr, "who is honored with particular devotion in the Latin, Greek, Muscovite, and Syriac calendars; but her history is obscured by a variety of false acts. Some say that she was a scholar of Origen, and suffered martyrdom at Nicomedia; but others say that she suffered at Heliopolis, in Egypt, about the year 306—there stood an old monastery near Edessa which bore her name."

I was surprised to see with what fidelity and enthusiasm the people kept this festival, and yet showed no curiosity to learn its origin or history. In fact, they keep all kinds of fasts and feasts, and perform all sorts of ceremonies, without pausing to consider what they mean. It is enough for them to know that they are "ancient customs"—and customs in the East are like the laws of the Medes and Persians. I do not pretend that in England we are altogether exempt from this kind of folly, but it is much more apparent among the Greeks and Latins of the East.

On Saturday, the 6th of December, I was playing at chess with Saleh Bek Abdul Hady, when one of his servants entered the drawing-room, and approaching his master, said, "A son is born to you, my lord." Mohammed Bek and Saleh Sekhali, who happened to be present, united with me in congratulating the father, but he received the tidings very quietly, and to my surprise persisted in finishing the game, which he did as coolly as he had commenced it. He afterward lingered to read some ancient Arabic poetry aloud to my brother, and did not leave us till long after sunset.

On Monday, the 8th of December, I visited his harem.

In the chief room I found a large number of people assembled, and in one corner there was a bed, consisting of two mattresses, on the floor, and Helweh, my favorite, was half reclining on it. When I approached her she threw herself on my neck and burst into tears, but quickly recovered herself, and said, "Welcome, O light of my eyes." I said softly, "You are very happy, Helweh, in being the mother of a son. Where is the boy?" She answered sadly, "I have no son. My child is a female child, and is made no account of."

I sat on the edge of her bed, and she lifted up the heavy coverings by her side, and handed to me a little figure swaddled in white and purple linen, and crimson silk, with its head bandaged and its eyelids blackened with kohl. I said, "What name shall you give your little girl?" She answered, "The Bek will name her—I have no power." I said, "Have you any choice?" She replied, "I should like it to be called Miriam, because that is your name, and it is a good name." I said, "That would please me greatly, and your little child would remind you always of me. I will ask the Bek if he will allow it." She answered immediately, "Then the child is named already—its name is Miriam."

A number of women were sitting round the room leaning against the walls. After coffee had been brought for me, and a narghilé had been prepared, the nurse, a strange-looking woman, with long ragged hair dyed with henna, till it had become a tawny red, began in a low monotonous key to sing a welcome to the first-born child of Helweh, and all the women clapped their hands beating the time.

I found that there had been a very serious quarrel in the harem, and to prevent mischief Saleh Bek had been obliged to hire a separate house for one of his wives, and she had gone there with her children and servants.

Soon after I returned home I saw Saleh Bek, and I asked him if he had seen his new-born child. He said, "No, custom forbids me to see it or its mother before seven days have passed." He added, "I have heard your wish that the child should be called 'Miriam;' it is sufficient, and I am reconciled to having a daughter instead of a son, because she may thus take your name. If after three years you will undertake the charge of her and teach her even as you have been taught, I shall think myself happy."

He afterward explained to me that the messenger who had brought the false tidings to him of the birth of *a son* knew perfectly well that it was *a daughter* which had been born to him; "but," he added, "in this land people are so foolish that my servant was ashamed and afraid to announce to me, in public, the birth of a female child, for it is thought no honor to be the 'father of girls.'"*

He assured me that he did not himself entertain this prejudice, though he certainly showed more pleasure and pride in his sons than in his daughters. This was natural, for he had the opportunity of educating the former and training them according to the best of his judgment, while the latter were a subject of great perplexity to him. He had become convinced that the civilization of a country depends very much on the character and position of its women, and he had liberal and enlightened notions about the advantageous influences of female education and freedom, but he did not know how to take any steps in the way of reform. He wisely observed that any sudden change would be dangerous, and lead to more harm than good. This was a subject on which I also had thought deeply and seriously. I found it rather difficult to come to any practical conclusions.

Reform in any system or institution, to be safe and sure, and on a firm foundation, must arise naturally and from

---

* Not only among the Moslems does this prejudice exist, but among the native Christian population also; and I am assured that in Southern Italy the same feeling prevails. Miss Cobbe, in an article on "Women in Italy, 1862," says: "An English lady, long resident in Naples, and married to a Neapolitan, informed me that till quite of late years it was customary among the poorer classes to hang a small black flag out of the window of the apartment wherein a girl was born, to save the painful necessity of informing inquirers of the unfortunate sex of the infant."

within. Women like my friend Helweb might do much toward effecting a change for the better in the mode of life in harems, and men like Saleh Bek would aid and encourage it.

It seems to me that all that we can do is to enter into sympathy with the Moslem women, and try to awaken and develop all the highest feelings of their nature, and to help them to understand and feel the power which they have of governing and elevating themselves, and to encourage them to exercise that power, and to think seriously. This may be done without the aid of books, and without perplexing them with new mysteries and dogmas. We might lead them insensibly to acknowledge and understand those ancient and universal laws of love which Christ declared to be the foundation of all religion—"The Lord our God is one Lord. . . . Love him with all thy heart, and with all thy soul, and with all thy strength, and with all thy mind, and love thy neighbor as thyself. This do, and thou shalt live." Words like these can rouse no anger or opposition, and they will daily become more clear and comprehensive to every one who truly takes them as a guide and rule of life. By striving earnestly to obey these simple laws, by measuring every thought and action by them, women shut up in their harems would become Christians, though they might still be called Moslems. Then their daughters would at an early age be led to love God with a trustful reverence, and taught to contribute to the happiness of all around them. Their sons, whose hearts and minds would naturally be ennobled and enlarged, would in manhood respect and honor their early teachers.

Thus, by degrees, women might be safely and surely emancipated, and the most jealously-guarded harems would be gradually converted into enlightened and happy homes. The character of the whole nation might thus be changed; but any attempt to exercise an influence from without, would certainly fail, if the religious prejudices or ancient customs of the people were directly attacked or condemned, for a dangerous spirit of antagonism and indignation would be immediately roused. All we can do is to try to excite Moslems to think more earnestly, and to endeavor to awaken in their minds the spirit of truth, by which they may be led to condemn all those customs and practices which are at variance with it, but which no mere words of ours will ever induce them to abandon. Indeed, they will probably be adhered to more obstinately than ever, if arguments be raised against them. "Overcome evil with good."

Missionaries, in the common acceptation of the word, would find it very difficult to obtain access to harems. I do not refer to men, for they, of course, could not enter. I am thinking of the persevering, enterprising, and talented Sisters of Mercy—who are now established in many parts of Syria in Latin convents, studying Arabic—and of the devoted wives of Protestant missionaries. But if they gain admittance they will certainly find that they will make no impression by teaching creeds or doctrines, or by trying to prove that Christianity is true, and Islamism is false—that the Bible is a Divine revelation, and the Koran a forgery—that Christ is the Son of God, and that Mohammed is an impostor. This would not touch the hearts, nor reach the minds of the matter-of-fact Moslem women; but any one who will help really to elevate them and reform their homes, will be helping indirectly to strengthen and confirm Turkey as a nation, for the men will be more vigorous and noble-hearted when the women are made free.

On the 13th of December, just a week after the birth of my little Miriam, I visited the harem of Saleh Bek again. I found it crowded with guests, for it was one of the days of congratulation. I heard the sounds of the tambourine and the voices of the singing women before I entered. When I was announced, there was comparative silence for a minute or two, and the women and girls made way for me, that I might approach Helweh. She was sitting up in a cushioned corner. She looked delicate, but prettier than ever, and was very gayly dressed. She had a rosebud and string of pearls in her hair. Her eyelids were newly dressed with kohl, and her hands with henna. There was a new joy in her face, and a striking expression of resolution, earnestness, and tenderness, when she placed my little swaddled namesake in my arms. I sat down by her side. A slave rose and put a small thin mattress on my knees, that I might rest the child on it.*

By this time the tambourine sounded again, and the chief singer commenced an impromptu song, having reference especially to the fact that the child had been named by me, and suggesting that it was a happy omen for the little one to have gained my love and protection from the moment of its birth. Then they sang songs in my praise, using extravagant similes, but so picturesque and full of imagery that I could not help thinking of the Song of Songs which is Solomon's. A third woman sang a sort of prayer for me, or rather wishes for my prosperity. In this song she forcibly portrayed the Oriental idea of the highest happiness—the delight of the mother, who in her youth opens her eyes upon her first-born son, and in her old age sees her children's children around her. It was a passionate outpouring of emotion, and every one present seemed to enter into the spirit of it. I do not suppose that it was an improvisation, but rather an adaptation of one of those old unwritten songs handed down from one generation of singers to another. Some dancing followed, and especial songs were sung in praise of the various guests as they arrived. The room was close and warm, and filled with smoke, for all the women were in turn supplied with narghilés, and I was glad to go out into the fresh air again.

On Christmas morning, at an early hour, the chief Moslems of Hâifa came to the Consulate to greet us, and wish us happy returns of the "*Eid el Miladi*," that is, "the Feast of the Nativity." About forty people came and staid long enough to take coffee and smoke a narghilé or

---

* These nursing mattresses are commonly used, and are covered with frilled or embroidered cases.

chibouque, and taste our preserves. Saleh Bek and Yassin Agha remained after the other guests had left us, and the former told me that he had sent his wife Helweh and little Miriam to Arrabeh, for change of air, as they were both delicate. I was surprised to hear that he had allowed the little one to go away without having once looked at her. Later in the day, after high mass had been celebrated in the Latin church, we were visited by the Christian population.

On the 2d of January, 1857, Dr. Kölle, a German, arrived in Hâifa, under the auspices of the Church Missionary Society, and I had the pleasure of welcoming his English wife and little daughter.

There was a threat of excommunication uttered from the churches against any one who would dare to let a house to the new missionary. Nevertheless, a good house was found, and his landlord was heard to say, " I shall be excommunicated for this, I suppose, but if so, I will learn the English religion, and the new priest will receive me into communion."

This arrival did not make any impression on the town generally, for the doctor lived a studious and secluded life. He had suffered severely in Damietta from brain-fever, and was sent to Hâifa to recruit his strength and to learn Arabic. He studied from books laboriously, and not from intercourse with people, so that the work was doubly difficult.*

On the 20th of January my brother invited all the best informed of the Arabs, without regard to creed, to meet at the Consulate in the evening, to make arrangements for the formation of a society for the acquisition and diffusion of useful knowledge, relative to the arts and sciences, and the history of civilization. The project was eagerly welcomed, and my brother was elected president. Mons. Aumann, the French Consul, delivered the inaugural address to a large assembly on the following Wednesday.

* Dr. Kölle and his family left Hâifa after having remained there about two years and a half.

He spoke energetically of the powers of the human mind, and the advantages of study and scientific research, and alluded with great feeling to the past history of the East, its grandeur, its scientific attainments, and its intellectual and moral influence over the world at large.

The subjects most eagerly studied were, the elements of geography, voyages of discovery, general history, and the rise and progress of civilization in different countries. Some of the members took especial interest in the history of the arts and manufactures. I was never present at any of these meetings. I used to retire to my room when the president took the chair.

One evening, when as usual I had retreated, and was busy writing an Arabic exercise, somebody tapped at my door. It was Yassîn Agha, one of the most wealthy and influential Moslems in the Pashalic. (See page 118.) He apologized for disturbing me, but said, "I entreat you to allow me to come and smoke my pipe here, that I may ask your counsel and help in a great matter." I welcomed him, and after having requested permission to close the door, he took a seat and said, "I have been greatly wishing to speak to you; it is now two months since you have been to my house—why have you ceased to come?" I answered, "Since the lamented death of your wife, there is in your house no one to receive me as a guest, therefore I no longer go there." He answered, "It is even as I thought; but now I have come to ask you to do me a great service. I wish to ask your advice about taking another wife. I have thought of one—you know her—and I want you to tell me if she is good and if she is beautiful. She is the daughter of Saleh Bek Abdul Hady, and her name is Asmé." I answered, "In all the country, I think, there is not a girl more beautiful or more pleasant than Asmé."

I had taken her portrait carefully, and I handed it to him. He was delighted with it, and said, gazing at the picture, "How tall is she? Does she speak softly? What is her age? Does her mother know you well?" I said,

"Yes." He answered, "Then she must needs trust you. Tell her, I pray you, how I wish to have her daughter for my wife—tell her all you can to make her have favorable thoughts of me—tell her I have a beautiful new house—tell her that my wife shall live like a princess. If you do this business for me, I will be your slave forever. I am fierce to marry that girl. Speak also to her father, Saleh Bek. Call him here to play chess with you, but do not think of the game; think only how to win this girl for me. Saleh Bek will take your counsel."

When he had concluded his vehement appeal, and began soothing himself with his chibouque, I told him that I must consider before I could promise to speak in his behalf; but I undertook to ascertain for him whether Asmé had been already betrothed, or promised. I knew that one of my Moslem friends had at one time thought of asking for her, so I questioned him, and found that he had abandoned the project.

Shortly afterward I called at Saleh Bek's harem. It did not seem like the same place to me now that Helweh and my little Miriam had been sent away. The senior wife, the Turkish lady, however, received me very kindly, and her daughters were gentle and affectionate in their greetings. I ascertained, in course of conversation, that Asmé was betrothed to her young cousin, the son of Mohammed Bek Abdul Hady, of Arrabeh, and that the marriage would take place very shortly. The bridegroom was only sixteen.

On my return home I sent for Yassin Agha to inform him of this, that he might at once abandon his project.

CHAPTER XIV.

LAST SCENES IN HÂIFA.

AFTER Easter, we frequently enjoyed the society of English travelers, who paused for a time in the neighborhood, either in their white tents among the trees outside the town, or at the convent on Mount Carmel.

On the 23d of April, the beautiful little yacht *Sylphide* arrived, and was at anchor for several weeks off Hâifa. I spent some delightful hours on board. Captain Leyland, who was then the owner, had truly made this yacht a home upon the waters, for he was accompanied by his wife, his daughter, with her governess, his son, with a tutor, and by Dr. Antony, a physician and amateur photographer.

Sunday, the 24th of May, was the first day of the great Moslem feast of Bairam, which follows the long and fatiguing fast of Ramadan. The little town of Hâifa was, in consequence, unusually gay. All the people were dressed in their best, and the yacht *Sylphide*, and Her Majesty's ship *Desperate*, a man-of-war, then in port, were decked with flags and streamers. 'Akka looked as if it were being besieged again, as the guns of salute flashed from the ramparts in quick succession, enveloped the city in clouds of smoke and boomed heavily across the bay.

On Thursday, 11th of June, there was a grand ecclesiastical procession, in honor of the *fête* of " Corpus Domini." The monks and priests of Mount Carmel, and nearly all the Consuls, assisted in the ceremony. The Moslems did not offer the slightest opposition to the display, although there had never before been such a demonstration in Hâifa. My brother was requested to raise the English flag on the occasion, and to allow his kawasses, *who were Moslems*, to walk before the priests, to clear and lead the way, in company with the kawasses attached to the other European Consulates. This he politely but firmly declined to do. His refusal was taken in a good spirit, and the request was not repeated.

In the afternoon we rode along the sands, round the bay, to 'Akka, and thence to the "Bahjeh," that is, " *The Garden of Delight*," about twenty minutes beyond the city. It is one of the prettiest places in the Pashalic. It was formerly the harem of Abdallah Pasha, who employed Greek and Italian artists to carry out his ideas of comfort and splendor.

The place is now the property of Mr. Girgius Giammal. He and his family occupy the large villa, built in the Italian style, which stands in the midst of the garden, where cypresses and pines rise above the fragrant orange and lemon trees and acacias, and where all kinds of pleasant fruits and sweet flowers abound. I had met the ladies of this family first at Yâfa, and had visited them at their town house in 'Akka. The gentlemen had often been with us at Hâifa, and had repeatedly invited me to the "Bahjeh;" so my brother left me there, while he made a tour in the interior, which had recently been disturbed by civil war.

Arabs who have associated much with Europeans, and who have obtained a slight European education, very often adopt European costumes and customs, and seem ashamed of their own; but this was not the case with Mr. Giammal's family, and though several members of it were pretty well acquainted with English, they had scarcely abandoned any of the Oriental fashions, either as regards dress or manners. Furrah, the youngest sister of Girgius, had been educated by the American missionaries, at Beirût. She spoke English freely, with fanciful Oriental idioms and expressions, which gave a charm to every thing she said. She was one of the very few native girls I knew who could read and write Arabic. She was betrothed to a studious and excellent man, an Arab, who at that time lived at Hâifa. He could speak no language except his own, but he knew that thoroughly, and my young friend enjoyed the unusual advantage of being able to correspond with him without the aid of a secretary.

One afternoon, as I was walking with her in the garden of roses, she showed me a little poem he had written to her, in the form of a letter, in which he complained of not having heard from her for several days.

Furrah is a happy wife and mother now, and I think that she will forgive me if I chronicle here a translation of the letter, which made her face look so bright on that 17th of June. I wrote it down in my note-book, as literally as I could, after she had kindly read it to me in Arabic two or three times, carefully explaining in English the meaning of every word which I did not understand. (Do n't be angry, Furrah!) The letter was dated Hâifa, June 15, 1857:

> "O my heart—where art thou?
> Be still, O my heart; have patience in thy sorrow.
>   Behold, God gave patience unto Job!
> I call to her, but she is silent;
> I speak, but she does not hear.
>   Why are my words unanswered?
> If they will not suffer her to write,
> Let her go down to the garden of roses,
>   And whisper her love to the fragrant air.
> I sit under the palm-trees,
> And the air will bring me her love.
>   The Palm-tree listens for the Rose-bud!
> I sat under the palm-tree,
> But no soft wind brought me her love.
>   Why does her love refuse to meet mine?
> My love is great: if she saw my suffering
> She would have pity! Her extreme gentleness
>   Could not give me such pain!
> Great is my love! If my love were in the Sakhara,
> The great and wonderful rock the Sakhara,
>   It would be broken into a thousand pieces.
> Great is my love! If my love were in the great mountain,
> The great mountain of Petra,
>   It would be moved.
> Great is my love! If my love were in the sun,
> The sun, the sun at noonday,
>   Her face would be darkened.

> Great is my love! When shall my heart rejoice
> With thee, O my 'Furrah ?'
> ' Furrah,' my ' true joy !' "

"*Furrah*" is the Arabic word for "*joy*," and it was the name of the young girl to whom this poem was addressed.

The *Sakhara* referred to, is the great rock at Jerusalem on Mount Moriah, and the beautiful dome above it, "Kubbet es Sakhara," "*the Dome of the Rock*," is almost always mistaken by travelers for the Mosque of Omar, which is in fact a comparatively insignificant building. The Arabs speak of the sun in the feminine, and of the moon in the masculine gender. There was a stanza about the moon in the poem, but I did not note it down at the time, and I do not remember it now.

In Mr. Giammal's service there were several pleasant, good-natured Abyssinian girls. They looked very picturesque in their holiday dresses made of scarlet woolen stuff, with silver necklaces and anklets, and glass bracelets, with red tarbûshes and bright-colored muslin kerchiefs fancifully arranged on their heads.

One day there was great rejoicing among them, and cries of congratulation echoed through the house. I inquired the cause. I found that a young slave girl, who had been hired by Mr. Giammal, had just been set free. She was the property of an Arab widow lady who resided at 'Akka. This lady had just arrived at the "Bahjeh," and had given freedom to her slave, and told her that she had made a will in her favor.

The poor girl was at first quite overcome with delight and wonder, but on reflection she seemed almost to tremble at the loneliness and responsibility of her new position. She asked her mistress if she could love her always just as much as she had loved her before, and said, "I would rather keep your love than gain my freedom." The lady explained that she was growing old, and could not live long to watch over her, and it was the thought of approaching death which had caused her to decide to give her young slave freedom.

Furrah told me that when this girl had been ill with fever in the Spring of the year, her owner came from 'Akka, and sat up two nights by her bedside, and did not leave her till she had recovered.

The girl still remained in Mr. Giammal's service. The only change in her position was that her wages were to be paid to her, instead of to her late owner. I questioned the girl a day or two afterward, as to how she felt. She said, "I am free and I am very glad-hearted, but I do not know what it is that makes me so glad. I am the same *one* that I was before, and I work and live as I lived before, but every body says it is better to be free."

Late on Friday night, the 19th of June, my brother arrived and told me that we must return to Hâifa as early as possible on the following morning, and start for Beirût by the next steamer, for he had been appointed to take charge of the Vice Consulate there for a few months, as Mr. Moore was about to visit England.

A busy fortnight followed, the last few days of which were spent in taking leave of my friends at Hâifa, many of whom I never saw again.

At half-past four on the morning of the 4th of July, a large number of people, Jews, Christians, and Moslems, walked down to the rocky landing-place with us, and watched us as we went swiftly over the waters in a little Arab boat, on our way to the Austrian steamer. We were accompanied by the French Consul and Mohammed Bek, who went on board, and remained with us till the last moment.

While my brother's duties detained him in Beirût, I had the opportunity of visiting the Lebanon, and becoming acquainted with the history of the inhabitants of the mountains—the Druses and the Maronites. My brother helped me to understand the complicated and threatening aspect of affairs, for he could even then foresee how, sooner or later, the mountains would become the scene of civil war—but of these things I will not speak here.

We did not return to Palestine till the following November. We steamed into the Bay of 'Akka at sunrise, and with pleasure saw again the range of Carmel, and the white convent, every window of which dazzlingly reflected the light of the morning sun. We were soon lowered into a little Arab boat, and the dusky palm-groves, the flourishing fruit-gardens, and the town of Hâifa, seemed to rise up by magic out of the sea to receive us as we rapidly approached the shore. How glad I was to land there again, and still more glad to see the well-remembered faces of my friends, and to hear their hearty words of welcome spoken in many tongues!

But there were many changes in the place—deaths, births, marriages, arrivals, and departures—old houses pulled down, and new ones built up. Saleh Bek Abdul Hady, with whom I used to play at chess, had gone with his family to settle at Arrabeh, and I heard with deep regret that his child, my little namesake Miriam, and her mother, my friend Helweh, were both dead. The child had died first, and the mother shortly afterward. Two of Saleh Bek's sons were at the French College at Antûra, near Beirût.

One of our neighbors, Signor Luïs Catafago, a widower, was the wealthiest and most influential of the Christian Arabs of Hâifa, and more learned in Arabic literature than any one in the Pashalic. He was well acquainted with Italian and French, and lived in Semi-European style. His sons were brought up at college, and dressed like Europeans, though his little girls were quite Oriental. He had married a second wife during our absence. She was a native of Damascus. The fame of her beauty and gentleness had gone forth throughout the land. Signor Luïs determined to try to win her, so he journeyed to Damascus, carrying with him offerings of rich silks from the looms of Lyons—wrought with gold—strings of pearls, and sprays of diamonds. He succeeded in his suit, and brought home his bride Lebîbeh in triumph, to grace the largest establishment in Hâifa. The bridegroom was above sixty, and the bride about sixteen years of age. She had never had any intercourse with European or even semi-European society, but with natural grace she accustomed herself to her new life and her new home.

I frequently visited her. She was the most perfect type I had met with of the truly-Oriental Christian female aristocracy, quite untinged by European innovations. Moslem female aristocracy is of a very different and far inferior order. It is comparatively barbarous in luxury and splendor.

The face of the bride pleased me exceedingly. It was a pure oval, and of that creamy, golden complexion, which looked almost fair, relieved as it was by glossy-black braids, long, dark lashes, and violet eyes. Her mouth was small and well formed. It is very unusual to see a refined-looking mouth among the Arab women. Girls often have prettily-shaped lips, but they almost invariably change in form and character in womanhood.

The first time I called on Lebîbeh it was on a Christian *fête* day. She was dressed in modern Damascus style. Her trowsers were long and very full, made of bright rose-colored silk, with a narrow pattern wrought in gold down each side Her jacket, which was short, made with tight sleeves, was of violet-silk velvet, richly embroidered, and quite open in front, exposing a lilac-crape shirt, which scarcely concealed her bosom. Round the neck and down the front of this shirt, a sentence, invoking a blessing on the wearer, was worked in Arabic characters, with fine gold thread, forming a rich ornamental border of about two inches wide. She wore a necklace of very large Oriental pearls, with a diamond cross hanging from it. Her black hair was parted on one side, and divided into fourteen long, straight, Grecian plaits. Each plait was neatly intertwined, and plaited with thick, black-silk braid to add to its weight and length. The ends of the braid were finished off with little pendants of pearls and gold.

Her head-dress consisted simply of a small piece of lilac crape tastefully arranged, and secured with sprays of diamonds and emeralds, and one rosebud. Round her waist she wore a fine white-muslin shawl, embroidered with gold. She showed me her trousseau and her needlework. She was very skillful in all kinds of embroidery, and designed and drew her patterns herself with taste and precision. She used a tambour-frame, or stretcher, fixed to a stand, and very prettily made of dark wood, inlaid with mother-of-pearl and ivory. On ordinary days she wore French muslins or Manchester prints, but she invariably looked nice, and generally had a flower in her head-dress, either a rose, a pink, or a bunch of everlastings.

I almost always found her in her private room, seated on cushions on the floor, with her embroidery-frame before her, and her youngest step-daughter, Carmella, a beautiful child of about three years of age, rolling on the divan by her side. The child was always attended by a laughing, merry-looking African slave-girl, gayly dressed in yellow or crimson, with gold coins round her neck, large rings—each one a potent protector from magic—on her fingers, bracelets of glass on her black, bony arms, and tinkling ornaments round her ankles. She wore at the back of her head a shallow, red-cloth tarbûsh, with a long blue-silk tassel, secured by a gilt crescent.

On the side of her broad nose a fine turquoise appeared. It was set in silver, and formed the head of a short, thick, blunt, silver nail, which was fixed in a hole made for the purpose in the wing of her nose.*

This girl always greeted me with some droll speech, and invented stories and tales unceasingly, to amuse the chil-

---

* This is a common custom, and I have frequently seen poor girls insert cloves, instead of jewels, into these holes. An artificial clove made of gold, clasping a pearl, which forms the round part at the top, is a very favorite nose-jewel. These nose-nails are worn by the younger girls, and are very fashionable; the elder women wear rings instead.

dren. She greatly admired her young mistress, and seemed to regard her as her especial property—as something very precious, which she delighted to caress, to embellish, and to protect.

Sit Lebîbeh could speak no language but Arabic, and could not read; but she was thoughtful, shrewd, and witty, and I always enjoyed her society. She was a member of the Latin Church.

After she had been in Hâifa about one year, she said to me, "My sister, you must not form an opinion of the character and customs of Arab women generally, from what you see of them here and in this neighborhood, for in my city, Damascus, and in Aleppo, they are much more civilized, although not Europeanized in the least degree. Here I find no companions like those I left in Damascus. Here nearly all the Arab women, both Christians and Moslems, live like peasants, and are very ignorant. They tattoo and paint themselves barbarously. They wear heavy silver head-ornaments, which are only fit to put upon the heads of horses. They do not keep their houses, themselves, or their children clean. I can not associate with them; while the few who have had the opportunity of learning some European language, and have married into European or semi-European families, have almost ceased to be Arabs. They prefer Italian or French to the language which their mothers taught them; so from them also I feel separated."

But there was happiness in store for Lebîbeh. A little while afterward her mother came from Damascus to stay with her, to help her to nurse her first-born son Yusef. When I paid the visit of congratulation, I found the young mother almost silent with delight, but the grandmother was eloquent in praise of the little swaddled boy, asleep in a swing-cradle made of walnut-wood, inlaid with ivory and mother-of-pearl, and curtained with fine muslin. The covering of the cradle was purple velvet, embroidered with gold thread. Lebibeh looked very pretty in her long, blue-cloth pelisse, lined and edged with light fur, and she smiled brightly when she heard herself called, "Um Yusef"—*the Mother of Joseph.* "Peace be upon her!"

New-Year's day was as usual a general holiday; visits and good wishes were being exchanged from early morning till sunset. On the first New-Year's day which I passed in Syria, I was surprised to hear our servants, and the servants of our neighbors, and all the Arabs of the poorer classes, greet us with the word "Bastrîna!" I found it was a common custom on the coast, and a present of a few piasters is always expected by the person who pronounces the word, and this is rarely refused. The custom is rather a tax upon people who hold a prominent position in Levantine towns.

I could not guess the origin of the custom, or the meaning of the word. The Arabs said, "Allah knows where the word came from; it is very ancient, but it certainly is not genuine Arabic." I inquired among the Europeans, but they threw no light on the subject. But an "Essay on the Fine Arts," by E. L. Tarbuck, led me to believe that this custom is a relic of pagan worship, and that the word "Bastrîna" refers to the offerings which used to be made to the goddess Strenia. We could hardly expect that the pagans who embraced Christianity could altogether abandon their former creeds and customs. Macaulay says, "Christianity conquered paganism, but paganism infected Christianity; the rites of the Pantheon passed into her worship, and the subtilties of the Academy into her creed." Many pagan customs were adopted by the new Church. T. Hope, in his "Essay on Architecture," says: "The Saturnalia were continued in the Carnival, and the festival with offerings to the goddess Strenia was continued in that of the New Year, with the gifts called in France *étrennes;*" to this I may add, that on the coast of Syria they are called "Bastrîna." The prefix "Ba," in Arabic signifies "on account of"—"for the sake of"—"for"—"by."

In April we visited Nazareth and its neighborhood with Mr. J. Lewis Farley, who has given an account of the trip in his work on Syria.

In July we went up to Esfia, a Druse village in the Carmel Range. I remained there for a short time, to enjoy the cool, fresh, mountain air, and was very kindly entertained by the people. I had excellent opportunities of becoming acquainted with their peculiarities and modes of life; but I hope to speak of these villages minutely on some future occasion, in connection with their coreligionists in the Lebanon and in the Haurân.

In August my brother went to Jerusalem, expecting to return in about a week, but he was detained on official business. I remained alone in Hâifa, and, as he had always allowed me to understand his pursuits and the principles which guided him in all his proceedings, I had the pleasure of being able, during his absence, to act as his agent in most of his affairs. Responsibility and plenty of work prevented me from feeling either dull, lonely, or timid. I am glad to be able to testify to the respectful kindness and good feeling shown to me by the Arabs, both Christian and Moslem, and to the courtesy and friendliness of the Europeans, while I was thus alone.

In November I went up to Jerusalem, and spent the Winter season there, at the English Hotel. It was a sad season for us; the Rev. J. Nicolayson was dead, Miss Creasy had been cruelly murdered, my friends at the Consulate were hopelessly watching over a suffering child, whose death they had to mourn before the close of the year. My brother was attacked by an alarming and dangerous fever, and in his delirium he was constantly taking leave of me, telling me that he was "dead," and could not rest till he knew that I was safe at home in England. But these dreadful days and nights passed away, and, thanks to the untiring attention and careful treatment of Dr. Edward Atkinson, the fever was subdued, and the new year commenced auspiciously for us.

I was surprised at the severity of the cold in Jerusalem. Twice I saw the city shrouded with snow, but the sun soon melted it away, leaving only white, fleecy wreaths on the northern sides of the domes and cupolas. There were a great many new buildings in course of erection outside the city. Large plots of land had been purchased by Russia,* France, and Austria, and foreign schools, hospices, and other institutions were being established.

Our friend, Kamïl Pasha, was no longer there. Surreya Pasha had succeeded him. He was a man of an entirely-different character. He had not so much sympathy with the Europeans. He was a strict Moslem, and kept the mosque and all the holy places religiously closed against unbelievers, and fostered a spirit of fanaticism. It was acknowledged, however, that he was in many respects a clever ruler, and an energetic and vigilant disciplinarian. It was said that he never took bribes, but caused the taxes to be regularly enforced. They had been neglected by some of his predecessors, on the principle that it is easier to take bribes than to collect taxes.

To facilitate the taxation of the citizens of Jerusalem, he had caused all the houses to be numbered, and large Arabic numerals now appeared on the doors. There was no division into streets or quarters, as in European cities, but the figures, commencing with units, rose up to hundreds, till every dwelling, however obscure, had its especial mark. Then a careful record was made of the names of the owners

---

* "Masons and builders are busy on the Meidan—the plain on the north side of Jerusalem. A portion of it, belonging to Russia, containing 16,000 square yards, has been inclosed by a stone wall. Several houses have been built there, and four large tanks constructed for the supply of water.

"A cathedral, dedicated to the 'Holy Trinity,' has sprung up as if by magic, and is now ready to receive its cupolas. A large house for the Russian Ecclesiastical Mission is nearly completed. A hospital to receive ten beds has reached the first floor; the next story will be finished during this year. Foundations are laid for an asylum capable of receiving 300 male pilgrims.

"Inside the city, the ground belonging to Russia, near to the Holy Sepulcher, has been cleared of the rubbish which formerly covered it to the hight of 35 feet. During the excavations, pillars and porticoes of the time of Constantine were discovered. Before the end of this year an asylum for Russian female pilgrims will be commenced."—*Jerusalem, August*, 1862.

and inmates. This was quite a novelty, and I was told that modern Jerusalem had never before been systematically numbered. The lower classes of Arabs regarded it as unlucky, and were strongly prejudiced against it—others spoke of it as a very *tyrannical proceeding*. Isaiah, in 22d chapter and 10th verse, says reproachfully, "Ye have numbered the houses of Jerusalem."

We left the Holy City in January, and rode over the hills of Judea, and across the plain of Philistia, many parts of which were dangerous to pass through, for the water rested in large lagoons, and the earth was swampy; but our guide knew the road well, and we reached Yûfa in safety, and in time for a Russian steamer which conveyed us to Hâifa.

Our little town was rising rapidly in importance; many large houses had been built during the year, and outside the western wall a hamlet was springing up, which was called by the Europeans the Faubourg of Mount Carmel. A handsome church with a large cupola had just been completed for the Greek Catholic or Melchite congregation.

The Russian Government had obtained a firman, which granted them permission to make a jetty at Hâifa, and Signor Pierotti, an architect and engineer in the Russian service, formerly Captain of Engineers in the Sardinian army, came to superintend the work, which gave employment to a large number of people, and created a great deal of animation in the place. The jetty was made of wood, and cost the Russian Government upward of three thousand pounds. There is not another such landing-place on the coast of Syria. It was freely used by all people, and no tax or toll of any kind was imposed.

A hospice adjoining the Greek Church was in the mean time erected. When these were finished, Signor Pierotti went to Nazareth to superintend architectural works for the Greek church there. He is now architect to the Pasha of Jerusalem.

When I inquired, "Why has the Russian Government gone to the expense of building a jetty and a hospice here and another hospice at Nazareth?" Russian employés and seemingly-satisfied Turks invariably answered, "It is for the benefit of Greek pilgrims, who come every year in great numbers to visit the holy places." But there were Europeans who shrugged their shoulders suspiciously, and said, "Perhaps this jetty is only built for the devotees of the Greek Church, but it would certainly, nevertheless, facilitate the landing of troops. Perhaps the hospices are only erected to shelter pilgrims, but they would, for all that, make excellent barracks." The generality of the Arabs were quite satisfied, and said, "God is bountiful!" and, "The Franjîs have long purses." Others said, "God knows what these things portend!" and then they silently smoked their pipes.

Russian influence was increasing every-where. A line of Government steamers had been established on the coast of Syria, and they called at Hâifa twice a week. We thus frequently came into contact with Russian captains and officers, and found them agreeable, well-educated, and liberal-minded men. Throughout the country Russia was well represented, and the consuls are almost invariably excellent linguists and independent of native interpreters. They thus avoid all those disputes and misunderstandings which arise out of the intrigues or the blunders of consular dragomen.

The Emperor of Russia had agents at work, eagerly investigating the ancient literary stores of Syria. For him the monasteries have been ransacked, and early manuscripts of the Gospels and of the Epistles have been brought to light. Through private Russian enterprise the Samaritans have been induced to part with some valuable MS. copies of the Pentateuch. Of one of these MSS. a fâc-simile has been made, and it is now—1861—being multiplied by means of lithography at Jerusalem, by Dr. Levisohn, who has devoted himself for some time to the study of Samaritan literature. He can read this ancient and rarely-acquired language as easily as Priest Amran the Levite can. Russian gold has been freely spent in the prosecution of such works as these—works of world-wide interest, and by which all the public libraries of Europe will be enriched. Dr. Levisohn will no doubt eventually publish the discoveries he has made of certain variations in the Samaritan and Hebrew versions of the Laws of Moses, which have not yet been noticed by commentators.*

In March, orders were issued for the thorough cleansing and sweeping of the chief streets of Hâifa, that they might be in a fit state to receive His Royal Highness Prince Alfred, who had landed at Yâfa and gone thence to Jerusalem, Hebron, and to the Dead Sea, or "Bahr Lutt," that is, *the Sea of Lot.* He was journeying through the interior toward Hâifa to meet his ship, the Euryalus, which had been in port for several days. The Pasha of 'Akka ordered all subordinate officers to hold themselves in readiness to go out with him to welcome the royal sailor-boy, who came from Tiberias by way of Shefa 'Amer, and arrived at Hâifa before sunset on the 4th of April—1859—with the commander and some of the chief officers of the Euryalus, attended by Mr. Finn, Her Britannic Majesty's Consul, and my brother.

The young Prince made a very favorable impression on all the people who were so happy as to see him in Syria. Every one had something to say in praise of his bright, frank face, and clear, quick-seeing blue eyes, or some story to tell, illustrative of his good-nature and good sense.

Those who accompanied His Royal Highness on his tour through Palestine, spoke of his love of fun, his brave, buoyant spirit, and his quickness of perception, but more

---

* In a letter dated Jerusalem, September 26, 1861, I am told that "Dr. Levisohn's work is delayed for want of funds." Will not the lovers of Oriental and ancient literature in Western Europe inquire into this matter, and assist Dr. Levisohn to complete his undertaking?

particularly of his implicit and ready obedience to his
governor and friend, Major Cowell. He was exceedingly
active, and he very much enjoyed outdoor exercises and
sports, and the freedom of tent life. He never sacrificed
comfort to state, unless etiquette obliged him to do so.
For instance, whenever a Mutsellim sent him a splendidly-
caparisoned horse, with a richly-wrought and embossed
saddle, he only mounted it for a few minutes, or on some
special occasion, just to acknowledge the courtesy, for he
preferred his own plain English saddle. When he approached Hebron, he was riding, as a duty, in state, on one
of the Pasha's favorite horses. Hundreds of people had
assembled to do homage to him. He good-naturedly and
cheerfully returned their greetings, then leaped from the
gorgeous saddle, ran through the crowd to the spot chosen
for the encampment, took up a large hammer, and began to
drive in the pegs for the tent-ropes most lustily, greatly to
the surprise of the stately Orientals. One of the ship's
boats was conveyed by camels from Yâfa to the Dead Sea,
that His Royal Highness, who is very fond of boating,
might have an opportunity of rowing on its heavy waters.
He also navigated the Lake of Tiberias.

On Wednesday, the 6th of April, the royal midshipman
explored 'Akka, and then joined his ship to proceed to
Beirût. He was the first English prince who visited the
Holy Land since the time of the Crusades.

On Sunday afternoon, April 17th, my brother and I were
reading together at the Vice-Consulate, when suddenly we
were disturbed by the abrupt entrance of a tall black slave
and six Moslem boys. They closed the door of the room
the moment that they were all safe within it. They looked
frightened, fatigued, and excited, as if they were seeking
escape from some great danger. The boys caught hold of
us, kissed our hands and our garments vehemently, and
cried out, "Ana dakhaliek! Ana dakhaliek!"*

---

* "Ana dakhaliek" will scarcely admit of translation into English. It means,
"I am your protégé." Among Bedouin tribes there is an ancient law called the

I immediately perceived that the boys were the sons and nephews of my old friend, Saleh Bek Abdul Hady. The slave who was with them explained, in a few hurried words, that Arrabeh was being besieged by Turkish troops, assisted by the Jerrar and the Tokan factions, and that the Abdul Hady family had no hope of being able to defend the town, so Saleh Bek sent his young sons away, to seek an asylum in Hâifa. The boys were fully persuaded that they should be in safety if they could only reach the English Vice-Consulate. They had met with many narrow escapes on the road. The slave concluded by saying, "Thank God, I have seen these children in safety under the roof of my lord, their protector!" Then he hastened away, before we could answer him.

The boys were very tired. They had crouched down on the carpet, close to my side, and two of them had taken firm hold of my dress. They said, "Ya habeebee! ya sittee Inglesi!" (O beloved! O my English lady!) "you will protect us—you will not let them take us to prison—you will not send us away!"

They watched my brother's countenance anxiously while he was speaking to me in English, for they did not know whether to hope or to fear. They said to me, "Speak to the Consul for us. Speak good words for us, O lady!"

We ordered food to be immediately prepared for the boys. They heard the order given, and one of them exclaimed, "We can not eat till the Consul gives us hope of his protection."

My brother then said; "I will do all I can for you, my boys. Eat now, and peace be upon you."

law of "dakhal." An escaped prisoner, or a man in danger of being captured by an enemy, may by this law claim refuge in the tent of an Arab, even in the encampment of an opposing tribe. The refugee enters the tent, takes hold of the robe of the occupant, and exclaims, "Ana dakhaliek!" and thus becomes a "dakhiel" or protégé. A true Arab will defend his "dakhiel" with his life. The law of "dakhal" is, however, only in full force among those tribes who are, by their strength or geographical position, independent of the Turkish government. Among tribes in which the law is maintained, a man who proved false to his dakhiel would be disgraced for life! The expression "Ana dakhaliek" is used by town Arabs as a term of endearment, implying perfect reliance and trust.

While they were eating, my brother reminded me that it was against the law for him to interfere to protect a Turkish subject; but that, as these boys were too young to have offended personally, he decided on writing to his superiors in office, the Consul and Consul-General, to explain the circumstances, and to consult them on the subject. He added, "I will take care of the boys till I receive instructions how to act. In the mean time, we may hope that Saleh Bek will be able to show that he is not implicated in this rebellion."

This plan he at once carried out, and sent special messengers to Jerusalem and Beirût. Soon afterward, as we expected, the Governor, with several soldiers, came to claim the boys as prisoners. My brother informed him of his decision, and the Governor politely withdrew; but a sentinel was placed to watch near the door of the Vice-Consulate, ready to take into custody any of the boys who might venture to go out. This watch was, however, abandoned in a few days.

We gave the boys the use of one room, and whenever we went out, they locked themselves in from the inside, and did not venture to open the door till they heard our voices. When they knew that I only was at home, they used to say, "Perhaps the Governor will come, and try to make you give us up—but you will be firm for us, and strong—you will not let him take us away to prison, even if he should ask for us ever so fiercely." They told me that their sister Asmé died soon after her marriage, and they said, "Perhaps we alone of our family remain living."

On Friday, the 22d, about midday, the sound of tumtums, and loud shouts, attracted me to the window, and I shuddered on seeing a regiment of Turkish infantry marching through Hâifa. They had come from Arrabeh. The town had been taken, and these soldiers had had the privilege of pillaging the place for an hour or more. It was said that they had secured some valuable jeweled pipes, ancient gold coins, necklaces, chains, head-dresses, and other valuables. They looked very barbarous and fierce, elated as they were with success and plunder. They had charge of a band of handcuffed prisoners from Arrabeh, who were to be conveyed to the galleys at 'Akka.

The poor boys, after this sight, were more alarmed and distressed than ever, for we had not been able to ascertain with certainty the fate of their fathers, though it was said that they had escaped beyond Jordan.

It was reported that the town had been quite destroyed, all the women and children barbarously murdered, and nearly all the men killed or taken prisoners. We did not discover, till some time afterward, that this was, to a great extent, an Oriental exaggeration. The poor boys were left in terror, suspense, and doubt. They could not tell whether they were orphans or no. The youngest boy, who was about ten or eleven, said to me one day, "If my father has been killed, God grant that I may live to be a strong man, that I may revenge his death!" It was difficult sometimes to know how to soothe or answer the excited children.

There were several other refugees from Arrabeh in town, but they were all soon taken prisoners, and conducted to 'Akka. My little protégés, or *dakhiels* as they were called, seemed to be forgotten. My brother removed them to a neighboring house, where they were taken care of by Moslems.

On Friday, May 6th, after the post had come in, my brother handed my packet to me, and then went out. I was absorbed in letters from England, when, suddenly, four of my protégés burst into the room, and jumped on to the broad divan where I was seated. Two of them got behind me, and threw their arms over my neck, and the other two tried to cover themselves with the skirt of my dress. They were all crying and trembling violently, and could only say, sobbingly, "Ana dakhaliek! Ana dakhaliek!"

Before I had learned from them the cause of their new trouble, the Governor, attended by two military officers and several common soldiers, fully armed, entered the room.

The boys actually shrieked with terror and despair, clinging to me more desperately than before. I half rose and asked the Governor to take a seat by my side. The soldiers stood in a row before the door, and the officers sat near to them. After we had exchanged customary greetings, the Governor showed me an official order for the apprehension of the boys, who were crying so convulsively that I could not help crying also; and the Governor himself seemed affected.

I said, as calmly as I could, "Tell me, my lord, to what place are these children to be taken?" He said, "To 'Akka, to the presence of his excellency the Pasha, O lady." The boys cried, "We will not go to 'Akka, unless our English lady, our protector, will go with us. You may kill us here, but you can not take us from her." They said much more, which I could not understand; for they spoke vehemently and rapidly, and all at once.

I tried to calm them, and inquired where the other boys were. The eldest one said, "They are prisoners. We were together, when we heard the footsteps and the voices of the soldiers. We jumped out of a high window into the street, to come to you; but our youngest brother fell and broke his foot, so that he could not run—and he and his cousin, who staid to help him, were taken away by the soldiers—but we escaped to this house."

The Governor then spoke kindly to the children, saying, "Your brothers are quite safe. Come with me, and I will lead you to them. Do not think that you are my prisoners; I will be as a father to you, and you shall be my sons." But the boys refused to be comforted. They had heard that a reward had been offered for the capture of their fathers, dead or alive, and they had no faith nor hope in any Turkish officer.

The Governor would willingly have saved them, had it been in his power, but, as he said, he was only acting as agent, and was bound to convey them all to 'Akka.

I had already explained to the boys that my brother

could only afford them conditional protection, but they had such unbounded and childlike confidence in my power and will to take care of them, that they were filled with astonishment when I told them, as tenderly as I could, that they must submit to the Governor, and go with him. Their renewed tears and sobs quite overcame me. As I tried to disengage myself from their embraces, they prayed passionately that I would not forsake them. One boy said, "Ask the Governor to give our little brother to you. He is sick—let him be brought to you. O, my brother—my brother!" Another said, "Darling lady, do not let him take us away. Protect us—save us!"

They were still clinging to me. The Governor rose. There were tears in his eyes, and he said, "Lady, I can not bear to see your sorrow"—then, to my great wonder, he took leave of me, spoke to the boys gently, and went out with all his attendants.

Shortly afterward my brother returned, and after speaking a few soothing words to the children, who were still sobbing, he said to me, "We will leave the boys here, while we breakfast." So I went with him unsuspiciously into an adjoining room. We had not been seated many minutes, when I heard the tramp of soldiers in the court of the house. I looked out, and saw the poor boys being led away down the steps. They were crying sadly, but offering no resistance. The Governor himself led the eldest boy with gentle firmness, and the younger boys were conducted one by one by the soldiers. I looked on in silence, and they did not see me again.

My brother then told me that he had received by post an order to give up the boys, and had hoped to be able to execute it without my knowledge. It was chiefly in anticipation of this order that he had removed the boys from the Vice-Consulate, that I might not see them made prisoners. He added, "When I came in just now, I met the Governor. He seemed quite disturbed, and said, 'O Mr. Rogers, I beg you to cheat your sister for us. The Abdul Hady boys are with her, and I can not take them from her. Her sorrow is too great for me. Cheat her, and let the boys be left alone, and I will come again for them.'"

On hearing this, I begged to be allowed to speak a word to the Governor. My brother did not object, so I sent a kawass to ask him to come to me for a minute, before starting for 'Akka. He kindly came, and I inquired seriously what he expected would be the fate of the boys. He said, "Because of their youth, and because they are of a high family, I think that they will be gently treated, and held only till they shall be redeemed. I will myself conduct them to the Pasha, instead of sending them with the soldiers, and I will in your name speak in their behalf." I said, "Will you let me have news of them as soon as possible?" He promised to do so, and kept his word. In a few days, a horseman came from 'Akka to greet me, in the name of the Pasha, to assure me that the boys were in good health, were well fed, and well lodged in an apartment of the seraglio; and though they were not allowed to go outside the city, or even into the streets, they walked every day on the ramparts as much as they pleased—they were detained simply as hostages, and were treated almost as guests. His Excellency wished me to know that he had given them each new tarbûshes, new shoes, and changes of under and outer garments, and had sworn by the life of his son that not a hair of their heads should be hurt. I received several messages afterward, all to the same effect.*

At this time we were busy making preparations for a visit to England. We had made arrangements to spend the Summer months there; but when all was in readiness

* To make this incident more clear, I must explain that Mahmoud Bek Abdul Hady, after having been displaced on account of serious complaints made against him, had in 1858 been reappointed to the governorship of Nablûs by the late Kourshîd Pasha, for the consideration, it is said, of a large bribe paid at the Seraï. But in January, 1859, Mahmoud was arrested without opposition and sent to Beirût, and Riza Bey, a Turk, succeeded him. In April, a military expedition was sent to Arrabeh to arrest all the leaders and factious members of the Abdul Hady family, and all those who were implicated in the Nablûs riots of 1856. The people resisted, and the town was besieged by the Turkish troops, assisted by two opposing and equally notorious factions. It is the Turkish policy to set one inter-

for the trip, the Vice-Consul found that he could not leave his post, and I was obliged to make up my mind to travel by myself, for loud voices were calling to me from my English home. All the Austrian steamers had been recalled, to swell the Austrian fleet; so my brother planned to take me to Beirût by a Russian steamer, and then to place me on board an English merchant steamship bound for England.

Hanné, my Arab maid-servant—a daughter of Angelina, the bride-dresser — an affectionate girl of seventeen or eighteen, who had been with me nearly three years, begged earnestly to go with me; and when I explained that I could not take her, she said, with passionate and impetuous eloquence, "Why did you *make me love you*, if you meant to leave me? Why did you take me from my mother, and teach me to like the life of the Inglese, if you must send me away to live like an Arab again? I can not live with Arabs any more." I had not attempted to teach her English, and she had only acquired three or four words. She had not in any respect changed her mode of dress, but had learned to appreciate neatness and order, and could not bear the idea of the uneven floors of earth and the unplastered and smoke-blackened walls of the houses of the poorer class of Arabs. I reasoned with her, and showed her how happy she might make an Arab home, and how she could render me a much greater service by remaining in Hûifa than by accompanying me to England.

On June 2d she came to my bedside, before sunrise, and awoke me, saying, "Ana dakhaliek, ya habîbî!"—"The

est against another, and affairs become very complicated when at one time the troops are fighting for and with a faction, and a few months afterward are employed to fight against it. The town of Arrabeh was not so much injured as we had at first been led to believe; the upper chambers only were demolished, and they were broken down by masons employed by the Turkish officers, because these upper chambers, with their battlemented terraces, which formerly made the town appear so picturesque, had been used as fortresses by the besieged. (See p. 236.) The power of the Abdul Hady faction is for the present destroyed. The leaders are banished, but Saleh Bek and some others, who had not been active agents in the affair, have been restored to favor, and the children, my protégés, have been restored to their parents.

steamer is here, and the day of our separation has come!" A number of our friends had already congregated at the Vice-Consulate, to say good-by, and an English traveler had come down from the convent to accompany us to Beirût. We were soon by the seaside, in the midst of a noisy crowd of boatmen, kawasses, porters, and heaps of luggage; for the French and Prussian Vice-Consuls of Hâifa, and the Père Vicaire of the Convent of Mount Carmel, were going with us.

I went off in the first boat, with Hanné and a few friends. I was anxious to hasten to the steamer, as I knew that Miss Frederica Bremer was on board. I soon found her in the saloon, and though we knew each other only by correspondence, we required no introduction. It was a great pleasure to clasp her hand, and to hear her voice. She speaks English distinctly, but with a musical foreign accent. I was in earnest conversation with her, when my maid, who was by my side crying, murmured, "Who is that stranger who is stealing from me my last moments with you? If she is not your mother, how can you look so glad while I am so full of sorrow?" I soothed her by saying, "The lady is a stranger here; she is my friend, and is traveling quite alone; she will land presently at Hâifa with you. For my sake you must try to help her. You, with the kawass, will lead her to the house of Dr. Kölle, where a room has been made ready for her."

With her usual impulsiveness, she kissed Miss Bremer's hand, saying, "I am your servant, O lady!" In about an hour I took leave of my Hâifa friends, with the expectation of seeing them again in a few months, and it was with conflicting emotions that I watched the little boats going toward the shore as we steamed out of the bay. The deck of the steamer was crowded with Russian and Greek pilgrims—men, women, and children—who had spent the Easter week in the Holy City, and to their great consolation had bathed in the waters of the River Jordan. In the pleasant airy saloon there were several passengers,

French, Italian, Prussian, and Swiss, most of whom I knew, but there were no ladies.

Soon after we had started the captain of the steamer came to me and said, speaking in French, "Mademoiselle, to-day is the fête-day of our Grand Duke Constantine—with your permission the Bishop of —— will celebrate it, and we shall be happy if you will assist at the service." Immediately afterward, four Greek priests in black robes came in and spread "a fair linen cloth" over a table at the end of the saloon, and placed on it a quaint old Byzantine picture, representing some sacred subject. The nimbus round the head of the principal figure was of gilt metal, and there were several precious stones introduced in the clasps and decorations of the dresses. The priests handled this picture with great reverence. They propped it up carefully, and placed in front of it a silver basin filled with holy water, and three large silver candlesticks, in which gilt and ornamented wax-candles were fixed and lighted. The captain and officers in full uniform, the sailors, the steward and waiters, and the first-class passengers stood in a group together, at the lower end of the saloon, facing the impromptu altar. Then a Russian bishop and an archdeacon entered. They were powerful and earnest-looking men, and were robed as gorgeously as if they were about to celebrate service in a cathedral.

They each had long brown wavy hair, which was parted in the middle, and hung down in front, so as to unite with their mustaches and their thick beards. They kneeled down side by side in front of the picture with their heads uncovered. One of the attendant priests placed a large missal before the bishop, who read the prayers and the Gospel and Epistle for the day in the Russian language; then a second priest prepared a censer and swung it, while the archdeacon chanted a litany. He commenced softly and plaintively in a minor key, but suddenly changed the melody to one of a more cheerful but very simple measure, and the concluding portions were like shouts of joy and triumph. The responses were very heartily made, especially by the sailors; and the sounds, evidently familiar, were caught up and echoed by the three hundred devotees on deck.

The bishop concluded the service by pronouncing a general benediction. He held in his hand a little cross, carved out of a piece of the rock of the hill on which the city of Jerusalem stands. It is a rather soft stone, and is about the color of Sienna marble. The captain solemnly advanced and kneeled down to kiss this cross, then the bishop dipped a finger of his right hand into the holy water, and with it made the mark of the cross on the broad, smooth, reverential forehead of the still kneeling captain.

All the officers in turn, and then the sailors, went forward with earnest simplicity and devotion to claim this benediction, and Mons. Aumann and several of our fellow-passengers—although they belonged to the Latin and other Churches—followed the example. Then the bishop went out on to the deck to give his blessing to the pilgrims there, and to let them kiss the cross, while the priests were sprinkling them with holy water and swinging the censers. When the bishop passed through the kneeling crowd, the pilgrims pressed the hem of his robes to their lips, and looked up to him as if they regarded him as an angel from heaven. Then followed a material feast. Large cans of meat and soup, and loaves of bread, were distributed to all the deck passengers, in the name and for the sake of the Grand Duke Constantine, the Emperor's brother; while the first-class passengers were invited by the captain to partake of a champagne *déjeûner à la fourchette*. The temporary altar was quickly removed, the picture was hung in its customary place at the end of the saloon.* The table was soon spread with fruit and flowers, tastefully arranged. The captain led me to a seat by his side, and the rest of the company followed. We were

---

* Pictures of patron saints, or of the holy family, are invariably seen in the saloons and cabins of Russian steamers.

twenty-two altogether, including the bishop and archdeacon. A very *recherché* Russian breakfast was served. The made dishes, which were numerous, were composed of curious combinations, and those which I tasted were piquant but peculiar.

A toast for the Grand Duke was proposed, and the captain requested my brother to start an English cheer for His Imperial Highness, and "hip! hip! hurrah!" resounded again and again through the saloon, echoed by Russian, French, Prussian, Swiss, and Italian voices, which mingled strangely together, with varied accentuations; and the pilgrims, on hearing or guessing the meaning of the cry, repeated it as well and as noisily as they could. [I observed that nearly every one at the table spoke French fluently, but I think that the only foreigner present who understood English was the learned linguist, Dr. Rosen, the Prussian Consul at Jerusalem.] After a few other loyal toasts and complimentary speeches, in which the Alliance was particularly alluded to, the piano was opened, and the national anthems of Russia, England, France, and Turkey were sung in chorus, while I played the accompaniments. We arrived at Beirût in the afternoon, and when we took leave of the captain and the ship's officers, they assured us that they had never had such a pleasant passage on the Syrian coast. We went to the Hôtel de Belle Vue, with our English fellow-traveler. From the lofty terrace, after sunset, I saw the Russian steamer brilliantly illuminated. Its general form was completely marked out by lines of light, and fireworks were thrown in rapid succession from the deck; while, from the residences of some of the Greek merchants in town, rockets were rushing and whizzing high into the purple night sky, and showers of stars were falling, all in honor of the Grand Duke Constantine. His Imperial Highness had been recently traveling in Syria with the Grand Duchess and a large suite.

The next morning I was in a pleasant, many-windowed room, surrounded by oleanders and roses in full blossom, and trees covered with large white bell flowers. I was comparing sketches and notes of travel with an English tourist, when my brother entered, to tell me that he had taken a passage for me in the *Demetrius*, a merchant steamer bound for Liverpool. I found it rather difficult to keep up my courage.

We went on board on the following afternoon, Saturday, June 4th. I was introduced to the captain, a good-natured, rough Sunderland sailor. I was the only cabin passenger, and although I was on my way home, I felt strangely desolate when my brother had taken leave of me, and we steamed away from the shores of Syria. But I was determined to try to enjoy the voyage, and I soon made friends with the captain, who seemed almost frightened at first of the responsibility of having me in his charge, and was nervously anxious to make me comfortable. I asked him if he had any books. He said, "Only ships' books, Miss—none that a young lady 'ud care to read." However, he showed them to me, and I found that they were very interesting guides to the Mediterranean shores, explanatory of the large charts with which the captain was provided. When he saw how pleased I was with these, he was at home with me directly, for he was an enthusiastic and practical seaman. He took pains to point out how we were steering, and to make me understand some of the principles of navigation. He showed me all his nautical instruments, and explained their uses, and promised to let me see him take his observations every day. On Sunday we were out of sight of land. The captain made a divan for me, of cushions covered with a union-jack, under an awning on the quarter-deck.

There was a very steady, orderly set of sailors on board. One of the mates, a self-educated man, spent all his leisure time in studying the rudiments of French, so I had the pleasure of helping him over a difficulty now and then.

On Monday morning, the 6th of June, we anchored in the port of Alexandria, where the *Demetrius* had to take in a cargo of cotton. Here all the deck passengers landed, with the exception of one man, a Jew of Aleppo, who was bound for Liverpool. The captain wished to give him some directions one day, while we were off Alexandria, but found that he could not make himself understood; so he requested me to act as interpreter. I went out on to the deck, and approached the solitary Syrian, whom I had not before observed, for he had occupied the other end of the ship. He was a man of about thirty years of age, and appeared very intelligent, but extremely timid. His dress, which was scrupulously clean, was of the kind usually worn by respectable town Arabs. When I was near to him, I said in Arabic, "God save you!" He started with astonishment, and, bowing down, kissed my hands vehemently, exclaiming, "God bless you, and God bless the voice which speaks to me in Arabic! I thought that I was left here alone!" When he found that I was going all the way to Liverpool, he said fervently, "Thank God! Thank God! This is good!" After telling him, in the captain's name, that a sheltered sleeping-place had been prepared for him in the forepart of the ship, I entered into conversation with him, and found that he was going to some Syrian merchants at Manchester, to whom he had been recommended; but he had never seen any of them, and knew no one in England. He asked me how he was to find his way from Liverpool, and begged me to help him. He made many inquiries, which proved to me that he had no idea of the wide difference which there is between life in the East and life in the West. He did not know a word of English. He wrote his name "*Shaayea*"—that is, Isaiah—"*Ateyas*," in Arabic characters in my pocket-book, and a day or two afterward I wrote for him, in English and Arabic orthography, the names of the three Manchester merchants of whom he had spoken. I also gave him a letter of introduction to a Syrian gentleman of Liverpool. From this time, whenever I was on deck reading, studying the charts, or sketching, Shaayea was by my side, and always watched impatiently for my appearance, greeting me with the words, "Ana dakhaliek!" He appeared to me to be a very good Hebrew scholar. He had several printed books and MSS. with him, and sometimes, at my request, he translated passages from the Hebrew Pentateuch into Arabic literally. Thus the time passed pleasantly. We did not leave the port of Alexandria till the 10th, for the *Demetrius* had, on the 7th, been struck by the *Meander*, a French steamer. Our figure-head and largest anchor were carried away, and the mainmast was snapped in two. The upper half fell on to the quarter-deck, where I was sitting alone. It came down as steadily as the funnels of the steamers do, when they stoop to pass under the London bridges, and so slowly that I had time to watch it and move out of its way. The collision was very violent; the head of the *Demetrius* was lifted up on to the *Meander*, and lodged there for about twenty minutes, causing great agitation and alarm, and a running to and fro on the decks of both the steamers. The mate said, "The *Meander* has hurt herself almost as much as she has hurt us, Miss!" The case was amicably arbitrated, the necessary repairs were quickly made, and the *Demetrius* proceeded on her way.

We reached Malta on the 14th, and passed through the Straits of Gibraltar on the 21st. I had seen the Mediterranean sometimes smooth and blue under a burning sun, and at other times plowed into deep dark furrows, which seemed as if they would swallow us up.

I observed that Rabbi Shaayea was by this time looking ill and weak. I think that the food which he took was not sufficient. He had brought provisions with him, for he could not eat food prepared by Christians, and he had nothing but bread and Aleppo conserves, lemons, coffee, and tobacco. I tried to induce him to kill a fowl and cook it himself, but he said that he could not do so, because he had not a properly-prepared slaughtering-knife.* I asked

---

* The slaying of food is a very important matter among the Jews, and it is under the immediate superintendence of the Chief Rabbi. No Jew may kill any

him if there was any kind of food we could give him, which it would be lawful for him to eat. He only answered, "I have plenty of bread, it is sufficient for me."

The captain was very anxious on the subject, and often said, in his good-natured, bluff way, "I do n't like to see a man starving while there's plenty of good food to be had;" and one day, as he was assisting himself to pea-soup, he exclaimed, "I wish you could get 'Solomon' to take some o' this soup, Miss—but I suppose it smells too much o' the pork!"

On the 23d we were off Lisbon, and as soon as I went on deck Shaayea came to me, threw himself on his knees, and caught hold of my dress, crying pitifully. I raised him up, and said, "Why is your heart trembling, Shaayea?" He looked terrified, and replied, "The sailors will kill me—they will kill me. I am afraid of them!" I said, "Tell me quietly, Shaayea, has any one hurt you?" He whispered, "I am frightened." I said, "Indeed, Shaayea, you have nothing to fear; I can protect you. Tell me what has happened." He took out his clasp-knife and opened it, and made signs as if he meant to say that he feared that the sailors would cut his throat. I said, "Put away that knife and answer me plainly, Shaayea. Did any one on this ship ever hurt you, or try to hurt you?" He said, "No—but they say dreadful words to me—they curse me!" I answered, "How do you know that they speak bad words, Shaayea? You do not understand their language. Tell me what they say." He was about to answer, but he looked cautiously round, and seeing that a sailor was near, busy at work, he would not speak, but took my pencil out of my hand, and wrote on the fly-leaf of a Hebrew and Italian grammar the Arabic letters which represent the sounds,

---

kind of cattle or poultry without a license. This license is never granted, till the person applying for it has been strictly examined as to his qualifications. The slaughtering of cattle is regarded as a religious performance, and requires rabbinical and traditional learning. The knife which is used is examined minutely, and whenever the slaughterer applies for a renewal of his license, he must submit his knife to inspection. The license is revocable at pleasure, either for misconduct or for any particular mistake or neglect.

"j, a, k." I thought that he intended this for some Arabic word, and I pronounced it accordingly, and said, "I do not think that I have ever heard that word; what does it mean?" He answered, "Hush, O lady! it is not Arabic it is in English." Then the signification of the word, which looked so unfamiliar in Arabic orthography, flashed into my mind, and I could not help smiling, as I uttered the word, "*Jack*," with its true English accent. He exclaimed, "Yes, yes, O lady, that is the word with which they continually curse me." "O Rabbi," I replied, "this is not a curse—it is not a bad word; 'Jack' is the English way of saying, '*Yuhanna*.' The sailors do not know that your name is Shaayea Ateyas, so they call you 'Jack,' and they would call me by the same name perhaps if I were a boy." He seemed satisfied, and was more composed. He smoked a few cigarettes silently, as he watched my pencil while I made sketches of the beautiful town of Cintra. But the next morning the captain said to me, "Solomon wants to speak to you, I think, Miss—he looks so miserable, and is watching at the door." So I went out to him before taking breakfast. I found him more distressed than ever. He told me that the sailors had called out to him, "Hallo, Jack!" and all my attempts to reassure him were in vain. He felt convinced that it was a curse which they pronounced. He asked me if I had felt afraid when I was first left alone among strangers on this ship; he added, "I saw the Consul leave you. Were you not afraid then?" I said, "No, Shaayea, I was sorry to leave my brother, but not afraid; we are quite safe here." He answered, "You are safe, because you are among your own people; but I am a Jew, and the Christian sailors curse me loudly." I tried to convince him to the contrary, adding, "The Christians of England love the Jews, and our country is governed and our laws are made jointly by Jews and Christians. We have Jews in our Medjlis, and people of all creeds and countries are safe with us;" but he refused to be comforted. After this he would not go to the forepart of the ship, but kept as near as he could to me all day, and at night slept in a nook between some bales of cotton, which were covered with tarpaulin, and stood opposite to the cabin-door. The captain kindly overlooked this breach of order, and allowed him to do as he liked.

I perceived that Shaayea's timidity and weakness increased every day, but his confidence in me, individually, was unbounded. "Where are you going after you land at Liverpool?" he inquired. "To my parents in London," I said. "Then I will also go to London—I will go with you," was his answer.

I told him that this would not be possible, and advised him not to think of altering his arrangements, saying, "Before you left Aleppo, you no doubt made your plans carefully, and now you must persevere in carrying them out. You are weak and timid from want of proper food and rest, but you will soon be strong and happy again, when you are with your fellow-countrymen in Liverpool and Manchester." I had asked the captain and mates to use their influence with the sailors, to prevent them from startling Shaayea in any way, especially with the terrible word, "*Jack.*" I also spoke to them on the subject, but although there was an exceedingly good feeling shown toward the poor fellow by all the men, this injunction was naturally regarded as a joke. However, I believe care was taken to avoid the word, though when sails were being taken in, or hoisted hastily, an occasional "Now, Jack," or "Out o' the way, Jack," escaped the most cautious and kind-hearted. Shaayea continued to express an overwhelming fear of the sailors, and told me how, whenever a Jew is alone among Christians, he is sure to be murdered, and he related instances which he said had occurred in Aleppo and Damascus. I tried in vain to inspire him with courage and hope. The captain, who invariably called him "Solomon," used often to greet him good-naturedly, but always in a very loud voice, and generally in broken English, with a word or two of French which he happened to know; as if he had the idea that in addressing a foreigner, it was only necessary to speak very loudly, and in some foreign language.

It was this habit, I believe, which caused Shaayea erroneously to imagine that the captain was angry with him. He used often to exclaim, "I pray you, O lady, ask the captain to forgive me!" and at my request the captain sometimes came out to comfort him, when he would tap him on the shoulder and say, "All right, old fellow, you not enough *mangez!*" or, if it were in the evening, he would say, "Cheer up, Solomon, it's all right; you'll be better to-morrow—*dormez! dormez!*" On the evening of the 25th of June, Shaayea startled me by declaring himself a Christian. I said, "Shaayea, for what reason do you say you are a Christian?" He astonished me still more by answering, "For the sake of the Messiah," and added, "Tell the captain, I pray you, that I am a Christian, and then he will not be angry with me any more." I said, "I assure you, Shaayea, that the captain is not and never has been angry with you; and whether you are a Moslem, a Christian, or a Jew, you are as safe in his ship as if you were in your home at Aleppo, and if you could understand his language you would know how kind he is." But he urged me still, and I consented to tell the captain what he had said, though I could very clearly see that he was only prompted to make this declaration by excessive and ill-grounded fear. I did all I could to inspire him with confidence. I reminded him of the courage of David and of Daniel, when they were in real danger, and of their trust in God. I told him that he might take food from us without doing violence to his conscience by calling himself a Christian. I said, "I think, if Rabbi Mûssa himself could speak to you, he would say, 'Peace be upon you, Shaayea; eat that you may live.'" I added, "Remember how David and his attendants, when they were hungry, did eat even of the consecrated bread." He said, "God bless you, O my protectress!" Soon afterward he took a cup of coffee from the steward, as he had frequently done before, and smoked a cigarette. He seemed more peaceful than usual when I wished him good-night.

The next day, Sunday, the 26th of June, when I saw Shaayea, I did not refer in any way to the conversation of the previous night, for fear of exciting him, but I led him to speak of general subjects, such as the commerce, the products, and the manufactures of Northern Syria, and I asked him to teach me the Hebrew alphabet. This amused him for a little time, and while I read to myself, he sat near smoking, reading silently from a Hebrew psalter. We had crossed the Bay of Biscay, and in the evening we stood by the cabin-door, watching the sun go down, red and glorious, behind the dark clouds which seemed to rest upon the broad Atlantic. Shaayea said that he was sorry that the night had come, and then complained of feeling very low-spirited, and very tired of the journey. I told him that after one more day we should land at Liverpool, and I gave him my London address, saying that he might write to me from Manchester to tell me how he was, whether he liked England, and to let me know if I could help or serve him in any way. He kissed my hands and cried, as if from extreme weakness. The captain requested me to advise Shaayea to rest that night in a sheltered place, as there was a heavy swell on the sea, and he would be likely to get wet if he remained in an exposed part of the deck. I explained this to Shaayea, but he said, "I can not go to the other end of the ship—I am afraid." He seemed very much agitated, and when the captain was going to his cabin, Shaayea caught hold of him, and kissed his hands and his feet vehemently, but the captain raised him up and said, "Come, Solomon, no more o' that; cheer up, be a man! *Dormez! dormez!*"

He asked for an effervescing draught, and I requested the steward to bring one for him, and he did so. Shaayea had taken one a few days before.

At half-past nine or ten o'clock, I said, "It is late,

Shaayea—you must go to rest now! Peace be upon you!" He said, "Good-night, O my protectress!" I answered, "A hundred good-nights to you, O Shaayea!" He took off his red morocco slippers, and placed them carefully side by side on a ledge, and then crawled into his favorite nook between the cotton bales, and covered himself with his wadded quilt. I never saw poor Shaayea again! On the following morning, as soon as I opened my door, I called to the steward, and said, "How is Solomon this morning, steward?" He answered very sadly, "I do n't know, Miss; he 's missing." I said, "What do you mean, steward?" He replied, "Why, Miss, the captain has been looking every-where for him, and can 't find him—and he 's in a dreadful way—he 's looked in every hole and corner, Miss, except in your cabin!"

On fully realizing these startling words, I reëntered my cabin, which contained two berths. I had always used the lower one as a wardrobe, and I drew its little red curtains aside with a trembling hand, hoping intensely, and yet fearing, that I should find Shaayea there, but it was not so. The captain entered at this moment, looking very much agitated. He told me that he had searched every nook in which a cat could be hidden. He said that he had never lost man or boy, under any circumstances, on his ship, and he did not know what to do. I said, "Who saw Shaayea last?" On inquiry we found that one of the sailors, who had been aloft in the night, remembered to have seen Shaayea at about midnight, leaning against the ship's side, beyond the foremast. He thought it rather strange, for he had never seen Shaayea in that part of the ship before; but as he did not suspect any thing wrong, he took no further notice. No one else could give any tidings about him. I noticed that Shaayea's slippers were exactly where I had seen him place them on the previous night.

Every one looked sad and thoughtful. The general impression was that Shaayea had thrown himself overboard, but I told the captain that a Jew was not likely to commit suicide, and I suggested that some accident might have happened to him. He begged me to go round the ship with him, that I might judge for myself whether there was any place from which a passenger could fall into the sea accidentally. After examining every part carefully, and making minute inquiries, I reluctantly came to the conclusion that poor Shaayea had, through excessive fear and an excited imagination, lost his self-control, and had either voluntarily or unconsciously thrown himself into the sea.*

All Shaayea's property was collected together: I assisted the captain to make an inventory of it, and then it was put under lock and seal.

We arrived at the Liverpool Docks on Tuesday morning, June 28th. I had an interview with the quarantine officer, and after having entered the name of the "*missing*" deck passenger in his book, in Arabic and in English, I hastened up to London.

An official inquiry was made into the history of Rabbi Shaayea's disappearance, by order of the Turkish Consul at Manchester; and as it was soon known that I was the only person on board who had conversed with the poor fellow, I was called upon to state all that I knew about him. I had kept a careful journal on the way, and was consequently able to furnish an account, which eventually satisfied the inquirers, that the balance of Shaayea's mind had been destroyed by his continual anxiety and groundless fears. I signed a solemn declaration of the above facts in the presence of a magistrate, whose signature was certified by the Turkish Consul-General in London, and a full report of the case was made to the Ottoman Government.

* I did not know that emotional disturbance was the cause and condition of insanity, or I should certainly have kept a continual and careful watch over poor Shaayea, but I never suspected that he was in any real danger. I was strongly reminded of his overwhelming dread of imagined dangers while reading lately the very important fact, that "the common causes of insanity are such as produce emotional changes, either in the form of violent agitation of the passions or that *chronic state* of abnormal emotion which pronounces itself in the habitually *exaggerated force of some one passion* or desire, whereby the healthy balance of the mind is at length destroyed."—See Bucknill's Psychology of Shakspeare, p. 133. Longman, 1859.

The history of poor Shaayea, and many somewhat similar circumstances which I had witnessed, prove to me that the Oriental Jews still regard blessings and curses with great awe. Even a blessing pronounced by mistake was declared by Jacob to be irrevocable, and Balak entreated Balaam to "curse the people of Israel," as if he thoroughly believed that a curse would act as a charm, and alter and determine the course of events. Shaayea's case is one example, out of many which I could give, of the excessive fear with which Christians are regarded by Oriental Jews, especially by the Jews of Northern Syria. This is a sad and striking proof that the Christianity of the East is not the world-embracing, harmonizing Christianity which Christ taught.

THE END.

www.ingramcontent.com/pod-product-compliance
Lightning Source LLC
Chambersburg PA
CBHW020538300426
44111CB00008B/716